STRATEGY FOR R&D:

Studies in the Microeconomics of Development

Ökonometrie und Unternehmensforschung

Econometrics and Operations Research

VIII

Strategy for R&D:
Studies in the Microeconomics of Development

by

Thomas Marschak
Thomas K. Glennan, Jr.
Robert Summers

With 44 illustrations

A RAND Corporation Research Study

Springer-Verlag Berlin Heidelberg GmbH 1967

Thomas Marschak
University of California
Berkeley

Thomas K. Glennan, Jr.
The RAND Corporation
Santa Monica, California

Robert Summers
University of Pennsylvania
Philadelphia

ISBN 978-3-662-39360-4 ISBN 978-3-662-40413-3 (eBook)
DOI 10.1007/978-3-662-40413-3

Originally published by The RAND Corporation in 1967
Softcover reprint of the hardcover 1st edition 1967

Library of Congress Catalog Card Number 67-28248

Title No. 6483

ACKNOWLEDGMENTS

The basic questions studied in this book were originally raised at The RAND Corporation, in a group whose membership changed over a period of some years. We are indebted to all members of this group, which included at various times Leland Johnson, Burton Klein, Andrew Marshall, William Meckling, Emmanuel Mesthene, Richard Nelson, and Edward Sharkey. We should also like to express our gratitude for the trenchant observations of Professor Edwin Mansfield of the University of Pennsylvania and John McCall and Robert Perry of The RAND Corporation, all of whom commented on an earlier version.

The work of the authors and the other members of the R&D policy group has been supported partly by the United States Air Force under the Project RAND research contract with The RAND Corporation, and partly by The RAND Corporation with its own research funds. Chapters 3 and 4 were supported by the Air Force and reported on earlier. For this support and for the contributions of numerous Air Force officers and civil servants we are deeply grateful.

Finally, we express our debt to Burton Klein, who first conceived the idea of extending a study of current military development practices into a broader inquiry into the nature of development, who first posed the questions that guided all the RAND work in this field, and who has given this book steady and extremely patient encouragement.

CONTENTS

LIST OF FIGURES

LIST OF TABLES

Chapter 1

THE MICROECONOMIC STUDY OF DEVELOPMENT

by Thomas Marschak

A. The Nature of the Studies

No one disputes that the production of new knowledge – Research and Development – is crucial to economic growth and to other national goals. Understanding the Research and Development process, however, must precede the formulation of intelligent policy, which aims to set the goals and the size of a nation's Research and Development effort, or to improve its management, or to insure that the institutions of a free economy direct resources to Research and Development in a satisfactory way. This book explores a number of distinct ways in which our understanding of the Research and Development process can be deepened.

The book concentrates on development rather than basic research. By development we understand the attaining of new knowledge, which, when combined with the existing body of knowledge, permits the creation of new and useful products. The relevant existing body of knowledge may be a set of physical laws learned through basic research or it may be a body of experience and practice. Whatever the sources, there are uncertainties as to the nature of the new products that will be developed and the effort required to achieve them. We consider development to be a process of uncertainty reduction or learning. One learns by the application of some strategy for allocating and reallocating effort among different uncertainty reducing possibilities as development proceeds and knowledge accumulates.

The four chapters that follow have two basic objectives: First, they characterize the nature of the development process and the alternative strategies that are available to a developer. In varying degrees they also contribute to an understanding of what one might mean by a "good" development or development strategy. Second, these chapters provide examples of distinct approaches to the study of the development process. A fundamental aim of this book is to provide evidence, by example, of the promise and problems of each approach so that other students of development may be stimulated to pursue them further.

The remaining chapters are autonomous and self-contained essays. Authorship and styles are different, and little attempt is made at integration or at cross-reference on the numerous occasions when one essay treats an issue that also arises in another. Nevertheless, all of them are concerned, in one way or another, with what it seems reasonable to call the economic properties of actual or ideal development projects. These properties have to do with the kinds of increases in knowledge that a developer can attain by allocating the resources available to him in different ways. The term "economic" is intended to suggest that properties that might be revealed by the tools of sociology or psychology – the impact of different modes of project organization on morale and creativity, for example – are not touched upon here. Since the studies in this book deal for the most part with the smallest economic unit in the national development effort, the development project, we label them as "microeconomic" studies.

Chapter 2 characterizes the issues that a developer must face and the strategies that are open to him in a general, verbal manner. As in the rest of this book, the discussion in this chapter is inspired by the learning techniques of current military development. Nonetheless, some techniques of uncertainty reduction – prototypes, component testing, and so on – are common to all development, and the issues and strategies discussed in Chapter 2 seem relevant to the task of the non-military developer, too.

The approach to studying development followed in Chapter 2 is a frustrating one. It is full of conditional statements, and no simple picture of development and of preferred development strategy appears. Yet this is a fruitful approach for two reasons. In the first place many decisions concerning the conduct of development activities must be made immediately. We cannot wait for more precise formulations and more concrete decision criteria to be evolved. In large government or commercial organizations, particularly, the development process tends to be, and probably must be, "institutionalized." Formal procedures, manuals of preferred practice, and organizational structures are adopted. Hopefully, the discussion of Chapter 2 combined with information on the nature of the development to be performed provides some basis for choosing better procedures or organizational forms or for writing better manuals.

In the second place the approach of Chapter 2 provides a framework and a set of problems for the three rather slow and arduous lines of study exemplified by Chapters 3, 4, and 5 of this book. The characterizations and conjectures advanced in Chapter 2 can be "tested" in three distinct senses, and these will be illustrated in Chapters 3, 4, and 5.

Chapter 3 is made up of a group of selective case histories of military developments. The purpose is to illustrate the manner in which a sufficiently well integrated and suitably comparable group of histories might test hypotheses about the nature of development and about the relative performance of specified strategies for conducting development. Chronologically these are the earliest research efforts in the book. The case histories were done at a stage in the total RAND program on R&D management when hypotheses were more crudely stated than today. Indeed, the case studies were perhaps the crucial step in the formulation of conjectures as to what constitutes a good or bad development. Because of their place in the history of RAND thought on development, the questions posed during the collection of data and the format for the presentation of the data are not the same as if the studies were started afresh today. Nevertheless, when these studies are integrated as they are in Chapter 3, useful insights emerge.

The study described in Chapter 4 is a unique attempt to collect data from many projects and to use this data to generalize about the development process. The difficulties of directly comparing development projects and drawing statistically significant conclusions are enormous. The military experience with development provides a rare opportunity to attempt such generalizations. Only here have the objectives of development remained so consistent, namely the seeking of superior weapons capabilities. Probably in no other area have such detailed records been kept, a condition of doing business with the government. In no other area has there been a sufficient number of potentially comparable projects that the myriad variables affecting development outcomes can be "averaged out" so that a study can concentrate on the relationship among a few key variables.

The origin of the study reported in Chapter 4 was the desire to characterize the learning process in development. One of the primary uncertainties in any development project is the cost of the product that emerges. Indeed, in military projects where a specified performance is sought, often as the primary objective, cost is perhaps the dominant uncertainty. The study relates the magnitude of the cost uncertainty to the improvement in performance sought and the elapsed development time.

At the time this study began, the question of using the results of such a study to improve cost estimates arose. If, for example, in projects seeking large performance advances a consistent bias downward in the cost estimates were discovered, should corrections to compensate for this bias be applied to such estimates in the future? Extended consideration of this point has suggested that the answer is no. There are several reasons.

The degree of technological advance is a hard variable to measure and a critical variable in the relationship. The value of this variable was obtained by an *ex post facto* examination of the projects included in the study, using the advice of a group of experts. Projection of this measure to future projects seems dubious, especially if one does not have access to the same group of experts. A second reason for questioning the use of the study's results to "debias" cost estimates is that the behavior underlying the data may have changed considerably. In particular, the practice of cost estimating has received a great deal of attention. The methodology has no doubt been considerably improved as we have learned from past mistakes. Moreover, development procedures have been changed by the government, in large part in response to the uncertainty shown in this study. These changes in procedures have resulted in a reallocation of initial development efforts in an attempt to reduce this uncertainty (as well as others) prior to the expenditure of large quantities of resources. The results of these changes [1] cannot yet be fully evaluated. There has not been sufficient experience. It is clear, however, that fundamental changes in development procedures have occurred since this study was prepared.

What remains, then, is a study that illustrates the application of statistical methods to the characterization of development projects. Moreover, it characterizes the developments that were typical of the time when RAND's case studies were made.

Chapter 5 considers elements of a normative theory of development, in which certain properties of the good conduct of development are deduced with some rigor from precisely stated assumptions about the developer's goals and the techniques that are available to him for acquiring knowledge. Here we no longer confine attention to the array of techniques actually used in current practice, the goals as currently stated, or the concrete language of development decisions currently in use. Instead we consider simple models—abstractions from the complex tasks a real developer faces. The reward for such simplification and abstraction is, of course, a set of models that lend themselves to analysis.

---

[1] Notably the application of Department of Defense Directive 3200.9, "Initiation of Engineering and Operational Systems Development," July 1, 1965.

A complete normative theory of the sort begun in Chapter 5 would have at least two useful results for the conduct of development in the real world and for its description. First, as Chapter 5 illustrates, a theory can test the validity of the various rules of thumb a developer may adopt as a very legitimate simplification of his task. To be more precise, the theory can find exact conditions that must be met by the developer's goals and his techniques of knowledge acquisition in order that the rules of thumb be good rules, as judged by his own goals. If the developer is unwilling to agree that his goals and techniques fulfill the required conditions, then he will want to re-examine his acceptance of the rules of thumb. The theory, in other words, has then uncovered an inconsistency between the developer's rules of thumb on the one hand and his goals and his beliefs as to the properties of his techniques on the other.

A complete normative theory would have a second useful result. Ultimately the prescriptions it yields would also serve as approximate descriptions of developers' actual behavior. A complete and realistic model of a developer's task would be a very complicated one and optimal behavior in the context of such a model would probably be very complicated behavior, requiring larger computing, observing, and communicating capacity than any development organization has. On the other hand the properties of optimal behavior in more simplified models might well have sufficient appeal, and be sufficiently easy to apply, that real developers would try to pattern their behavior after these models. The normative theory would then become approximately descriptive as well.

The theory could be made more accurately descriptive by modifying it to take account of a developer's real limitations wherever these prevent the following of difficult prescriptions. Such limitations are discovered through "behavioral" studies of observed development. Behavioral studies may use project histories or statistical analyses but would also use other tools of various social sciences. Normative studies should be regarded as complementary to behavioral studies in the task of describing the development process in a way that is not only accurate at the moment but is enduringly so.

As we have noted, the studies that follow can be considered as microeconomic in nature. They concern the individual efforts that make up the total national development effort. Little attempt has been made in the past to relate microeconomic aspects of development to broader national issues. Some comments on the relation now follow.

B. The Microeconomic Study of Development and Its Relation to Broader Economic Issues

We shall briefly consider the implications of the microeconomic knowledge of development for three broader economic issues. The issues are as follows, listed in order of increasing remoteness from the microeconomic knowledge of development: (1) the management of the government-financed portion of the national Research and Development effort; (2) the market allocation of resources to Research and Development; and (3) the role of Research and Development in achieving technical change and economic growth.

1. The Management of Government-financed R&D

If the entire government-financed development effort has been identified as a collection of well-defined development tasks, the value of much microeconomic knowledge is fairly clear. The developer in charge of each task is to achieve a new item (a moon landing, a weapons system of certain capabilities, and so forth). *If* he is given a fixed budget for this task then he wants to achieve it as quickly as possible, and any knowledge about the properties of strategies that minimize expected completion time is highly pertinent. If each task is to be given a fixed budget, moreover, then such knowledge is pertinent if a total government budget is given, if the development tasks to be performed are to be selected, and if the share of each in the total budget is to be chosen.

Whatever cost-benefit analyses are performed in making such an extremely difficult allocation decision, knowledge about the tradeoff between the time (or expected time) required to complete a task and the task's budget is valuable knowledge. It would be a valuable result, for example, if analysis such as that of Chapter 5 or historical studies such as those of Chapter 3 were to reveal certain broad and reasonable conditions to imply a diminishing returns property: successive increases in a task's budget decrease its expected completion time, but by a successively decreasing amount.

It is easy to see, however, that for an individual development task it is *not* optimal to choose the best budget *before development starts* and then to allocate that budget in the best possible way as development proceeds. This is a point that is quite unaccountably overlooked in some general discussions of development that devote considerable attention to the question of time-money tradeoff (that is, the tradeoff between size of fixed budget and expected completion time). The essence of development, as all the studies in this book emphasize, is learning, or the sequential acquisition of knowledge, with the developer making a sequence of responses to his changing knowledge. The developer is interested in displaying, at the end of his task, a good history. The goodness of the task history depends on the time and the money (the budget) that task completion required (and perhaps on other things as well). The developer would like to undertake the tasks assigned to him in such a way that they exhibit, on the average, a good history when they are completed.

It is clearly an annoying constraint for him to be given a fixed budget at the start of each task, even when the fixed budget is chosen so as to yield a better average history than would any other fixed budget. What the developer wants is to be free to choose at the start of each period (each week or month) in the course of development the money he will spend in that period. He wants to be able to base this choice on the knowledge he has gained so far. The budget he will finally turn out to spend, when the task is completed, is then a random variable just as is the time required to complete the task. Since the problem of the optimal allocation of a fixed budget is artificial and does not permit optimal behavior, it is dealt with only relatively briefly in the models of Chapter 5. There may be compelling institutional reasons why the individual developer must be given a fixed budget when development starts, but there seems to be little empirical evidence that such institutional constraints are widespread.

On the level of a large, multi-task R&D effort, however, or even a large firm's total R&D effort, there may indeed be strong institutional pressures for imposing a fixed budget ceiling on the total effort before the several individual developments are under way. The government has to present a total proposed effort, broken down into many projects or areas, for congressional review (although later supplemental requests may lend some sequential character to the choice of total budget). Similarly, the R&D department of a large firm must typically propose a fixed R&D budget to the board of directors.

One may conjecture, moreover, that the larger the development organization the less the damage done when the problem posed is the best choice of fixed budget instead of the best sequence of budget adjustments. Large development organizations have a large backlog of unattempted projects that are candidates for a share in the total development budget. It seems reasonable that if a fixed budget must be chosen in advance for such an organization, then it will be optimal to choose a large fixed budget, permitting the pursuit of many of the backlog projects. The share of each project in the fixed budget is then sequentially determined, and the high share of some projects offsets the low share of others. To be more precise, as one increases the number of projects that are candidates for a share in the fixed budget, the smaller (absolutely, or proportionately, or both) is the penalty due to insisting that the total budget be fixed in advance rather than sequentially adjusted. If this conjecture[2] is true under reasonable conditions one then has a stronger case for concentrating on the problem of best choice of fixed total budget and best sequential allocation of that total budget, regardless of institutional pressures, at the level of the government or the very large firm.

The shortcomings of the best fixed total budget approach remain if one allows the development projects supported by the budget to yield items of uncertain value (uncertain performance) instead of assuming that each project is a well-defined development task, certain (after some uncertain effort) to yield an item of specified performance. The sequential allocation of the budget is then much more complex, since it must take into account, at each step in the sequence, the alternative development times and the alternative performances that every possible project budget could achieve. At each stage, performance goals for each project may have to be adjusted, as well as the budget of the project.

Microeconomic knowledge of development is relevant not only to the question of optimal size and composition of the government R&D effort, but also to various broad questions of the government's procedures in conducting its effort. A major question of this sort has received considerable attention; namely, the nature of the government's contracting arrangements when it is the sole buyer of one or more private firm's development services. In perhaps its simplest form the problem arises when the government faces a single firm which is to perform a given development task, and the firm does not share the government's preferences with respect to the alternative time-money combinations that could characterize the task when completed. These preferences imply a certain attitude toward risk when the true time-money combination is uncertain, and they may be assumed representable by some sort of payoff function. The government's contracting problem is then essentially to set the rewards for completion of the task in alternative time periods so that the firm, responding to the announced rewards in its own way (optimally in the light of its own preferences or as close to optimally as it can) behaves in a manner

[2] The conjecture may be stated and investigated in the spirit of the models of Chapter 5.

yielding the government an expected payoff at least as great as any other schedule of rewards.

To solve the problem, the firm's techniques of knowledge acquisition in pursuing the task must be characterized; and appropriate properties of the firm's optimal procedures must be studied, or its observed behavior in such situations must be studied, or both. A wide class of microeconomic analyses, then, would have implications for the character of good contracting policies.

2. The Market Allocation of Resources to R&D

The difficulties that arise when a competitive market determines society's allocation of resources to the production of knowledge are now well known and have received some excellent discussions.[3] For an economy with appropriate "classical" properties a competitive equilibrium exists and achieves an optimal allocation of resources so long as knowledge is not produced. When knowledge production is introduced into such an economy then neither for the competitive mechanism nor for any simple modification of it is the optimality of equilibrium preserved and even the existence of equilibrium is doubtful. In the real world in which there are departures from the conditions guaranteeing existence and optimality of competitive equilibria quite unrelated to knowledge production, the presence of knowledge production further aggravates these departures.

Two of the main difficulties are the inability of the producer of knowledge to capture the full social benefit of his new knowledge, and the fact that knowledge, once produced, has a dissemination cost of essentially zero. Once produced, it is socially optimal for knowledge to be disseminated free of charge, but if it is disseminated free of charge then there is no reward for the knowledge producer, even though potential social benefits of the new knowledge could provide a reward quite sufficient to stimulate the knowledge producer and cover his costs. The patent system is a somewhat arbitrary attempt to deal with this dilemma.

A third difficulty is that the outcome of knowledge production activities is uncertain. Now many uncertainties as to future "states of the world" can, in fact, be incorporated into the model of the

---

[3] See Kenneth J. Arrow: The Allocation of Resources to Inventive Activity, in R. R. Nelson, ed.: *The Rate and Direction of Inventive Activity: Economic and Social Factors*, Princeton: Princeton University Press, 1962; R. R. Nelson: The Simple Economics of Basic Scientific Research, *Journal of Political Economy*, Vol. 67, No. 3, June 1959, pp. 297–306.

economy for which competitive equilibria exist and are optimal.[4] To do so one assumes that it is not commodities that appear on the market but rather many different kinds of tickets; a ticket of a particular kind will yield the holder a unit of a particular commodity if a certain state of the world in fact occurs and nothing if it does not. If each consumer's preferences over all bundles of tickets satisfy the classical sufficient conditions and if the same is true of the production of commodities in *each* of the possible states of the world, a competitive equilibrium will exist and be optimal. The principal classical sufficient conditions are convexity of the economy's total production possibilities (no indivisibilities and no non-decreasing returns to scale) and, for each consumer, convexity of the set of bundles preferred or indifferent to a given bundle.[5]

The trouble is that the huge number of tickets that would be required do not exist in the real world, for the very good reason that such an elaborate set of ticket markets would be very costly to operate. For lack of such markets the optimal allocation of risk bearing in knowledge production, and in other production in which there is heavy uncertainty, is not achieved.

But there is a further difficulty, not so far discussed in the literature, that would not disappear even in an economy with tickets. This difficulty stems not from knowledge production's uncertainty itself but from the peculiar character of the learning that the development phase of knowledge production typically exhibits. In the typical development activity, resources are used to acquire information; the information, and the resources that turn out to be needed, are unknown states of the world from the point of view of the knowledge production "firm" (the developer).

It can readily be shown that if one tries to incorporate production units engaging in such development activities into the ticket model, then the classical condition of production convexity is in general automatically violated for such firms, and therefore quite probably for the whole economy's production possibilities as well. Existence and optimality of competitive equilibrium may well fail, therefore, if an economy contains not only all the ticket markets but also firms that produce knowledge. Since the microeconomic study of development is in large part the study of activities that consume resources to acquire information, it should eventually shed more precise light on the extent of the difficulty.

---

[4] G. Debreu: *Theory of Value*, New York: John Wiley and Sons, 1959, Ch. 7.

[5] A set of bundles is convex if, when two bundles are in the set, the bundle equal to α times one of them plus $1 - \alpha$ times the other ($0 \leqslant \alpha \leqslant 1$) is also in the set.

Besides helping to clarify the theoretical inadequacies of market allocation when knowledge production exists, the microeconomic study of development also bears more directly on the usefulness of certain public policies designed to offset these inadequacies. It may be contended, for example, that the encouragement of large industry-owned research laboratories is desirable, or possibly that an industry with a few large firms makes a socially better allocation of resources to knowledge production than an industry with many small firms. For the study of either contention, microeconomic findings relating to the question of returns to scale for different laboratory sizes would be very useful. Suppose that laboratory size can be increased only quite slowly and that it is natural to require that one size be chosen for a long period. Then the discussion of best choice and best allocation of a fixed budget (laboratory size) becomes relevant. It may turn out that the best size is indeed a large one, even when one faces rising incremental costs as size increases. To deal with the best allocation portion of the problem for fixed laboratory sizes, one would have to draw on knowledge, normative or descriptive, of the properties of individual development projects and the strategies that they can follow.

3. R&D, Technical Change, and Economic Growth

In this most aggregative of the economic issues relating to research and development, microeconomic findings about development have only a remote role to play. This is not just because of the high level of aggregation at which one typically studies economic growth, the magnitude of ultimate interest, but also because it is technical change, not knowledge production itself, that is a condition of growth. Technical change does not occur until the new knowledge has spread and has been embodied in the commodities that appear in the market.

At the level of certain highly simplified experimental theorizing, however, in which the knowledge spreading and adoption process is suppressed, there may be some links between microeconomic properties of knowledge production and economic growth. One could, for example, follow the spirit of a number of recent investigations of "optimal" growth[6] in each of which the maximization of the discounted sum of future national incomes is studied for a particular model.

In the simplest case there would be one commodity (called "output") in the economy and a (possibly growing) labor force as well. In

[6] See, for example, H. Uzawa: Optimal Growth in a Two-sector Model of Capital Accumulation, *Review of Economic Studies*, 31 (1964), pp. 1–25.

each of a sequence of periods, a fixed proportion of output is consumed. The remaining output can go to investment (additions to the capital stock) or to knowledge production. Each period's output depends on the current labor force and the current capital stock, in accordance with a production function that shifts through time, its level in any period depending on a magnitude called "accumulated knowledge," which also changes through time.

The time path of accumulated knowledge depends in a specified way on the time path of expenditures on knowledge production. (In particular there may be a long lag between current expenditures on knowledge production and their first effect on accumulated knowledge.)

In each period full-employment measures insure that the portion of output not consumed does in fact go to investment and to knowledge production. The policy problem is to find an optimal rule governing the amount of each period's unconsumed output to be devoted to knowledge production rather than investment, given the preceding history of the economy. An optimal rule maximizes the discounted sum of outputs (or perhaps per capita outputs) summed from now into the indefinite future. The solution would be affected by various properties of the relation between knowledge-production expenditures and the level of accumulated knowledge, including the extent to which the time lag mentioned above can be reduced, for a given improvement in the level of accumulated knowledge, by increasing current expenditures on knowledge production. A guess at which properties are reasonable ones to assume might be based (under some suitable aggregation assumptions) on the corresponding properties of the individual knowledge-production project – on whatever returns to scale or time-money tradeoff properties the microeconomic study of projects might discover.

The preceding survey of the possible links between the microeconomic study of development and the study of broader issues is very sketchy and incomplete. It would be premature to attempt to derive more accurate, specific, and precisely demonstrable links until the microeconomic knowledge is itself much more firmly based. The self-contained essays in this book are steps in that direction.

Chapter 2

ISSUES IN THE CHOICE OF DEVELOPMENT POLICIES

by THOMAS K. GLENNAN, JR.

This chapter describes the development process and identifies the important elements of development decisions. Any development is unique: it is the creation of some product or process that did not exist before. Generalizations about a creative process are difficult to make, and discussions of efficiency in such projects lack precision and concreteness. It is possible, however, to create a model of the development process and to identify the important determinants of cost in such a process. Such a model helps to clarify the issues facing a developer by providing a basis for describing alternative development policies or strategies. It does not provide the basis for choosing one policy as dominant. *There is no one right policy for all development efforts.*

This chapter has its origins in empirical studies of the development policies adopted by the Air Force and other government agencies. It is important to keep that orientation in mind. The RAND Corporation has been particularly interested in identifying development policies that afford advantages over those used in past Air Force projects. Some of the development experiences in aircraft, airborne radars, missiles, and aircraft engines that have been examined are included in the next chapter of this book. These projects have a number of characteristics that distinguish them from many non-military developments. They are unusually large as measured by the number of scientists and engineers involved in each project. Military developments have frequently placed very high value on large performance advances and relatively lower emphasis on costs. The work has been done for the government, which frequently leads to constraints on development decisions in the interests of promoting broad government objectives. There has been a shifting division of duties in the development process between the military development commands and industrial contractors. Government project offices have recently exercised greater authority over them. Nonetheless, these factors do not affect the basic structure of the development process, but instead restrict the alternative policies available to the military in conducting developments. The civilian sector of the economy faces the same issues in setting up development projects, but because it has a different value structure from the military it may frequently choose different policies.

A. What Is Development?

It is very difficult to define development precisely. Initially let us say development is the obtaining of a proven capability to produce a product or process that differs significantly from anything obtained in the past. It is always conceptually possible to trace the origins of a new product or process back to fundamental scientific research, even though at the time the research was conducted the research personnel may have had very little perception of the use to which their work would be put. It serves little purpose to consider development so broadly. Instead development will encompass those activities between the time a developer decides that a product possessing fairly specific qualities has sufficient value to merit the application of resources, and its achievement. The development process will be considered to continue during the time the developer is consciously looking for a product with the given qualities. Thus, we do not consider all of the issues facing a businessman in his R&D activities. How much fundamental scientific research a firm should conduct or where resources should be applied to obtain unique technical capabilities are not of concern. The important quality is that the end use of the product and its qualitative characteristics are perceived by the developer at the beginning of the process. The development, then, can be viewed as the sequence of steps leading to a product that fits the broadly conceived characteristics.[1]

[1] This view of development is too restrictive to serve as the sole basis for determining official development policies. In particular, there are times in military developments when obtaining a capability to produce may be inappropriate. Sometimes development activities are purposely carried through a stage short of production as a hedge against possible actions by enemies. In such cases, development activities may be carried through a model or prototype stage only. If the enemy threat requiring the developed article as a counter materializes, the development may be concluded. If the threat fails to materialize, the development is dropped. Although the discussion here, particularly in the concluding sections, does not exclude this possibility, the focus is on a situation where there is a reasonably high degree of certainty concerning the environment into which the developed product or process will be introduced.

A "significantly different" new product suggests that this notion of development does not include activities consisting solely of routine engineering jobs. The product is sufficiently different from previous products that there are substantial uncertainties surrounding its technical aspects. Tests, analyses, or literature searches will have to be performed to resolve these uncertainties. Expert opinion may have to be sought outside the developing organization. The commitment of a design to production before such activities have resolved some of the uncertainties runs a large risk of serious difficulties when the product is put into use. Thus, a styling change of an existing product would not be considered as a development. But, again, the distinction is not completely clear. Sometimes styling changes can be so great as to involve substantial uncertainty in the manufacturability of the new style. It is perhaps more appropriate to consider developments to exist upon a spectrum from little or no uncertainty in its concept and design to great uncertainty. The discussion focuses on the more uncertain end of this spectrum.

The second element of the definition is the acquisition of a capability to produce the design. This is emphasized for two reasons. First, many of the problems surrounding a newly designed product appear only during the initial phases of production when the capital equipment and tooling jigs necessary for production are being assembled. The mere design, manufacture, and test of a hand built prototype is generally not sufficient to eliminate all problems. For a variety of reasons, the development is not complete when only such activities have been accomplished. One of the important qualities of a design is its manufacturability. Although the construction of a prototype can go far toward providing information on manufacturability, hand built, experimental products are no substitute for experience with the full manufacturing process. Moreover, the final stages of development frequently involve intensive testing of a product by potential users. Such testing turns up many problems that must be corrected before a product is marketed. This type of testing requires a large number of examples of the product, usually more than can be provided by an experimental shop, and there has to be production activity to produce these test items.

A second reason for treating the acquisition of a capability to produce as a part of the development process is that many of the most important questions in the selection of development policies revolve around the creation of the production process. When should the investment in this process be made? What type of tooling should be purchased? What financial risks are involved? There are many conflicting pressures brought to bear upon the capital investment decision. The desire to obtain production equipment early so as to be able to test a large number of examples of a design quickly must be balanced against the desire to delay a commitment of large quantities of resources to a production process before major technical uncertainties in the product are resolved. These concerns are central to the analysis, hence the emphasis on the acquisition of a manufacturing capability in this definition of development. It seems unrealistic and oversimple to view the development process as, first, the design of a new product and, second, the decision to invest capital to produce it.

The final element of this definition of development is the verification of the performance of the product. The inclusion of testing in the definition emphasizes the role it plays in development. The end point of development is not simply a paper design or a piece of experimental hardware. Development is finished only when the product is demonstrated to have utility and (frequently) to meet the specifications laid down at the beginning of the project. Such a demonstration is an important factor for the decisions concerning the capital investments that must be made to obtain the capability to produce the product.

B. The Structure of a Development: Uncertainty Reducing and Routine Tasks

Any development has associated with it a great number of routine tasks. The production of drawings necessary to communicate the design to workers, the decision on which proprietary components of outside manufacturers to use in a product, and the scheduling of the production activities required by the development are examples of such routine tasks. These tasks are characterized by the low levels of uncertainty associated with them. The worker responsible for the task has or will receive sufficient information to allow him to carry out his task. These tasks require only the performance of routine investigations or calculations. One can imagine these being the activities required if the firm were merely duplicating an existing product.

But, as noted above, development activities are accompanied by considerable uncertainty. Not enough is known at the beginning of a development to be able to instruct the doers of the routine activities. This gives rise to what will be called uncertainty resolving activities.

Suppose, for instance, that a manufacturer seeks to fabricate a part out of an aluminum alloy and that two such alloys are available. Suppose also that the shape of the part makes it impossible to use standard handbook information to obtain the metal's characteristics. Although many characteristics of the material are important let us concentrate on just one, say strength. Initially the manufacturer is uncertain about the strength of the part made of either alloy but he has some crude estimates or guesses. These estimates are portrayed in Figure 1a. Not only is there a best guess estimate, as represented by $\bar{a}$ and $\bar{b}$, but there is also some notion of how certain the manufacturer is about the estimates as indicated by the variance or spread of the distribution. If he were forced to choose an alloy immediately, he would probably choose Alloy B as more likely to have superior strength qualities. But he would have a chance of being wrong and of, in fact, selecting an inferior alloy in terms of strength. For instance, the true strength of Alloy B could be less than b* whereas the true strength of Alloy A could be a*, thus making Alloy A superior to Alloy B.

The option is open to perform a test prior to making the selection of the alloy. The manufacturer can fabricate some test parts and subject them to stress. As a result he might reformulate his estimates of the strength of the alloys. Such a reformulation is shown in Figure 1b. As a result of the test he can now pick Alloy B with far higher confidence.

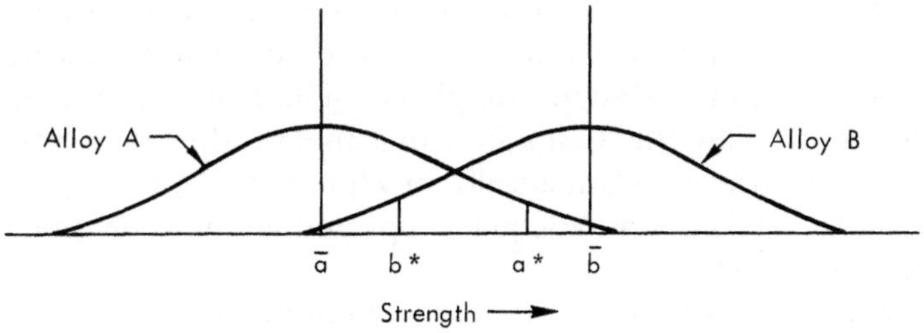

Fig. 1a. Subjective probability distribution of strength before test

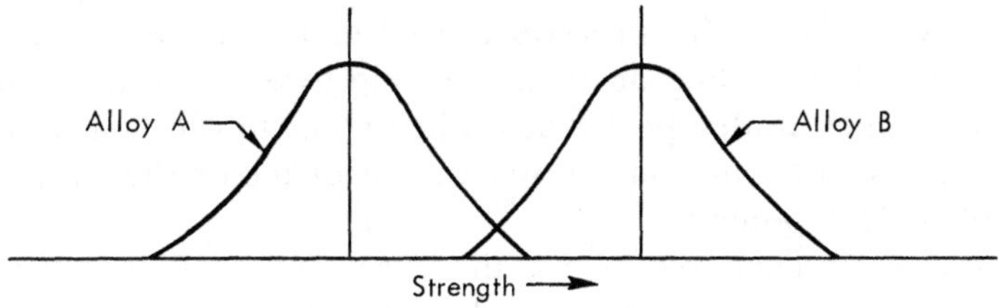

Fig. 1b. Subjective probability distribution of strength after test

There are two types of benefits to be drawn from such testing activities. In some cases, given other design constraints on a fabricated part, a strength of less than a* would be inadequate and result in an inadequate design. If a commitment to such a design were made, a costly redesign would be required when the error was discovered. On the other hand, either alloy might have a high probability of adequate strength but the stronger could lead to the redesign of the part, which might provide a superior final system.

The fact that one does not need to make decisions in the face of major uncertainty but can instead take steps to reduce uncertainty is an essential quality of the development process. There are a variety of ways of reducing uncertainties. Most important, perhaps, is the performance of tests such as described above. Tests of materials and models in simulated environments or tests of prototypes in actual environments are important sources of the information necessary to resolve uncertainties. But there are many other ways of reducing uncertainties as well. Mathematical tools of analysis help in the understanding of the elements of a design. Experts can review a design from a variety of specialized viewpoints. Sometimes a search for other similar experience to guide the designers will help to resolve uncertainty. These means of resolving uncertainties will be examined later in this essay.

The traditional view of development has tended to separate the uncertainty resolving tasks from the routine tasks. First the uncertainties are resolved and a design completed. Then the routine activities needed to translate the design into an actual product take place. This notion is portrayed schematically in Figure 2. Generally, however, this breakdown is not an adequate representation of the time history of a development.

Seldom is time so unimportant in a development that all the uncertainty resolving tasks can be accomplished before the routine engineering is started. Usually there is a contraction and an overlapping such as in Figure 3. Those parts of components that have the least uncertainty and the least interrelatedness are sent through the routine activities first. This procedure has the advantage of permitting activities such as tooling or manufacturing to proceed in a smoother fashion without undue peak loads. The degree to which such overlap is appropriate depends on the time pressures and on the interrelatedness of the components.

There is a second reason for the overlapping of uncertainty reducing tasks with routine tasks. To demonstrate capability of the product or system, the complete system must be tested many times,

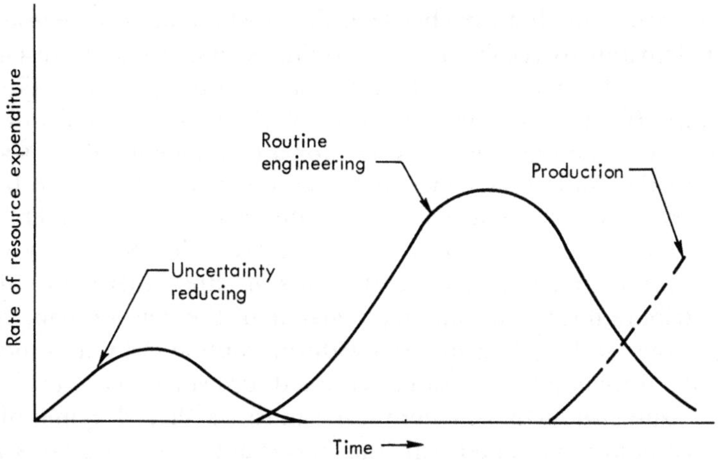

Fig. 2. Traditional view of distribution of effort in development

which may require a substantial number of representatives of the final system. To provide such test articles, a production line may have to be set up requiring the routine tasks attendant to such an action. All this occurs prior to the final testing of the test articles; hence the overlapping of the two types of activities may be necessary, even if time is not an important factor in the development.

The time shortening pressures plus the need for large scale, full systems tests provide a note of qualification to the earlier statement that developers simply do not have to make decisions in the face of

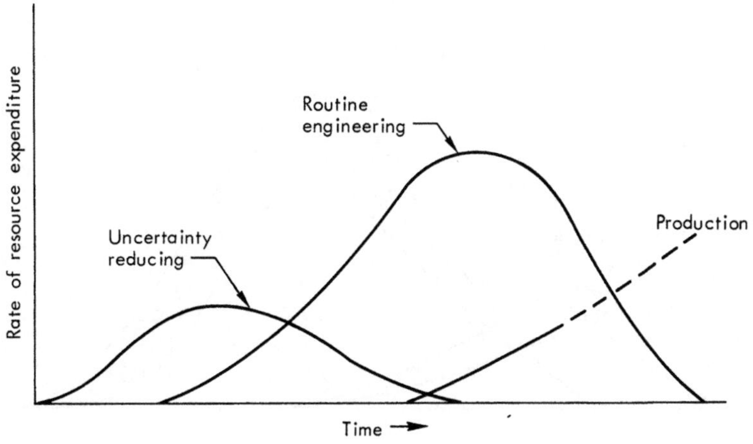

Fig. 3. Overlapping of tasks

major uncertainty but can choose, if they wish, to undertake tests and other activities to resolve the uncertainties first. In some situations there is no alternative to making decisions in the face of major uncertainty. If such decisions must be made then the probability of mistakes may be substantial. A design for a component will be started through the routine activities and subsequently may have to be redesigned. The routine activities associated with this component may largely have to be repeated and some efforts will have been wasted. These will be called error costs, the costs of efforts that turn out not to contribute directly to the final outcome of the development. Such error costs are largely associated with the routine tasks, and include the cost of tooling that must be scrapped, drawings that must be redrawn, and production planning that must be altered. Some of the error costs are associated with the uncertainty resolving tasks also. Tests are performed on components that turn out not to be used. Analyses are done on problems that turn out to be irrelevant. The uncertainty resolving tasks associated with the extensive field testing of the system and the possibility that error costs will arise are of a continuing nature. This is shown graphically in Figure 4. Crudely speaking, the non-shaded portion of the areas under the curves indicates the cost of the surviving design whereas the shaded areas represent the cost of activities not directly incorporated in this design.

A critical part of development policy is the control of the error

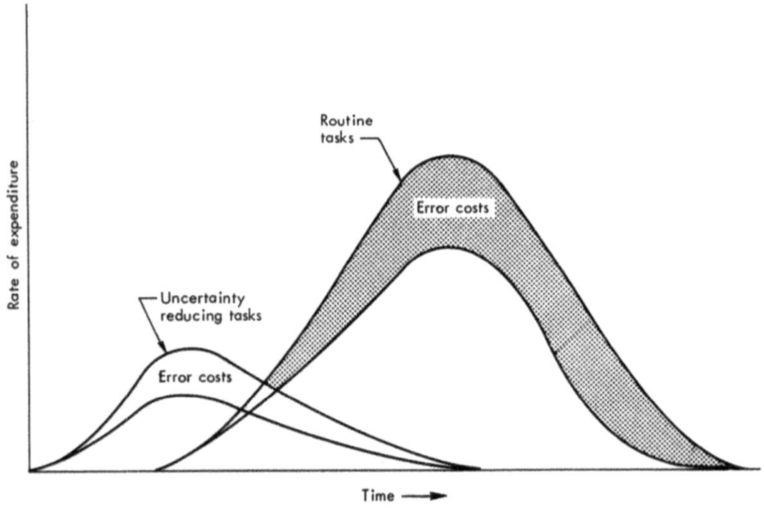

Fig. 4. Distribution of development costs through time

costs. The size of the error costs will be affected by the timing of the various tasks and by the interrelatedness of the components of the system being developed. But the critical question is the degree of uncertainty inherent in the project.

C. The Nature of Internal Uncertainties in Development

It is possible to divide the uncertainties facing a developer into internal and external categories. There are uncertainties surrounding the value of the product when it is completed. These include uncertainties as to how the product will be used, and what competing products or systems are available at the conclusion of the development. They can be viewed as external to the development process itself. The amount of such uncertainty will have an important effect upon the way in which a development is conducted. This section considers only a group of uncertainties that are internal to the project.

The internal uncertainties facing a developer are extremely complex. It is quite difficult to describe these uncertainties without reference to a specific development and development plan. For a simple example, consider a power supply and an amplifier, as shown schematically in Figure 5. The power supply takes energy from the primary power source (perhaps a gas turbine) and converts it into electrical energy which, for purposes of this example, is characterized solely by its voltage and its maximum current capacity. The amplifier uses this power to provide the desired qualities of amplification, such as gain, signal distortion, and so on. Each of the units is characterized by weight, cost, reliability, and size.

Development can proceed in a variety of ways. It is possible to take the desired amplifier capabilities, to design and fabricate the amplifier and determine through test of the amplifier what power supply capabilities are required, and then to design the power supply. Al-

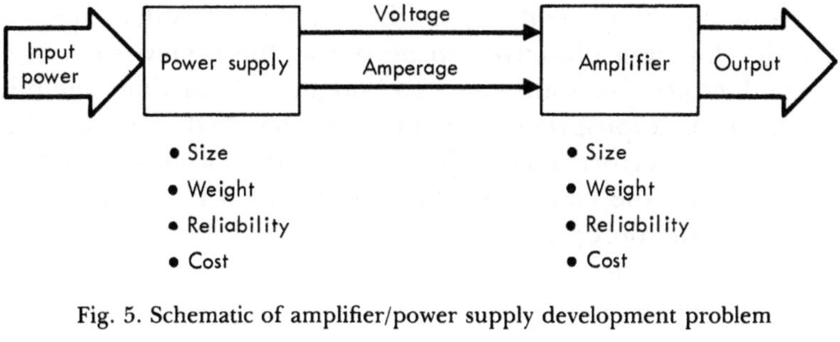

Fig. 5. Schematic of amplifier/power supply development problem

ternatively one could design the power supply, measure its capabilities, and design an amplifier capable of producing the desired output using the achieved power supply input. These are sequential development approaches. They take time because one task must be completed before the next begins. Moreover, it may be impossible to achieve the desired characteristics in the component designed second, given the design of the first. For instance, the amplifier might require more current than provided by the initial power supply design.

A preliminary design will frequently reduce the development time and lessen the occurrence of unexpected redesigns. Such a design sets out objectives for both components which, if achieved, will lead to a satisfactory system (power supply-amplifier combination). This design will be based upon theory, experience, and component specifications. With such a preliminary paper design, work can begin on both components simultaneously.

Typically, as a part of such a design exercise, budget levels are specified and a schedule for the work is laid down. In addition, permissible limits with respect to qualities such as weight, size, reliability, and production cost are established. As a result of applying the budget over the length of time planned and constraining the design in parameters other than A and V, there are a variety of possible outcomes. These can be represented by a probability distribution, in our case, of the two variables voltage and amperage. Such a distribution is shown in Figure 6. The uncertainty is represented by the amount of dispersion that the distribution has around the design points A^* and V^*. (In a realistic case, of course, there are many more variables than shown, including, for example, the parameters treated as constraints in this example.)

There are many possible ways to represent this uncertainty. One could start with a fixed schedule and budget and show the distribution of performance outcomes. One might just as well have fixed some of the performance outcomes and described the probability distributions of costs and time required to achieve this outcome. The choice of representation depends upon the situation. Crudely speaking, if the development objective can be put as the achievement of the best product possible within a given budget and schedule, the initial formulation is appropriate. On the other hand, if more emphasis is placed on performance objectives for the product developed (as is generally the case in military developments), the second approach is more appropriate.

The impact of uncertainty in a given component on a total development project is not indicated in this example. Figure 6 suggests that there is a substantial probability that the values V* and A* will not be precisely achieved. To understand the impact of this uncertainty, the consequences of failing to achieve the desired A* and V* must be known. In the case of the power supply example, because the amplifier draws only what current it needs, any value of A greater than A* will be satisfactory. If the voltage deviates slightly from the plan some simple changes in the amplifier are possible, though at some cost. Conceptually one can attach to each point in the A-V plane a cost necessary to make the system operate satisfactorily. Some of the points will have zero cost. Others may have quite high costs, equivalent to complete redesign.

These costs are determined by the nature of the technology and by other development decisions already alluded to. For instance, suppose that in the interest of minimizing the time required to get the power supply amplifier combination into production, production on the amplifier had been initiated before the actual power supply characteristics were determined. If this power supply then failed to come up to specifications, it is conceivable that all the amplifiers produced would need modification. (Alternatively, of course, it might be possible to redesign the power supply. Relative costs would determine the alternative chosen.)

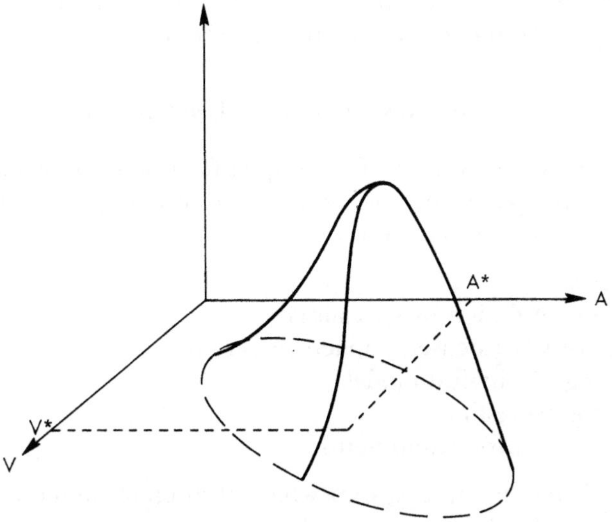

Fig. 6. Probability distribution of outcomes of applying fixed budget over a given time toward achieving A* and V*

In discussions with people concerned with development projects, much confusion arises with these concepts. Typically, an engineer will refer to a project as risky if there is large dispersion in the probability distribution shown in Figure 6. This might be referred to as technical risk. The overall project manager on the other hand looks beyond simply the technical risk: to him, the risk also involves the cost. Thus, he frequently takes action to lower the costs of correcting technical deficiencies (for instance by withholding a production go-ahead until he is sure the equipment has satisfactory technical characteristics). To the manager the riskiness of the project is represented by the cost *and* time uncertainty he faces. It is conceptually possible to obtain a measure of this by combining the probabilities of obtaining different combinations of A and V with the costs of bringing the piece of equipment up to adequate performance levels if the A and V obtained are unsatisfactory. This would result in a transformation of the probability distribution shown in Figure 6 into a probability distribution of cost outcomes.

Of course, the given example is very simple. When realistic examples with many interrelated components occur, technical uncertainties associated with each component quickly compound. This means that the preliminary design has a very high probability of being modified. Indeed the initial stages involve modifying the preliminary design by undertaking activities that reduce the uncertainties surrounding the technical components. The next section considers the means by which these uncertainties are reduced.

D. The Resolution of Uncertainty

There are a great variety of techniques for resolving the uncertainty facing a developer at the initiation of a project. These techniques can be collected into six categories:

1) analysis
2) review of design by specialists
3) test activity (focused applied research)
4) testing of physical models
5) prototype testing
6) testing of production items

These activities are at least somewhat substitutable and the emphasis placed upon the different types of activity is an important aspect of a development policy.

Analysis is probably the most important single part of the uncertainty resolution process. Generally it uses mathematical analogs of the physical world. Using these analogs, a wide variety of hypothetical designs can be investigated and at least preliminary judgments can be made on the suitability of alternative designs.

Although analysis is an indispensable tool of design, it has serious shortcomings. The mathematical analogs must always abstract from reality. They may provide satisfactory insight into the first order aspects of a design, but they seldom can reflect the multitude of extremely important second order effects. Moreover, the analyses frequently must concentrate upon only one attribute of a component where many attributes are important. A variety of analyses must be undertaken that frequently lead to conflict, requiring design-analysis iterations. The growth of computer capabilities has allowed more complex analogs to be constructed and has allowed rapid computation (once a computer program exists) which tends to counteract these problems.

The degree to which analyses can fill the uncertainty resolving needs will vary from project to project depending on the richness of the theory in different technologies. Improvements in the capabilities to do analyses such as are represented by computer growth will tend to increase the role of analysis. On the other hand analyses require data inputs concerning the environment in which the product is presumed to function, and the role of analysis will vary with the degree of understanding of the environment in which the product is expected to function. Finally, we believe that analyses are relatively more useful in programs that lead to highly specialized products. Such a conjecture is based upon the belief that highly specialized equipment can be based more nearly upon theory. A product that must be flexible requires design compromises and a richness of detail that analytical techniques frequently cannot meet. Products of this sort perhaps are best perfected through tests. This is, of course, a matter of degree. Analysis will be essential to any program.

The second method of uncertainty resolution is the use of experts to review designs from the point of view of their specialties. This method can be viewed as the use of analysis since the review frequently would involve analytic activities. However analysis is not always a part of such review. For instance a design for a new product must at some time go to the manufacturing people and they will often attempt to modify the design to ease its manufacture or perhaps lower its cost. Such a review may be institutionalized as a part of the design process. The importance of such activities depends upon the scope of the project and the degree of specialization that the technology seems to require. In many product developments, the designer (inventor) may be so familiar with manufacturing methods and the technologies involved with his product that such review is absent. In the military areas, particularly, this is not the case because there has been a great growth in specialization. The designer seldom has the detailed knowledge necessary to consider all the ramifications of his design; hence the use of specialist review groups. But it is possible to retain flexibility here even in the face of a given technology. Designers can be broad as well as narrow. They can be "generalists" as well as specialists. It probably takes more capable men to be generalists, but such men can be found. The degree to which a development organization is made up of this type of individual is an important element of a development policy.

The third type of uncertainty resolution is called "focused applied research." Once a basic design has been selected for development, there will be many questions surrounding the materials, manufacturing techniques, or similar technical inputs to a design. These questions will be similar to those investigated prior to fixing upon a design except that there will be a clearer focus, a narrowing of the areas of interest. The output of this testing activity is information that is frequently the input to the kinds of analyses discussed above. Indeed, the performance of these tests may frequently be motivated by the needs of the analyses.

Again, the importance of this form of uncertainty resolution will depend upon the technological area of the development and, more importantly, the degree of advance being sought. If the development seeks merely a permutation of existing components and technologies there will be little of this type of effort.

It should be noted that these types of tests share with analysis the quality of abstraction. The test of the strength of a piece of material is usually conducted with a standard test sample of the material. The shape of the material is determined by the testing procedures and the strength will be measured according to some standard method. However, in actual usage the material will be shaped differently, subjected to different stress levels and dynamics, and will no doubt have peculiarities of fabrication. The ability of a designer to translate the test results into valid information concerning the actual design will be a function of the degree to which the design differs from past practice. Such focused applied research results should be more cautiously applied when the product differs greatly from previous ones. Again this is a matter of degree and relative emphasis.

The fourth category of uncertainty resolving tasks is model testing. It differs from the focused applied research in that a model represents a partial synthesis of components and it differs from prototype testing in that it seriously abstracts from the final product. It should be clear, therefore, that there is no hard and fast distinction between these categories; rather there is a continuum. Nonetheless, it is useful to place particular emphasis on the specific parts of the spectrums.

The use of a model in development follows a recognition that the complexities of a design prohibit complete analysis perhaps because of the complex interaction of components or because the second order effects are important. Thus a model of an aircraft control system will insure the compatibility of components of the system and test the component interactions under various sorts of stress. Also in aircraft design wind tunnel models are used (among other things) for study of the airflow interactions between the different aerodynamic shapes that constitute a configuration. It is possible to analyze the airflow over a wing or the fuselage, but combining the two flows and their interaction on one another analytically has been impossible.

It is generally true that these models must be tested in a simulated environment. Because of this, a calibration of the environment is required. A wind tunnel test requires corrections for the peculiarities of scale and discontinuities. To the degree to which the environment is known and understood, the calibration is relatively straightforward. We are reasonably confident, for instance, of test work in subsonic wind tunnels because of the wide range of past experience with the translation of wind tunnel results to actual practice. These tunnels and experiments are generally "well calibrated." When we seek to extend our results beyond our experience, however, the problems of calibration increase and our confidence in the tunnel results should decrease. Thus, model testing would seem to share many problems with other techniques of uncertainty resolution. Serious problems can be expected in interpreting the results when significantly different (advanced) products are being developed.

The fifth category of uncertainty resolution is the use of prototypes. The word "prototype" has many connotations, particularly in connection with military developments. For present purposes a prototype will be a full sized, or nearly full sized, model that can be tested in the true physical environment in which the final product will be used. Because it represents a first approximation of a product and is expected to be changed as a result of testing, it will generally be built with a minimum of specialized capital equipment so as to save both money and time. Moreover, a prototype can be either a subsystem or a collection of subsystems, depending upon the needs of the development project.

Prototypes do overcome some of the disadvantages of analysis and model testing. Since prototypes are usually full size, results obtained in tests do not have to be scaled. And since they operate in the environments in which the final products will be used, there are no calibration problems. Prototypes also have a rather intangible advantage. They can be clearly seen, felt, and worked over. There are no problems of visualization. Many changes can be made and tested quite quickly.

But prototypes also have possible problems that may weigh against their use. As they are likely to be made more nearly by hand, they may differ in an important but quite possibly unanticipated fashion from the final product produced with specialized tooling. They can be quite expensive both in terms of resources and time. Because of this, frequently only a couple of examples are built and the amount of testing that can be done, therefore, is limited. Finally, although the prototypes will serve to resolve many uncertainties, there are many others that it will not resolve. A prototype will determine the feasibility of a design and resolve the uncertainties surrounding its performance. To a lesser degree it will tend to resolve the cost uncertainties surrounding manufacture, though true resolution awaits the actual construction of the capital equipment needed to produce the product. Similarly, manifestly unreliable components are likely to be discovered and, to this extent, uncertainties about reliability reduced. But much of the reduction of uncertainties and, more important, the improvement in reliability, come only through extensive testing. Because of the limited number of test articles, prototypes frequently cannot provide this type of testing. Further, a prototype often requires considerable time to build. Where time is an important consideration this form of uncertainty resolution may appear infeasible.

When testing a sample piece of equipment involves the destruction of that equipment, there is another qualification. This has been the case in our missile and space programs. In order to do any reasonable amount of testing, 15 to 20 examples of a design must be constructed and it may well be necessary to set up limited production lines. Still another problem may arise if specialized tooling is required even if only one example is built. It is simply not possible to build an aircraft like a B-70 or an A-11 without quite extensive and sophisticated tooling.[2] However, this is a matter of degree. It is not necessary to build the full production tooling required for volume production either.

The final category of uncertainty resolution is the building and testing of production vehicles. This is the ultimate test. Cost uncertain-

---

[2] Brigadier (now Major) General Ascani, Press Conference, Los Angeles, May 10, 1964, p. 10.

ties will be nearly fully resolved, reliability will be observed, and producibility will be demonstrated. This type of testing will be the culmination of any development that runs its full course. It is hoped that only minor difficulties arise at this point, for virtually all commitments to production facilities have been made; changes are very expensive. The question with regard to this type of testing is not *whether* to do it, but *how soon* to do it.

We reemphasize that development policy is concerned with the distribution of effort among these methods of uncertainty resolution, not the choice of one method or another. Prototypes cannot profitably be built without being preceded by analysis and model testing. But if a prototype is built, less analysis and model testing will be required than if the first full scale testing is done on production articles. The choice of these relative levels of effort is an important element of development policy or strategy and the following section treats that choice, among others.

E. The Elements of Development Policy

For the purposes of this discussion the assumption is that the required development is precisely known. The world external to the development is characterized by certainty. In military development this is equivalent to saying that there is a firm, valid, and clear requirement throughout the development.

The system to be developed is made up of several components. The system can be any of a variety of types. It could be considered as a combination of subsystems as in a missile. Here propulsion, airframe, guidance, reentry vehicle, and warhead, together with the associated ground support equipment, constitute the system. Alternatively, each subsystem could be considered as a system itself. In the case of the guidance system, for instance, there are gyros, computers, computer programs, and the associated equipment. Breaking it down even further, a gyro could be considered as a system and its parts as components. From the point of view of the decisionmaker, the system includes all components whose design is within his control.

When the developer begins work on a preliminary design, he must make decisions on four major questions. He must make a judgment on the approximate performance attributes for each of the components or subsystems comprising his system. He seeks to set out the degree to which he wants to push the state of the art in each. Second, he must settle on the degree of what we have called interrelatedness among the components of his design. Basically this is equivalent to deciding how sensitive a component is to the characteristics of other components in the system. Third, he must make a decision on the distribution of effort among the various uncertainty reducing tasks outlined above. Finally, he must make decisions on the number of parallel approaches or backup developments to take on each component, if any.

It is important to recognize that each of these decisions, or more precisely each of these groups of decisions, is closely related to all the others. Decisions cannot be made in one of these areas without consideration of decisions made in the other. There is no one best way to conduct all developments.

F. The Component State of the Art Advance

The first element of the development decision was the set of attributes that each component of the system is to have. In development, because the developer is trying to create a product or process different from anything produced before, the attributes of the components frequently will be "beyond" anything previously developed. For instance, a new automobile engine may achieve a greater output per cubic inch of displacement or per pound of engine weight. A new microphone may achieve a more even response than previous microphones. Frequently the degree to which these performance characteristics exceed previously achieved characteristics is referred to as the degree to which that component advances the state of the art.

The term "state of the art" is very vague. It refers to the degree of knowledge that exists, but for present purposes this is an insufficient definition. One could say that if any person knows how to build a piece of equipment, the knowledge exists. Hence if another person sets out to build a system possessing similar characteristics, but this second person does not know of the first development, the second person can be considered not to have advanced the state of the art. For determining a development strategy this is an unimportant question. Clearly what is important in determining the effort and time required to develop a component is the knowledge possessed by the developer conducting the development. It should be the state of his art that enters the development decision.

This may seem to be a trivial distinction and perhaps a mere manipulation of words. It is not clear, however, that this is the case. Quite possibly, the reason that "the" is used rather than "his" is a common assumption that knowledge is readily transferred from one developer to another at least when those developers work within similar product areas. It is by no means clear that this is true. Experiments in group learning, such as those performed in the 1950's at The RAND Corporation, suggest that an organization's capabilities are more than the sum of the individuals' capabilities within those organizations.[3] The fact that a design organization has accomplished a task, that it has published the detailed final results of the development, and that some individuals within the organization have moved to other organizations does not mean that other organizations can be said to have reached the same level of knowledge. On the other hand, if a developer has obtained published literature on other developments or hired individuals who have experience with other developments, then he does have greater knowledge than that incorporated in the developments he has actually accomplished.

It is fair to say that how knowledge is transferred from organization to organization is imperfectly known. An understanding of this process is central to meaningful national policies in science and to source selection procedures in military development. In any case, an advance sought by a developer must be considered relative to the state of knowledge within the developing organization. How does one quantify even the description of the advance, much less measure such an advance? It is clear that in making a decision on how far to extend the performance of a component a developer is making very intuitive judgments. It is likely, moreover, that as he pushes further into the unknown there is a significant increase in the degree of uncertainty surrounding the length of time for and the cost of achieving those attributes.

In setting down his initial and preliminary design, the developer must make decisions on each component. Usually he can trade off advances between components. In the case of an automobile, for instance, he can make advances in the engine, or the body, or both. If the objective is to get more performance, he can increase the output of the motor or he can lighten the body. The choice of which direction to pursue would depend upon where his special talents lie (engine or body design) plus many other factors such as cost and ride quality.

In summary, then, in seeking to achieve a given set of attribute goals, the developer must make a series of preliminary decisions on what the attributes of each component will be, and these in turn determine the state of the art advance to be sought in each component.

---

[3] R. L. Chapman, J. L. Kennedy, A. Newell and W. C. Biel: The Systems Research Laboratory's Air-defense Experiments, *Management Science,* April 1959.

G. Component Interrelatedness

Another set of qualities that a developer must consider during the initial design may be called interrelatedness. The components or subsystems of the total system will be interconnected. Because of this interconnection, changes in the final design of one component compared with the design originally contemplated may require changes in other components.

This can be illustrated by an automobile body and engine. The handling qualities of a car depend on the weight of the engine. The engine compartment can hold only a certain size of engine with its accessories. The drive shaft and differential can handle only a limited amount of torque. Changes in the weight, size, or output of the engine may necessitate changes in the body of the automobile. These interrelations and many others must be taken into account in the design of an automobile.

Actually, in the case of the passenger automobile there is a good deal of flexibility with regard to the body-engine match. The engine compartment is usually large, the parts of the suspension are easily changed, and the drive shaft probably has plenty of excess torque-carrying capability. Engines of a variety of shapes and sizes are frequently placed in the same body. But this need not be the case. In high performance automobiles, the size of the engine compartment is frequently sharply constrained by aerodynamic considerations. There may be efforts to lighten the whole automobile by making the parts of the drive system and body as light as possible, given the required strengths. In such a situation, the flexibility in the size, shape, and performance of the engine placed in the body is sharply reduced or eliminated.

This example illustrates a system of tightly interrelated as opposed to one of loosely interrelated components. There is engineering slack in the design if a deviation of any component from its preliminary design specification does not require other components to be redesigned. Designers often put such engineering slack into their designs. Buildings are designed to support more than the expected weights of the occupants. Bridges contain a safety margin of strength over the strength required to support the largest expected or possible load. Auxiliary power systems in aircraft may have excess capability over initial design requirements to support growth in power needs.

It is not difficult to see that the tightness of the component interrelatedness can be traded off against the uncertainty surrounding a component. If a developer is uncertain about the attributes of a component and other components must be simultaneously developed, then the presence of engineering slack in the preliminary design can enhance the probability that the components will function properly together. On the other hand, if it is desirable to build a tightly interrelated design, the risk associated with each component should be low; the components should be nearly "off the shelf." So far as possible, such tradeoffs should be carefully considered during the planning of the development efforts and, no doubt, intuitive attempts to do so are made in most projects.

The growth of systems analysis and the generally enlarged scope of the design has led to attempts to obtain engineering optimization in design. Crudely speaking this means that in the interests of achieving "efficient" systems, as much slack as possible is squeezed out of a design. Under conditions of *certainty* this can probably be shown to lead to an efficient use of resources—that is, a system that is efficient in an engineering sense is efficient in an economic sense, too. For instance, achieving the greatest number of pounds in a particular orbit for a given number of pounds of thrust is equivalent to achieving the greatest number of pounds in orbit for a dollar expenditure. Under conditions of uncertainty this may not be the case. The achievement of high engineering efficiency will require that engineering slack be cut down, frequently leading to a general heightening of interrelatedness. But, as noted above, this substantially increases the risks of redesign. If the routine activities necessary to begin the production process are started early, as has been recent practice, there is a greater risk of cost escalation. The risks of such redesign are extremely sensitive to the degree to which a design reaches beyond what has been accomplished in the past. Engineering optimization is far less likely to correspond to economic optimization when a designer is working with components that are all intended to be improvements over current practice than in the case where the components are relatively close to current practice.

Requirements to use existing components can be viewed as constraints on a design. If such components to be used are specified, the designer will try to optimize his design subject to these constraints. It is easily demonstrable that as one relaxes constraints and allows a reoptimization, the payoff must increase, or at least not decrease. Putting this another way, it will always seem that a superior design can be achieved in an engineering sense with a *smaller* rather than a larger proportion of existing components. This can be viewed as a partial explanation of the tendency to want to extend the state of the art in many subsystems simultaneously in many modern military systems.

H. The Use of Parallel Developments

When the requirement for state of the art advances is thought to be important, it is possible to hedge some of these uncertainties through the use of parallel developments of one or more components. If the system is of high priority and requires for its achievement a significant advance in one component, one would expect such an approach to be quire desirable. This was the case, for example, in the Air Force's ballistic missile program.[4] If such a program is followed with respect to a component, it is less likely that changes in other components will have to be made because of a failure to achieve the performance levels envisioned in the preliminary design. It may also mean that greater flexibility must be maintained in the rest of the design, so it can utilize either of the components designed. Such flexibility is equivalent to a decrease in the level of interrelatedness. The conditions under which parallel approaches in development seem desirable have been discussed elsewhere.[5] This is one alternative for meeting uncertainty in component design.

I. Distribution of Effort Among Uncertainty Reducing Tasks

The final element of a development decision is the distribution of effort among the various types of uncertainty resolving activities. The discussion of uncertainty resolving activities provides some insight into such decisions. Clearly the desirability of alternative distributions of effort depends on the level of advance being sought and the level of interrelatedness of the components.

If a high level of advance in the state of the art is being sought, the problems of "calibrating" analyses and simulated tests are difficult. Previous experience is not a particularly good guide to a good design. In such a case, testing a full scale prototype in a realistic physical environment may be desirable. Of course, if the level of advance is small and there is extensive previous experience with the performance level, analysis and scale model testing may be quite satisfactory and may cost a good deal less than full scale prototype testing.

---

[4] Robert L. Perry: The Atlas, Thor, Titan, and Minuteman, *The History of Rocket Technology*, E. M. Emme, ed., Wayne State University Press, Detroit, 1964, pp. 142–161.

[5] Richard R. Nelson: Uncertainty, Learning and the Economics of Parallel R&D Efforts, *Review of Economics and Statistics*, November 1959; see also Ch. 5 of this book.

A decision to make a system highly interrelated will be reflected in the distribution of effort in several ways. More analysis will be required because the design of each component must reflect the additional constraint provided by other components. Making a system more highly interrelated may well reduce the value of information derived from prototype (or full system) tests. Because the design of each component of a highly interrelated system is so constrained, improvements in a component design based upon prototype testing of the component may be difficult or impossible to make. This is of course true only if the components are designed simultaneously. If the components were designed sequentially, the early ones at least would be less constrained and hence the information from a prototype test may be useful.

J. The Impact of Available Time and Resources upon Development Strategies

This discussion of the elements of a development strategy has ignored two important considerations in every development plan, the time and resources required to complete the development. If the component state of the art advance and the component interrelatedness are specified, there is a probability distribution of resource-time requirements. Conceptually the problem could be turned around and the acceptable probability distribution of resource-time requirements specified. Associated with such a distribution would be a number of combinations of component advances and interrelatedness. Higher levels of component advance would be associated with lower levels of interrelatedness. Introduction of parallel development approaches in some of the component developments might lead to an increase in the expected cost of the development but a reduction of the dispersion or risk of the outcomes and possibly a reduction in the expected development times.[6]

Some of these notions may be made clearer by an example. Consider two qualitative effort distribution alternatives. One is associated with development policy based primarily upon complete analysis, intensive model testing and careful design review. The result of this design activity is a set of drawings that go directly to manufacturing and lead to the production of a series of test articles using full production tooling. If the approach is successful this test activity will be more in the nature of a proof of the design than a step to help modify the design. Only those uncertainties that cannot be resolved before this vol-

[6] Nelson: Uncertainty, Learning, and the Economics of Parallel R&D Efforts.

ume testing should remain at the time of such testing if this form of development is to be successful.

Contrasted with this method is one that places heavy emphasis upon a prototype as a learning device. Here prototype testing is substituted for some of the analysis, model testing, and review. The prototype is used to point up problem areas and as a method of verifying design fixes.

Prototypes can be built of a subsystem or a full system. They can provide testing of feasibility and performance. Unless they can be built in large numbers (which tends to force them into the production test category), they cannot provide the kind of design *refinement* provided by extensive testing of production articles.

Given a development objective, the choice of which of these two alternatives to follow (or whether an intermediate strategy should be adopted) depends upon the issues raised in the discussion on uncertainty resolution. The dominant element of those discussions was the degree to which the design went beyond current experience. There is difficulty in calibrating tests or performing analyses if the performance levels of the design exceeded levels at which there is considerable design experience. Figures 7a and 7b consider two designs, one of which is well within the state of the art in most of its components (say a cargo aircraft such as the C-141) and one of which is considerably beyond the state of the art in most of its components (an aircraft such as the Lockheed A-11). These two figures relate the expenditure of resources to what we shall call the level of confidence—the probability that the design will have no major errors when it is released to production.

In both cases there is a similar initial increase in the confidence level during the expenditure of initial resources because preliminary design is being done in both. In the non-prototype development (Strategy I) the confidence level continues to increase at a high rate whereas in the prototype case (Strategy II) some resources are devoted to building the prototypes and confidence grows at a lower rate. At some point in the development using Strategy I, further increases in the confidence level become quite expensive and the developer will begin to release the design to manufacture. In Strategy II the learning (or increase of confidence) increases with the initiation of testing and rapidly reaches a high level. Note, however, that in the program that does not push the state of the art (Figure 7a), using Strategy II the levels of confidence achieved do not exceed by any significant amount those achieved using Strategy I. Moreover, the amount of resources required to achieve the desired level of confidence is also higher using

Strategy II. Thus, in this case, the return to the use of a prototype does not seem worth the cost.

In the case portrayed in Figure 7b, however, Strategy I fails to achieve the desired levels of confidence and Strategy II does provide the confidence levels desired prior to a commitment to production (portrayed in Figure 7a). If the design were committed to production (drawings released to manufacturing) on the basis of work

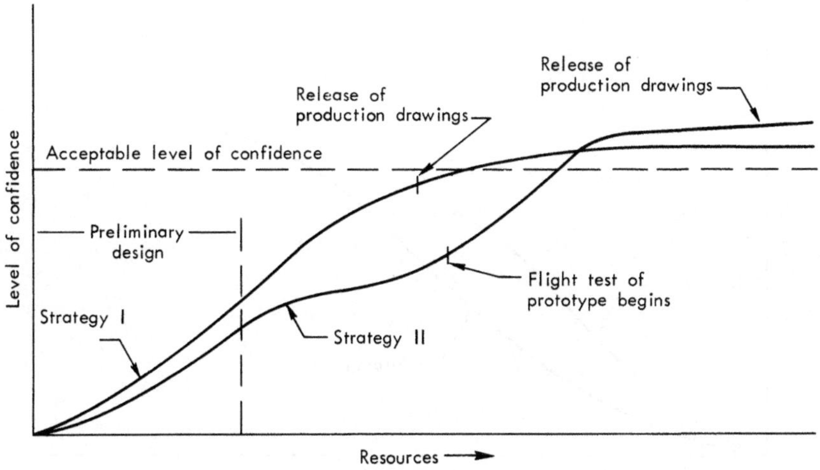

Fig. 7a. Design within the state of the arts

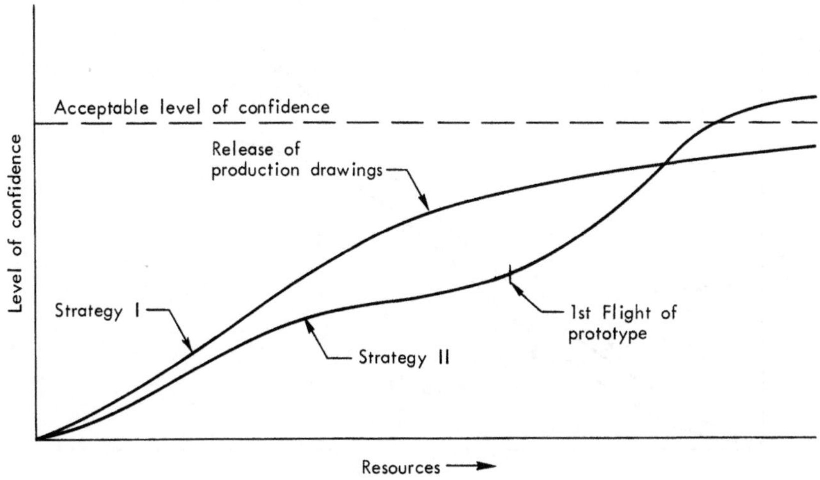

Fig. 7b. Design beyond the state of the arts

done in Strategy I, there is a high probability of the need for substantial changes in the system once it is in production. These two diagrams do not tell the entire story, however, for one of the important factors in most development decisions, time, is missing.

Figures 8a and 8b attempt to provide the missing insight by plotting time and resources. The case within the state of the art is clear. Not only does achieving the desired confidence levels in this particular

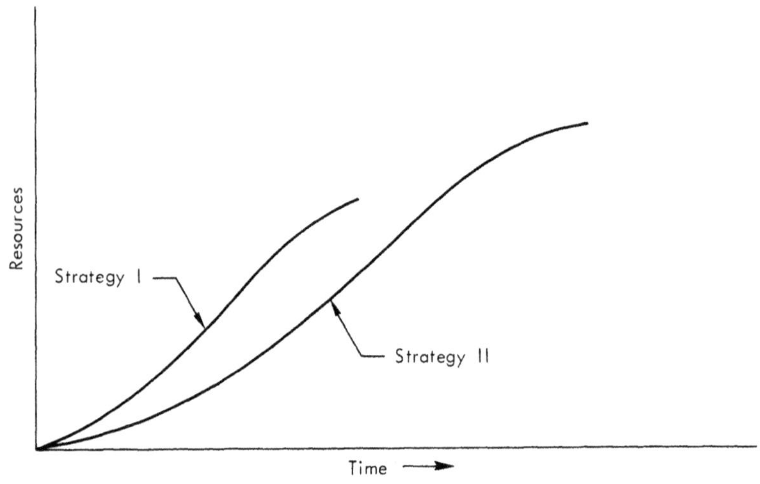

Fig. 8a. Time and resources plotted within the state of the arts

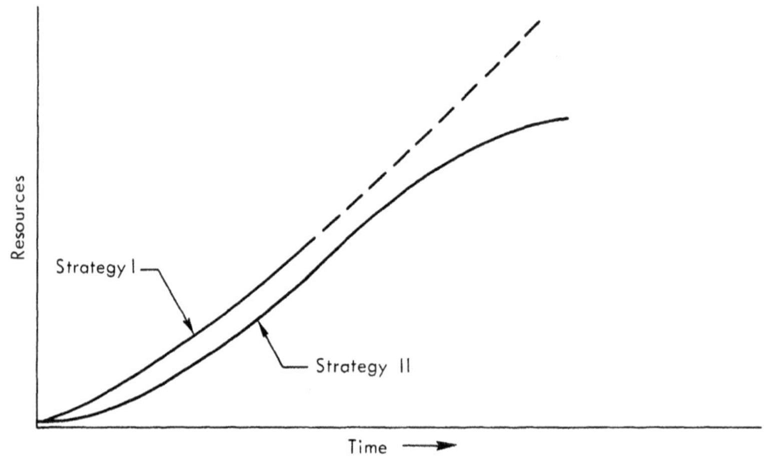

Fig. 8b. Time and resources plotted beyond the state of the arts

example require fewer resources in Strategy I than in Strategy II, but it requires less time. The situation is less clear in the case portrayed in Figure 8b. In this case it requires a greater time to release the drawings to manufacturing in a case using Strategy II than in a case using Strategy I, but since the desired level of confidence is never achieved using Strategy I, there is a high probability of serious difficulties occurring during the production phase which could delay the program and add to its cost. Thus, to compare Strategy I and Strategy II in the advanced state of the art case the production activities must also be considered. The key questions surround the time and cost required to make changes once the system has entered production.

These questions are not easy to answer. Several of the case studies in Chapter 3 suggest that (in military programs at least) high costs and time slippages are occasioned by the necessity of changes after production commitments have been made. The time slippage can be minimized by following parallel development paths for critical components (a possibility not considered in the simple example above). This adds some costs initially for the additional developments, but may ultimately save resources by reducing the difficulties encountered in production. It is also possible to retain varying degrees of production flexibility to allow rapid changes in tooling or scheduling to be made. If such steps are not taken in developments involving large state of the art advances the costs *and* development time associated with Strategy I are quite likely to exceed those associated with Strategy II.

K. External Uncertainties

A development project will be initiated only when the developer feels there is a high probability the product or process resulting from the development will have a value exceeding the cost of development. In most cases this calculation is a crude one. The uncertainties are so great that a development will be undertaken only if its expected value exceeds its expected cost by a substantial margin. Uncertainties external to the project refer to uncertainties with respect to this value.[7]

These uncertainties fall into two categories. There is a static uncertainty. Imagine that a development takes place instantaneously and a product appears having exactly the characteristics desired by the developer. He cannot be certain of the value of this product. If it is a

[7] It can be argued that there are external uncertainties affecting cost too. Technological achievements external to the development might lead to significant savings in the project because of the improved information. These external cost uncertainties seem to be far less important quantitatively than uncertainties with respect to value.

commercial product, he is uncertain about its acceptance. If it is a military product, he is uncertain of its effectiveness. The magnitude of this type of uncertainty is positively related to the degree to which the developed product differs from existing products.

Other uncertainties arise because of the changes that constantly take place during a development. All development activities take time. During the course of the development many of the market or threat conditions that existed at the start of the development change. Naturally the magnitude of the uncertainties is related to the length of the development period. These changes may occur more or less autonomously because of conditions entirely unrelated to the development itself or they may occur as a result of actions taken by a competitor or enemy who has learned of the development. These uncertainties are called "dynamic" uncertainties.

Static value uncertainties would primarily encompass uncertainties as to precisely what attributes the product should have if it could be developed instantaneously. In the case of a microwave telephone transmission system it would include uncertainties as to the volume (quantity) of transmissions to design for and the quality that the transmissions should have. In the case of synthetic shoe leather it would include qualities such as porosity and flexibility and the tradeoff the consumer is willing to make between these qualities and ease of maintenance, appearance, and durability.

In these same product areas can also be indicated the nature of the dynamic uncertainties. In the telephone transmission development there is the uncertainty as to the availability of alternative transmission systems such as communications satellites and there is uncertainty as to the nature of the communications as between data, voice, or television for instance. In the case of artificial leather, uncertainties surround the availability and cost of real leather, possible technological improvements in the processing of leather, and actions of competitors who have somewhat different synthetic substitutes.

These types of uncertainties are perhaps a bit more spectacular in the case of military developments. In developing a fighter bomber, even if the enemy posture does not change, there are uncertainties as to what qualities will provide the best penetration capabilities and what types of ordnance and delivery tactics will be most effective. The uncertainties due to the dynamics of military development would include changes in the posture because of the introduction of new defense missiles or aircraft, changes in the enemy tactics, or the generation of superior alternative means of weapons delivery by various kinds of missiles.

There are numerous examples of military developments whose value has been lessened by changes in the threat. The SAGE (Semi-Automatic Ground Environment) system of directing air defense efforts against manned bombers is a particularly good example. This system was conceived at a time when there was thought to be a massive buildup in the Soviet bomber forces. The system was designed to combat large coordinated bomber attacks on the North American continent. Two major changes occurred. First, the bomber threat failed to materialize in the numbers foreseen. The sophisticated capability to handle these large attacks semi-automatically was not as valuable as expected. Second, the highly centralized system was very vulnerable to attack by ballistic missiles.

It is easy to criticize the developers of this system for proceeding the way they did with the hindsight we now have. But the problem is complex. Why did the Russians fail to develop the bomber force we thought they would? The most probable explanation, perhaps, is that they recognized the potential of the ballistic missile. It is quite possible, however, that a part of the reason was that the SAGE system was being developed. They made an assessment that with SAGE in place, the value of their bombers would be low because of the high attrition to be expected. Thus the development of SAGE may have had the effect of *deterring* the acquisition and deployment of a Soviet bomber force. This example is an important one, for it suggests that there are times when one undertakes military developments without feeling completely confident they will ultimately be used, because their development alone may eliminate the need for their deployment.

Another example of dynamic uncertainties in military development was the cruise missile program of the Air Force encompassing both the Navaho and the Snark. At the time these programs were initiated they appeared to be logical complements to the bomber force. Their development required a longer time than expected, but there is little doubt that if they had been deployed extensively they would have had military usefulness. However, an alternative technology came along in the ballistic missile development that promised even greater usefulness, so that the programs were canceled. Even though they were canceled these programs did not constitute a total waste of resources for the propulsion and guidance technology they generated have been useful in numerous other projects.

Finally, in military developments, not only does the enemy threat and the alternative technological means of meeting that threat remain uncertain, but the objective to be accomplished may change. Over the past 15 or 20 years U.S. strategy for meeting enemies has changed radically in response to new enemy force deployments and technological capabilities. The early history of the Minuteman missile illustrates the impact of changes in strategic objectives. Although the origins of the Minuteman concept are a little unclear, it appears that it was initially thought of as a very cheap, fairly inaccurate missile. It was to be fired in salvos against large area targets such as cities. It was simply a deterrent weapon. At about the same time, however, counterforce attacks in central war were being reexamined and the doctrine of controlled response was beginning to evolve. As a result, the Minuteman system has undergone rather continuous change to improve both its counterforce capability and the flexibility with which it can respond. Because of the initial conception of the missile as a low cost, relatively unsophisticated system, these changes have been expensive. Improved guidance required greater weight carrying capability or great reductions of guidance weight. These have been obtained, but not cheaply.

Changes of this kind are inevitable because the uncertainties are an inherent quality of the environment in which developments take place. It is also evident that the more a new product differs from its predecessors or the longer the development process takes, the greater the impact of the uncertainties. Because of the nature and size of military development tasks meeting such uncertainties effectively is particularly important to the military. In the civilian area, the advanced and the inherent project size seem generally to be of a much smaller scale. Although these external uncertainties remain important, they are perhaps not so dominant.

Clearly, external uncertainties cannot be resolved in the same manner as uncertainties internal to the project. Dynamic uncertainties in particular are resolved only by time, and the final resolution may depend in part on the actions taken in the development project, as may have been the case in the SAGE system. Static uncertainties are somewhat more amenable to resolution. In the commercial area, market research of various types will help to resolve some of the uncertainties. In the military area, exercises and operational analyses will clarify many of the issues. But we must reiterate the fact that as a product increases in distinctiveness as compared with past products, the ability of market research, operations analyses, or simulated field exercises to resolve the uncertainties decreases.

L. The Relation of Development Strategies to External Uncertainties

Development strategies must be considered in the context of the development efforts. The military establishment has a comprehensive responsibility for all development activities associated with national security. As a consequence, its total development policy must provide the best possible assurance against technological surprise by an enemy as well as provide opportunities to enhance our position of superiority. The comprehensiveness of this task is in marked contrast to that of an individual firm developing products for a commercial market. The military establishment must have balance in its program. A commercial firm can and frequently does choose to concentrate its resources in narrow areas. The character of the total R&D program of a firm is related, among other things, to its technological area and the structure of the market in which it operates, subjects that are outside the concern of this essay.

With this distinction in mind one can suggest the impact that external uncertainties have on the decisions that combine to define a development strategy. Of particular importance are the decisions having to do with the distribution of effort among uncertainty resolving tasks and the degree of production flexibility that is planned for. The greater the uncertainty about the future military threat, the longer to delay the final establishment of a product configuration in the development process and the more alternatives to have under consideration (and in development) in order to meet the developing threat. Because of these considerations, as uncertainty in the threat increases (or putting it another way, as uncertainty about the ultimate product value increases) Program A will be preferred to Program B in Figure 9, and Program C to Program D in Figure 10, all other things being equal.

In Figure 9 there is less time between the definition and the deployment of the system in Program A than in Program B. This means that it is more probable that the threat envisioned at the definition stage will remain relevant at deployment. In order to minimize this time between definition and deployment, under conditions of considerable threat uncertainty, the developer might be willing to accept either some increase in cost or some increase in total development time. These are prices he would be willing to pay under some conditions.

Similarly, if there is some probability that a program will be can-

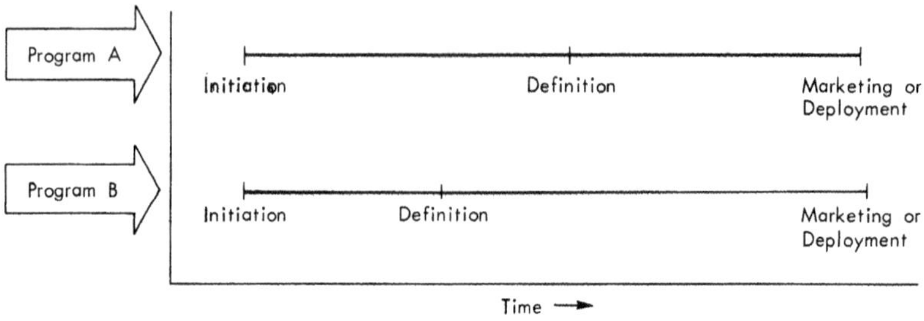

Fig. 9. Key events in development

celed or severely redirected as a result of a change in the threat, then Program C is preferable to Program D in Figure 10. At any time, if the programs are canceled, less resources will have been expended in Program C than in Program D. Again, to obtain these benefits, a developer might well be willing to accept a somewhat higher cost or a somewhat longer overall development time. Thus under some conditions of uncertainty surrounding the future he might prefer Program E to Program D.

The primary means for obtaining differences in programs such as are shown in Figures 9 and 10 are through shifts in the relative effort

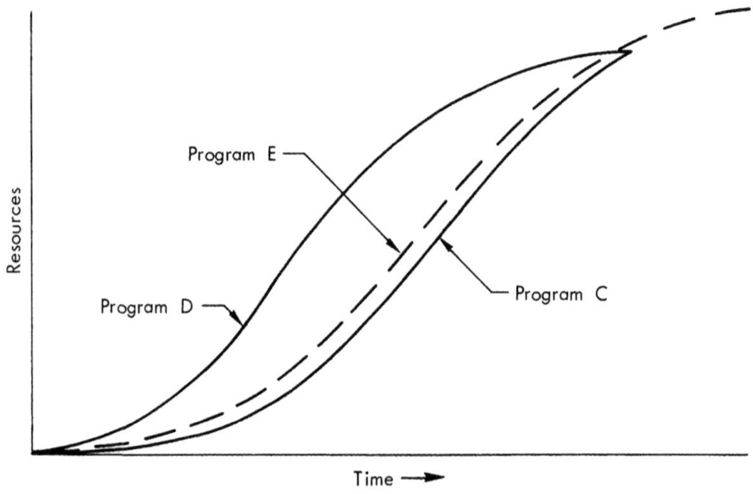

Fig. 10. Cumulative costs of development

among the various uncertainty reducing activities. For instance increased analysis, model testing, or prototype testing prior to the final definition of the system could lead to a lessening of the time between that definition and deployment by lessening the time to get a production line in operation and by lessening the number of changes required as a result of testing production systems. Similarly the delay of tooling and production expenditures will lead to an expenditure curve like that associated with Program C or E in Figure 10.

The feasibility of these shifts varies with technology. There are considerable differences between missile and aircraft programs for instance. In missile programs virtually all flight tests result in destruction of the component and hence to carry on any volume of tests requires a corresponding volume of test vehicles and production capabilities. Aircraft flight tests ordinarily do not result in destruction of the vehicle and hence require few vehicles and less production capability. Within each technology, however, there is considerable scope for tradeoffs among the various types of uncertainty resolving activities. The important point to recognize here is that the choice of a development strategy cannot be made solely on the basis of information internal to the project.

When there are static uncertainties (uncertainties as to use, tactics, and so on), the tightness of the interrelations of the subsystem should be an important concern. A highly interrelated system is harder to modify to perform tasks not anticipated during initial design than is a more loosely interrelated one. Again it must be noted, however, that a price is generally paid to achieve this. For example the airframe of a fighter aircraft may have to be larger, hence the engines will be larger and the total system cost will be higher. Similar remarks apply to a missile. As a result of this, the costs of producing the final system may be higher. If this results in a more useful system, it may be worth the price that the developer is willing to pay.

M. Conclusion

This chapter has been largely taxonomic, concerned with characterizing development decisions and pinpointing critical variables. There are, however, a number of more positive conclusions concerning good or bad development policies. Where there is great uncertainty about the ultimate value of the developed product or where a large state of the art advance is being sought, strategies that emphasize sequential decisionmaking are generally more attractive than those that do not. On the other hand, if these uncertainties are relatively small, projects that are more completely "planned" at their initiation may be, in some sense, more efficient. Certain types of uncertainty reduction are more appropriate to large state of the art advances than others. Systems interrelatedness will have an important bearing on the project outcome with the effect again dependent upon the state of the art advance and the nature of the uncertainty reducing steps.

The RAND work on development led to a number of conclusions about the manner in which development activities were and should be conducted by the Air Force. These conclusions were based upon the experience of the 1950's and possibly are no longer true because of Department of Defense and Department of the Air Force changes. Nonetheless, an examination of some of the conclusions here may provide some insight on how the material in this chapter can aid in organizing one's thinking about development.

One of the primary conclusions, based upon examination of numerous histories, was that the uncertainties inherent in Air Force projects of the 1950's were very great. Certainly this is illustrated in several of the case studies shown in Chapter 3 and in the statistical examination reported in Chapter 4. The size of these uncertainties was occasioned by the state of the art advances being sought and to some extent by the time constraints placed on the developments. The discussion in this chapter suggests that two things are appropriate in such a situation: (1) A sequential learning process should be followed, and (2) the components of the total system should be relatively loosely interrelated.

The observations suggested, however, that frequently neither of these two factors seemed to be adequately considered. Two trends were occurring in the early 1950's. In the first, the view that a development is a system was gaining increasing acceptance. There were important reasons for this. In particular, several developments were plagued by the fact that their components did not work together initially, requiring expensive and unexpected fixes. But the trend toward viewing new products as a system seemed to lead to a tendency to want to optimize systems, and the process of optimizing tended to give insufficient attention to the uncertainties. The net result was that the interrelatedness of the subsystem seemed to increase substantially.

The difficulties arising from this trend were compounded by another trend, the adopting of procedures designed to shorten development times. Various terms were applied to these policies, the most frequent being the terms "Cook-Craigie procedures," or "concurrency."[8] Many argued about the meaning of these terms, and some felt that they were, in fact, the same procedure. The common thread in their use, however, was that they attempted to reduce development times primarily through careful planning. Although it is true that these procedures did not preclude the use of any particular type of uncertainty reduction techniques, they did tend to favor analysis and model testing over prototype testing of component subsystems because of the time (and expense) required for such tests.

The emphasis on careful development planning had much the same effect that careful system planning had. It tended to suppress the uncertainties and to reduce the sequential character of decision-making. This latter tendency occurred because of the need for constraint of the outcome of a particular development task so that it meshed with the outcome of other such tasks. It can be seen that the outcome of such a situation when compounded by the tendency to tighten the interrelatedness could lead to considerable difficulty, which would require resources and time to resolve, possibly eliminating time and cost advantages expected to accrue to the projects from the use of these procedures.

Several of the case studies suggested that this was indeed so. The case of the F-102, reported in Chapter 3, is notable. However, the case studies also indicated examples of "good" developments and suggested possible rules of thumb to guide the developer. If time was very important, a solution was to try not to seek very large advances in components and use a non-sequential development planning approach. This is illustrated by the case of the F-100. Alternatively, if time and performance were both deemed to be important, a sequential approach could be taken, particularly if tight interrelations were not required. The F-104 is an example of such a program. Finally, high performance could also be achieved quickly if sufficient parallel development activity were undertaken on critical components. Notable here is the early ballistic missile program (whose history is not reported in this book).

It is important to recognize that any one of these combinations of

[8] The Cook-Craigie procedures emphasized the building of a relatively large group of prototypes of the total system (15 to 30 aircraft) to allow rapid testing of the total system. Because of the need to produce the large quantity of examples of the system, production tooling was required and thus the design essentially entered production before very much full scale testing was done. See Chapter 3.

state of the art advance, interrelatedness, and short development time is potentially desirable. It has been the tendency of most large organizations to adopt procedures appropriate to the image they hold of the "ideal" development. Experience has shown that there is no ideal, and that procedures should be flexible enough to allow strategies appropriate to each development.

Chapter 3

THE ROLE OF PROJECT HISTORIES IN THE STUDY OF R&D

by THOMAS MARSCHAK

A. INTRODUCTION

The purpose of this chapter is to illustrate one approach to the study of development: the compilation and analysis of intensive histories of completed development projects. We shall be interested in the sorts of conjectures about development on which a group of related histories can shed light.

The project histories with which we shall deal are histories of airborne radars, aircraft engines, fighter aircraft, bombers, and an air-to-air missile.[1] When sufficient in number and sufficiently closely related, a group of histories can provide strong support for general conjectures about the nature of development, and specific conjectures about the consequences of (1) alternative strategies for the conduct of development in a given area of technology, and (2) alternative modes of organizing the team of people who make up a development project.

Project histories, on the other hand, have several serious limitations. The main one is that a strong subjective element often enters the interpretation of a history and the decision as to whether or not it supports a given conjecture. This is, of course, the classic difficulty of all historical analysis.

We shall illustrate here both the possibilities and the limitations of the project-history method. To do so we shall focus on two main topics and shall investigate the extent to which our collection of case

[1] Two histories of non-military developments have appeared elsewhere: T. A. Marschak: Strategy and Organization in a System Development Project (a study of the development of a large microwave transmission system); and R. R. Nelson: The Link Between Science and Invention: The Case of the Transistor, both in R. R. Nelson, ed., *The Rate and Direction of Inventive Activity: Economic and Social Factors*, Princeton: Princeton University Press, 1962.

histories can support a hypothesis about each of them. First we shall try to see whether the histories support the hypothesis that major uncertainty, at least in the earlier phases of development, is a natural and inevitable property of a program that seeks a real technical advance. Second, we shall try to see whether the histories support a hypothesis about the consequences of making heavy or light commitments in the early phases of development. Stated very broadly, the hypothesis is as follows: When the predictions available at the start of a development program are used as the basis of heavy commitments to a highly specified design, then in the fortunate cases when the predictions turn out to be correct, time and money may have been saved compared with the postponing of such commitments until later in development. If the predictions are seriously wrong, however, costly revisions will be required. The initial uncertainties of development are such that the gains due to heavy initial commitments in the fortunate cases are outweighed by the costly revisions of the unfortunate cases.

The studies that follow all deal with military projects because all of them were prepared as part of a broad effort to understand military research and development. For several reasons the studies differ from one another in scope and style. The original studies, on which the sections that follow are closely based, were prepared by several different authors. Furthermore, the availability of historical material varied considerably; some projects were voluminously documented, and others required patient interviewing and searching through files to construct even a fragmentary history. Again, the original studies differed with respect to the amount of material that had to be deleted here because of (a) military security or (b) the privileged status of the material (revealed in confidence by private firms).

The following histories contain a fair amount of historical and technical detail. The aim is to preserve, as much as possible, the true flavor of the histories, the concrete form taken by development strategy, and the uncertainties of development.

Finally, a strong word of caution is in order about the interpretation of the histories. The criticism of past development procedures, or the past performance of any development agency, is *not* our purpose. Nor is our purpose to advocate one kind of R&D management policy as opposed to another. Any such interpretation of the histories entirely misses the point of this chapter: to illustrate an important method for acquiring knowledge about the research and development process.

B. Airborne Radars [2]

In the development of a military airborne radar, the final item is an operational radar, satisfactorily performing in one or more specific aircraft in a specified military environment (combat, reconnaissance, and so on). We shall consider several programs that differed in important respects.

1. "Side-looking" Radar

Developmental History

Early in 1954 some reconnaissance radar photographs taken by the Royal Air Force were seen at the headquarters of the Strategic Air Command. The radar used was a "side-looking" radar, photographing a strip several miles wide on either side of the plane. The reflected radar signals were received through fixed linear antennas mounted on either side of the plane. Previous radars had photographed a circular area, using a rotating antenna. The side-looking radar operated at a frequency in the K_a-band.[3] Its photography represented a startling improvement over previous radar photography; in information content it approached the quality of poor-resolution optical photography. At that time there happened to be an acute need for an all-weather, high-resolution reconnaissance capability to be used for the detection of air bases. The principal existing reconnaissance radar—the APS-23—rarely met the need. Moreover, no U.S. Air Force radar then under development was capable of results at all comparable to the RAF photography.

In February 1954, personnel from Wright Air Development Center and from SAC went to Britain to examine the British photography and equipment in more detail. On March 25, SAC officially requested the Air Research and Development Command to initiate a 90-day program to develop a side-looking radar capable of detecting runways of a certain width from an altitude of 40,000 feet, considerably higher than the altitude from which the RAF pictures had been taken. On April 11, the Commander of the Air Research and Development Command ordered this program started on a high priority.

Early in May, Westinghouse Electric Company was given an informal go-ahead with the understanding that one K_a-band radar set

[2] This section is closely based on a study prepared by B. H. Klein and E. Sharkey.

[3] A frequency band in the neighborhood of 35,000 megacycles per second.

would be designed, built and installed in a SAC reconnaissance bomber – an RB-47 – within 60 days. (The 60-day period was set to comply with SAC's earlier 90-day request.)

Although the British model might have been copied to meet this short deadline, for several important reasons it was not. First, SAC wanted a set that would operate at much higher altitudes than the British design; second, the system had to be designed to fit in an RB-47. There was no certainty that K_a-band radar could "see" all the way to the ground from 40,000 feet, and the question of K_a-band performance degradation by weather was still unanswered. It was necessary to get answers to these and other basic questions from the initial model, and quickly. Accordingly, the requirements put on the contractor were simple: to make a set that would *detect* (but not necessarily provide detailed photographs) runways of a specified width from 40,000 feet out to a range of 10 miles on at least one side of the aircraft. The flight test would show whether these requirements were met or whether it was possible to meet them. No other more detailed requirements were insisted upon, and no sophisticated features were asked for. The Air Force expected the contractor to come up with as good and reliable a set as was possible in the short time available, but there was no insistence on equipment details. The first model looked to only one side of the aircraft; to make it look to both sides would have increased the time required to achieve a working set.

The Air Force's arrangement with Westinghouse, concluded on May 15, took the form of an amendment to an existing Air Force-Westinghouse contract, and had several unusual provisions. In the first place, specific compliance with JAN Specs (Joint Army-Navy Specifications) was not mentioned in the contract. Such specifications, often assigned at this stage of development, would have constrained the dimensions, performance, and reliability in a detailed manner. The informal understanding was that Westinghouse would choose components with an eye to making the equipment highly reliable and maintainable; and that the particular choices would require approval only of the Air Force people directly in charge of the project. Second, the contractor was given the task of maintaining the equipment for one year.[4] Third, the contractor was given responsibility for installing the radar in a SAC-furnished RB-47, and for working directly with Boeing (the plane's manufacturer), to make structural changes in the airplane so that it could accommodate the antenna.

[4] Giving the contractor the maintenance responsibility undoubtedly made it easier to sell the idea of waiving technical specifications. The presumption was that if the contractor had to maintain the equipment he would not be likely to use components that would complicate the task of keeping it in good working order.

The radar was designated the AN/APQ-56. The total amount provided in the initial contract for the development, installation and maintenance of the first model—the XA-1—was $370,000.

Although the XA-1 did benefit considerably from the British side-looking radar work (and also from Westinghouse's previous experience in K_a-band radar work), major development problems remained. To get a 10-foot linear-array antenna to perform satisfactorily, for example, required an antenna design and construction effort that continued far beyond the time the XA-1 was first tested. Because side-looking radar involves an entirely different type of presentation than does a scanning (rotating) radar, new problems were faced in getting a satisfactory recorder and camera, as well as the usual problems encountered in making the first model of any kind of new radar.

Despite these difficulties, however, 59 days after Westinghouse was told to go ahead, the XA-1 was test-flown in the SAC RB-47, and succeeded on its first flight in picking up runway patterns from the required altitude. The antenna pattern was not satisfactory, but the initial flights of this first model showed that at 40,000 feet operation was feasible, that runways were easily detected, and that weather was not much of a problem in the K_a-band.

Shortly after the XA-1 was flown, and after bids had again been solicited from three contractors, Westinghouse was awarded a contract for building ten improved models (the XA-2). The schedule called for the first delivery to be made on December 1, and for one additional set to be delivered every three weeks in the period following. Westinghouse was to deliver the sets directly to Lockbourne Air Force Base and install them in SAC RB-47s.

Westinghouse then proceeded to redesign the radar. A more complete system, looking to both sides of the aircraft, was designed and developed, and a number of improvements were made (for example, improved signal-to-noise ratio, smoothing of the antenna pattern). Other possible changes, for example, to insure better mapping accuracy, to get a larger film size, or to get in-flight processing of the side-looking radar photography, were not incorporated in this second design; the emphasis was still on *quickly* giving SAC a small, all-weather, high-resolution reconnaissance capability, now that it had been shown to be feasible.

It turned out to be very fortunate that no attempt was made to incorporate these peripheral improvements and, consequently, to delay testing, for when the radar was tested early in December, it was found—as it has been found in the course of almost every airborne radar development—that there were some fairly basic difficulties (for example, reliability, antenna pattern, and so on) that still had to be overcome. A series of modifications (resulting in the XA-2 Model II) was then undertaken to correct the difficulties and to make the radar operationally more useful. (SAC asked for a larger film size and a compass heading repeater.) In the main, however, improvements were aimed at overcoming the technical difficulties encountered in the Model I version of the XA-2. The already delivered models were modified by being run back through the factory.

The first Model II set, which was flown early in May 1955, performed much more satisfactorily. At SAC's request, attention was then turned to increasing the operational suitability of the radar. Changes were made to improve the radar's mapping accuracy and to add other features that the tests showed to be necessary. The Model III was delivered for testing in September of 1955.

During the latter part of 1955 the airborne reliability of the equipment was improved to about 80 per cent. By the standards of postwar airborne radar development this is a rather remarkable achievement, especially considering that modifications were still underway during the period. (The malfunction rate of approximately 20 per cent includes the effects of shakedown flights on factory modified equipment.)

Organizational Aspects

The side-looking radar project had important organizational properties. The test and development programs were run as one, with a very wide measure of decisionmaking authority and responsibility vested in only a few on-the-spot Air Force people: two from Wright Air Development Center's Aerial Reconnaissance Laboratory, and two officers at Lockbourne Air Force Base. Higher echelons did not have to be consulted on changing a detailed "General Operational Requirement" or a previously prepared "Development Plan," because there were none. The contractor had responsible engineering personnel at Lockbourne AFB, where the test program was being conducted, and which was only a short distance from WADC. This facilitated quick decisions. By virtue of these arrangements the problem of communication between the operational command, the R&D command, and the contractor was minimized.

The integration of the test program into the development work not only permitted modifications to be made on the basis of realistic test results, but it also gave SAC a considerable amount of operational experience in the use of a new technique. This seems to have been an important reason why the developed radar was attained with such relative speed.

The contractor displayed an enthusiasm and effectiveness that Air

Force personnel reported to be exceptional. This cannot be attributed to any definite assurance of a large procurement contract for this radar, for the original commitment was for only ten XA-2s. Moreover, Westinghouse had no reason to regard itself as a unique source for side-looking radars. (Concurrently, Bell Laboratories was testing a side-looking radar of another frequency in a SAC plane, with very good results.) On the other hand, Westinghouse certainly did have reason to believe that there might be a substantial market for such a radar if it could be successfully developed, and, indeed, subsequently received a contract from the Navy.

It seems reasonable to assume that the organization of the project stimulated the contractor's eagerness to do a good job. Since it was able to get quick and relatively well-informed decisions, the company was able to keep its engineering staff fully and productively occupied from the time development on the XA-1 was initiated to the completion of the ten test models (the XA-2 Model III) of the Q-56, and thereby to keep the cost of the program low. There were no lulls in development activity while equipment was waiting six months or more to be tested. There was no long period of uncertainty between the completion of Phase I development (the XA-1) and the award of a Phase II contract (the XA-2). The blanket exemption from "Joint Army-Navy (JAN) Specifications" made it unnecessary for the contractor to apply for necessary exemptions piecemeal, and to wait the customary interval (in some programs six months or so) for approval. (Approximately 60–70 per cent of the Q-56 parts were not on the approved JAN list; 20–30 per cent actually had never been built before.) Long periods were not spent ironing out differences among the contractor, the R&D people, the agencies responsible for testing the radars, and the operational command.

2. World War II Radars

During World War II at least five different USAF airborne microwave radars were developed to a quite adequate degree of operational usefulness and reliability, and were used extensively in combat.[5] These radars were developed similarly in important respects to the strategy used in the Q-56 program. The need for each of the radars was urgent. Their development was not based on any elaborate requirement. There was no long-term, highly detailed consideration of all the factors of the operational environment in which they were going to be used; a "best" set of specifications for meeting this en-

[5] Some other radars were developed through the initial testing phase, and then canceled.

vironment was not imposed. Rather, several radars (often of different design) were quickly readied for flight testing. After testing, one or more was chosen to be brought quickly to combat useful status. A small-scale combat operations test was usually the final phase. Production of a final model then began. The argument for quickly getting models into a highly realistic test environment seemed to be that there was simply not time to do otherwise. It is true, of course, that some of the accelerated test programs turned out poorly; but a radar that was not good enough was discovered quickly.[6]

The development of the SCR-717-B radar along with the APQ-5B computer for low-altitude bombing is an example of such a program. Development of the radar and computer as experimental models was begun in 1942. In August 1943, following a quick R&D flight test, a realistic one-squadron combat flight-test program was initiated (the test area happened to be in the Solomon Islands), during which many modifications, both in the radar and the computer, were made. Within five weeks, the reliability of the radar and the computer on combat missions was improved to over 90 per cent.[7] It is worth noting that the equipment was used in fair quantity for the rest of the war with no further changes (except for the switch from "S-band" to "X-band" in the radar when this became possible).

The SCR-517 series of radars (the first USAF microwave radar) was used primarily at low altitude in the antisubmarine campaign. The APS-15, the APQ-13, and the APQ-7 were high-altitude bombing radars; they were basic radar sets with a very simple bombing computer included. Figure 11 shows the development times for all of these wartime microwave radars.

3. Some Postwar Radars

For postwar radars completed by 1957 other than the Q-56, the time elapsing between the start to development and the start of operational use ran from about four to seven years.[8] Most of these radars

[6] In so characterizing wartime radar development, we certainly do not want to imply that all the wartime radar programs were conducted in exactly the same manner. Not all the models that were tried in combat tests were "development" models, some were "research" models. The line between research and development was at times hard to define. But the tendency to push even very crude experimental models into operational aircraft was one important difference between the wartime and later conduct of radar development.

[7] Radar reliability was then defined more stringently than became the case after the war: a flight was "successful" only if the radar functioned satisfactorily during the entire flight.

[8] The bombing radars developed include the APS-23 (part of the K- and Q-24 bombing systems), the HSBR (part of the MA-2 bombing system), the APS-64 (a tunable

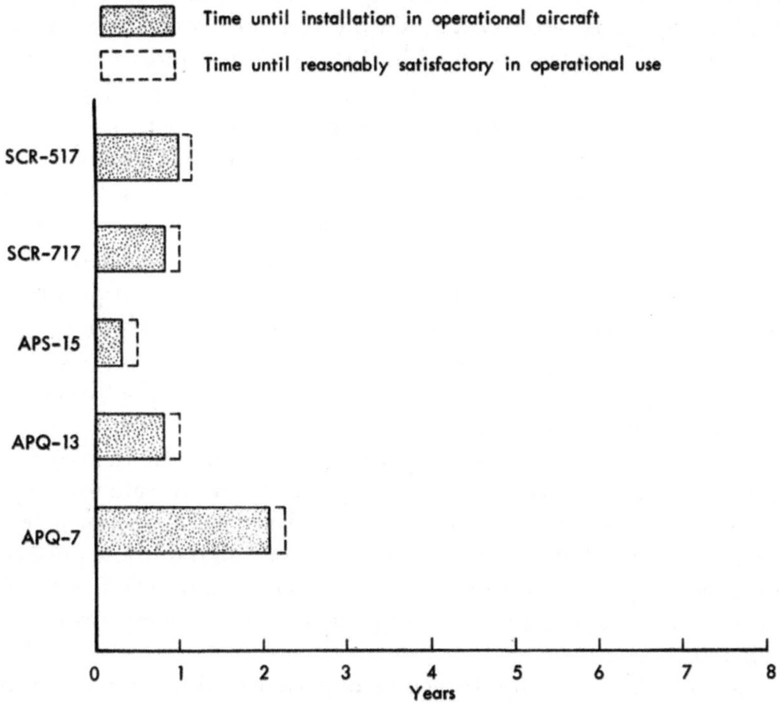

Fig. 11. World War II radar development

proved to be far from satisfactory. Where the radar in question was already in production, correction of the faults was difficult and expensive.

The APS-23 is one example of a radar that took a long time to develop and was found to be unsatisfactory. In terms of inherent technical difficulty, this radar should not have been essentially more difficult to develop than a number of other radars, including the Q-56. Design of this radar began in 1945. It was first put in SAC planes in 1949, four years later, but after a relatively insignificant amount of testing (compared with the Q-56). It was combined with a computer to form the Q-24 bombing system but the immediate

modification of the APS-23), and the K-5 radar (part of a bombing system developed for the Tactical Air Command). Although the associated computers had the same problems as the radars, only the radars are discussed here because the radars are all roughly comparable as a development problem. The all-purpose search radars were the APS-42 and the APN-59. (The APS-42 was actually a Navy design which has been widely used by the Air Force.)

impact of the introduction of the Q-24 was a significant loss in SAC's combat capability—the system simply did not work often enough. Two years after it was installed in SAC airplanes, and a full six years after the initiation of the program, many faults of the radar (and the associated computer) still had not been overcome. A major program (Project Reliable) was undertaken to bring the performance of the Q-24 computer-radar system up to acceptable standards. Within half a year, a limited number of sets assigned to a special test and modification program were brought up to a reliability of over 90 per cent; but it was some time later before all of SAC's sets were appropriately modified. The cost of the modification program per radar system exceeded the original purchase price of the equipment.

There was similarly slow progress in the case of the K-bombing system, which also used the APS-23 radar but with a different computer. From the first installation of the K-bombing system in SAC aircraft to the achievement of a 10–15 per cent failure rate took about five years. During this period the APS-23 radar was responsible for roughly half the failures. Many factors contributed to these poor performance difficulties, but it seems safe to say an important factor was the insignificant amount of testing the systems received prior to installation.

As a result of the unsatisfactory experience with these two radar bombing systems, interest became focused on equipment reliability in the development of the next radar bombing system. (This was the MA-2 system, previously called the HSBD, and later the ASB-4; the radar portion is called the HSBR.)

The HSBR took more than six years to develop. Flight experience began late in the program. It was then necessary to modify the MA-2 radar and computer extensively in order to satisfy SAC with respect to operability and reliability, even though reliability had been heavily emphasized from the start. SAC's dissatisfaction with the system developed soon after SAC personnel got their first real flight experience with the system.

The other postwar radars have not had as serious problems when they were introduced into operational use, but for the most part these radars represented relatively small departures from existing equipment. The relative speed of the Q-56 program is shown in Figure 12.

The development histories of a number of postwar radars contrast sharply with those of the Q-56 and some of the World War II radars. For these postwar programs the aim was to avoid successive modifications and to proceed directly, by careful planning, to the final production models. Detailed requirements were issued before the start of development. The requirements were determined after considering in detail the capabilities of the radar observer; the logistical and training difficulties, and what was then known about the performance of alternative possible designs. Following the issuing of detailed requirements, a detailed design proposal and a detailed development schedule were approved by the appropriate agencies.

Since the approved development plan and the approved requirements were the result of such an intensive effort, it was hoped that major design changes would not occur in the course of development. When they did appear necessary, the organization of the program often made it difficult to get them approved. Responsibility for the project was divided into a number of functions (for example, formulating the initial requirements, programming the development effort,

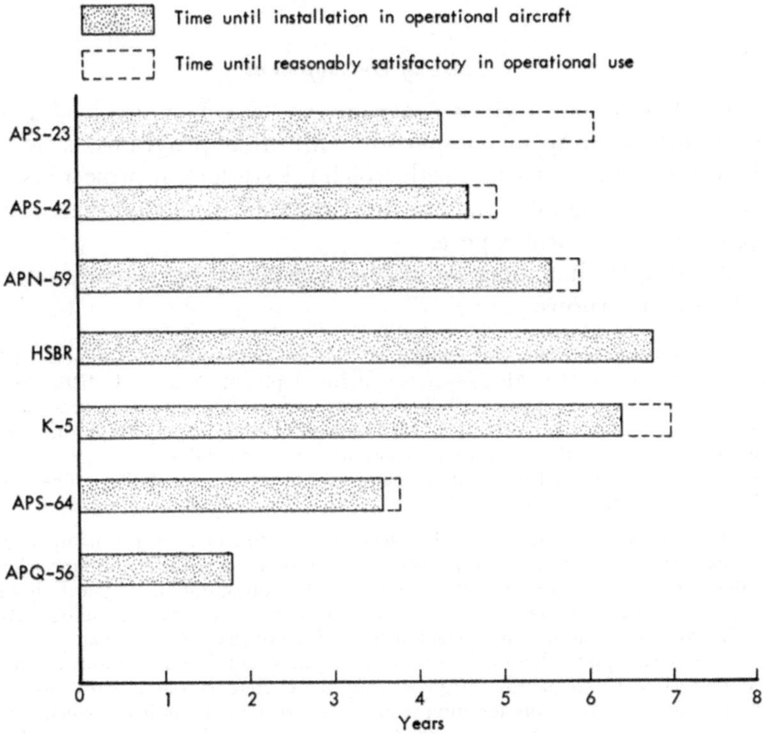

Fig. 12. Postwar radar development times

supervising the program, testing the development equipment) which were performed by a number of different specialist agencies. Many design changes required the concurrence of all of them, and this, of course, took time.[9]

Much of the testing effort in the postwar programs consisted of lengthy series of "R&D tests." Members of the operating command (the final customer) played only a minor role in these tests, as compared with the Q-56 and the wartime programs. The R&D tests were generally not as realistic as those of the wartime programs.

4. Interpretation

What tentative explanations can be proposed for the relatively short development time of the Q-56 and the World War II radars? Were they perhaps (1) "easy" development jobs, or (2) projects in which short development time was bought by the expenditure of an unusual amount of money?

Ease of Development

Whether or not a given program was "easy," or involved a small technological jump by comparison with other programs, is perhaps the most delicate problem with which the student of project histories has to deal. Generally one has no choice but to rely on the personal opinions of technical experts.

We suggest that there would be substantial agreement with the following assertions:

---

[9] The best evidence for this characterization of postwar development is Manual 80-4, issued by the U.S. Air Research and Development Command, *ARDC Program Management Procedures,* August 1957, to define approved development procedures in Air Force-sponsored projects. The Manual describes the many steps (involving a number of agencies) that must precede issuance of a development contract, as well as the procedures required in obtaining approval for subsequent changes. The Manual interprets these procedures as follows:

> "This concept of performing work in accordance with a plan sets up an implicit requirement that no individual or agency will make a change affecting time schedules, technical and performance requirements, configuration, physical characteristics, or cost, without consulting with other agencies concerned and obtaining full agreement and approval. The approval of the original R and D plan validates the technical approach and the resources required but does not authorize initiation of work. Consequently, an agency must not change its commitment and must not undertake any action deviating from the approved plan until all participating, coordinating and approving agencies have been notified, the over-all impact of the proposed change evaluated and a decision in the form of a changed directive issued."

1) The many advances incorporated into operational airborne radars during the few years of the war far overshadow the relatively few real advances that have been made in the decade following the war. The primary difference between the wartime and the postwar airborne radars is that the latter are better integrated into the associated bombing computers; however, the extra complexity has appeared primarily in the computers, not in the radars.

2) Although the Q-56 did benefit considerably from the experimental flight test work of the British, it can hardly be characterized as a "relatively easy, off-the-shelf, components-assembly job." A number of the main components were unusually large departures from their counterparts in preceding radars. The novelty reflected the fact that the Q-56 was to operate in a frequency range in which there had been little relevant experience; that it was not to be a scanning radar with rotating antenna like previous radars; and that unlike other radars, which could supply information directly to an observer, it would be useless without very high-speed photography. In particular an antenna and lens system different from the British one had to be designed, and the construction of the K-band linear-array antennas to the needed tolerances proved to be an especially difficult job.

3) Though the other airborne radars developed since World War II have all had special problems, their development has not involved many radically new techniques. The basic design of the APS-23, for example, was completed during the war.

Development Costs

Approximate development costs for a number of wartime and postwar radars are given in Table 1. The figures in the first column relate to the actual development costs; the figures in the second column have been adjusted for increases in engineering and materials costs in order to indicate their approximate price levels.[10] It will be noted that in presenting the cost of the wartime programs, we have lumped together as a single program those radars that were developed from the same general design.

The table shows that the wartime "emergency" programs were not expensive compared with the postwar radar development program. On the contrary, in terms of 1957 engineering and materials costs, the cost of developing the wartime radars averaged not much more

[10] These adjustments were made on the basis of contractor-furnished information on wage and material costs.

TABLE 1

RADAR DEVELOPMENT COSTS [a]

Time Period and Radar Problem	Actual Cost (million $)	Approximate Cost in 1957 Dollars (million $)
Wartime		
SCR-517-19-20	3.5	7.2
SCR-717 A, B, C	3.2	6.6
APQ-13	3.0	6.3
APQ-7	2.5	5.3
Postwar		
APS-23	8.0 [b]	11.1 [b]
HSBR	15.6	17.2
APQ-56	5.1 [c]	5.3 [c]

Notes:

[a] Includes cost of fabricating initial flight test models, service tests, and subsequent engineering services.

[b] Does not include Project Reliable costs.

[c] Includes the cost of contractor maintenance and the cost of SAC's ten operational radars.

than half the cost of the APS-23 program, and not much more than one-third the cost of the HSBR program.[11]

Ease of development and money spent do not, then, explain the speed of the Q-56 and the wartime programs. A strong contender as an explanation is the set of differences between the general development strategy of the World War II and Q-56 programs on the one hand and the development strategy of the indicated postwar radars on the other. Organizational differences between the two groups of programs supplement this explanation.

In the wartime radars and the Q-56, detailed operational and

[11] In making the cost comparisons we did not include in the cost of the wartime radars the amounts spent for research and initial development work on them by the M.I.T. Radiation Laboratory. The above figures cover costs on *development* work done on getting radars designed for production for use in combat aircraft; they do not include research program costs. If the cost of Project Reliable were adjudged to be a development cost, the total APS-23 development costs would be substantially larger than shown above. It might be noted, however, that even including amounts spent at the Radiation Laboratory on the wartime radars, which would increase the wartime amounts shown by about one-third, the wartime programs still stand out as costing less than the postwar programs (in which no research costs are included).

technical requirements were absent. The initial emphasis was on getting out preliminary flight test models quickly. The test program for these models, moreover, consisted of a rapid, concentrated series of *realistic* tests; equipment was flown and tested by the operating Air Force command in the same environment in which the final item was to perform.

These properties of the program seem to have had the following consequence: The absence of detailed requirements made it *possible* to get flight test models quickly. It was not necessary to spend time ensuring that a flight test model was consistent with requirements imposed on the final model. The speed with which the test data were in fact obtained, and their realism, made it possible to determine the faults of the tested models very quickly—faults that are unpredictable, inevitably occur, and can be spotted only through realistic testing. (The cost of obtaining this information was a small fraction of the total development cost.) Correction of these faults was quick and inexpensive at this stage of development, as compared with modification of models already in or near the production stage. Moreover, the broad definition of a "satisfactory" version of the radar permitted a wide choice of corrections to be made.

Organizational aspects of the Q-56 and wartime programs seem to have reinforced these effects of the strategic properties. Responsibility and authority were held by a small group of on-the-spot people. Changes in the programs were approved very quickly. Those in charge of operational matters were quickly able to obtain information and advice about the equipment from the developing engineers.

The strategy and organization of the postwar programs, on the other hand, was, as we have shown, quite different. Commitments were made to detailed designs and detailed schedules at a stage when knowledge about designs was unreliable. Realistic early testing was not stressed and there were organizational obstacles to the quick approval of major advances.

C. Aircraft Engines [12]

The turbojet and turboprop engines discussed here were all completed between the end of World War II and the end of 1957. Most of the histories that it proved possible to compile are brief and fragmentary. Only one is detailed.

Although the histories are deficient, we shall preface them with a

[12] This section is based on a longer study by T. A. Marschak.

largely illustrative attempt to characterize the general nature of engine development. We do not attempt such a characterization for any of the other areas of technology with which the project histories in this study deal, although such an attempt would be useful in all of them. The main hypotheses whose possible testing concerns us in this study have to do with the way the developer's knowledge changes as development proceeds and the performance of different development strategies, that is, different ways of responding to the changed knowledge. For each of the areas of technology we consider, it would be useful to have a model of the typical development project, in which the changes in knowledge that occur are described concretely. In such a model the main magnitudes characterizing the item emerging from the typical project are considered, and the learning that typically occurs with respect to each of them as development proceeds may suggest a natural division of the project history into stages.

There are a great many ways to divide development into stages. If, in each of the stages chosen, there are relatively great gains in the developer's knowledge about some of the magnitudes defining the final item, and relatively small gains in knowledge about others, it is easy to describe development strategies. Suppose it is in fact possible to define stages A, B, and C of the typical project such that there is relatively great reduction in the developer's uncertainty about magnitude 1 in stage A, about magnitude 2 in stage B, and about magnitude 3 in stage C. Then a strategy involving heavy commitments when uncertainties are still large could be described as a strategy that bets heavily on predictions about magnitude 1 at the start of stage A, magnitude 2 before stage B, and magnitude 3 before stage C.

We shall make a rough attempt at a division of this kind for the case of engine development. The model is intended primarily to be an illustration of the sort of model it would be useful to have for any technology. Its realism in the case of many past engines is certainly open to question. The stages do not correspond to stages that have been generally defined for the purposes of official project administration, and, of course, they are not intended to. In actual practice the stages have often overlapped in time. They may also blend into each other so that it may be hard to say whether a given development event belongs to the beginning of a certain stage or to the end of the preceding stage.[13] For a number of engine histories in

[13] The model's stages are particularly in need of modification for the case of engines in the Mach 3 range. Development of such engines got under way after the period with which we are concerned.

the period with which we are concerned, however, the suggested sequence of stages seems a reasonable approximation, and for some of these the model will serve to make the characterization of the development strategy more concrete.

1. The Nature of Engine Development: An Illustrative Model

General Observations

An engine is characterized by a number of magnitudes – performance, weight, durability, unit production cost, spatial dimensions. The development of a new engine yields knowledge about the effort needed to attain certain values of these magnitudes. Spatial dimensions have an important peculiarity: an engine may be made larger or smaller within wide limits, that is, it may be scaled up or down, while preserving its basic internal design arrangements.

As development of an engine proceeds, there is less and less uncertainty about how difficult it will be to attain alternative sets of values of the engine magnitudes. More precisely, the decline in uncertainty and the acquisition of knowledge during the course of development may be approximately described as follows:

a) At a given point in the course of developing an engine of a given internal design, suppose that x dollars per week are available to the project for y additional weeks. Suppose also that the scale of the engine is approximately fixed. One then wants to make a prediction about the engine magnitudes that will characterize the engine at that scale when the x additional dollars have been spent and the y additional weeks have passed. Such a prediction may take the form: "the values of the engine magnitudes will lie in a certain region R" (a region in the space of these magnitudes). To such a prediction one may attach a degree of confidence – say 60 per cent. This means, roughly, that one expects predictions made in such programs to be right 60 per cent of the time provided the region R is always chosen to have the same size. A higher degree of confidence can be attained by taking R to be a larger region; if R is taken to be the entire space of the magnitudes, then the degree of confidence is 100 per cent.

The statement that at a certain point in the course of development magnitude 1 is more accurately predictable than magnitude 2 then means that for any degree of confidence, and for any fixed values of x and y, the associated region R permits much less variation with respect to magnitude 1 than with respect to magnitude 2. If, for example, there are just two magnitudes (other than scale) then the region R lies in a two-dimensional space. The figure below indicates a situation in which magnitude 1 is more accurately predictable than magnitude 2.

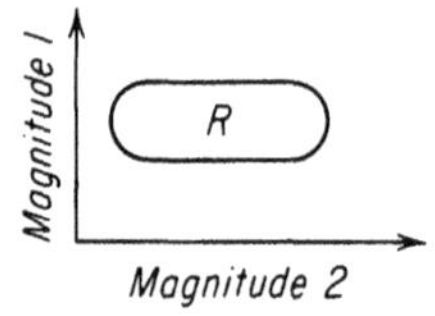

R: region in which final engine magnitudes are predicted to lie, for fixed degree of confidence, fixed engine scale, and fixed remaining budget to be spent over fixed remaining time interval.

b) Suppose, in the course of development, that one considers the effect of changing to a new engine size. Suppose also that for the old size engine, performance is very accurately predictable but the other engine magnitudes are much less accurately predictable. Then for the new scale, performance remains predictable with high accuracy but predictability of the other magnitudes may decline somewhat further. Performance predictions, in other words, can be scaled up or down without much influencing their accuracy; predictions about the other magnitudes lose in accuracy when they are scaled up or down.

c) As development of an engine proceeds all predictions increase in accuracy.

d) At any point in development, performance is generally more accurately predictable (for fixed engine scale) than the other magnitudes. Durability is often the least accurately predictable magnitude, until the very last stages of development.

An Idealized Division of Engine Development into Stages

We shall now describe the development of a new engine in terms of the following successive stages: (1) collection of "on-the-shelf" component test data without application to a specified complete engine (this stage may not occur); (2) the general design study stage; (3) the stage of performance-oriented development; (4) the stage of weight and durability oriented development; (5) the final prototype stage. Beyond the final prototype stage "operational development" may occur, that is, a long sequence of minor modifications that may be quite costly and are stimulated by operational experiences with the engine. But we shall consider development to be complete once operational engines exist. One or more of the stages (2), (3), and (4) may be performed by a developer for several alternative designs, each holding some promise of providing the new engine.

Within the second and third stages, a demonstration in the sense of a sharp increase in knowledge (predictability) of one or more engine magnitudes may occur. The demonstration may be achieved by running "demonstrator" engines (described below) or by testing critical components, or both. The sharp increase in knowledge may take the negative form of determining that a running demonstrator engine or testable components can be built only at extremely great cost over a long period of time so that a decision may be made not to attempt the building but rather to drop the project.

Collection of "On-the-shelf" Component Test Data

In several past engines it is possible to identify one or more components (for example, the compressor) that incorporate design innovations taken "off the shelf." Those innovations were contained in experimental components built *prior to the inception of the engine and without reference to any specific using engine.* Extensive test data obtained from the experimental hardware were then placed "on the shelf" to await the start of a complete engine in which components incorporating the same design innovations (but perhaps of a different scale) could be used. In providing performance predictions for such an engine, the on-the-shelf test data are very useful.

The General Design Study Stage

In this stage, the basic principles of a complete engine's construction are specified—for example, whether it is to be axial or centrifugal flow, single rotor or dual rotor, fixed stator or variable stator, and so on. In addition, dimensions and shapes of the major components—compressor, combustion chambers, turbine, and so on—are tentatively specified. These specifications then also approximately imply the frontal area and over-all dimensions of the engine, though not the weight. The scale of an engine incorporating the basic principles, in other words, is chosen for further study. On the basis of these design specifications, using whatever on-the-shelf test data are available and relevant, and using thermodynamic cycle studies describing the family of theoretical thermodynamic cycles to which the engine's operation may be expected to correspond, performance curves for the engine are obtained.

These curves show specific fuel consumption versus thrust (or versus equivalent shaft horsepower (ESHP) in the case of a turbo-prop)[14] for alternative given air speeds, altitudes, and durations. Several points on this family of curves serve as standard numbers that are frequently used to characterize an engine, for example, maximum thrust (or ESHP) at sea level and zero speed for 5 minutes' duration and for 30 minutes' duration, maximum thrust (or ESHP) at 35,000 feet and 500 knots for 5 minutes' and for 30 minutes' duration. The coordinates of such points may be considered performance parameters roughly defining the performance curves. In computing the performance curves, it is necessary to consider other variables upon which the performance variables depend: for example, airflow, nozzle and inlet temperatures and pressures, and fuel flow. Curves relating these variables are also obtained to use in estimating how great are some of the problems of materials, of detailed component design, and of accessories.

The performance curves of the study yield fairly accurate performance predictions. Relevant on-the-shelf test data further improve these predictions. Alternatively, an engine can be built of the same basic design but of different scale; and for this engine, "scaling" of the original performance curves and the original on-the-shelf test data yields similarly accurate performance predictions.

Weight, durability, and unit production cost are much less accurately predictable at this stage than is performance because they depend on the solution of many individual problems of materials, of detailed component design and construction, and of accessory design and construction. The paper design studies of the variables underlying the engine's performance – temperatures, pressures, airflow, and so on – together with general knowledge about the state of the art for materials, components, and accessories, and data on the specific on-the-shelf components to be used, yield only very rough estimates of the time and money needed to solve most of these problems.[15]

The Stage of Performance-oriented Development

If the design innovations in the engine's major components have previously been extensively tested (though perhaps in a scale different from that of the final engine), so that a collection of on-the-shelf test data is available, then the stage of performance-oriented development may be very short and inexpensive. Its purpose is to achieve

---

[14] Pounds of fuel per hour per pound of thrust (or per equivalent shaft horsepower).

[15] In the design study stage, the developer may also pay attention to the accessibility of components for maintenance of the proposed engine. There may be preference for a design promising great accessibility.

very accurate predictions of the performance of the complete engine, and the component test data when pieced together in the general design study stage may already have yielded such predictions for the scale chosen in the study.

If, on the other hand, no major component test data can be taken off the shelf and if the engine incorporates major design innovations, this stage may require considerable time (perhaps a year or more) and money. To achieve sharp increases in performance predictability beyond that of the general design study, one possible method is the building and running of (or the attempt to build and run) a performance-oriented demonstrator engine. This is an engine incorporating the design principles of the general design study but whose durability is only great enough to permit its running for a short time and whose weight may be quite high compared with the engine of the same scale that emerges at the end of development. Thus, none of the detailed problems of reducing weight and increasing durability has been attacked in building the demonstrator, and it may be built in any scale that is convenient for available test facilities. The performance data obtained by running it may be "scaled" so as to provide nearly as accurate predictions about performance for an engine of different scale as about performance for an engine of the demonstrator's scale. The performance predictions after a demonstrator is run can be expected to be quite accurate.

The same kind of sharp increase in performance predictability may be achieved by constructing and testing those components that have a major effect on performance and for which no test data exist. Generally, such components may be built to a convenient scale. This is the method that has prevailed in the engines studied. If the uncertainty as to performance at the start of the stage hinges only on one or two major components of novel design, then it is probably quicker and cheaper to achieve the sharp increase in predictability by component tests than by building a complete demonstrator.

The Stage of Weight- and Durability-oriented Development

In this stage serious efforts are made to select materials of light weight and high durability for constructing the components of the chosen design.[16] In addition, there are numerous minute configuration details of the major components, and details dealing with the

[16] In turbojet engines in the Mach 3 range—more recent engines than those considered here—materials able to withstand high temperature are much more critical than in previously developed turbojets. Thus, serious consideration of the engine's materials problems may have to begin earlier, perhaps as early as the design study stage.

spacing, mounting, and connecting of the components that affect durability but do not significantly affect performance. Many of these details are worked out during this period.

In this stage, as in the previous one, a sharp increase in knowledge may be achieved by means of a demonstrator engine, component tests, or both. The engine or its components may be run in wind tunnels to simulate high air speeds and altitudes. In this stage, however, the increase occurs in knowledge of weight, durability, and unit production cost. (In solving weight and durability problems knowledge is gained of the cost of fabricating components out of the materials chosen and alternative materials.) The demonstrator and the test components differ markedly from those of the previous stage.

The demonstrator that may be used in this stage has the purpose of demonstrating that the design principles "work" (which means, generally, that performance is consistent with the performance data previously collected) for an engine of a certain scale, a certain weight, and a certain durability. Hence, it is possible to make predictions of much greater accuracy about the further reduction in weight and increases in durability that may be expected after specified further efforts. It may be possible to achieve the same result by testing components that have been constructed with materials problems in mind. If the uncertainty as to weight and durability at the beginning of this stage hinges on one or two major components only, then again it is probably cheaper and quicker to build and test those components rather than to build and complete a demonstrator engine.[17]

The scale of the demonstrator engine and the test components cannot be chosen as freely in this stage as in the previous one. Scaling up or down of weight, durability, and unit production cost predictions obtained from observing a demonstrator or from testing components of a given scale is much less accurate than scaling up or down of performance predictions. Hence the scale most likely to be "best" in the final engine is chosen with some care. Since the "best" scale depends on the changing knowledge mentioned several times before, and since the greater the accumulation of such knowledge supporting the scale decision the less likely it is that the decision will be regretted by the developer, he has a strong incentive to perform the weight- and durability-oriented development after the performance-oriented development (the order could conceivably be reversed). We shall not attempt to define the end of the stage of weight- and durability-

[17] In the case of engines in the Mach 3 range, the predictions obtainable from a demonstrator engine are more limited since air speeds in this range cannot be simulated in existing wind tunnels.

oriented development except to say that it is the beginning of the final prototype stage.

The Final Prototype Stage

In this stage, a complete operational engine, meeting required standards of durability, is achieved. Accessories take final shape. Investigation of the major problems of tooling and fabrication that must be solved before quantity production may begin may also be started in this stage. In this stage, moreover, the design details (mounting arrangements, accessibility for maintenance, controls, and so on) that depend on the detailed configuration of the airframe to which the engine is to be matched, are worked out and incorporated. To do so often requires some predictions as to the detailed configuration of the airframe; and if these predictions turn out to be wrong, some of these "matching" tasks may have to be repeated.

Within the prototype stage, two milestones have generally been used: the passing of the 50-hour Preliminary Flight Rating Test and the 150-hour Qualification Test. Both of these tests are run according to precise military specifications. They are not run continuously but in a series of periods of specified lengths. Each period is further divided into segments in which specified conditions with respect to acceleration, thrust, control positions, fuel, lubrication, and so on must be met. The 150-hour test, in addition, includes numerous tests of separate components. After an engine has completed its running under test conditions, it is disassembled and the parts inspected to determine whether or not the test has been passed.[18]

Following the 50-hour test, there generally begins a series of tests in which the engine is run while flying in, though sometimes not powering, a testing plane. These tests are necessary in order to learn about the engine's durability at higher air speeds and altitudes than test facilities can simulate.

Passing the 150-hour test generally qualifies the engine for production. It is run under conditions of much greater variety and severity than the 50-hour test.

Between the two tests many highly detailed problems are solved. The prototype stage is generally much more expensive (though not longer) than the previous stages combined. However, the only recorded figures that bear this statement out with any precision relate to (1) the task of proceeding from the start of the design study stage (when there are no off-the-shelf test data for major components) to

[18] For Air Force sponsored engines, inspection has generally been performed by the Propulsion Laboratory of Wright Air Development Center.

the passing of the 50-hour test, and (2) the task of proceeding from the passing of the 50-hour test to the passing of the 150-hour test. In the period of this study the first task has taken something like one-third of the development costs and from 2 to 4 years; the second task has taken the remaining two-thirds of the costs and from 1 to 2 years.

Following the passing of the 150-hour test, the typical engine is by no means free from further alterations. Numerous troubles and deficiencies generally occur in operational use and, as we remarked above, "operational development" may occur through much of the engine's life. This may lead to separately identified later models of the original engine. The passing of the 150-hour test, moreover, may make it possible to predict with high confidence that the interval between overhauls of the average engine will be acceptably large; but the dispersion around this average interval is often very great.

In addition to "fixes" on the engine of the first model there are often subsequent models, incorporating design modifications, new materials, or additional accessories. The later models usually account for considerable improvement in performance, weight, and durability. Sometimes an engine may be developed of basically the same design as an existing engine but of different scale.

2. Issues to Be Examined in the Engine Histories

In some engine development programs the developer's task was to achieve an engine meeting certain conditions; no using aircraft was specified. In other programs a using aircraft was specified; it is important to bear in mind that the complete development task in such a program is most accurately thought of as the achievement of a satisfactory airframe-engine combination. In either case one can investigate the commitments and choices made in the successive stages of development, and the knowledge that was available at the time. This we shall do, as far as possible, for the programs to be considered.

3. The J-79

The J-79, which at the close of 1956 was nearing the end of its development (production of early models had begun), incorporates important design innovations and represents a distinct advance. An unusual aspect of its history, compared with previous engines incorporating design principles of comparable novelty, is the accuracy of performance predictions (for the scale chosen) made after the first general design study. The accuracy seems principally due, as we shall see, to testing and placing its major critical component on the shelf prior to the development of the J-79 proper. The accuracy is indicated by Table 2.

TABLE 2

ACCURACY OF PREDICTIONS AS COMPARED WITH ACTUAL PERFORMANCE, J-79 ENGINE

	Predicted Performance of XJ-79, Autumn 1952 [a]	Official Performance (1956) of YJ-79-GE-1, First Production Model
Maximum thrust, sea level, static	14,346	14,500
Specific fuel consumption at maximum thrust (lbs/hr)	2.05	2.00
Military thrust,[b] sea level, static	9,242	9,600
SFC at military thrust	.86	.87

Notes:

[a] In addition to the comparisons shown, predictions made in a General Electric report dated June 1953, with respect to performance at high altitude, appear to have been substantially met by the first production model except that a slightly larger afterburner diameter than that predicted seems to have been required.

[b] Military thrust, or military rated power, is the maximum power or thrust specified for an engine by the manufacturer or by the Air Force as allowable in flight under specified operating conditions for periods of 30 minutes' duration.

The precise origins of the J-79 are both complex and obscure. Probably sometime in 1951 General Electric became aware that there was great Air Force interest in engines capable of speeds around Mach 2 whose specific fuel consumption was sufficiently low that high pressure ratio compressors were required. The Air Force interest became explicit when in February 1951, both Convair and Boeing were given contracts for design studies of a high altitude supersonic strategic bomber.

Two general engine (or compressor) design principles which seemed capable of producing the high compression ratios required were recognized at this time: the dual rotor with fixed geometry and the single rotor with variable stators. The latter principle had been unexplored in actual hardware (although long known in the literature). It offered the possibility of providing the same performance (for a given engine scale) at considerably less weight and for considerably less development effort than the dual rotor, since it was thought to be a less bulky and less delicate mechanism. Sufficient interest in the variable stator principle emerged at General Electric so that in June 1951, work was begun to modify a 14-stage, fixed-stator, single-rotor research compressor (with which unsuccessful attempts to achieve high pressure ratios had been made) into a variable-stator design. Six months later, enough testing of this compressor had been done to demonstrate by providing fairly accurate performance predictions that a variable-stator compressor would be capable of providing high pressure ratios and would not stall at low speeds. In late 1952, design study work was begun on a complete variable-stator engine – a "demonstrator" engine from which the J-79 derived.

The dual-rotor approach was not yet rejected, however. A series of "paper engines" were shown to the Air Force after the testing of the variable-stator research compressor. In these proposals high pressure ratios were achieved by means of dual rotors. Within G. E. the dual-rotor approach still had strong advocates.

A month later, Convair was awarded a development contract for the B-58 with a General Electric engine of specified scale and performance. For several months afterward, there was still disagreement within G. E. as to whether the engine was to have dual rotor or variable stators. The variable-stator viewpoint finally gained ascendancy and the engine for the B-58 became the variable-stator J-79. Design studies for this engine were then completed. As a result of the data previously obtained from testing of the research compressor (on-the-shelf component test data), it was possible to predict with high confidence the performance that would correspond to the design scale chosen. (This scale was considerably smaller – 165 pounds per second airflow instead of 240 pounds per second – than the scale of the research compressor.) However, considerable uncertainty remained as to the levels of weight and durability (and unit production cost) that would be attained (for this scale) after given expenditures over given time periods. But it *was* believed that a given expenditure over a given time period would permit lower weight and greater durability under the variable-stator approach now selected than under the rejected dual-rotor approach.

The J-79 development proper began, then, about 6 or 7 months after construction of the research compressor began, and 1 or 2 months after work on the demonstrator engine began. The demonstrator program continued, with the original large engine scale, simultaneously with the development of the J-79. A separate team was assigned to it. It was not a "boiler plate" engine intended to demonstrate the previously tested research compressor (which was of approximately the same scale) with little attention paid to problems of weight and durability. Rather it was, in the words of a G. E. brochure, a "light-weight engine built as a flight type research vehicle." It was first run a year after it was begun in December 1953. Tests continued for a number of months afterward. Its cost was a small proportion of the total development cost of the J-79.

At the same time that the demonstrator was being completed, the J-79 team was engaged in its own attack on weight and durability problems for the J-79 proper. This work involved building and testing components. It merged gradually into the accessory design, airframe matching, and complete flight engine construction work, which form the prototype development phase. The J-79 was first run in June 1954. After some detailed redesign work on compressor attachment arrangements (necessitated by an initial compressor failure), a 50-hour test was passed in August 1955, and a 150-hour qualification test was passed in December 1956.

The increase in knowledge ultimately due to the demonstrator dealt not with the performance made possible by a variable stator compressor (for this knowledge was obtained earlier through tests of the research compressor) but rather with the attainable level of weight and durability for a variable-stator engine of the demonstrator's scale. This knowledge implied (by application of "scaling" principles) some predictions about attainable weight and durability for a variable-stator engine of the J-79 scale. There is some evidence, however, that the brief period of work on the demonstrator had already yielded enough such predictions partially to support the final decision in favor of the variable-stator design. It is clear, on the other hand, that somewhat more accurate predictions were obtainable later, after completion and testing of the demonstrator.

Thus, in the case of the J-79, extensive testing of the design of what turned out to be the major critical component, and placing the test data on the shelf, made it possible to predict performance accurately after the general design study stage; hence the stage of performance-oriented development was short. The stage of weight- and durability-oriented development overlapped with (rather than succeeded) both the performance-oriented stage and the general design study stage, for the weight- and durability-oriented demonstrator was in fact begun when the design study was in progress. The demonstrator's development overlapped, moreover, with prototype work on the J-79 itself. The demonstrator was built to a scale considerably larger than that of the J-79 itself and work on it was allowed to proceed only a short time before separate weight and durability work for the J-79 itself was begun. Had the demonstrator been close to the J-79 scale (which was specified in the general design study), and had its development not overlapped so extensively with the work of the team assigned to the J-79 proper, it might have better served to provide a sharp increase in predictability with respect to weight and durability. Nevertheless the largest uncertainties had been removed before any heavy commitment to the final J-79 design and scale was made *and* before heavy commitment to a using airframe. The J-79 reached the prototype phase relatively quickly considering the novelty of its design. It ultimately became one of the few engines to enter the commercial market.

4. The J-57 and J-75

The history of these two important Pratt and Whitney engines is very sketchily documented; critical decisions made within the development company are particularly hard to verify. The J-57, probably the most successful of all U.S. turbojet engines, was first contracted for by the Air Force in December 1948 after completion of a preliminary design study. It was an axial-flow engine obtaining considerably higher pressure ratios than previous U.S. engines; and it was the first U.S. engine to use a dual-rotor compressor.

A design close to that of the J-57 had apparently been incorporated, prior to the first contract, in a turboprop engine, the XT-45, which may or may not have run; the turboprop was canceled at the time of the J-57 contract. Moreover, there is evidence that prior to the first Air Force contract Pratt and Whitney conducted intensive component tests and completed and ran an engine that essentially was not only a performance-oriented, but also a weight- and durability-oriented demonstrator for the J-57. Hence, there is reason to believe that Pratt and Whitney could predict with high confidence that the levels of performance, weight, and durability specified to the Air Force in the design study that preceded the contract, could be attained by an expenditure of the predicted amount over the predicted time period.

Nothing has been found in Air Force documents to indicate awareness of the existence of the demonstrator, and hence the Air Force could not have had the same high confidence as Pratt and Whitney. Nevertheless, the first large commitment to the J-57—the decision of late 1949 to use it in the B-52 bomber—was made at about the same time as the signing of the first J-57 contract. Thus the Air Force may have thought it was making a large commitment in the face of major uncertainty but from the point of view of Pratt and Whitney (who knew the performance of the demonstrator that preceded the commitment) this was not the case. Other aircraft commitments were made shortly before and shortly after the first passing of a 50-hour test (August 1951) and during several years after this date.

The notably long list of military aircraft using the J-57 is included in Table 3 below. (In addition, the J-57 and J-75 have been the principal engines for commercial jet liners.) In none of these aircraft, it would appear, did major difficulties in the J-57 cause major delays or deficiencies.

It is worth noting here that Pratt and Whitney's own development expenditures (the initial pre-contract investigations probably constitute the bulk of them) seem to have played a large part in the success of the J-57. This success, in any case, appears to have established Pratt and Whitney as the leading engine firm, receiving the largest procurement orders and possessing the best reputation as a developer. The company's investment of its own resources seems to have yielded a return that justifies the investment.

The design of the J-75 was not quite as novel as that of the J-57: it had a different compressor, but it incorporated some features of the J-57. Nevertheless, Pratt and Whitney apparently were able to achieve the same high level of confidence, for the same kind of predictions, as in the case of the J-57. In this case, however, the Air Force was apparently aware of most of the effort, for according to the 1953 History of Wright Development Center:

> The contract had not been awarded to Pratt and Whitney until December 1952, yet by June the basic aerodynamic and mechanical design layout was complete, 95 per cent of the detail parts drawings had been completed and released for manufacture, and the remaining 5 per cent were drawings of internal parts which had a short manufacturing lead time. More than half of the parts for the first experimental engine were complete and the remainder were in the process of fabrication. An experimental J-57 had been modified to incorporate some of the unusual design features of the J-75 and instrumented to investigate some of the problems peculiar to that engine.

The high confidence turned out to be justified, for the J-75 exhibited closer conformity than any previous engine to the first official predictions of engine magnitudes. These official predictions were made only after the first major jumps in knowledge were past. Airframe commitments, moreover, were not made until these high-confidence predictions were available. The aircraft programs that used the J-75 experienced no important engine difficulties.

5. The J-40

Since this case is very well documented,[19] we shall present its history in some detail. The J-40 was a Navy engine, but the difficulties experienced do not seem related to any difference between Navy and Air Force procedures.

On June 30, 1947, the Navy signed a contract with Westinghouse for the development of the J-40. Westinghouse was selected, according to Admiral Russell, head of the Navy's Bureau of Aeronautics, because "it offered to develop an engine with greater thrust or power than that proposed by any other concern and in a shorter time and at less cost." In the original proposed design, the J-40 was an axial-flow single-spool engine weighing 3,500 pounds, developing 7,500 pounds maximum static thrust dry, 10,900 pounds with afterburner. No other engine in this thrust class was begun until 18 months later.

At the time of the contract signing, Westinghouse's reputation as an engine developer was very good. They had built the first American turbojet, the A-19. This had led to the first engine to pass a 150-hour test, the J-30, a generally successful engine. This had been followed by the J-34, a highly successful engine of which 4,500 had been built. It had performed well in Korea, powering the Banshee (McDonnell F2H) fighter.

After the first year of work on the J-40 program, Westinghouse had designed, still largely on paper, two families of engines. One had the thrust ratings of the original proposal and the other had considerably higher thrust (about 12,000 pounds maximum static thrust with afterburner). The higher-thrust engines, though of the same frame size (scale) as the lower-thrust group, *were of substantially different design in their turbines and compressors.*

Towards the end of 1948, after some 16 months of initial development work, Westinghouse received contract authorization to proceed with both the high-thrust engines (the J-40-10 was the principal high-thrust engine) and the low-thrust group (of which the J-40-8 was the chief representative). It is fairly clear that at the time this final authorization was made, the Navy had little more basis for prediction than a detailed design study with complete performance curves and Westinghouse's promise that a flyable J-40-8 engine would be delivered in 20 months and a flyable J-40-10 engine in 30 months.

[19] As a result of Congressional Hearings. See *Navy Jet Aircraft Procurement Program,* Hearings before a Subcommittee of the Committee on Government Operations, House of Representatives, Eighty-fourth Cong., 1st Sess., October 24–27, 1955, U.S. Government Printing Office, 1956. The history given here is based on this document.

In December 1948, the Navy held a design competition in the aircraft industry for a short-range interceptor. McDonnell was the winner of the competition with the F3H Demon using the low-thrust J-40. Although the Navy asserted that other engines could have been used, R. J. McDonnell testified, and the House investigating subcommittee concluded, that no other existing or prospective engine could have been seriously considered at that time.[20]

In March 1951, the low-thrust engine passed a 50-hour test, only three or four months behind schedule. A prototype Demon, using the engine, flew in August 1951, with few engine troubles.

In January 1951, however, the Navy decided to change the mission of the Demon: it was now to be a medium-range, general-purpose, all-weather fighter. The major change in design which this required increased the weight of the plane from 22,000 to 29,000 pounds. The J-40-10—the high-thrust version of the J-40—was expected to be suitable for powering the redesigned plane.

In March 1951, the Navy placed a contract for 150 planes; 378 more were ordered in 1952 and 160 more in early 1953, making a total order of 688 planes in March 1953. With a J-40-10 engine yet to be run, the Navy let a contract to the Ford Motor Company for the production of 200 J-40-10 engines under license from Westinghouse. In December 1952, the order was increased to 800, and Westinghouse was given a production order for 700 of the J-40-10s. In addition, Ford was given $50 million to build a government plant. Delivery of the engines was to begin in mid-1954. At the time of the Ford contracts there were orders still in effect for some 70 of the low-thrust engines to be produced by Westinghouse.

In July 1951, four months after the Ford contract, the first doubts about Westinghouse's promises appeared. McDonnell expressed fear that development of the J-40-10 was lagging far enough behind so that the projected aircraft delivery schedules could not be met. In the following months, the possibility of using engines other than the J-40 (in particular a modified J-46) was considered, but no action was taken.

At the end of 1951, the Navy, now quite sure that development of J-40-10 was proceeding far slower than it should, authorized McDonnell to plan for interim installation of the low-thrust engines, some of which could be delivered in a year or so, in the first 12

[20] There is evidence that for several months after May 1948, serious consideration was given to the use of the J-40 in the B-52; the notion had been abandoned by October, however (with the J-57 selected). The Air Force also very seriously considered (and then abandoned) the possibility of using the J-40 in the B-66.

Demons. By spring, 1952, prospects for the J-40-10 looked worse still, and McDonnell asked permission to install the low-thrust engines in 150 aircraft with retrofitting when the J-40-10 became available. The Navy agreed and, moreover, increased the order for the low-thrust engine by several hundred. At the same time McDonnell stated that aircraft so fitted would be disappointingly underpowered.

In the autumn of 1952, the Navy decided that the Allison J-71 of which an early version had just passed a 50-hour test, should be installed when available in some of the Demon airframes. The J-71 availability date was very uncertain, however, and no cancellation of any part of the Westinghouse or Ford commitment was made. McDonnell continued to plan for installation of the low-thrust J-40s in the Demon aircraft. The Navy was still hoping for ultimate success with the high-thrust J-40-10, and regarded the J-71 as equally uncertain (strangely, since it, at least, had passed a 50-hour test). The Navy, at this point, regarded the uncertain J-40-10 and the uncertain J-71 as insurance for each other.

Delivery of production models of the low-thrust engines began in November 1953. They were installed in a number of Demons. In March 1954, there began a series of 11 crashes of planes using the low-thrust engines, four of them with pilot fatalities. The low-powered Demons were reduced to the role of "limited life land-based development vehicle for the indoctrination and familiarization of pilots." Flight operations of these planes were canceled.

As for the high-thrust J-40-10 engines, the Navy finally abandoned these in September 1953, when the development program was terminated after engine development expenditures of some 40 million dollars. Another 40 million dollars had been spent for production tooling. Ford had built the 50-million dollar plant for the government. Westinghouse was paid 10 million dollars in termination costs and Ford 15 million dollars.

Far greater than the cost of the abandoned engine program, however, was the total development and production cost of the Demon airframe, estimated to have come to more than one-half billion dollars. What the Navy finally had to show for this expenditure is roughly this: 60 aircraft containing low-thrust engines not suitable for combat use; and some 200 airframes, some of which were eventually backfitted with J-71s at a conversion cost of about $450,000 each. These aircraft, the only usable ones, were not available until well after the original intended date for operational Demons. They soon became obsolete.

In the J-40 case, it seems fair to say, the unfortunate consequences resulted from making a large engine-airframe commitment in the face of great technical uncertainty as well as uncertainty about the mission of the aircraft, on the basis of knowledge contained in an engine design study.

6. Some Shorter Histories: J-46, J-33, J-35, T-35

The J-46

The history of the Westinghouse J-46, an engine begun in late 1949, is fragmentary. The fragments, however, give a rather clear impression of a "classic" case of engine-airframe commitments being made in the face of great uncertainty about all engine magnitudes.

The engine's design was new as were its performance goals. One important aircraft (both engine and airframe) was planned from the very beginning around the J-46. This was the experimental Douglas X-3 whose mission was to explore supersonic turbojet-powered flight. Two other fighter aircraft—the Navy's Cutlass and the Lockheed XF-90—were later scheduled to use the engine.

The delays beyond the original schedule in attaining the performance, weight, and durability intended for the J-46 proved extreme. The highest powered model of the engine, which was to permit maximum information to be obtained from the X-3, receded so far into the future that the incorporation of a much lower powered model became the aim. By August 1952, however, the lower powered model was 14 months behind schedule. In order to salvage any usefulness from the X-3, the plans to use the J-46 were canceled in late 1952. The X-3 flew with a much lower powered J-34 and never achieved supersonic speed.

As for the Navy's Cutlass, it finally received J-46s, lower powered than had been intended, and the program was greatly delayed and therefore greatly cut back. The Lockheed XF-90 was finally scrapped, largely for lack of a satisfactory engine.

The J-33 and J-35

These were the first U.S. turbojets to be produced in quantity. The initial proposals for both were made by General Electric in May 1943, and G. E. developed both simultaneously. The J-33 was first available for test in January 1944, and the J-35 in April 1944. The first 50-hour test was passed by the J-33 in June 1945, and by the J-35 in February 1946. The first 150-hour test of the J-33 (actually a later model) was passed in April 1947, and the first 150-hour test of the J-35 was passed in December 1947.

The J-33, a centrifugal-flow engine, did not involve (at the time of its inception) great unpredictability as to the difficulty of accomplishing the design study and performance-oriented development stages. There was considerable uncertainty, however, about the difficulty of achieving a durable engine, and a great deal of uncertainty about the difficulty of tooling and organizing for large-scale production of the J-33 (large-scale jet engine production had never been done before). Elaborate schedules for production and delivery of aircraft (principally Lockheed P-80s, intended originally for use in the war) were set up early in the J-33 development. They were based on equally elaborate schedules for production of J-33s.

It became evident in late 1945 that the planned J-33 schedules would not be attainable at G. E. and that the P-80 program would be greatly delayed. In addition, durability, as measured by times between overhaul, promised to be considerably less than anticipated and hence the P-80 promised to be a less useful aircraft. The production difficulties were partially resolved by designating Allison as a secondary production source. In 1945, sole production responsibility was given to Allison.

Nevertheless, the failure of predictions as to engine durability and production schedule feasibility to be borne out by subsequent events led to an aircraft delivery schedule that lagged well behind, and an aircraft usefulness inferior to that originally assumed in making the choice of engine and airframe.

The J-35 was an axial-flow engine. In response to an Air Force proposal to finance development of a new engine (in addition to the J-33) and to let G. E. decide whether the design was to be taken from a British engine or to be "started from scratch," G. E. chose the latter course. The Air Force apparently recognized that there was considerable uncertainty about performance, and no specific aircraft commitments dependent on the engine were made until this uncertainty had greatly declined.

When commitments were made, however, in October 1944, there was still uncertainty as to the additional effort required to attain a producible engine and to prepare for large-scale production. The commitments required use of the engine in the Douglas XB-43, and the Republic XP-84 and P-84; they involved the ordering of 5,000 engines according to a detailed production schedule. The schedules proved impossible to attain, even though production sources in addition to G. E. were obtained, first Chevrolet, then Allison. (Allison, as in the case of the J-33, was given final responsibility for the engine, in 1948, to alleviate the pressure that several simultaneous engine programs imposed on G. E.)

The original schedules rested on the assumption that production tooling could be done while development of the engine was still far from complete, and that this tooling could remain usable. The assumption proved false. Thus it was discovered, in spring of 1945, that production drawings that G. E. was scheduled to have prepared for Chevrolet some five months earlier were not ready. The delay in completion of these drawings, it was explained, "had been due to the amount of development difficulty encountered which had required detailed changes in design, so that the original drawings required extensive revision for production purposes."

In May 1945, the new knowledge about the difficulty of achieving large-scale production and a reexamination of the aircraft programs involved (in the light of the possibility of using J-33s instead of J-35s) led the Air Force to cancel 3,200 of the 5,000 J-35s which had been ordered. The planned P-84 program was cut down correspondingly, and a considerable delay in the scheduled delivery of the aircraft was accepted.

It may have been the J-33 and J-35 experiences that led to an attitude of caution in some Air Force quarters toward the next large engine-aircraft commitments that were expected to be made. The attitude was expressed by General Spatz in November 1945, when he said that the Army Air Forces "could well afford to delay allocation of funds for development of the new medium and heavy bombers in favor of maximum emphasis on development of new types of engines, because until engines with adequate performances are available, airplanes with desired characteristics cannot be built."

The T-35

The T-35 was a centrifugal-flow turboprop developed by Wright. The first design studies were completed (following an initial Air Force contract) at the beginning of 1945. The first intended application was to be to the B-36, but this idea was soon dropped. As the first designs for the B-52 were completed, the T-35 began to look attractive for this application. The original design of the T-35 was revised (a compressor stage was added) and greater power and lower specific fuel consumption were predicted for the final engine. In January 1947, a B-52 design study incorporating the T-35-3 (the revised T-35) was submitted to the Air Force by Boeing and adopted (temporarily, as it turned out). Total accumulated work on the T-35-3 at this point consisted of the general design study and some detailed component drawings. No component construction had been begun. Uncertainty about all the engine magnitudes was considerable.

The result of the B-52 design adoption was that by the end of 1947, approximately 30 million dollars of Air Force funds had been committed to development of the T-35. In 1947, the T-35 (together with a much less extensive turpoprop program—the T-37—regarded as providing a "backup" for the T-35) absorbed about 60 per cent of the year's engine development budget.

Beginning in 1947, there were simultaneous development efforts to construct testable units of the T-35 turbine engine component (that is, the compressor combustion section and turbine) and of its propeller, driveshaft, gearbox, and power control components. The difficulties that arose in constructing the latter four components proved to be much greater than anticipated. As a result of this difficulty, and of information acquired about the turbine engine component, it began to appear that a combination of the turbine engine with a dual-rotation propeller instead of the single-rotation propeller originally planned would be preferable. This major change (which would require a coaxial shaft instead of the shaft so far developed) was decided upon, and a considerable delay in delivery of the first flyable engines for the B-52 was anticipated.

In February 1949, the intended B-52 design was changed; turbojets replaced the T-35-3 turboprops. The difficulties that had arisen in the T-35 program as revised to achieve the dual-rotation engine, and new information about the J-57 turbojet which promised to make possible the range required, were principally responsible for the change. The T-35 program was thereupon ordered terminated.

It seems clear that in the case of the T-35 there was a large commitment to engine development for a specific airframe when the uncertainties remaining with respect to the engine were still very great. Changes in knowledge of other engines as well as information acquired about the T-35 led to a reevaluation of the commitment and a decision in favor of a turbojet. Sufficient information about the T-35 to justify a reevaluation might well have been attained, however, after a far smaller commitment than the one made, chiefly by inexpensive preliminary test work on propeller, gearbox, and driveshaft. This might have indicated, at much less cost, the advantages of, and an estimate of the difficulty of attaining, a dual-rotation engine.

7. Tabular Summaries of Uncertainties in the Engine Projects Studied

We shall now summarize some of the uncertainties that characterized a number of past engine projects. We want to stress our contention that these uncertainties are a natural and unavoidable property of engine development. The best predictions that can be made in the face of these uncertainties have a useful role in engine development strategy even though they may be very inaccurate predictions.

Table 3 deals with predictions made early in the development of 15 major engines (in most cases the predictions were made within a year of the award of the first development contract). They are predictions made by the Air Force (or Navy) as to the dates at which the 50-hour and 150-hour tests would be completed, as to the weight of the engine after the 150-hour test, and as to two of its performance parameters after the 150-hour test, namely "military thrust" and "specific fuel consumption at military thrust." Table 3 also shows the actually realized dates, weights, and values of the performance parameters after passing of the 150-hour test. In a few cases predictions and realizations for the first running of an experimental engine are also shown.

The prediction about the 50-hour test proved optimistic by one to three years in five cases and by at least six months in all but one case—the sole case in which the actual date preceded the predicted date. The predicted date of passing of the 150-hour test proved early by one to three years in eight cases and by only a few months in the exceptional cases of the J-57 and J-75; a plausible explanation for the exceptions has been discussed above, as has a third exception, the J-79, not included in Table 3.

An uncritical glance at the predictions and realizations for weight, thrust, and specific fuel consumption might suggest that in many cases these predictions turned out to be accurate. But it must be recalled that a meaningful prediction as to these characteristics must also specify a time at which they will be attained. Thus the complete, meaningful prediction for each engine includes the predicted date for passing of the 150-hour test (after which the characteristics were observed) as well as the engine characteristics themselves. The total predictions made for each engine were, it is seen, generally far from accurate, and the extent of the inaccuracy varied widely.[21] It is this *variation* in the accuracy of predictions that suggests accurate predic-

[21] A prediction for each engine as to the expenditure required to realize the predicted test dates, weights, and values of performance parameters was unavailable. Such a prediction must have been made for each engine if the total set of predictions was to be meaningful. It could conceivably be the case that it was predicted that at some expenditure the indicated predictions would be met, and that at some other expenditure (the expenditure actually incurred)—the actually realized test dates, weights, and values of performance parameters might be attained. In this case Table 3 would falsely indicate inaccuracy of prediction. But there is not the slightest evidence to support this explanation of the discrepancies shown in the table.

TABLE 3

EARLY PREDICTIONS IN THE DEVELOPMENT OF 15 ENGINES

Engine (turbojet)	Date of Predictions	Date of First Running, "Experimental" Engine: Predicted	Actual	Date of Passing of 50-hour Test: Predicted	Actual	Date of Passing of 150-hour Test: Predicted	Actual	Weight: Pred.	Actual[a]	Military Thrust/ESHP: Pred.	Actual	SFC at Mil. Thrust/ESHP (lbs/hr): Pred.	Actual	Maximum Thrust/ESHP[b]: Pred.	Actual	SFC at Max. Thrust/ESHP (lbs/hr)[b]: Pred.	Actual
J-46-1,-2	Mar. 1950	Oct. 1950		May 1950	June 1951	Sept. 1950	Feb. 1952	1,863	1,863	4,080	4,140	1.01	1.09	6,100	5,800	2.50	2.54
J-47-21 (later the J-73-3)	June 1951	Aug. 1951	Apr. 1952	June 1952	May 1953	Sept. 1952	Aug. 1953	3,528	3,880	9,100	8,920	.905	.917	8,100	8,100	.905	.917
J-48-5	June 1950			none (test covered by J-48-1 test)		Jan. 1951	May 1952	2,725	2,760	6,350	6,350	1.16	1.17	10,900 ±100	11,000	2.50	2.35
J-53-1	June 1950	June 1951	Mar. 1951	Mar. 1953	Dec. 1952	none	none	6,500	8,000[c]	17,500	15,750[d]	.856	.938	17,500	?	.856	?
J-57-1	June 1950					Feb. 1952	Oct. 1952	4,390	4,200	9,250	9,500	.775	.795	9,250	10,000	.775	.795
J-57-3	Dec. 1950			Jan. 1951	Aug. 1951	none	none	4,348	4,250	8,700	8,700	.84	.84	8,700	8,700	.84	.84
J-65-1	Mar. 1951			Sept. 1951	May 1952	Jan. 1952	Dec. 1953	2,600	2,695	7,220	7,220	.92	.92	7,220	7,220	.92	.92
J-65-1	Nov. 1951			Feb. 1954	Dec. 1955	June 1954	not yet	5,000 (dry)	5,100[e]	13,200	13,800[e]	?	?	21,500	21,500[e]	2.1	?
J-67-3	Apr. 1953	July 1954	July 1954	Oct. 1954	Mar. 1958[f]	Dec. 1955	Mar. 1959[f]	6,904	7,600[g]	12,950	14,050[g]	.795	.855	22,350	23,000[g]	2.35	2.40
J-71-3	Aug. 1950			Feb. 1952	Nov. 1952	Sept. 1952	Feb. 1954	4,350	4,350	9,700	9,700	.92	.92	9,700	9,700	.92	.92
J-75-1	Aug. 1952	Dec. 1953	Nov. 1953	Sept. 1954	Apr. 1955	Sept. 1956	Nov. 1956 (J-75-5)	6,200	6,100	15,500	15,500	.82	.82	23,500	23,500	?	2.03
T-34-3	July 1952					Apr. 1953	July 1954	2,590	2.590	11,000	11,000	3,440	3,685	11,000	11,000	3,560	3,685
T-47-1	Nov. 1951	Dec. 1951	Dec. 1954[h]	July 1953	no test	Jan. 1954	May 1956[i]	4,825	4,859[i]	11,400	11,400[i]	6,380	6,380[i]	11,400	11,400[i]	6,380	6,380[i]
T-49-1	Aug. 1951			June 1952	Dec. 1954	Oct. 1952	no test	4,357	4,466	9,000	8,500	6,815	6,815	9,000	8,500	6,815	6,815
T-56-1	Sept. 1952			May 1953	Sept. 1953	Nov. 1953	Dec. 1954	1,510	1,595	3,507	3,507	2,046	2,025	3,507	3,460	2,046	2,025

Notes:

[a] At 150-hour test, or at last recorded date in engine's development, whichever is earlier.

[b] ESHP at take-off.

[c] WADC History, July 1 to December 30, 1952, p. 298.

[d] "Historical Resume of XJ-53 Program," WADC Technical Report 53-467, December 1953.

[e] Prediction in April 1955. WADC History, January 1–June 30, 1955, p. 160.

[f] According to Aircraft Engine Characteristics Summary, 10 September 1956: "Phase 1 Preliminary Flight Rating Test Scheduled March 1958, Phase 2 Preliminary Flight Rating Test Scheduled March 1959."

[g] Prediction in Aircraft Engine Characteristics Summary, 10 September 1956.

[h] Prediction in Aircraft Engine Characteristics Summary, 21 December 1952. Funding subsequently stopped and no test occurred.

[i] Prediction in Aircraft Engine Characteristics Summary, 21 December 1952.

tions are very difficult to make—that the size of the confidence regions R, discussed above, is small. That the error was almost always on the side of optimism is perhaps explained by the fact that contractors were the primary source of most of the predictions. Whether or not *successive* predictions for each engine were increasingly accurate—as our general description of engine development suggests—is not revealed in the table because records of successive predictions were not available.

No predictions were available for durability and production costs. If our model of engine development were correct, these would have been less accurate than the performance predictions. So far as weight predictions versus thrust predictions are concerned, the average of the prediction errors (when the errors are taken to be percentages of the true value) is less for the thrust predictions shown in the table than for the weight predictions (2.3 per cent versus 4.6 per cent).

Table 4 shows successive engines used in a number of aircraft. It is difficult to determine in many cases whether two or more successive members of the sequence of engines shown were *planned to be successive engines* in successive versions of the aircraft, or whether *each* successive member of the sequence arose because the predictions used in choosing the preceding engine turned out to be wrong. In either case, the same point is illustrated: it is extremely difficult to make a good choice of engine for a given aircraft when some of the engines to be considered are in early stages of development. If the whole sequence of engines shown for an aircraft was a planned sequence, because the "ultimate" engine was too far in the future and had to be preceded by others, then this illustrates that the choice may be extremely difficult, for it may sometimes have to be the choice of a sequence. If the sequence shown arose unintentionally, the original choice being the choice of a single engine, the difficulty is illustrated again. Very few aircraft end up with the engine chosen at the start of development.

Table 5 shows, for each of several major engines, the list of aircraft (many of them considered to be "successful" aircraft) that have used the engine. The list for some of the engines is very diverse. A "good" engine is used in many aircraft of different types regardless of its assignment to a particular aircraft at its inception; and the airframes that end up using such an engine are often developed quite independently of the engine, incorporating it only when its development is near completion.

TABLE 4

SUCCESSIVE ENGINES PLANNED FOR USE IN VARIOUS AIRCRAFT

Aircraft	Engine Sequence [a]
Air Force	
F-84	J-65, J-73 [b]
F-86	J-35, J-65, J-47
F-89	J-35, J-71, J-65
F-100	J-57
F-101	J-57, J-67, J-75, J-79 [c]
F-102	J-33, J-40, J-67, J-57 (several models), J-75 (in F-102B, later called F-106)
F-104	J-65, J-79
F-105	J-71, J-67, J-57, J-75
F-107	J-57, J-67, J-75
B-47	J-35 (used in first two planes), J-47, J-57 (B-47C), T-49 (B-47D), T-47 (B-47D), J-65 (B-47D)
B-52	T-35 (several models), J-40 (seriously considered), J-57
B-57	J-65, J-57 (B-57D)
B-58	J-57 (originally planned for use in first 15 planes), J-79
B-66	J-40, J-71
SNARK	J-71, J-57
YC-130	T-56, T-38 (tentatively planned when delay of T-56 became apparent)
C-133	T-34, T-40 (tentatively planned when delay in T-34 threatened)
X-3	J-46, J-34
Navy	
F7U	J-34, J-46, J-35
F8U	J-57, J-75
F4D, F5D	Similar airframes, first used J-57, then J-79
F3H	J-40-10 (high-thrust model), J-40-8 (low-thrust model), J-71
F9F	J-42, J-48, J-33, J-65
F11F	J-65, J-79
XP6M	J-71, J-67 (seriously considered), J-75

Notes:

[a] These engines were either planned for use or actually were used by the Air Force and Navy for the designated aircraft. The engines in each sequence are listed according to approximate date of first decision for use in the indicated aircraft. No sequence extends beyond 1956.

[b] The J-65 was the intended (and is the current) engine for the F-84F. But in 1953 it was planned to fit two of the aircraft (to be called F-84Js) with J-73s "on the chance that the J-65s might have to be junked" (History of WADC, July 1–December 31, 1953, p. 165).

[c] General Electric proposed use of J-79-2s in the F-101A and received one F-101A from the Air Force for test installation of the engine.

TABLE 5

USE OR PLANNED USE OF MAJOR ENGINES IN AIR FORCE AND NAVY AIRCRAFT[a]

Engine	Air Force Aircraft	Navy Aircraft
J-33	F-80, T-33, XF-92, YB-61, YB-62, F-94 (A, B), TM-61 (tactical missile)	AJ2, F9F-7, TV-1, T2-V, P4M-1
J-34	X-3, XF-88	F3D, F2H, F6U, F7U
J-35	F-84 (B, C, D, E, G, H)	FJ-1
J-47	B-45, XB-51, XF-91, B-36, B-47, F-86 (D, F, K)	
J-48	F-94C	F9F
J-57	B-52, YB-60, F-100, F-102A, F-101 (A, B), SNARK, F-105A, F-107, KC-135A, B-57D, X-16	A3D, F4D, F8U
J-65	F-84F, B-57	F11F, A4D, FJ-3, FJ-4, F9F
J-69	YQ-1, YQ-2, T-37	
J-71	SNARK, YF-89E, B-66	
J-75	F-101, F-102B, F-105, F-107	F8U, XP6M
J-79	B-58, F-104, F-101A (see note c, Table 4)	F5D, F11F, A3J, F4H
T-34	C-133A, YC-97J, YC-121F	R7V-2
T-40	XF-84H	R3Y, XFY, A2D
T-56	YC-130, YC-131C	

Note:

[a] Aircraft in which engine was used or was planned to be used. For at least one (and generally more) of the aircraft in the list associated with a given engine, the decision to use the engine was made when the engine was in the final stages of development. (In the case of the J-57, J-79, and J-75 this is true of nearly all the aircraft listed.) No list extends beyond 1956.

Summary

For an engine developed independently of an airframe the developer may constrain the performance, weight, and size of an engine at the start. The developer then heavily relies on the findings of the design study stage, even if these are unsupported by data on on-the-shelf components that are to be used in the engine. He decides, after that stage, on a single, highly specified design that will "best" meet the constraints. Assuming that the chosen paper design will be that of the final engine, the developer then tries, to some extent, to telescope the several stages of development. He also permits extensive simultaneous (rather than sequential) work on major components (compressor, turbine, and so on), even though the failure of one component to meet the predictions of the design study stage might require scrapping the work performed on another component.

In the case of an engine intended, at the start of development, for a specific airframe (which may itself just be starting development), the engine developer pursuing a strategy of the same type may display all of the above tendencies. In addition he is highly influenced from the start by the design of the proposed airframe. He makes his choice as to size and weight, for example, so as to fit the proposed airframe, as soon as some predictions about its relevant characteristics are available.

Alternatively a developer, whether or not a using airframe is specified, can avoid early commitments and can stress instead the quick attainment of some of the sharp jumps in knowledge that occur in engine development. A number of alternative designs may be explored, and the jump will serve to narrow the number considered. In the exceptional cases in which a very critical component of a proposed engine already exists, tested and on the shelf prior to the design study stage, the second type of developer may permit himself a somewhat closer reliance on the predictions. Such an exceptional case was the J-79.

D. Fighter Aircraft [22]

1. The F-100

Early Development History

North American Aviation was unsuccessful in the competition for a new interceptor held in 1950–1951. The winner was the F-102, to be discussed below. North American then, at its own expense, continued development of its unsuccessful proposal, an advanced version of the F-86, a fighter in satisfactory operational use.

The company spent about a year working on design studies and conducting wind-tunnel tests before receiving an Air Force contract for what was to become the F-100. Because of the desire of the Air Force for a new air-superiority fighter to combat the MIG-15 encountered in Korea, a decision was made in November 1951 to pro-

[22] This section is closely based on a longer study by Leland L. Johnson.

cure two prototype aircraft. Thirty million dollars were committed to the program, but only $12 million were allocated in this initial phase. As a result of its earlier work, North American was able to provide a mock-up for inspection at the time of the Air Force decision to proceed with the F-100.

Negotiations leading to a letter contract were conducted during the rest of 1951. A clause was inserted calling for a production program (94 aircraft were mentioned), including the purchase of long lead-time items, spare parts, and tooling. The letter contract was signed in January 1952. Delivery of the two prototypes was scheduled for December 1953 and January 1954.

Amendments made soon thereafter radically increased the size of the program. Amendment No. 1, dated February 1952, called for 23 F-100A aircraft to be delivered from December 1953 through July 1954. Delivery of the prototypes was advanced six months, to June and July 1953. Amendment No. 4, dated 11 March 1952, authorized fabrication of tooling (jigs, dies, and fixtures) to support a production rate of 25 aircraft a month and capable of a peak rate of 175 a month. Amendment No. 7, dated 26 August 1952, specified 250 additional vehicles to be delivered during the period August 1954 to July 1955.

The definitive fixed-price incentive contract covering these and other items was signed in December 1952. Some of the major items were:

Item	*Estimated Cost*
2 prototypes	$ 13,579,950
23 aircraft at $1,530,825	35,208,975
250 aircraft at $299,426	74,856,500
Static-test article	1,530,825
Flight test	4,074,781
Spare parts	29,480,598
Spare parts	500,000
Engineering changes (allotted)	1,728,549
Other (wind-tunnel models, manuals, and so on)	11,262,364
Total	$172,222,542

The prototype and production versions were to be identical except for the engine (the former had the XJ57-7; the latter, the J57-7), the afterburner nozzle, and the aft fairing of the fuselage underbody. Specifications of 18 May 1952 described a plane with a wing span of 36.58 feet, a length of 45.19 feet, and a gross takeoff weight (clean) of 24,989 pounds. Government-furnished equipment included a specified radar set, gunsight, and armament. Maximum speed was estimated at Mach 1.31, service ceiling at 55,700 feet, and combat radius at 505 nautical miles.

A major reason for the large commitment to North American prior to completion of a prototype was the feeling that the program did not entail a major advance in the state of the arts.

> The selection of (this design) for production had been predicated on two principal circumstances: ". . . the confidence that our people have in the ability of North American to produce good equipment, and . . . the fact that this airplane design does not represent major unknown areas of development." The Air Materiel Command considered the airplane to be no more than ". . . a moderate advancement from the proven F-86 design." Early production availability of a high performance air superiority fighter was the major consideration in the decision to buy the "Sabre 45" on an "off the shelf" basis, "without benefit of the usual experimental program." [23]

On the other hand, there was some reason for believing that major unknown elements did exist in the program, for the plane had several novel features in wing construction, landing gear supports, and fuselage materials. In February 1954, moreover, North American commented in a report that "major development" would be required since the F-100 was to be the first combat aircraft capable of combat maneuverability and sustained flight at supersonic speeds.

The Air Force expressed considerable apprehension concerning the conduct of the program. The first production model was due only six months after delivery of the first prototype, a time plan that would not allow many changes in the aircraft following test-flight evaluations. In fact, the test-flight program as originally conceived was such that *all* the F-100s on contract would be delivered before flight testing could be completed. But the program was subsequently modified to include 36 aircraft in flight-test inventory to permit a more rapid completion of flight evaluation; nevertheless, the evaluation was to be completed only after a substantial number of aircraft had been produced. Moreover, the prototype itself was to be a production-engineered aircraft constructed with hard production tooling; any major changes found necessary during flight test could be time consuming and costly to incorporate on the production line because of the large tooling program planned by the time of first flight. In September 1952 (after the additional 250 aircraft had been programmed) Major General Albert Boyd stated that because several features of the F-100 would prove troublesome, a rapid production build-up

---

[23] Air Force Systems Command, Wright Air Development Center, *Historical Résumé of the F-100 Program* (n.d.).

should be delayed until evaluation of the first 25 aircraft had been completed. In the same week, Colonel V. R. Haugen, Chief of the Weapon Systems Division, warned that ". . . the early and rapid acceleration of this airplane into full production will cause considerable difficulty in reducing it to a practical, reliable weapon suitable for operational employment . . . the schedule allows no opportunity for an orderly test program to uncover any unsatisfactory features which may well exist, before the production line is operating at full capacity."[24] In November 1952, General Partridge said, "I can only foresee that as now programmed, we are headed for another rash of groundings, retrofittings . . . and all the things that have plagued us recently in the B-47, F-94C and F-89 programs."[25] Nevertheless, the delivery schedule was not revised in any substantial way from that established in 1952.

The first YF-100A flew in May 1953, about 16 months after the initial implementation decision. Flight evaluation was completed four months later:

> The test results indicate that the craft is superior in performance to any production fighter in the USAF. The most serious defects of the aircraft are the inadequate visibility over the nose during take-off and landing, the poor low-speed handling characteristics, and the negative to neutral static longitudinal stability experienced in level flight from approximately .8 Mach to maximum level flight speed.[26]

Flight testing continued into 1954 while North American proceeded with large-scale production. A follow-on letter contract for 230 aircraft in the C version was let in February 1954, and a definitive contract for 564 F-100Cs was signed in June. The first squadron delivery of the F-100A took place in September 1954.

During this period, stability problems, in particular, plagued the program. Late in the test-flight series in November 1954, a fatal crash caused by inertial coupling led to the grounding of the approximately 100 vehicles that had been produced during the 18-month span subsequent to first flight. To cope with these problems North American instituted a retrofit program on completed aircraft (consisting mainly of installing a larger vertical fin and adding a 12-inch extension to each wing tip) and incorporated modifications into the production line. The retrofit program was completed by August 1955. The first wing of F-100As was operationally equipped in June 1955, four and

---

[24] *Ibid.*

[25] *Ibid.*

[26] Air Force Flight Test Center, *Phase II Flight Test of the North American YF-100A Airplane,* p. ii.

a half years after the development program had been started. Supplemental Agreement 43, signed in June 1955, provided for a cost increase on the contract of about $7 million, which presumably covered the cost of the retrofit and modification program.

In mid-1955, two years after first flight, the F-100A underwent its operational suitability tests at Eglin Air Force Base. Even at this late date many problems were noted. For example:

Deficiencies in the engine limit the kill probability of the F-100A. These include compressor stalls with throttle manipulation and afterburner failure to ignite on many initial selections.[27]

The F-100A is severely restricted from optimum combat performance because of compressor stalls. Experience has demonstrated that compressor stalls may occur at any combination of altitude, power setting and flight condition. . . . Once compressor stall commences, the pilot has little or no choice except to break off any attack and regain control of the engine by all means at his disposal.[28]

In combat it will be difficult to tell if explosive projectiles are hitting the aircraft or compressor stalls are occurring.[29]

Serious limitations presently exist in the F-100A weapon system hindering its ability to deliver ordnance on an aerial target.[30]

The results of an evaluation involving 29 sorties indicate that pilots flying the F-100A aircraft, as presently equipped with the MA-3 fire control system are not capable of firing satisfactory air-to-air gunnery scores. The exact cause of this limitation is unknown at this time, since on some passes with good tracking and with the pipper on the targets no hits were obtained. In addition, all pilots attempting air-to-air gunnery in the F-100A stated that smooth tracking was very difficult and that reticle vibration during gunfire was excessive.[31]

When guns are fired at altitudes above 40,000 feet, an inverter failure indication sometimes occurs during the time of gunfire [this renders the gunsight and radar, as well as other equipment, inoperative]. Of even more significance, at altitudes above 50,000 feet a delay of up to five seconds often occurs between triggering and gunfire. The cause of these discrepancies has not been determined.[32]

---

[27] Air Proving Ground Command, *Final Report on Operation Suitability Test of the F-100A Aircraft,* September 1955, p. 6.

[28] *Ibid.,* p. 12.

[29] *Ibid.,* p. 35.

[30] *Ibid.,* p. 6.

[31] *Ibid.,* p. 12.

[32] *Ibid.,* p. 13.

These deficiencies were eliminated in subsequent development of the aircraft. A series of engine modifications and an intake duct redesign reduced the frequency of compressor stalling so that the operational capability of the aircraft was not seriously compromised. The fire-control system in the early aircraft was not modified satisfactorily. This system, which was developed during the time of the F-86, could not make adequate correction in the steering and target data presented to the pilot because of the flight characteristics of the aircraft, namely, a general lack of stability as a gun platform and a tendency to "porpoise" at certain speeds and altitudes. However, pilots well accustomed to the characteristics of the weapon system were able to achieve satisfactory target-practice scores by calling on their own judgment to aid in the operation of the fire-control system. For example, if they found that at given speeds and altitudes the system provided erroneous information regarding the amount of target lead, they could learn to make allowance for it.

In the spring of 1955, 70 aircraft of the 250 that had been ordered under Amendment 7 were transferred to another contract covering production of the C version of the F-100. The initial contract, the only one under which the F-100A was procured, therefore covered the two prototypes and 203 production vehicles. The last aircraft on the initial contract was delivered in the summer of 1955.

During the time these aircraft were produced there were many other changes and amendments to the contract that generated both cost increases and decreases. For example, a reduction totalling about \$8 million was occasioned by a decrease in spare parts procurement. Small cost increases occurred because of numerous minor modifications, procurement of 500 wing tanks (\$740,000), and a second mobile training unit (\$495,000).

A firm (reset) target price for the 206 airframes (two prototypes, 203 production version aircraft, and one static test article) was established in March 1955 for a total of nearly \$136 million. This figure corresponds to a \$103 million figure calculated according to the terms of the original contract—not a wide discrepancy by comparison with other projects. In March 1957 a final renegotiation took place on this contract. The final price of the 206 aircraft came to about \$134 million. With the renegotiated prices for the rest of the items covered in the contract, the over-all total (including fee) was about \$186 million.

Besides the 205 F-100As, over 2000 F-100s in the C, D, and F versions were ordered by the Air Force. Over 1000 were delivered by the end of 1956, with little slippage from original schedules. The C,

D, and F differed from the A primarily in modifications for larger external stores in fighter-bomber roles, and alteration in subsystems. The F-100D, for example, could carry either a number of rockets in six underwing clusters for a primary mission as a fighter bomber or or four Sidewinder missiles as a day fighter, in addition to its guns.[33]

Remarks

Several points in the F-100 history are important. First, it is notable that the aircraft, though originally designed as an air-superiority fighter, apparently proved quite versatile, for it was adaptable to a fighter-bomber role. North American was able to add various combinations of off-the-shelf items to the basic airframe and roll out a weapon system that the Air Force bought in large numbers. Although only about 200 aircraft were procured in the version originally planned, and although there were a number of difficulties with this particular version, ten times that number were procured in the subsequent versions. This illustrates two kinds of uncertainty: (1) components often turn out adaptable to weapon systems for which they are not originally designed, and (2) the preferences of the Air Force may change through time. Even if the Air Force gets the system it originally ordered more or less as planned, it may find another system preferable. While the whole F-100 program was begun on the premise that an advanced air-superiority fighter was needed, the Air Force, apparently finding a few years later that a fighter-bomber was more badly needed, procured ten times as many fighter-bombers.

Second, although great caution is necessary in comparing one aircraft with another (there are features that are simply not comparable), it is notable that the development time of the F-100 program was less than that of any other of the "Century Series" (which included the F-101, F-102, F-104, F-105, F-106). Even allowing for the year spent by North American on its own, the first wing was operationally equipped four and one-half years after initiation of the program. Time spent from USAF implementation to first *squadron* delivery for other Century Series aircraft was in no case less than five years.

Third, the cost of development through the initial contract was relatively low. Of the other Century Series fighters only the F-104A appears to have been equally inexpensive.

Finally, development of the F-100 proceeded smoothly. Aside from the inertial coupling problem, the airframe showed no serious aero-

[33] The addition of the Sidewinder missile to the F-100D system gives the aircraft a satisfactory capability as an interceptor within certain environments.

dynamic deficiencies and there were no significant delivery slippages. The design proposed in 1951 was developed without major change. The F-100 is the only one of the Century Series in which the engine originally selected appeared on the finished plane. Cost overruns were modest in comparison with those found in some of the other Century aircraft; and major performance parameters of the finished product were not far different, except for range and ceiling, from those predicted by North American at the time the definitive contract was signed.

How can the relatively short lead time, low cost, and reasonably straightforward character of the program be explained? While no complete answer is possible, there appear to be three factors of particular relevance. First, the design was based roughly on the configuration of the F-86, an aircraft that was well proven and by any reasonable standard quite successful. At the low supersonic speed required, and for the tactical roles planned for the F-100, the basic design simply did not exhibit major deficiencies. There were no unexpected transonic drag rises, pitch-up problems, or unexpected weight increases, characteristic of certain other programs, that might have degraded performance. In short, there was a wide range of configurations—delta wing, straight wing, swept wing, single-engine, twin-engine, nose air intake, side air intake, and so on—from which to choose in designing an airplane with the general capability of the F-100, and some would in all probability have been better than others. North American chose one in which the uncertainties were known to be relatively few because of its close relation to the F-86.

Second, the airplane was based on off-the-shelf procurement of proven major components other than the airframe. The electronics (including the radars) and gunsight had been developed earlier and had already seen operational use. This procedure helped the aircraft program in two ways: (1) no major problems arose concerning availability of these components when they were needed on the production line; (2) the principal area of uncertainty was confined to the airframe-engine combination. Such is not the case when all major components are designed at the paper stage to work together as a weapon system before they are tested in hardware form. In such situations, if unforeseen problems occur in the development of any one component they can have a serious effect on the development of the whole system. It should be pointed out, however, that despite the fact that the subsystems did not involve any major development problems, problems did arise in getting them to work properly after the airplane had been put into operational use. As for the engine, it is true that the J-57 was still in development when North American selected it. However, it had passed its 50-hour test in August 1951, three months prior to Air Force implementation of North American's proposal, and it had already powered the B-52 prototype, which made its first flight in April 1951. Although this selection did not preclude compressor stall and afterburner deficiencies, North American did get an engine that in general met specifications, was relatively reliable in operation, and was available more or less on schedule.

Third, and perhaps most important, it is notable that the Air Force had a better basis for committing itself in the F-100 program, in terms of quantity of information available to it, than it did in other Century Series developments. It had the benefit of the information gained by North American during the year the company worked alone: the mock-up inspection was held at about the time the Air Force gave the initial go-ahead. In other Century programs, mock-up inspection was held some time after initial commitment. The importance of this observation lies not in the fact that mock-up itself is of primary importance, but in the fact that typically many of the changes and modifications occurring in aircraft programs are made on the basis of wind-tunnel tests, rocket tests, and paper calculations performed prior to mock-up. By the time mock-up is completed, the specifications of the aircraft provide a more reliable basis for Air Force commitment than those drawn up earlier. In the case of the F-100, the Air Force's initial "bet" was a heavy one but it was placed late in development compared with other fighter programs.

2. The F-102

Developmental History

In the late 1940's several factors were of particular importance in shaping the concept of air defense out of which the F-102 emerged. First, the interceptors soon to enter inventory were expected to have only marginal capability against Russian jet bombers expected to become operational in the early 1950's. Flying at near Mach 1 speeds at altitudes of around 50,000 feet, these bombers would provide elusive targets for the existing interceptors—the North American F-86D and the Northrop F-89, which were subsonic and had combat ceilings of under 50,000 feet.

Second, successful interception of such bombers involved reliance on the continued development of air-to-air missiles, rockets, and radar fire-control systems to provide all-weather capability in detecting and identifying enemy aircraft, in positioning the interceptor in the optimal flight path for the kill, and in preparing and firing weapons at the proper instant of time. In the new era of extreme speed, visual methods of aiming and conventional machine gun armament became hopelessly obsolete. At the same time, the increasing complexity of electronic equipment threatened to make impossible demands on the single pilot during the final intercept phase. Use of a second crewman to ease this burden, as in the F-89, involved weight and space penalties that made this solution only a stop-gap measure. Making the "ultimate" fire-control system as automatic as possible was therefore stressed.

Finally, in the late 1940's a strong body of opinion emerged in favor of designing airframe, engines, fire control, and other equipment to be operated together from the outset in an integrated weapon system. This approach stood in contrast to the more or less piecemeal fashion in which technological advances (such as the B-29, P-51, and F-80) of World War II and the early postwar years had been made. Typically, under the latter approach an airframe was developed, after which the engines and supporting equipment, developed under separate programs, were requisitioned off the shelf to complete the system. Problems arose because components so tied together were not always compatible: an airframe might be developed for which no suitable bombing-navigation system was simultaneously available, or environmental conditions imposed by the aircraft might be outside the tolerance levels of its electronic equipment. Because it was felt that the attainment of ever higher levels of aircraft performance in the future would entail progressively more restrictive environmental conditions, more stringent space limitations, and greater difficulty in keeping component development in phase, the notion of applying the new "weapon system concept" to subsequent aircraft development became increasingly popular.

In 1949 Air Force Headquarters accepted the idea of a coordinated development program of an interceptor system capable of dealing with the enemy threat during the 1954–1958 time period. A directive to the Air Materiel Command (AMC) called for "an interceptor competition . . . to meet military characteristics now awaiting approval."

In May 1949, Air Force officials held a series of presentations in Washington before industry and military representatives. Among other things, they outlined the problem of air defense and broached the subject of the weapon-system concept in which they envisaged the various components such as airframe, armament, ground and airborne radar, communications, servicing facilities, and so on, as forming an integrated, complete defense network.

Since the Air Force believed that development of a fire-control system would take longer than development of the airframe, and since the airframe was planned to be tailored to the requirements of the electronic and control system, a competition for the electronic and control system was held prior to the competition for the airframe. Requests for proposals and an outline of requirements for the electronic and control system were sent to 50 firms in early 1950. By early April, 18 companies had offered proposals. Cost estimates for the development program ranged from $1,680,000 to $14,250,000. In July 1950, Hughes was named winner of the competition, and a first-year contract was subsequently negotiated for its MX-1179 electronic and control system.

In September 1950, AMC sent requests for airframe proposals to 19 aircraft companies. Requirements were written around an interceptor to be operational in the 1955–1959 time period and capable of intercepting bombers that have a maximum speed of Mach 1.3 and fly at altitudes up to 60,000 feet. Armament and combat radius were specified. The aircraft was to be directed automatically to the target area by the ground-based aircraft-warning and control system tied directly by data link to automatic intercept-course computers and an automatic flight-control system in the aircraft. After the aircraft locked onto the target, the armament was to be aimed and fired as directed by the fire-control system. It was planned that the pilot have only a monitoring function during the intercept. That the new weapon-system concept was to govern the development of the interceptor was emphasized in an introductory statement to the request for proposals:

> The problem of interception can be solved successfully only by effecting the highest degree of integration of electronic and control equipment into the design of the airplane. To insure the success of the new interceptor, it will be mandatory for the aircraft and the electronic and control system manufacturers to coordinate extensively both developments. In this respect, the prime responsibility for the satisfactory functioning of the airplane as a weapon will rest with the aircraft manufacturer.

By the end of January 1951, the deadline for replies, six firms had submitted a total of nine proposals. Republic offered three, North American two, and Chance-Vought, Convair, Douglas, and Lockheed each proposed one design.

For our purpose, we need discuss in detail only the Convair proposal for the aircraft that became the F-102. It called for a delta-wing, single vertical-fin configuration. The advantages claimed for this configuration were:

1) Low weight and high rigidity with very thin wing sections.
2) Low drag at transonic and supersonic speeds.
3) Adequate stability and control without addition of a horizontal tail.
4) High maneuverability and freedom from buffeting with a smooth stall development and excellent spin recovery characteristics as compared with conventional swept-wing configurations.

Convair specified the Wright J-67, an engine presumed to be available by June 1954, for use in the ultimate version. In addition, it suggested the Westinghouse J-40, programmed to be available nearly 3 years earlier, for use in early test-flight vehicles. A prototype, using the J-40, was expected to fly in 1952 or early 1953. Intended specifications for each version of the aircraft are shown in Table 6.

TABLE 6

SPECIFICATIONS FOR TWO VERSIONS OF THE F-102

	J-40 Engine (13,700 pound thrust with afterburner)	J-67 Engine (21,100 pound thrust with afterburner)
Maximum speed (Mach)	1.88	1.93
Combat ceiling (ft)	56,500	60,200
Combat radius (n.mi.)	715	768
Take-off weight (lbs)	22,472	22,940

In each version the first three estimated specifications were a substantial improvement over the minimum performance requested by the Air Force. Convair provided cost estimates for two prototype airframes, for the first 25 production airframes, and for the first 300 production airframes. Convair further predicted that given an order for 300 units, a March 1951 go-ahead, and availability of Hughes' MX-1179 (the Air Force specified fire-control system) in June 1953, deliveries would start in 1954 and a production peak of 15 per month would be reached in the spring of 1955.

On the basis of these predictions and similar predictions for the other interceptor proposals in the contest, Air Force Headquarters announced in July 1951 that Convair, Lockheed, and Republic were the winners of the competition, that each would be given a Phase I contract, and that one would be given a production contract on the basis of the results of Phase I work. Phase I comprises "preliminary design and mock-up." (Succeeding phases, which have sometimes been separately contracted for, are Phase II, "fabrication"; Phase III, "preliminary flight tests"; and Phase IV, "final performance tests.") It appears, therefore, that the intention of the Air Force was to keep several contractors in the program but to make only small commitments to each of them early in development in order to "purchase" information and delay the *major* decision concerning a production contract, because of the relatively high costs involved, until more knowledge was available. But the decision to sponsor closely competing programs was soon revoked. Only a month later Lockheed was notified that it would not be given a development contract. In addition, Republic was informed that development of its aircraft would continue as a separate, long-range program because its success would rest on development of the J-67 in combination with a novel ram-jet arrangement utilizing the afterburner, a joint development that would take some years. Consequently, by the end of September 1951, Convair remained the only contractor upon which the Air Force could depend for development and production of an interceptor whose characteristics might have been expected to meet the requirements set forth in the competition. The original commitment to Convair, however, remained quite small in dollar terms until the fall of 1951.

When the pressure of events in Korea mounted, Air Force Headquarters concluded that none of the proposals would result in an operational aircraft by 1954. It appeared that Convair's J-67 version would not be available before 1956 because of expected delays in delivery of the fire-control system and the engine. An obvious candidate for an "interim" interceptor for the 1954–1956 time period was the J-40 version; this could at least serve in an extensive flight-test program. Cost estimates were requested in October from Convair covering development through two prototypes and production of 25 airframes in the first year, with tooling to support a buildup to 50 per month. Other candidates for the interim role, from other contractors, were also considered.

In November 1951 the Air Force decided in favor of Convair's J-40 version, to be used in an accelerated test-flight program, involving 50 aircraft. The J-57, however, was now substituted for the J-40. These 50 aircraft were designated the YF-102; the follow-on version of the interim aircraft was designated the F-102. (The "ultimate" version of the aircraft was designated the F-102B in late 1952.)

Production was to be conducted under the so-called "Cook-Craigie" plan in which Convair was given the green light to proceed with production tooling prior to first flight of the prototype. While Convair was eliminating troubles in the airframe in accordance with flight-test results, it could simultaneously be modifying its tooling, and presumably be in a position to move into large-scale production buildup within a relatively short time.

This was a major decision involving expenditure of many millions of dollars for tooling, manufacture of hardware, and flight testing, in contrast to the hundreds of thousands of dollars involved in the Phase I contracts planned at the time of the aircraft competition. The Air Force did not immediately award a definitive contract to cover this additional work. However, in January 1952 Convair's original letter contract was increased by several million dollars to start a production-engineering and tooling program. No large-scale production schedule was set at that time, but in early 1952 Convair was authorized to proceed with two YF-102 prototypes to be delivered in June and September 1953 and seven production-version aircraft to be delivered from January through August 1954.

There were several factors that apparently motivated the Air Force to make this major commitment early in the development of the aircraft. First, there was a growing preoccupation in the Air Force with reducing "lead-time" consumed in moving from paper-stage planning to operationally suitable aircraft. Under the development approach previously followed, typically one or two prototypes were "hand-made" with relatively crude and inexpensive tooling, and the procurement decision postponed until after flight-test data were available. That this procedure might involve excessive time and duplication is well expressed in a May 1952 statement:

> It is not believed that an airplane produced partially by hand and partially with temporary tooling is a true representation of the final production article. As a result, much of the flight testing may have to be repeated on the first airplane fabricated with production-type tooling. Also, the fact that some parts can be satisfactorily fabricated by hand does not always mean that some parts can be readily produced within the acceptable tolerances with production tooling. . . . Should the results of the first six months' flight testing be favorable and a decision made to produce the aircraft in quantity, *the time consumed in manufacturing the first article with production tooling would be essentially the same as for producing an entirely new aircraft.*[34]

In addition, a rapid production buildup on the basis of limited flight testing of nonproduction prototypes had in the past frequently resulted in major defects being uncovered only after a large number of production aircraft had been built. (One of the best examples here is

[34] Letter from Air Materiel Command to Headquarters, USAF, 16 May 1952, subject: Initial Production Rate for New Model Aircraft.

the B-47 experience, discussed below.) This alteration resulted in expensive and time-consuming retrofit programs.

A proposed solution to these problems, the Cook-Craigie plan, enjoyed increasing Air Force support in the early 1950's, and the F-102 became the first aircraft to follow this plan. By constructing production-engineered aircraft with production tooling at the outset and holding output to a low level for about 18 months during the test program, the manufacturer would presumably discover and remedy the major difficulties before undertaking large-scale production. Furthermore, it was hoped that time and money would be saved in moving from an experimentally designed article to one suitable for mass production; that development, production engineering, and tooling cost of the interim version of the interceptor would not have to be duplicated for the ultimate version, since the original plan was to construct a common airframe for both. Only the engine and possibly the fire-control system and other supporting equipment were to be different. Consequently, the Air Force had no reason to believe that costs for the over-all program would significantly increase because of the independent interim effort. The "best guess," moreover, was that the MX-1179, the designated fire-control system, would be available for the interim aircraft and that no separate interim system, which would involve additional development cost and possibly delays in the MX-1179 program, would be necessary. So far as engines were concerned, the J-67 remained programmed for the ultimate version, to follow the J-57-powered interim version.

It is notable that the Air Force had only limited knowledge concerning the performance and cost of the interim aircraft at the time it authorized the interim program in November 1951. It had the cost estimates provided by Convair in October; it also had Convair's estimate of performance with the J-57, which included a maximum speed of Mach 1.5 and an altitude of nearly 60,000 feet. But neither the aircraft laboratory at Wright Field nor the National Advisory Council for Aeronautics (NACA) had yet conducted wind-tunnel tests to verify Convair's figures.

During 1952 and early 1953 several things happened to bring about a radical shift in fire-control system programming. Hughes was beset with continuing delays, and the MX-1179 was falling behind schedule. In addition, during the summer of 1952 the Air Force canceled the F-89F interceptor program, the aircraft that had been intended to precede the interim F-102 in the inventory of the Air Defense Command. This decision made it even more imperative that the over-all interim program remain on schedule, which in turn forced a reappraisal of the availability and capability of alternative fire-control systems. The best bet for an interim system appeared to be the Hughes E-9, originally programmed for advanced F-89 interceptors, appropriately modified for use in the YF-102. Hughes estimated that a crude system would be available for installation in an early YF-102 by July 1954 and a refined version available in production quantities two years later.

A decision regarding the E-9 presented the Air Force with a dilemma. If no interim fire-control system program were interjected, it was felt that the MX-1179 would be ready for testing by December 1954, in phase with the YF-102 test flight program, and that production quantities would be available by April 1957, about a year behind the schedule for the E-9. However, with an interim fire-control system in the picture, the MX-1179 might be delayed an additional 18 to 24 months. Moreover, the E-9 as then developed had few of the automatic features of the MX-1179. The pilot would have to fly manually to and from the target area as directed by verbal ground instructions; he would not have the benefit of automatic flight itself, and there was no provision for an autopilot, which was considered essential for long intercept flights.

In early 1953, Headquarters USAF decided in favor of the E-9 and shortly thereafter approved a proposal to develop an E-9 autopilot to be available for retrofit by September 1956. In addition, the decision included initiating work on a program involving pilot-assist subsystems aimed at providing automatic flight control and automatic attack modes. Possibly because of the increasing cleavage between the interim and ultimate versions of the aircraft, the nomenclature was revised: the interim version was redesignated the F-102A, while the ultimate version was designated the F-102B. In the words of the Air Research and Development Command in March 1953:

> Every effort should be exerted to expedite the availability of the F-102A whose configuration has been determined as incorporating the E-9 Fire Control System and the J-57 engine. The F-102B configuration with the MX-1179 and J-67 engine will be phased in at the earliest date without affecting E-9 availability for the F-102A.

An important point concerning the E-9 is that much more than a repackaging job was involved in the initial program. About half of the equipment had to be designed specifically for the F-102A in order for the system to operate at altitudes up to the combat ceiling of the aircraft. The original E-9 had been developed for lower altitudes. Because of the major changes involved, the fire-control system for the F-102A was redesignated the MG-3.

During 1952 and early 1953, major changes were also made in the airframe involving substantial weight penalties, which were later to play a critical role in the performance of the airplane. As originally designed, the aircraft was to carry its air-to-air missiles in a bay directly below the engine and the rockets in a forward bay. This arrangement was based on a missile wingspan of 20 inches. Later the developer of the designated missile discovered that the missile would have to be enlarged, and, in particular, its wingspan would have to be increased. The corresponding increase in the size of the missile bay and the resulting increase in fuselage diameter would substantially reduce the top speed of the F-102A; therefore, a complete redesign of the armament bays was necessary. The missiles were installed in two tandem bays and the rockets placed in the doors of each bay. The fuselage was lengthened and with resulting changes in controls, wiring, and so on, the airframe weight increased. There was a roughly equal increase in missile weight. Changes in armament and additional airframe changes led to a still further weight increase. The total weight increase was substantial.

Late in 1952 the Air Force negotiated a definitive contract (cost plus fixed-fee) for nearly $100 million covering production of the 42 aircraft to be delivered in 1954 and 1955. In 1952 and 1953, there was a debate about the drag of the F-102A that culminated in an extensive modification of the aircraft. Early in 1952 Wright Field engineers disputed Convair's prediction as to ceiling and combat range for the J-57 version, believing that insufficient allowance had been made for "trim drag." NACA subsequently conducted an analysis of drag and came to conclusions that were disquieting: actual ceiling was estimated at 5,000 feet less and combat range at one-third less than the Convair prediction. Even the supersonic capability of the aircraft was held in doubt, all because of an expected "unusually high transonic drag rise." NACA, furthermore, had developed the "ideal body theory" and recommended that it be incorporated in the F-102 design. Very briefly, this theory, based on the work conducted in 1952 by Richard Whitcomb and R. T. Jones, indicated that in order to compensate for the drag of a delta wing at transonic and supersonic speed, the fuselage would have to be indented at the juncture of fuselage and wing, and elongated to conform to a minimum acceptable ratio of fuselage length to cross-section area.[35] By early 1953, wind-tunnel and rocket tests of models incorporating the indented and elongated fuselage confirmed the belief that Convair's early

[35] The "Coke-bottle" modification was intended to improve performance in the transonic region, and a different modification, later developed by Jones, was intended for aircraft flying in the Mach 1.2 to 2.0 regions.

estimates were wrong. In August 1953 Convair accepted the "ideal body theory" and joined in recommending the appropriate modifications.

These modifications were fairly extensive. Besides the indentation, they involved lengthening the fuselage by seven feet and moving the wing and vertical fin rearward. In addition, a cambered leading edge to increase lift and "warped" wing tips to reduce trim drag were included in the program. The modifications amounted to a 1100-pound weight increase. New specifications for the F-102A were issued. They called for a lower ceiling at combat speed than the previous specifications.

The configuration change complicated the program because under the Cook-Craigie plan Convair had already tooled up for production of the old configuration. Changes in tooling would involve scrapping about two-thirds of the tools already procured. Because hardware fabrication was well along for the first few aircraft, Air Force Headquarters authorized that the two prototypes (having the old configuration), be delivered in October and December 1953 as scheduled, that an additional eight of the old configuration, already far along in development, be completed during 1954, and that beginning with the eleventh aircraft all the remaining 32 incorporate the modifications. The first ten were designated YF-102, and the new version, F-102A. (The "ultimate" version, the version proposed originally by Convair with the J-67 engine and the MX-1179 fire-control system, remained the F-102B.)

The prototypes, built with production tooling, were delivered on schedule. Flight tests confirmed the fear that the plane would be subsonic. Maximum altitude tests in April 1954 indicated a combat ceiling below 50,000 feet, well under that originally intended.

At the beginning of 1954 it became apparent that more than the "ideal body" modification would be necessary to provide adequate performance in air defense. By itself the modification was expected to add only .1 Mach to maximum speed (with the J-57 engine), while combat altitude would remain below 50,000 feet. The F-102A had simply grown too much in weight since it had been originally conceived in 1951. Take-off weight with all the preceding modifications, and many others, had risen to about a third more than the original estimate. Air Force officials felt that only an engine such as the J-67, in the 20,000 pound thrust class, as compared with the J-57's 15,000 pound thrust, could provide the kind of performance needed. But prospects for the availability of the J-67 were growing bleaker and bleaker. In fact, there was increasing talk of substituting the J-75 for the J-67 in the "ultimate" version (F-102B). Rather than halt development pending availability of a larger engine, it was decided to make a drastic reduction in the weight of the airframe of the F-102A. The airframe had been designed to withstand the stresses that would be exerted in flight with an engine producing over 20,000 pounds thrust. With the 15,000 pound thrust J-57, it would be possible to reduce the dimensions of structural members without reducing structural integrity within a lower-stress flight environment, but this involved serious problems. First, the airframes originally planned for the F-102A and the F-102B were to be identical, thereby requiring only one set of development and tooling costs. With two distinct airframes in the program, new F-102B airframe development and tooling costs would have to be added to all the costs incurred in the interim program. Furthermore, the tooling needed to produce "ideal body" F-102As beginning in early 1955 was modified from that employed in constructing the ten YF-102s. To carry out a second program involving weight reduction, even more tools would have to be replaced or modified and substantially more engineering changes would be needed.

The Air Force decided that the second modification program held sufficient promise of salvaging the F-102A so that it was worth the expected cost. The program involved not only reducing weight by about 2400 pounds, but also modifications involving nose lengthening, canopy redesign, intake redesign, and aft wing fillets. Even so, the planned take-off gross weight of the final lightweight version was still about one-fourth more than the original estimate made in 1951. Rather than produce the remaining 32 aircraft under the contract with only the "ideal body" modification, Convair was not directed to apply both modifications to 28 of the aircraft. Only these last 28, therefore, were expected to enter the air defense inventory. In summary, the following is a tabulation of the models comprising the 42 aircraft:

Production prototypes (YF-102)	2
Unmodified production versions (YF-102)	8
"Ideal body" modification, heavyweight versions	4
Both "ideal body" and weight reduction modifications	28
Total	42

Convair produced the remaining eight of the first (unmodified) version during 1954. These were used in various phases of flight testing that did not involve supersonic flight. The first "ideal body" aircraft flew in December 1954. In order to approximate the flight characteristics of the later, lightweight aircraft, it underwent an arbitrary weight-reduction program in which over a ton of equipment was eliminated. Flight tests with this aircraft indicated substantial improvement in speed and an altitude capability superior to that of the YF-102. After discarding about one-half of the tools used to manufacture the four heavyweight F-102As and adding a somewhat greater number of tools to the production line, Convair completed the first lightweight version in June 1955. The 28 lightweight aircraft were produced at the rate of 2 to 3 a month; the last one was delivered in March 1956. All of these, it will be recalled, were to be used as test-flight vehicles.

Phase IV performance tests on the F-102A (lightweight, "ideal body") were conducted at Edwards in early 1956. The evaluation, which for the most part covered testing of the airframe-engine combination (*not* the complete weapons system), was very favorable. The aircraft was pronounced "greatly superior" to any all-weather interceptor then in use.

The total cost of attaining these 42 aircraft, excluding the flight-test costs, turned out to be about double the original allotment for this purpose. Some of the additions involved the two major modification programs; others involved new items.

It turned out in 1956 that the *complete* weapon system, including missiles and fire control system, was unsatisfactory. The following two years saw an extensive program of modifying the troublesome components and retrofitting the aircraft. When the program was completed in late 1958, the F-102A weapon system attained an acceptable level of over-all effectiveness.

As for the "ultimate" version of the interceptor, the version with which Convair had won the competition back in 1951, a contract was let in 1955 for a number of these (redesignated the F-106). An engine switch from the J-67 to the J-75 was made in 1955; the original fire-control system remained. Numerous modifications, delays, and improvements, not foreseen at the signing of this contract, followed. Budgetary constraints and the success of competing fighter programs led eventually to a substantial cut in the number of these aircraft finally procured. Their maximum speed and combat ceiling fell short of the original 1951 specifications (for the J-67 version).

Remarks

The F-102 and F-106 programs had two outstanding and related properties:

1) A complex "system," made up of many components, was highly

specified from the start and heavy commitments were made quite early on the assumption that the initial performance predictions would be met in the specified time interval.

2) An attempt was made (the Cook-Craigie Plan) to telescope two of the most time-consuming steps (testing and production tooling) in the task of attaining the required number of operating aircraft. All testing was to be done with production aircraft rather than with "hand-made" vehicles. ("Hand-made" vehicles have played an important role in resolving early development uncertainties in many aircraft programs, for example the F-104, which we consider next.) Had all the initial predictions turned out to be accurate there seems little question that the program would have been cheap and quick as compared with programs involving a similar technical jump. Unfortunately, crucial predictions about the airframe, engine, fire-control system, and air-to-air missile turned out to be substantially wrong. So closely integrated was the planned system that each wrong prediction implied a delay, not only in the satisfactory completion of the component in question, but also in the development of other components. The telescoping of testing and tooling, finally, did not achieve the saving in time that it was intended to achieve; the unexpected need for the weight-reduction program meant scrapping the early tools.

The F-102 case strikingly illustrates one of the major *external* events that can make major revisions desirable. This event is the discovery, outside the project, of new principles that advance the whole state of the relevant art. Such a discovery was the "ideal-body" rule.

3. The F-104

The F-104 series is related to the design Lockheed entered in the competition of 1950–1951 out of which grew the Convair F-102/106. After the screening in mid-1951, only Convair and Republic were left in the running. This came as a surprise and was a serious loss to Lockheed since at one point in the evaluation the firm had received a letter from the Air Force stating that Lockheed's proposal, the L-205, would be placed under development. With this turn of events Lockheed had fears for its long-run future in the fighter field. Its last fighter development prior to the L-205 proposal was the XF-90, which had been a failure partly because it was designed around the Westinghouse J-46 engine which, as we saw in Part C, did not perform as expected. Because of the failure of the XF-90, and the lack of a contract enabling Lockheed to keep its hand in the fighter field, Lockheed foresaw its future ability to compete with other companies for fighter business endangered.

In order to remain in the fighter field, Lockheed continued work on the L-205 and renewed its efforts to win a contract. A subsequent version growing out of this work, the L-224, won support in some circles of the Air Force in early 1952, but the model was judged by WADC to be not enough better than the Sabre 45 (the F-100) to justify its development.

Lockheed returned to the drawing board and in May 1952 presented WADC with another proposal, design L-227. This proposal, at one time on the verge of acceptance, was rejected in June. The rejection marked the emergence of a new concept that was to affect the type of aircraft Lockheed subsequently developed. In mid-1952, military circles were concerned about the possibility of future wars resembling the Korean War. Attention was focused, therefore, on exploring the implications of peripheral wars for the kinds of military hardware required. For a tactical fighter it was suggested that a cheap, mass-produced lightweight plane be developed. Proponents of this approach argued that it was profitable to trade quality for quantity, and that we had gone too far in insisting that our planes be equipped with a number of "luxury items." This position was supported by the testimony of many ex-Korean combat pilots, who asserted that much of the equipment on their planes was of little value. This concept stood in direct contrast to all Lockheed's earlier proposals, which had called for gross weights in the 26,000-pound class.

The new proposal was far from unopposed. Another faction in the Air Force, contending that such a development policy would lead to inferior equipment and a second-best Air Force, strongly urged development of aircraft such as the L-227. The lightweight fighter proponents were strong enough at the time to block the contract with Lockheed for the L-227 but not strong enough to initiate development of a lightweight fighter. As a result, neither a heavy- nor a lightweight fighter contract was let in mid-1952.

The rejection of the L-227 by the Air Force touched off a lengthy debate over the relative merits of light- and heavyweight fighters. Within the Air Force the strongest supporters of lightweight fighters were those in the Tactical Air Command responsible for maintaining theater air superiority. Most strongly opposed were those in Air Defense, who insisted that they wanted an all-weather fighter, which in turn would require a heavyweight design. Within Lockheed, the emergence of the lightweight concept was viewed as a threat to its heavyweight proposals. Consequently, Lockheed stepped actively into the debate on behalf of the heavyweight design. Other companies, Northrop, North American, and Republic in particular, submitted specific lightweight proposals to the Air Force.

During the course of the debate certain developments in technology affected the relative merits of the two positions. The most important were in the field of engines, where it appeared that better thrust-to-weight ratios, lower specific fuel consumption, and better ratios of thrust to frontal area would shortly be available. These factors implied that a reduction in aircraft weight was possible with no reduction in over-all capability. Some of these advances had already been embodied in the British Sapphire engine, the predecessor of the Wright J-65. Although the various models of the J-65 weighed about the same as most models of the J-35 and J-47 (the engine in the B-47), the J-65 provided a considerable increase in thrust. Specifically, the J-65 had 7800 pounds static thrust dry and 11,000 pounds thrust with afterburner, as compared respectively with 5400 and 7500 for the model 17 of the J-47. The specific fuel consumption of the J-65 was .93 dry at sea level and 2.0 with afterburner, compared respectively with 1.12 and 2.3 for the J-47. Furthermore, it appeared that even more substantial gains would be achieved with the General Electric J-79 engine, which was at that time in the paper stage. Developments in radar and armament also made weight reductions feasible without loss of capability. In particular, development of rapid-fire cannon made it possible to reduce gun weight without reducing fire power.

For these reasons, the lightweight proponents successfully argued that it was possible to build a first-class fighter much lighter than the F-86F and the F-100. Early in 1953, then, the Air Force was ready to let a contract for such an aircraft.

Although Lockheed had been a very active proponent of the losing side of the debate, it was quick to adjust to the turn of events. Lockheed took only about three weeks to come up with a proposal. The L-246, a 15,000-pound airplane, was hardly more than one-half the weight of the previous proposal. Contract negotiations between Lockheed and the Air Force proceeded in early 1953, and a letter contract was approved by the Air Force in March of that year. It covered the procurement of two prototype XF-104s (the redesignation of the L-246), mock-ups, spare parts to support 100 hours of flying, and rocket and wind-tunnel models, all for an estimated price of a few million dollars. The plane was to be equipped with a J-65 engine having a maximum thrust with afterburner of 12,000 pounds. Armament was specified. Empty weight and maximum take-off weight were to be 10,720 and 18,570 pounds respectively. For the basic mission (take-off weight 16,145 pounds), maximum speed was given as 1.82 Mach (1048 knots at 35,000 feet), sea-level rate of climb as 49,200 feet per minute, a combat ceiling of 52,900 feet, and a combat radius of 375 nautical miles.

The definitive contract, signed in November 1953, covered the same items but at a price several million dollars higher. The two prototypes were to be delivered in March 1955. A subsequent change in orders increased the cost coverage to include items such as modification of afterburners, and development of the fire-control system.

Construction of the two prototypes began in March 1953 and first flight took place only 11 months later, a month ahead of schedule. Total cost of the two planes, including development of the fire-control system and some flight testing, amounted to less than fifteen million dollars.

Lockheed's performance in constructing the XF-104 reflected a number of circumstances. In the first place Lockheed felt that its F-104 would be crucial in determining whether or not it stayed in the fighter business. Consequently, it took the project very seriously. In the second place, whether by accident or intention, Lockheed was given a relatively free hand in development. The requirement for the system, issued almost simultaneously with the contract, imposed few constraints on Lockheed; it had little to say in detail, being couched for the most part in generalities. In the third place there was extensive and very fruitful use of wind tunnels. Lockheed was able to rely upon testing facilities of the National Advisory Council for Aeronautics to resolve uncertainties associated with the F-104. Fortunately for Lockheed, NACA was particularly interested in a number of problems that were of concern to Lockheed in developing the F-104. By comparison with most aircraft under development, the F-104 was therefore able to command an unusual amount of wind-tunnel time for proving its aerodynamics. In the fourth place Lockheed's task was made substantially easier by the availability of information, particularly wind-tunnel data, gathered in the course of the Douglas X-3 program. Although the X-3 program (initiated in 1943 and terminated in 1951) was generally thought a failure, largely because it was designed around the ill-fated J-46 engine, the experience gained had a carry-over value for the F-104 program. Finally, the vehicles were virtually handmade, few tools being designed specifically for the purpose of constructing it. Later when Lockheed did in fact tool for production, it took as long as a year and a half to construct some of the tools required. Had the first two test aircraft awaited production tooling, they would have been available only much later than they were.

In addition to building an aircraft in less than a year, a record unequalled by any other of the "Century Series" aircraft, Lockheed also developed an afterburner for the engine. When the J-65 was delivered in the fall of 1953 for use in the XF-104, it was a relatively proven engine, having passed its 150-hour test in its nonafterburning version. An afterburning version was being readied by Wright for the Navy, but not on a schedule suitable for use in the XF-104 prototypes. Because the success of the F-104 program was at stake, Lockheed itself undertook the development of the afterburner and succeeded in making available a J-65 afterburner version for the early XF-104 flight-test program.

The XF-104 made its first flight in February 1954 and completed Phase II testing 13 months later. Most deficiencies in the aircraft's performance, shown in Table 7, were attributed to the low power of the J-65 engine, even in the afterburning version. The airframe itself was highly praised.

In mid-1954 the Air Force was undecided about the program. The old heavyweight proponents were in favor of dropping the project. A second group, concerned with the possibility that the United States might soon become involved in a war in Indochina, contended that the F-104 should be procured immediately with the J-65. A third group, whose views eventually prevailed, suggested adding more equipment to the F-104 and improving its performance by switching to a more powerful engine. These suggestions were supported by the fear that with the J-65 engine the F-104 would have inadequate altitude capability in air defense. Enemy bombers, it was argued, would very likely attack from an altitude in excess of 50,000 feet and would, therefore, be invulnerable to attack by the F-104.

In view of the relatively low thrust of the J-65 engine, an official decision was made in mid-1954 to switch to the J-79 in the production version. At the estimated 14,350 pounds maximum thrust, the air-

TABLE 7

PERFORMANCE OF THE F-104

	Actual (Phase II flight test)	Specification 24 March 1953
Engine thrust (lbs)		
Maximum	10,300	12,000
Military	7,800	8,300
Basic weight (lbs)	11,800	11,406
Sea level rate of climb (feet per minute)	32,000	49,200
Combat ceiling (ft)	48,650	52,900
Maximum speed (Mach)	1.59	1.82

plane was expected to attain Mach 2, have a rate of climb of 20,000 feet per minute at 35,000 feet, and have a combat altitude of 60,000 feet.

There was considerable risk associated with substituting the J-79 for the J-65. In mid-1954 a 50-hour test had not been completed on the J-79 while the J-65 had already passed its 150-hour test. Yet it was felt that the expected increase in performance was sufficiently great to warrant taking the risk.

An implementation program involving obligations for production planning and tooling was begun in mid-1954. In the fall of 1954 Lockheed signed a $39 million contract for 17 F-104A airframes. Deliveries were run from January to October 1956.

As a result of the switch to the J-79, the F-104 fuselage was lengthened by five feet and increased in diameter. From the point of view of production, the J-79 version was virtually a new airplane. If Lockheed had tooled for production of the J-65 version, a switch to the J-79 would have meant scrapping nearly all these tools.

The first F-104A made its first flight in February 1956, two years after the first XF-104 flight. The early flight-test program of the F-104A suffered considerable delay, at least partly because of some difficulties with the J-79 engine. Development of the engine was not yet complete; the main engine difficulties were resolved when the J-79 passed its 150-hour test in June 1956. The F-104 attained a progressively higher top speed in subsequent tests, attaining 1.95 Mach late in April. By the first week in June, just prior to the delivery of the second F-104A, the plane had made 16 flights. Phase II flight testing was completed six months after first flight.

The test evaluation disclosed deficiencies in the new airframe somewhat different from those found by the test on the XF-104 model. While the two principal deficiencies of the F-104A were lack of range due to low fuel capacity and "pitch-up" (an aerodynamic problem), neither was mentioned in the earlier evaluation. The latter was largely caused by the combination of the higher thrust engine and the peculiarities of the modified airframe, which gave the aircraft some of the characteristics of a ballistic missile. When pitch-up occurred, the wing blanketed the airflow to the empennage, the pilot lost virtually all control of the aircraft, and because of its extreme speed and inertia the aircraft followed a ballistic flight trajectory.

However, a good deal was learned from the XF-104 experience that was applicable to the F-104A program. Although much of the detail engineering planning that went into the XF-104—the drafting and blueprinting—was not transferable in a body to the F-104A program,

Lockheed did learn from the XF-104 a considerable amount about general manufacturing problems, about how to handle the metals going into the aircraft, and about particular tooling problems. For example, the fuselage of the aircraft is built around a central keel that is the main structural weight-bearing member. Since this feature appeared in the XF-104, Lockheed gained early experience with it and found the experience applicable to the F-104A program. Furthermore, test flying the XF-104 disclosed certain deficiencies that could be corrected; hence it was possible to some extent to accelerate the test-flight program for the F-104A. This carry-over from the XF-104 may partly explain the seven month difference between the time taken to carry the XF-104 through Phase II flight testing and that taken by the F-104A.

Early wind-tunnel tests had shown that there might be a pitch-up problem, although it did not appear in the earlier Phase II evaluation. It was not until early 1957 that development of a satisfactory pitch control was completed for the F-104A.

Unexpected major difficulties with the designated gun also complicated the F-104A program. The aircraft reacted in an undesirable way to firing. These difficulties were partially responsible for the decision to replace the gun in Air Defense Command (ADC) interceptors with two Sidewinder infrared missiles. While the F-104 was originally designed to serve the Tactical Air Command, ADC later decided to procure four squadrons, but for various reasons did not favor use of the gun. Besides the mechanical difficulties with the gun, ADC felt that guided-missile armament was superior in air defense and that provision for guns on the F-104A would require a return to the ground-support provisions that ADC had long since abandoned in its general changeover to missile and rocket armament for all other interceptors.

Although subsequent changes in force requirements sharply reduced the value of the F-104 to the Air Force, the generally high capability of the F-104 system as a lightweight, low-cost fighter accounts in part for Lockheed's success in the stiff competition among U.S., English, French, and Scandinavian manufacturers to sell lightweight, low-cost fighters to NATO and SEATO governments. The West German Air Force procured a license from Lockheed for manufacture of the aircraft in Germany. A number of other countries have also procured the aircraft.

The F-104 history illustrates that research and development in one program can have a great carry-over value to another. Lockheed's success in building and flying a prototype less than a year after go-ahead would very probably not have been possible without the knowledge derived from the Douglas X-3 program. Although the value of this experimental effort in the F-104 program could hardly have been anticipated when Air Force money was advanced to finance it, the value to the Air Force of the X-3 program extended far beyond its immediate results.

The F-104 history also illustrates the inevitable uncertainties of development. The unforeseen difficulty with the chosen gun is typical of the troubles that can beset a program when reliance is placed on components that are only in early development at the time the aircraft program is initiated. Although the aircraft was first envisaged as an air-superiority fighter, it has gone into ADC inventory as an interceptor, and in the tactical version it was given a nuclear bomb capability. Its major customers turned out, in the end, to be foreign governments. Although it was originally designed to have only gun armament, the Sidewinder missile (which was developed quite independently) has been successfully added. Although the aircraft was originally designed for considerably less than Mach 2 performance, the engine switch provided maximum speeds and rates of climb and ceilings (zoom climb) that broke speed and altitude records for operational USAF aircraft.

A notable aspect of the F-104 program was that the initial commitment to Lockheed covered only the construction of two experimental prototypes that were virtually handmade. This had two advantages: first, Lockheed was able to get the aircraft flying more quickly than would have been possible if production tooling had been used. Furthermore, the absence of tooling greatly facilitated the switch from the J-65 to the J-79. The merits of lightweight fighter design were quickly and (relatively) inexpensively tested in an early flight program, and modifications were added to the production version at modest expense. Although the initial financial commitment to Lockheed was small (with the emphasis placed on early experimental flight test rather than on production of an operational weapon system), the total time of five years between the start of the program in 1953 and the first squadron deliveries in 1958 is a record exceeded in the Century Series by only the F-100A.

E. Two Postwar Strategic Jet Bomber Programs [36]

1. The B-52

Early Developmental History

The B-52 was developed under military characteristics issued November 23, 1945. Those characteristics specified a plane with the following as "minimum" performance requirements:

1) High speed at tactical operating altitude for 15 minutes	450 mph
2) Tactical operating altitude	35,000 ft
3) Service ceiling	40,000 ft
4) Service ceiling, one-half of engines	15,000 ft
5) Tactical operating radius with 10,000-pound bomb	5,000 mi
6) Average speed for above radius	300 mph
7) Take-off over 50-foot obstacle at design gross weight	7,500 ft
8) Landing over 50-foot obstacle at design gross weight less droppable fuel and bombs	4,500 ft

In addition, the characteristics set forth some specific and some general requirements regarding armament, crew, equipment, and structure and design features.

A directive inviting design proposals was circulated February 13, 1946. The letter accompanying the directive stated:

> It is desired that the requirements set forth be considered as a goal and that the proposal be for an interim airplane to approximate all requirements, except that emphasis must be placed on meeting the high speed requirement . . . It is the intent that design proposals should present the best possible over-all airplane consistent with power plants or combinations of power plants that will integrate with combined Phase I and Phase II program of approximately three years.

Boeing, Convair, and Martin responded with cost quotations and preliminary designs. The evaluation that followed concluded in favor of Boeing's model 462, and a Phase I development contract was authorized. The price quoted by Boeing in its proposal dated April 18, 1946, for the Phase I work, was $1,785,176. It was notified of its award on June 5, 1946, and a letter contract was approved June 28, 1946.

[36] This section is partly based on studies by W. Meckling.

The most prominent feature of the early history of the B-52 is the succession of major design changes that occurred. From the time Boeing was adjudged the winner in the original design competition until the swept wing turbojet version finally prevailed, one configuration after another was proposed, studied, and then supplanted by the next. Some of these never went beyond paper studies, others were the subject of Phase II development contracts. Table 8 summarizes pertinent physical and performance characteristics for some of the models.

The ink was hardly dry on the contract authorizing Boeing to go ahead on model 462 before dissatisfaction with the B-52 became apparent. The office of the Assistant Chief of Air Staff, Major General E. E. Partridge, indicated in September 1946 that the B-52 was "an unrealistic type" because of its monstrous size, and that the B-52 design failed to meet Army Air Force requirements. At a Wright Field conference held on the 17th and 18th of October in 1946, Boeing proposed model 464, and on November 26th, General Craigie, Chief of the Engineering Division, recommended that the B-52 development be converted to essentially that design.

However, at another conference held the next day the whole concept of the B-52 was changed materially. Instead of developing a general purpose plane, it was decided to make the B-52 a special purpose plane designed for the specific mission of carrying an atomic bomb over a long range, taking advantage of surprise, apparently by night. The minimum requirements for crew and armament were to be reduced substantially, thus permitting a large weight reduction. The airdrome problem was also to be alleviated by equipping only a few wings.

In an effort to meet this new concept, Boeing proposed two models, 464-16 and 464-17, which were essentially alike, except that 464-17 was still a general purpose plane with a maximum bomb load of 90,000 pounds; whereas 464-16 could carry a maximum of only 10,000 pounds. At a conference on January 7, 1947, it was decided that Boeing should go ahead with model 464-17, the general purpose version. New military characteristics superseding those of November 1945 were issued June 23, 1947, reflecting the new version of the B-52. Working toward the desired 10,000-mile range, Boeing evolved model 464-29, which was to use a more advanced type of T-35 engine. The 464-29 was the first model that purported to meet the range requirement.

The new B-52 configurations by no means assuaged all fears regarding the advisability of its development. Heavy pressures for a

TABLE 8

B-52 MODELS—DESIGN DATA

Model Number	Date	Engine Type	Number of Engines	Design Gross Weight	Radius (statute miles)	Maximum Speed	Cruise Speed
462	April 1946	T-35-1	6	360,000	3,110	440	410
				(alt.) 400,000	3,570		
464	November 1946	T-35-?	4	230,000	2,500	430	400
464-17	February 1947	T-35-5	4	400,000	3,750	440	420
				(alt.) 480,000	4,610		
464-29	? 1947	T-35-3	4	400,000	5,005	455	415
464-35	January 1948	T-35-3	4	280,000	3,540	512	500
464-40	July 1948	J-40-WE-6	8	280,000	3,375	536	500
464-49	October 1948	J-57-1	8	330,000	3,060	572	520

change became evident again in the summer of 1947. In September 1947 a Special Bombardment Subcommittee of the Aircraft and Weapons Board drew up and recommended a new set of military characteristics that reduced the required range from 10,000 to 8,000 miles, increased the required cruising speed to 550 mph, and specified air-to-air refueling. Subsequently the cruise speed requirement was reduced to 500 mph, with a maximum speed of 500+ mph. New military characteristics embodying these changes were issued December 7, 1947.

Some controversy and confusion over whether a new competition should be held followed the issuance of the new requirements. At one point the B-52 contract was ordered canceled, but the cancellation was later rescinded and Boeing was authorized to proceed with a new model. The new model was 464-35, a four-engine, straight-wing turboprop still utilizing the T-35-3 engine.

In May 1948, Boeing discussed with Wright Field personnel a preliminary study of the B-52 using J-40 turbojets, and was requested at that time to expand the study. The results, which appeared encouraging, were sent to Wright Field in July.

When Boeing personnel came to Wright Field on Friday, October 22, 1948, to discuss the turboprop model 464-35, they were informed that the Air Force was seriously interested in a turbojet. The Boeing officials drew up the design and constructed scale models of the present B-52 with swept wings and eight J-57 engines. In January 1949 the Board of General Officers met and decided to let Boeing go ahead with model 464-49 in place of the turboprop without a new design competition.

The B-52 configuration was not yet settled. Dissatisfaction still existed, especially with regard to radius, which at that time was estimated at 3,050 miles. In November 1949, Air Force Headquarters expressed dissatisfaction with in-flight refueling as a means of getting the required range, but agreed to accept a B-52 if it had a radius of 4,250 miles. Boeing engineers responded by increasing the take-off weight to 390,000 pounds, thereby increasing the radius not to the figure requested, but to 3,530 miles. Only in a much later version, the B-52C (weighing 450,000 pounds), did the radius reach an estimated 4,170 miles.

Developmental History After 1949

Even with the essential configuration decided upon—the swept-wing design, the engines, the intended weight, radius, and speed—numerous uncertainties remained. Although the flights of the B-47 (starting in 1947) had resolved some major uncertainties about large, swept-wing aircraft, numerous problems of fabrication and detailed design peculiar to the B-52 had to be solved. Fairly confident predictions about the J-57 engine could be made (at least by the developing company) for early versions of the engine had been running for some time. In the face of the remaining uncertainties the Air Force was committed, at the end of 1949, to two prototype aircraft, the XB-52 and YB-52. It appeared to be the intention, at least in 1950, that a production commitment was to await the flying of at least one of the prototypes.

Early in 1950 it was decided that both prototypes should use not the nearly qualified first model of the J-57, but rather the more advanced J-57-3 which the production planes were later to use. In July 1950, an inspection board, observing the engine mock-up as well as the relevant information acquired in developing the preceding J-57-1 version, concluded that the range requirement could be met with the engine. Shortly afterward several problems arose in developing the J-57-3 model, notably a surging condition during acceleration and deceleration. These fairly normal engine difficulties might themselves not have caused delays in the test flights of the two B-52 prototypes had not two other changes occurred: (1) The J-57 became increasingly important to other aircraft programs (the F-100, for example); and (2) the entire B-52 program was accelerated, in part, presumably, because of the pressures generated by the Korean War. While the first test flight had been scheduled for February 1952. Boeing announced, in early 1951, that it hoped to make a test flight before the end of the year.

The tightness of engine deliveries, however, caused this prospect to vanish. It was in April 1952 that a prototype (the YB-52) first flew. Engines had to be used that did not yet contain the large bleed valves chosen to solve the surge problem. Speed and altitude were consequently restricted. The engine scarcity problem continued until early 1953 and somewhat hampered the YB-52 flight test program.

The role of the swept-wing B-47 in resolving aerodynamic uncertainties throughout the period 1949–1952 was an important one. By the time Boeing was ready for the first B-52 flight tests, the B-47 had had more than four years of flight tests, and many difficulties of large swept-wing aircraft had come to light. A number of important "fixes" were copied from the B-47 experience to solve difficulties that appeared in the B-52 flight tests.

The YB-52 flight test program (despite the late availability of suitable engines) was considered to be unusually rapid. Its results were encouraging, although a number of needed alterations were discovered. The other prototype, the XB-52, though built earlier than the YB-52, first flew in October 1952. The problem of engine surge did not disappear for a few more months and the XB-52 test program was hampered, as the earlier test program had been. Engine company facilities were still strained by competing demands and it therefore took fairly long to find an appropriate fix. The initial solution (large bleed valves) turned out not to work well. Other serious problems arose in connection with crew safety (leakage of fumes into the cabin) and flight control surfaces.

By May 1954, however, most flaws had been corrected. Air Force opinion about the plane had become enthusiastic and one Air Force general in the Air Materiel Command is reported to have suggested that "someone should try to discover how we accidentally developed an airplane that flies so beautifully."

What production commitments were made through the years 1950–1954? The acceleration that occurred in 1951 meant the abandonment of the plan to let flying prototypes precede production commitments. In February 1951 the Air Force and Boeing signed a letter contract for 20 production aircraft. In May 1951 there was a mock-up inspection, and in October 1952, after the first YB-52 flights, final production specifications were approved. They differed somewhat from those of the letter contract, but not enough, apparently, to require any scrappage of tooling already accumulated. The first production airplane rolled from the plant in May 1954, and the first delivery of a B-52 to the Strategic Air Command took place in June of 1955. This was ten years to the month after the preliminary conference out of which grew the first military characteristics for the B-52. It is most unlikely that anyone at the earlier date had in mind a plane very much resembling the one delivered.

Remarks on the Early History

It is clear that the basic design of the B-52 changed frequently in the years 1946–1949, and that differences between basic designs were not negligible. The Air Force did not start out by analyzing the alternatives, selecting the one "best" alternative, laying down a detailed schedule of development and then proceeding forthwith to build a number of prototypes, for the Air Force could not be certain what was best; and the best guess kept changing as new knowledge was acquired.

In retrospect it is difficult to appreciate the magnitude of the uncertainty about what kind of bomber should be developed. In early versions, for example, the central question was whether the Air Force was buying a useful capability by insisting on a plane with a range of 10,000+ miles. There was disagreement as to how much such a plane would have to weigh, and hence disagreement about how much it would cost. The cost disagreement included not only the airframe, but also cost of facilities, bases in particular. Those who felt the plane would be heavy and expensive argued that the Air Force would do better to spend money developing a lighter, shorter range bomber. Similarly there was uncertainty about how much speed should be sacrificed in order to achieve range. Some argued that a 10,000-mile bomber would be so slow that its vulnerability would render it ineffective. In regard to configuration there was the question of the flying or delta wing versus the swept or straight wing. The engines furnished another major source of uncertainty: should they be turboprop or turbojet? On all these questions and many more, individuals or organizations voiced concern, and sometimes vigorous controversy. Because of these uncertainties the Air Force accepted any particular concept only tentatively. It did not treat development as though the central problem was simply to get "a B-52" as quickly as possible. Rather it concerned itself with the question of discovering what B-52 would in fact be best.

Moreover, as efforts to develop a plane proceeded, new knowledge was constantly being acquired that impinged on the current program. Although the period from 1945 to 1949 was hardly one of unusually rapid technological change (there was nothing that might be described as a technological breakthrough) in just a few years the technological outlook for bombers changed materially. Gradually the Air Force was better able to estimate weights, costs, timing, the penalties imposed by large crews, and the penalties imposed by all-around defensive armor. The success of swept wings became apparent with tests of the B-47. Enemy defensive capabilities were reevaluated. Development work at Pratt and Whitney disclosed the possibility of obtaining very significant advances in the performance of the turbojet.

Thus the central theme in the early B-52 development is the process of revision based on new information. The proposal of the much lighter, shorter range model 464 reflected a conviction that the long-range version was not optimal. This conviction had been materially influenced by a growing feeling that a 10,000+ mile bomber would be much heavier and more costly than had been anticipated. The original stimulus for model 464-17 was similar. In this case the answer to excessive costs and weights was to sacrifice defensive armament, bomb load, crew comfort, and crew size in order to preserve range. As it turned out, however, new engines appeared on paper at least, and a new general purpose plane resulted. Model 464-29 represented no new change in concept, but did reflect improved aerodynamics, and once again a new engine.

New knowledge of two classes was important in the adoption of model 464-35. For one thing, great strides had been made or were within sight in air defense, and it was clear that the slow speed of the long-range plane was going to be a serious handicap. For another, aerial refueling developed and began to appear much more attractive as a means of achieving long range than before. Model 464-40 occupies a unique position in this list, because it was never seriously considered as a plane to be developed. Its purpose was purely to investigate the feasibility of turbojets. Model 464-49 grew partly out of the studies of 464-40, but was influenced heavily by early paper studies of the J-57 engine, and by the success of the swept-wing B-47 which had first flown in December of 1947. Furthermore, it had become quite apparent by this time that developing a 500 mph turboprop engine, gearbox, and propeller was much more difficult than had been anticipated.

In retrospect it might seem that the factors that resulted in the decision on the final model of the B-52 should have been apparent much earlier. But the uncertainties that plagued the decisionmakers were not of a kind that might be quickly and easily resolved. Even the best experts could not agree, and as a result the advice the Air Force obtained on technical matters was equivocal. On the question of weight, for example, studies by Boeing yielded weight-range curves considerably more optimistic than similar studies made elsewhere, and the question of which was more nearly correct was a very controversial matter. On the question of configuration, there were many experts backing the flying wing or delta wing for long-range bombers. And it was not until December 1947, when the B-47 first flew, that flight data began to be available on the performance of the swept wing for large aircraft. And then, of course, there was the question of which type of engine: turboprop or turbojet? In terms of potential advantages, it could be quite convincingly demonstrated, the turboprop was a better choice. But despite the fact that in the period 1946 through 1948 about 60 per cent of the engine budget was being used for turboprop development, it was far from clear when a satisfactory turboprop would be available. On the other hand, it also was very uncertain if within a reasonable period of time a turbojet could be developed to power a bomber over the "minimum" range believed necessary. As late as 1948 a respectable body of opinion held that such turbojets were very far in the future. It is clear that the picture painted for turbojet development relative to turboprop was much blacker than what actually proved to be the case.

Inability to foresee the future was not limited to technical matters, however. It is doubtful if anyone in those early years could have foreseen very accurately the political and strategic environment in which the B-52 was destined to operate. Many of those who became the strongest proponents of a large B-52 force then contemplated a small one.

Remarks on the Later History

After the decisions of 1949 the Air Force, it seems, was well aware that uncertainties remained. It was decided to try to continue developing the B-52 so that changes could be made relatively easily. The backlog of B-47 experience, moreover, decreased the likelihood of major design changes. The originally unintended acceleration of 1951 contributed heavily to at least one of the major development difficulties (the scarcity of suitable engines). Even so, however, major difficulties following the flying of prototypes were few compared with other bomber programs—the B-47, for example.

2. The B-47

The B-47 grew out of military characteristics issued in November 1944. They called for a plane having a minimum high speed of 500 mph, a tactical operating altitude of 35,000 to 40,000 feet, and a range of 2,500 to 3,500 statute miles. The first version proposed by Boeing in December 1944, and accepted by the Air Force, was model 432; a straight wing, four-engine turbojet, with the engines mounted on top of the fuselage. However, in 1945 on a visit to Germany, Boeing's chief engineer uncovered valuable information on the performance of swept wings. This prompted Boeing to propose model 448, which had swept wings and two additional engines in the tail. Finally, in the fall of 1945 model 450 was proposed and accepted. It was a six-engine version with the engines slung on wing pylons essentially like the B-47 that finally emerged.

The swept-wing design promised to permit attainment of high speeds, given the performance expected of advanced versions of the existing J-35 engine. There were, however, major aerodynamic uncertainties in applying the swept-wing principle to aircraft of this size as well as some engine uncertainties. Accordingly, the early stages of the development of the B-47 were conducted on an experimental basis. There were only two prototypes, the XB-47s, and these were essentially stripped down experimental planes. This meant that the cost of buying the early flight test information was very small. The total amount paid to Boeing for the two prototypes was in the neighborhood of $12 million, but there was a substantial amount of government furnished equipment. According to B-47 project personnel the cost of that equipment was probably equal to the amount paid Boeing. This would put the total cost somewhere between $20 and $30 million, a very low figure compared to later programs.

The first XB-47 flew in December 1947. Subsequent test flights in the next few months established that the aircraft would perform satisfactorily in the 600 miles per hour speed range. Fourteen months after the initial flight the XB-47 established a transcontinental speed record. The plane also "ran away" from the currently operational jet fighters.

A number of changes were still needed to make the aircraft suitable for mass production and operational use. For example, a rocket-assisted take-off device, not yet developed, appeared necessary in order to get the fully loaded combat version off the ground. Nevertheless, basic airframe and engine uncertainties had been resolved when the first production contract was signed. This occurred in November 1948 and covered the procurement of 10 B-47As and later procurement of 41 B-47Bs, with the delivery period extending from January 1950 to March 1951; the initial delivery date was soon changed to April 1950. The B-47B was to have more powerful engines than the B-47A or the XB-47; but the intended engine, designated the J-47, had the same basic design as the J-35 that powered the X and B versions. The B-47B was also to have more equipment, notably in-flight refueling equipment, than the B-47A; the B-47A, in turn, was to have more equipment than the XB-47. Otherwise the three versions were to be very similar. Most of the B-47As and a number of the B-47Bs were intended not for immediate operational use but for flight-test programs, designed to eliminate inevitable "bugs."

Compared with its subsequent revised form the first production schedule was a rather relaxed one. It seemed reasonable to expect that the remaining engineering problems could be solved without much delay beyond the intended delivery schedule.

By June 1949, however, the number of B-47Bs ordered had approximately doubled, with the delivery period extended only to

December 1951.[37] This was the first acceleration of the original production schedule. The outbreak of the Korean War in June 1950 led to much more acceleration. In December 1950 the Air Force began to seek B-47 production sources in addition to Boeing. Douglas and Lockheed were selected. By April 1951 the number of B-47Bs on order (including a reconnaissance version) had risen to 1500. A high monthly production rate (utilizing a six-day week) was authorized for all the producing plants.

At the same time there was heavy emphasis on getting the aircraft from factory to combat readiness as soon as possible. A number of aircraft previously designated to serve initially for testing were now assigned to operational use. Installations of several of the later models of the J-47 engine were made in planes destined for operational use before these models had passed their 150-hour tests. There was a similar acceleration with respect to the rocket-assisted take-off device and other components.

As a result the early operational history of the B-47 was marked by a series of delays, equipment failures, equipment deficiencies, substitutions of provisional equipment, equipment voids, and so forth. Early production aircraft had no ejection seats; an interim fire control system substituted for a development that failed completely; the bombing system was so unreliable as almost to destroy the usefulness of the plane as a bomber; there were dangerous fuel tank leaks; canopies cracked and blew off; and there were numerous other major and minor difficulties.

At the same time that the decision was made to seek production sources in addition to Boeing, plans were begun for a modification program. It was realized that those B-47s delivered late in 1951 and in 1952 would need modification in order to incorporate the major engineering changes that would be made during this time. A retrofit center was established in late 1951 and two more centers in 1952. Several hundred aircraft passed through these centers at costs ranging between one-tenth and one-fourth of the estimated cost of the unmodified aircraft.

The delays, difficulties, extra costs, and general dissatisfaction to which the accelerated production program gave rise should not be

[37] At about the same time, Boeing became interested in the promised J-40, at that time a paper engine, whose ultimate fate was described in Part C above. If it met specifications, the high-thrust version of this engine would achieve better fuel consumption and range than the J-47. This possibility did not lead to a change in the intended engine for all the production aircraft on order, but only (in August 1949) to the decision that one B-47B should be fitted with J-40s for test purposes. In late 1950 the dubious future of the J-40 led to cancellation of this plan.

allowed to obscure the advance achieved by the B-47 nor the flexible manner in which the program began and might well have continued. The United States was much earlier than either Britain or Russia in having a medium jet bomber operational. It is safe to say that since World War II no other advance (except perhaps thermonuclear weapons) has given the United States a comparable strategic advantage.

Until the attainment of a flying prototype, aerodynamic uncertainties were great because of the novelty of the basic design. Requirements, on the other hand, were broad and commitments small; the use of new information was possible without major costs of revision. It was the deliberate speeding up of production that broke this pattern.

F. The Sidewinder Missile [38]

Finally we consider an air-to-air missile program that seems to have been a classic example of an important type of strategy, and had striking organizational properties as well.

1. Development History

Sidewinder, a passive, infrared-homing, air-to-air guided missile was developed at the Naval Ordnance Test Station (NOTS), China Lake, California. The outstanding characteristics of the development program were as follows:

1) Only very broad requirements were imposed on the missile throughout its development. The goal was a simple, reliable, inexpensive, and easily maintained missile for use primarily in tail-chase attack from single-place fighter aircraft. In this use it was to have better kill probabilities than existing weapons for some useful altitude and speed ranges. More detailed performance specifications were not imposed and neither were dimensions or weight. No specific using aircraft (with accompanying specific stowage requirement) was designated.

2) The developing laboratory had authority for all design decisions and was free to pursue parallel approaches to the design of individual components, using contractors if desired.

3) Emphasis was placed on early testing of all components and early and numerous firings of test missiles. Extensive test facilities were available at the developing laboratory.

---

[38] This section is based on a somewhat longer study prepared by T. A. Marschak.

Origins

The history of Sidewinder begins in 1947 with a NOTS survey of air-to-air homing devices. The survey concluded that infrared homing held great promise for accurate and inexpensive missiles. According to another, roughly contemporary NOTS study, a pursuit tail-on attack (hence an attack aimed at the target plane's principal infrared source) was the optimum interception path for a fighter against a high-speed bomber. In 1948 a third NOTS analysis, concerning fire-control systems for air-to-air rockets, was completed. The study found that by far the largest source of error in fire-control of rockets is movement of the target after firing; such errors far outweigh the errors due to computing, or to angle of attack, aircraft skid, and rocket dispersion. It was concluded that putting the guidance in the missile was a far more promising approach to reduction of error than that alternative of making fire-control systems vastly more complex (and hence unreliable).

In the same year, laboratory models of an infrared tracking device and of a hot-gas servo control valve (a promising means of steering a missile) were demonstrated at NOTS, and a target-radiation survey showed that radiation levels from jet aircraft were high enough so that existing photo-sensitive lead sulphide cells could be used as target detectors.

In June 1949 these studies and demonstrations resulted in a formal "Proposal for a Heat-homing Rocket." The proposal was written by W. B. McLean, who became the chief organizer of the Sidewinder program; it contained the basic design principles of Sidewinder.

Basic Design Principles

1) Guidance is based on a gyro-stabilized target detector in which infrared radiation is converted into a usable signal as it passes through a rotating chopper and strikes a lead sulphide cell. The detector is not mechanically coupled to the missile body, so that tracking is independent of the body's motion. Oscillation problems which such coupling has generated in other missile programs are eliminated.

2) A torque-balance control (servo) system governs the missile's steering fins (the fins assume an angle for which the control torques exerted on them balance the aerodynamic lift forces). Variations in required torque are very small compared with the variations in fin position required in a control system that directly commands fin angle rather than torque. Such large variations have posed serious problems in other missiles. Moreover, the torque-balance principle

eliminates the need for gain compensation (a further problem of other control systems) to allow for changes in velocity or altitude.

3) The torque-balance servo system generates torques on the steering fins which are kept proportional to the torques generated by a second servo in the guidance unit. The second servo's function is to keep the seeker head always aimed at (precessed toward) the detected signal. The result is "proportional navigation" (the missile's flight path is turned at a rate proportional to the seeker's precession rate), so that the missile takes a collision-intercept course relative to the moving target. The alternatives of pursuit navigation and constant-bearing navigation are more difficult to achieve.

4) There is a single primary energy source—a gas-generating grain of chemical fuel—for the entire guidance and control system. Difficulties of multiple power sources are avoided, and the use of a pneumatic control servo (the torque-balance servo) actuated by the generated gas eliminates problems of valves, pressure maintenance, pipes, oil cleanliness, and so on that have arisen in other missiles containing complex hydraulic servo systems.

5) The guidance and control components are placed in the easily detachable forward section of the missile. Other detachable sections contain the warhead, an influence fuze, the rocket motor, and the rear stabilizing fins. The field-maintenance problems associated with electrical and hydraulic connections between sections (which have arisen elsewhere) are avoided.

6) A previously developed and proven on-the-shelf rocket motor propels the missile.

7) Forward concentration and detachability of the guidance and control section suggested use of a canard-type airframe. The warhead and rocket motor form part of the airframe and the rocket motor chiefly determines the missile's length. For this length the forward controls of the canard-type airframe, together with independent gyros placed in the rear fins, achieve aerodynamic stability. Stabilizing tubes and gyro circuits, which are required in missiles with rear control surfaces, are avoided.

8) The only missile control in the launching aircraft is a button that causes ignition of the propellant grain and so launches the missile. The button is pressed after visual sighting and verification that the missile is "locked on" to the target (a simple circuit delivers an audible signal to the pilot when "locking on" occurs). Once the button is pushed the aircraft neither controls the missile nor illuminates the target.

The overriding considerations in the choice of these basic design principles were simplicity and the avoidance of complex approaches that had caused difficulties in other programs.[39]

Initial Authorization and Funding

The work preceding the formal Heat-homing Rocket proposal had been carried on from NOTS Exploratory and Foundational Research Funds and had included voluntary after-hours work by a number of laboratory scientists. After submission of the proposal, Bureau of Ordnance officials felt that because of the number of untested principles involved, further work should continue with the same funding plus some additional Bureau support for fuzing development. Accordingly, the ensuing effort was aimed at demonstrating the feasibility of proposed but untested principles.

In the spring of 1950 an airborne detector detected a jet aircraft three-quarters of a mile away. Also in 1950 there was a demonstration of a laboratory hot-gas control servo that was sufficiently advanced for use in a practical missile. In the same year it was demonstrated that, given the missile length imposed by the choice of an on-the-shelf rocket motor, aerodynamic stability could be obtained by installing gyro wheels, powered directly by the airstream, in the rear stabilizing fins. Test missiles were ground-launched to demonstrate roll-control feasibility.

In March 1951, two tests of sun-seeking, free-flight, ground-launched missiles demonstrated that the hot-gas servo could control the missile in flight. Later in 1951 two complete, packaged seeker heads, each of different design, demonstrated tracking ability against light-bulb targets. One seeker (Type A) was designed at NOTS and had essentially the design given in the original Heat-homing Rocket proposal; the other seeker was developed by Avion Company, a contractor. The NOTS design exhibited a wobble, subsequently eliminated. Design studies of two additional seeker systems were initiated, one at Eastman Kodak and the other again at NOTS. The four competing designs differed with respect to independence of the optics from the gyro and with respect to the precession system (magnetic or pneumatic) used. (The design finally perfected and adopted, however, was the Type A design of the original proposal.)

In the autumn of 1951, as a result of the demonstrations, the NOTS group felt "technically certain that all problems were capable of solution if a full-scale program could be established" and proceeded

[39] The Heat-homing Rocket proposal included also a free reference gyro and a fire-control system in the parent aircraft for initial correction of the infrared-guidance path. Both were dropped in 1950.

to convey this conclusion to various groups within the defense establishment. They included the Bureau of Ordnance, the Guided Missile Committee of the Research and Development Board, and the presidentially appointed Guided Missile Coordinator. Money for new missile development was at that time very hard to obtain; support had to be sought at levels higher than the Bureau of Ordnance, and the novel contributions of the proposed program compared with others had to be stressed. The Guided Missile Committee approved the proposed program late in 1951, and Bureau of Ordnance funding of Sidewinder on a development level began with an initial budget of $3,000,000.

The Bureau of Ordnance, however, still declined to issue a requirement imposing performance, size, and weight specifications. Requirements of that sort have constrained other missile programs starting at a far earlier stage of development.

Main Events in the Chronology of Full-scale Development

In 1952 a redesign of the airframe followed free-flight and wind-tunnel tests. The most promising seeker head (Type A) was improved and the turbogenerator, supplying all electric power in the missile and dependent on the same hot-gas source used by the control servo, was successfully adapted from a British design. In August 1952, the first air firing of a complete missile (using the Type B seeker, later rejected) took place, and in November the first of 30 more custom-made missiles (those with Type A seekers) was delivered.

In 1952 Philco Corporation was selected as prime contractor responsible for the production of test and (later) operational guidance and control sections. Philco's task was to achieve efficient production of the guidance and control section, redesigning its components where possible so as to obtain lower production costs without impairing performance.

In 1953 satisfactory performance of the Type A seeker head was achieved (wobble was eliminated), and, after a final demonstration of the Type B seeker, Type A was selected for the missile. A new gas-generating fuel was developed, and as a result the servo time lag was substantially reduced. The design of the chopper through which the infrared target radiation passes was greatly improved and the tracking of targets against some kinds of cloud background was demonstrated with the new choppers.

A total of 16 missiles, all launched from aircraft, were fired against targets (propeller-driven drones) in 1953. As a result of these tests successful development of a prototype Sidewinder—one distinctly worth producing—was considered achieved, except that fuze development was still incomplete. It was not until December 1953 that a requirement including performance specification and dimensions was issued by the Bureau of Ordnance. Although continuing improvement in the performance of most components was made a goal for the ensuing years, the basic design of the guidance and control section was "frozen" for production at Philco in March 1954.

Later in 1954, development of an influence fuze—a completely self-contained, detachable section of the missile—was completed at Eastman Kodak, and development of a contact fuze was completed by Bulova Research and Development Laboratories. Both fuzes went into production (and improved versions of both were later developed). Throughout 1954 there were further test firings, including night and high-altitude firings, using missiles made in the Philco model shop.

In 1955, design of the controlled-fragmentation warhead to be used in operational missiles was completed (previous missiles had been fired with dummy warheads) containing telemetering packages. A total of 88 more missiles were fired in 1955 including firings at supersonic jet targets. The last missiles fired came from the initial Philco pilot assembly line (rather than the model shop). The result of these tests was release of the missile, in January 1956, for Operational Development Force (OpDevFor) evaluation, the final step before introduction of the missile in fleet use.

The missile went through OpDevFor evaluation very quickly relative to other Navy missiles. This was due in part to the availability of field maintenance experts at NOTS who, during the latter phases of development, suggested minor design modifications affecting maintenance. Approval of design details affecting maintenance could be very quickly obtained.

Parallel Component Approaches by NOTS and by Contractors

There was extensive exploration of parallel approaches to certain components within NOTS and (in at least two important cases) by contractors. Different approaches to the lead-sulfide cell, the rotating chopper, the servo valves, the amplifier, the generator, and the propellant grain were, at some time in the course of development, pursued by groups at NOTS. The major set of parallel efforts was directed at the seeker head itself, as described above; two contractors and two groups at NOTS explored competing paths. Each of the contractors had a good expectation of obtaining a production contract should his approach prove to be the more successful. The same was true of the two contractors developing influence and contact fuzes, on which some independent exploration was concurrently being performed at NOTS.

Development Cost, Development Time, and Military Value of Sidewinder

The annual development costs, up to 1957 (which marked completion of development of the improved Sidewinder 1A), are given in Table 9; the costs of development by contractors are shown as well as total costs. The cost of all test missiles up to but not including those delivered for OpDevFor evaluation are included.

TABLE 9

ANNUAL DEVELOPMENT COSTS, SIDEWINDER MISSILE, 1950–1957

Fiscal Year	Total Costs (thousands)	Contracts (thousands)
1950	100	
1951	365	
1952	1,360	
1953	2,930	626
1954	3,172	593
1955	4,291	818
1956	8,992	2,918
1957	11,513	3,449
Total	32,723	8,404

This is a very low total development cost and a short development time relative to other air-to-air missiles. Sidewinder, moreover, proved a distinct success in its mission. It proved easily adaptable to a variety of aircraft. At no point in its development was it "matched" to any one of them. Improved versions of Sidewinder gradually broadened the mission in which it could be used.

Remarks

The development strategy pursued in the Sidewinder program seems to have been made particularly easy by the main *organizational* property of the project—the great amount of authority given to the developing laboratory, and in particular to its head, who happened to be a gifted designer as well as the originator of Sidewinder. There was, in this case, an unusually intimate connection between strategy and organization.

G. Conclusions

We shall now examine the limitations and the possibilities of the preceding studies for the support of two hypotheses about development in the areas of technology we have considered. The first hypothesis is simply that major uncertainties are inevitable in development. Such uncertainties appear in all the cases considered. Predictions about the effort required to make a given design attain a specified performance are subject to large errors, especially at the start of development. Another study of a large group of projects, prepared by R. Summers, further supports this conjecture in a statistical manner.[40] In addition to such "technical uncertainties," there are often great "strategic uncertainties," for there typically occur outside the development project during the course of development, events that affect the relative desirability of the design being pursued: the relative value of different missions changes, fundamental state-of-the-art advances occur, and other projects turn out to have an unforeseen bearing on the project under study.

The second hypothesis is much harder to formulate and to test. It concerns the commitments made in the early phases of development, when crucial predictions are often necessarily inaccurate. Early commitments can be large or small. A large commitment permits one to start certain tasks that take a long time but that also require fairly detailed knowledge of the final form of the item. Such tasks are the preparation of production facilities and the selection and development of other items that are to be "mated" to the item in question in order to form a system. A small commitment may mean that these tasks have to be postponed; but a small commitment may also fairly quickly produce a large jump in the accuracy with which one can make predictions about the final form of the item under development.

Thus two opposite extremes of development strategy can be roughly defined. It will be convenient to label the first extreme the "inflexible" strategy. This strategy takes very seriously the best predictions available at the start of development as to the effort required to achieve alternative, highly detailed specifications. One such set of specifications is chosen and large commitments to it are made,

---

[40] See Chapter 4.

namely the commitments that would achieve rapid development if the predictions turned out to be correct. At the other extreme is a strategy we shall call "flexible." This avoids all but the broadest specifications to start with and makes no major commitment until there has been a substantial jump in knowledge. It concentrates at the start on achieving such a jump quickly by actually building and testing one or more crude versions of the item's least predictable parts. In this way it obtains predictions about the effort required to achieve alternative detailed specifications – predictions generally much more accurate than the initial predictions on which the other strategy bases its large, early commitments.

When the developer who uses the inflexible strategy is lucky, all of the critical initial predictions turn out to be correct and there are no external events that cause him to revise his initial choices. He may then well have saved time and perhaps money as compared with his experience if he had used the second strategy. When the developer who uses the first strategy is unlucky, the chosen specifications will turn out to be much harder to achieve than predicted; this, together with external events, will make the initial choice appear unfortunate. The developer may then be faced with the alternatives of abandoning the program or revising it; in either case parts of the initial heavy commitment (production facilities, programs aimed at another highly specified item to be mated to the item in question) are scrapped.

Suppose a developer undertakes a large number of programs in one of the areas of technology we have considered. His total experience, when all the programs are completed, is composed of the programs' development times and costs, as well as the items finally obtained. If he uses a fairly inflexible strategy in all the programs then, according to the hypothesis, his total experience will be inferior, in terms of his own preferences, to his experience if he had adopted a fairly flexible strategy. That is to say, the gains in time and money of the luckiest cases are outweighed by the revisions required in the unlucky cases.

There are a number of difficulties in using the preceding collection of histories to test this hypothesis.

1) In the first place, few of the programs fall close to one or the other of the two extremes. Those that do not are not relevant to the hypothesis. It requires some subjective interpretation, moreover, to place even the less ambiguous programs in one category or the other.

In the case of radars, the side-looking radars and probably most of the World War II radars can plausibly be argued to fall close to the light commitment or flexible type of program. Some postwar radars, developed according to official procedures that *required* early commitments to highly specified designs, fall close to the heavy commitment or inflexible type of program. In the case of aircraft engines, the J-79, J-57, and J-75 lie close to the flexible type, while the J-40, the J-46, and the T-35 lie close to the inflexible type. Other engines are harder to place. In the case of fighter aircraft, the F-102 seems to be a program of the inflexible type. The F-100 is more ambiguous. On the one hand the initial commitment was a heavy one; on the other, the initial uncertainties were not as large as for most fighter aircraft programs because of the closely related aircraft preceding it. The F-104 program can reasonably be placed close to the flexible extreme.

In the case of the two bombers the situation is again not clear-cut. In the B-47 case the very early commitments were small and much information was obtained from the prototype phase. But immediately afterward, the program was accelerated and very heavy commitments were made to production. In the B-52 case there was a similar acceleration, even before the prototypes flew.

The Sidewinder, finally, falls as clearly as any program can into the flexible, low commitment category.

2) A second difficulty in testing the proposed hypothesis is that of grouping the projects studied into significant pairs. In such a pair one project is of the inflexible type and the other of the flexible type, while both are similar with respect to the other circumstances that might explain major differences in the projects' total experiences. In the ideal "laboratory" test of the hypothesis the same project would be duplicated; it would be run once in a flexible manner and once in an inflexible manner, and the cost, time, and usefulness of the final item would be compared for the two versions. We can hope to approximate this ideal test only very crudely. One reasonable way of doing so is to find pairs in which one project was flexible and the other inflexible while both achieved the same order of technical advance. This approximation is valid only when the achievement of the same order of technical advance by the two projects also meant that the two achieved equally useful items. This would not be the case if external events drastically altered the usefulness of one of the two projects. In studying the project pairs, size of technical advance is certainly a subjective matter, and one can probably do no better in determining it than to poll experts. Such a poll would probably reveal that the side-looking radar, the F-140, the Sidewinder, the J-57, the B-47, and the B-52 (all essentially flexible programs, as argued above) can each be paired with a program that was essentially inflexible and

involved at least as great a technical advance. For the case of the J-57, the J-40 is probably an inflexible program involving a comparable advance; and for the case of the F-104, the F-102 is probably such a program. For the case of the side-looking radar at least one of the postwar radars probably plays a similar role. The inflexible member of each of these pairs took distinctly more time and money to develop than the flexible member. We have not here considered programs that pair up in the same way with the Sidewinder or with either of the bombers.

Some of the histories, then, fall into pairs that support the proposed hypothesis and others do not. None appears to fall into pairs that directly conflict with the proposed hypothesis, that is, a pair of comparable programs, one clearly flexible, the other clearly inflexible, the latter having required distinctly less time and money.

3) Finally, if the histories presented are to support the hypothesis they either should be roughly a random sample from each of the areas of technology or they ought to cover these areas completely (for the postwar years, say). Since histories often take a very great effort to compile, one has to strive for the former alternative. The preceding histories, however, were not chosen quite at random—they were largely chosen because the programs seemed interesting and their study promised to be feasible.

Although our first hypothesis seems well supported, our second conjecture is far from settled, one way or the other, by the preceding collection of histories. In at least one area (engines) the pairing of projects seems clear-cut enough to provide substantial support; in other areas many additional studies would be needed. We hope nevertheless to have sufficiently illustrated the project-history method so as to make clear its possibilities and its limitations.

We note, finally, that even if the project-history approach falls far short of confirming a hypothesis, it may still be useful to the policy-maker. For the policy-maker, unlike the student of R&D, must make decisions here and now. If he has to choose now between two strategy types he must probably be content with incomplete groups of studies such as those presented here. Although he cannot be certain his choice is the correct one, such studies can make his uncertainty a great deal smaller.

Chapter 4

COST ESTIMATES AS PREDICTORS OF ACTUAL COSTS: A STATISTICAL STUDY OF MILITARY DEVELOPMENTS

by ROBERT SUMMERS

A. INTRODUCTION AND SUMMARY

1. Aims and Scope of the Study [1]

A major uncertainty in military development, and no doubt in nonmilitary development as well, has to do with the production cost of the developed item. Sometimes the actual costs of major military hardware articles (aircraft, missiles, and so on) have been five or ten times the estimated amounts. Early estimates, made near the beginning of a development program, have been particularly unreliable.

The purpose of this study is to subject cost uncertainty to statistical analysis. We seek to be precise. We ask, quantitatively, How unreliable are cost estimates and in what directions are they unreliable? How widely do the estimates depart from actual costs, and do they tend to center upon the actual costs or are they systematically biased on the low side? In attempting to answer these questions, and in isolating some of the variables that "explain" past mistakes in estimation, we may obtain fresh insights into the research and development process as well as suggest ways to improve estimating procedures. We seek particularly to illuminate errors in estimates for systems that are in early stages of development.

[1] This chapter was originally prepared as a RAND Research Memorandum designed to help Air Force officers and other government officials in assessing the probable accuracy of cost estimates for major hardware articles of military systems still in development. It was believed that the methods presented provided a sensible way of using imperfect information about the past to decrease the uncertainties about future hardware costs. At this much-later date, the empirical formula devised for debiasing early cost estimates is no longer applicable. The author firmly believes, however, that although the particular formula arrived at was vulnerable to the passage of time, neither the methodology nor its information about the research and development process has been as perishable.

The users of cost estimates, rightly made cautious by past experience of underestimation, have sometimes been driven to apply rule of thumb adjustments to increase the estimates to more realistic magnitudes. Such adjustments are recognized by those who use them as being crude and precarious, being based upon impressions derived from experience with only a few weapon systems. A principal aim of this study, therefore, is to provide a rationale for adjustment based upon refined statistical techniques. This chapter offers a formula relating estimates to actual costs in terms of various characteristics of the development program.[2]

Ideally, we should like to investigate simultaneously the reliability of all types of estimates for new weapon systems, not only estimates of all kinds of costs for whole systems, but also estimates of system performance and time of availability. For practical reasons, however, we concentrate here on one aspect of the estimating problem: the early cost estimates for major hardware articles. But some observations will be made about other aspects of cost also.

Although most users will take it for granted that it is worthwhile to improve cost estimates of major hardware articles, a later section attempts to deal quantitatively with the consequences of cost-estimating errors; we ask whether errors of the observed magnitudes are large enough to affect the outcome of cost-effectiveness studies. A number of cost-effectiveness studies are examined to see how sensitive their conclusions are to variations in costs of major articles. In addition, the budgets required to support two Air Force strategic-force structures are estimated under several different assumptions about the costs of the major articles of a number of future systems.

It should be emphasized that the aim here is not to assign responsibility for the observed inaccuracies in cost estimates. The sources of error appear to be numerous and complex. There are exogenous factors such as changes in the general level of prices and wages; there are inadequacies in the system specifications and errors in the procurement quantities, items usually taken by cost estimators as given data; and in addition to these there are various difficulties in cost estimating itself. To identify all the sources of error would be difficult and would require very complete and finely detailed information about the estimates, the estimators, the system specifications, and the course of the system development programs. The aim of the present study is more modest. It attempts to answer the questions: How useful are typical early cost estimates as a basis for making judgments

[2] This aspect of the study has lost precedence to the method of analysis and to the information about research and development that has been revealed by the analysis.

about future weapon systems and force structures? What can we learn about the research and development process from looking at the cost-estimating histories?

2. Outline of Methods and Results

The empirical basis for most of this study is the history of estimates for the major hardware articles of 22 existing or former weapon systems (a total of 68 cost estimates). The cost chronologies for these systems are analyzed in considerable detail in relation to the development process, but the individual case studies are not discussed here.[3]

A superficial examination of the raw data seemed to indicate that many early estimates were wildly inaccurate. In nine of the 22 systems studied, the actual procurement cost per article was more than three times an early estimate of cost; and in two cases the actual cost was more than ten times an early estimate! This, however, badly overstates the inaccuracy of cost estimates. Actual costs depend very much upon the quantities produced, or, what is much the same thing where weapons are concerned, upon the quantities procured. But cost predictions by cost estimators have been based for the most part upon forecasts (usually made by others and often rather inaccurate) as to the quantities to be procured. The raw data have therefore been adjusted to reflect the costs the estimators would have predicted if they had known the actual procurement quantities.[4] These adjustments are quite important where the actual procurement quantities turned out to be much lower than was expected when development was initiated. Nearly all the gross inaccuracies disappear when this adjustment is made.

Another factor generally outside the sphere of the cost estimator is

---

[3] The author is grateful to members of The RAND Corporation Economics Department, especially to E. R. Brussell, for making available extensive unpublished notes on these case histories. Published reports that have been particularly useful in analyzing the case histories, and in other ways, include: B. H. Klein, W. H. Meckling, and E. G. Mesthene, *Military Research and Development Policies,* The RAND Corporation, R-333, Santa Monica, California, December 1958; T. A. Marschak, *Strategy and Organization in a System-Development Project,* and A. W. Marshall and W. H. Meckling, *Predictability of the Costs, Time, and Success of Development,* in R. R. Nelson, ed., *The Rate and Direction of Inventive Activity,* National Bureau of Economic Research, Princeton, N. J., 1962; and D. Novick, *System and Total Force Cost Analysis,* The RAND Corporation, RM-2695, Santa Monica, California, April 1961.

[4] Ideally, in making a cost-effectiveness study the system analyst has available the estimated cost schedule expressed as a function of the number of units procured, rather than a single cost estimate corresponding to a single procurement number. In practice, however, the procurement number is often a datum given to the cost estimator, and he should not be held responsible for cost differences due entirely to the difference between the given number and the number actually procured.

the secular change of wage rates and material costs. Price-level changes would no doubt have differential effects in a number of cases, for example, hardware-intensive versus personnel-intensive systems, and short-term versus long-term R&D and procurement programs. But even if price-level changes could be forecast, the effect on the *relative* costs of alternative systems would generally be much less than that of other uncertainties. For this reason price-level corrections are usually not taken account of in cost-effectiveness studies, and cost estimates are made in terms of the price levels current at the time of estimation. In comparing estimated and actual costs, however, it is desirable to eliminate this source of difference, and we have therefore made a further adjustment of each estimate to allow for increases in procurement cost due to price-level changes.

The cost estimates adjusted to take account of both procurement-quantity and price-level corrections were still, however, very far from being accurate. In the chronologies studied, the estimates adjusted for these two factors were occasionally higher than the actual costs, but they were usually much lower, and the ratio of adjusted estimate to actual cost varied widely. This is illustrated in Figure 13, where the 68 cost estimates studied are represented by a cumulative distribution curve.[5] The bias of the estimates is clearly seen: about four-fifths of the estimates were less than actual costs, and as many as one-fourth were less than half of actual costs. The fact of variability is also clear: as a percentage of actual costs, some estimates exceeded others by a factor of five to ten.[6]

It appears, therefore, that the user of such cost estimates is faced with substantial difficulties of interpretation. Our analysis leads to results that can be helpful to him by identifying the situations in

[5] It should be clear that since cost estimates made at different times within the same development program are not independent, this curve must be regarded as no more than a convenient descriptive device.

[6] For the 22 systems (68 estimates) studied, the actual costs of major hardware items were never more than seven times the adjusted estimates. Expressed as a percentage of actual costs, adjusted estimates ranged from 15 to about 150 per cent, a factor of ten. It should be emphasized that the cost estimates that have been in error by enormous margins—by factors of 30 or more—and have consequently received unfavorable publicity, have been *unadjusted* estimates in cases where (a) there was such a significant upgrading in the performance required during the course of development as almost to mean a change in kind rather than in degree, or (b) there was a substantial cut-back in the procurement number, or both. But even if these errors are discounted, factor errors of five to ten are serious enough. Even greater factor errors would no doubt have been observed had we always been able to include the *earliest* cost estimates for each of the chronologies studied. But it was often impossible to document these with sufficient precision as to the date and the amount of the estimate, and where this was true the earliest estimates were excluded. Factor errors of five or ten may therefore be regarded as on the conservative (low) side.

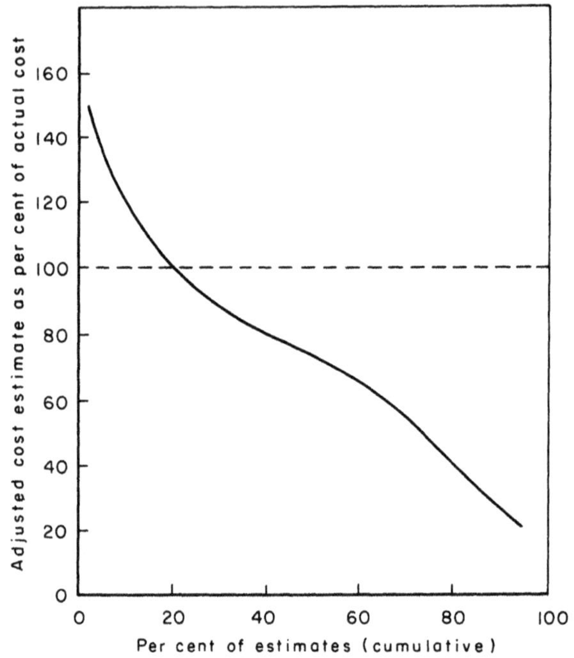

Fig. 13. Bias and variability of adjusted cost estimates

Note: This cumulative distribution curve is based on the data for 68 estimates given below in Table 11, columns (1) and (3). The adjusted cost factor F referred to there is the reciprocal of the "adjusted cost estimate as per cent of actual cost" used here.

which the variability is likely to be large and when the estimates are likely to be particularly low.

Much of the variability in the ratio of adjusted estimate to actual cost can be accounted for by the character of the development program and the timing of the estimate. Cost estimates were generally poor for development programs that required the state of the art to be significantly advanced; estimates were usually good if only a small technological advance was being sought. Almost universally, if the early estimates were poor, later estimates were better.

Various other factors are considered here in an attempt to obtain a better explanation of the variability of cost estimates. We find (1) that, other things being equal, cost estimates improved significantly between 1945 and 1955; and (2) that inaccuracies were greater for long development programs than for short ones, even after taking the degree of technological advance into account.

The critical factor determining the accuracy of a cost estimate seems to be the degree of uncertainty, at the time the estimate is made, about the exact configuration of the article at the end of the development program. When the final configuration is known only vaguely, or perhaps specified only in terms of performance requirements, an estimate is likely to be poor; when it is known with precision, the cost estimate is likely to be good.[7] Great uncertainty about the final configuration is encountered early in programs involving large technological advances. There is much less uncertainty (1) when the major article is being developed in a program involving only small technological advances, and (2) when a program with major advances has reached a point at which most of the development problems have been solved. Considerations of uncertainty go a long way toward explaining the differences in accuracy of the various cost estimates studied here. The argument from uncertainty would lead us, however, to expect the estimates to center on the actual costs, some being higher, some lower. The fact is that in situations of uncertainty the estimates are pretty consistently below actual costs.

How much were the estimates in the 22 weapon system programs biased, and what are the possible reasons? Various causal explanations are examined and it appears that the evidence is inconclusive as to the cause of bias although conclusive as to the fact.

In the next section a debiasing formula is developed by the multiple regression technique to show how much too low a cost estimate is likely to be, given:

- t, the timing of the estimate within the development program expressed as a fraction of program length,
- A, the degree of technological advance required in the program (on a numerical scale), and
- L, the length of the development period (in months).

This formula has the form:

$$F = \{11.929\}\{\exp [.097t - .032tA - .311A + .015A^2 + .008L - .075(T - 1940)]\} \cdot v$$

where F is the ratio of actual cost to adjusted estimate, T is the calendar year, and v is a residual. In the nature of the case, this formula cannot be of universal application, and if used numerically it should

[7] Even in this case, if radically new manufacturing techniques are used about which little experience has been accumulated, cost estimates may be poor. The cost of fabricating stainless-steel honeycombed structures might well be difficult to predict, even given the blueprints of the structures.

be used with full knowledge of the limitations inherent in its derivation. As an inference from past experience, it may not be equally applicable in the future. In particular, the form in which T is introduced brings F down to zero for a large enough T. The formula probably captures the effect of improvements in cost-estimating procedures over time for the period covered by the data (1945–1958). However, it is unlikely that the formula extrapolates satisfactorily very long after this period. New types of hardware may present more difficult problems for estimators. On the other hand, estimators' skills may improve as better understanding of the problems of estimation is developed through research.

If future development program cost histories and cost-estimating methods are like those in the past, this formula should be helpful to those who use the cost estimates. If proper allowance is made for the excessive numerical precision of the results, an Air Force planner could hardly be misled if he took the results into account in the course of making decisions.

The relationship stated in the formula can be expressed in words as follows: The ratio of actual cost to adjusted [8] estimate is not far from unity for cost estimates for major hardware made (even early in development programs) when only minor technological advances are sought and the development time is short. But when major technological advances are sought and the development time is long, the ratio is significantly different from unity. In such cases the initial estimates are generally too low by a factor of between two and three.

It goes without saying that one cannot correct a cost estimate perfectly merely by multiplying it by a factor by which similar estimates were in error in the past. But the data suggest that, in the absence of such a correction, a cost estimate for a long-term program requiring major technological advances will almost certainly be too low. Even for the period 1945–1958, multiplying by a debiasing factor of two or three would not make the estimate "right." There would still be a problem of variability, but the revised estimate would inspire more confidence than the original one because it would not be more likely to be low than high. It would almost certainly be closer to the true cost than the original estimate.

The *consequences* of inaccuracies in the cost estimates of major hardware articles are examined in the last section of this chapter. The effect of these inaccuracies is considered in relation to the many other

[8] "Adjusted" means, as explained earlier, that the correct procurement number is used and the secular change of prices is taken into account.

uncertainties surrounding a weapon system at the outset of its development program (for example, its final performance characteristics and its operating concept). It is found that typical errors in the cost estimates of major hardware articles can affect total estimated system cost as significantly as a variety of errors in the initial specifications of the system.

What has just been said refers to problems of bias. Even if the estimates are debiased, however, they are not likely to be correct. The last section also considers the consequences of estimate variability in cost-effectiveness comparisons. It offers a tentative answer to the question: How large must the difference be between the estimated costs of two major hardware articles before we can be confident that the one that initially appears to be cheaper will actually turn out to be so?

The practical importance of cost-estimating errors is then assessed by analyzing the mistakes that could result from the making of weapon-system choices without correcting the cost estimates for bias *and* taking variability into account. A number of actual cost-effectiveness studies are examined and the question asked: Would the recommendations made as a result of these studies be upset if the original cost estimates had been corrected? The answer is not always "No." Cost estimating errors of the kind encountered in the past can make a significant difference in choices based on cost-effectiveness studies.

Like the choice between individual systems, force-structure planning requires accurate information about the cost of alternative systems. Alternative structures for the strategic force are analyzed to determine the effects on cost totals of incorrect hardware estimates. When "official" cost estimates for highly futuristic weapons are employed, the total-force cost pattern over time is significantly lower than it would have been if the cost estimates had been corrected in accordance with past experience.

Before going on to the detailed statistical analysis of the cost estimates, it must be emphasized that the crudeness of the data precluded the possibility of obtaining anything like a precise description of cost-estimating errors in the years following World War II. But the cost-estimating experience of the recent past is so relevant to an assessment of the accuracy of present day estimates that we must try to extract what information we can from the data, unsatisfactory as they are. What is claimed is that the methods employed in this study constitute a reasonable way of looking hard and close at the information available. The merit of the formulation offered here lies in its explicit method of derivation and in the possibility it offers for future refinement with more complete data and with experience of new kinds of systems and new production techniques.

B. An Analysis of Cost-estimate Chronologies

3. Errors in Nonmilitary Cost Estimating

Twenty-two chronologies of cost estimates of major articles of Air Force weapon systems constitute the basic data of this study. Even a cursory examination of the chronologies suggests that the estimates leave much to be desired. It should be recognized, however, that predicting how much something will cost that is to be produced a long time in the future is always a hazardous activity. The United States is studded with railroads, canals, tunnels, bridges, and highways that cost a great deal more than was originally expected. For example, the final cost of the Troy and Greenfield Railroad was more than ten times as much as the original estimate, principally because tunneling four miles through Hoosac Mountain turned out to be enormously more difficult than the railroad's geologists had predicted. The Welland Canal cost many times more than was expected because the height of a major cut, estimated at 30 feet, was actually 60 feet.

The Suez and Panama Canals tell much the same story. The earliest cost estimate for the Suez Canal, a half-century before it was finally built, was low by a factor of twenty; the year before digging actually began, the estimate was still low by a factor of three. The early abortive effort by the French to build a canal across the Isthmus of Panama was undertaken as a result of a substantial underestimate of the magnitude of the task. The total outlay on the project by the French and subsequently the United States was about twice what the French originally thought would be necessary. Even though the United States had the French experience to learn from, and a portion of the job was already done, the American outlay was 70 per cent more than anticipated when the American work began.

The nuclear power plants recently built offer another example. Almost without exception, the initial cost estimates for these plants were too low. Costs climbed from 50 per cent to 100 per cent, and in some cases are still climbing. It is instructive to examine the breakdown given by Consolidated Edison for the cost increases they experienced in their Indian Point plant. Though the total cost went up about 90 per cent, expenditures on the strictly nuclear portion of the plant went up by a factor of three; the increase for the conventional elements, on the other hand, was only 37 per cent. If one allows for general price-level increases and a slight change in gross capacity, the increase for the nuclear part of the plant still amounts to a factor of about two-and-a-half.

A characteristic common to each of the projects just described is the substantial degree of initial uncertainty about what difficulties would be encountered in the course of the project. For the most part, the uncertainty was technological.

4. Model of the Development Process (I)

A careful examination of the 22 chronologies requires a framework of analysis. The facts speak for themselves but only after they are arrayed in a meaningful way. We begin by describing a "typical" weapon system program. Needless to say, no actual program would closely resemble this highly idealized version. Implicit in this approach is the assumption that much of the explanation for cost-estimate inaccuracies can be found in the research and development phase of the program. Another assumption might be that, at the beginning of development programs, contractors submit cost estimates known by them to be too low. In this case, the cost-estimating problem is one of incentives in Air Force contracts. This possibility will be discussed briefly in the next section.

A program can be characterized by (among others) five goals: the performance characteristics of the system's various parts, its date of availability, the cost of carrying out the research and development required to make it feasible, its operating costs, and its investment cost. Of these costs a large share is the cost of the major hardware article. There are trade-offs possible among these five goals. Other things in the program remaining the same,[9] development costs will be lower if the time allowed is longer. A greater development effort may lead to simpler, and therefore cheaper, installations and major articles, or to reduced operating costs. By accepting lower performance, it is possible to achieve earlier availability and reductions in all elements of cost. In the initial planning of a weapon system program, these trade-offs may or may not be taken explicitly into account.

What happens, however, when difficulties are encountered in the course of the program that necessitate revision of the program goals? The performance characteristics decided upon initially are often held to tenaciously. Adjustment of the date of availability is made with reference to the additional cost of keeping the program on schedule and the expected savings achievable if time-slippages are tolerated. It

[9] This is an important qualification; long development programs may invite new (and more demanding) specifications and requirements.

is essential, therefore, that an analysis of changes in planned development expenditures should be carried out in conjunction with an analysis of program slippages, and vice versa. This is not true, however, for an analysis of changes in major article costs. The expected cost of the major article is likely to rise when the program runs into trouble. A safe generalization about most programs is that, although the initial development plan may have taken into account possible substitutions between cost of major articles on the one hand and development expenditures and development time on the other, rarely is additional money or time made available later on so as to reduce these costs if they have risen. Thus, an analysis of changes in estimates of major article costs may be legitimately carried out without immediate reference to changes in other program goals.

We will now briefly describe the cost estimate chronologies and explain how the data were translated into a form amenable to analysis, and then we will return to the description of a typical weapon system program.

5. Preliminary Description of the Data

Cost estimates of the flight vehicles listed in Table 10 were collected from a variety of sources. Although most of the estimates originated in The RAND Corporation, some came from Air Force consultants, some from within the Air Force itself, and some from contractors. The estimates given in the source documents were not presented according to a uniform plan, and it was necessary to interpret the sources somewhat in order to provide comparable data. The unit of study is the flight vehicle with all of its on-board gear, excluding ground-support equipment. Although much might be learned from examining how cost estimates changed over time for individual components of the flight vehicle, sufficiently detailed data on components were not available for all the chronologies to provide a basis for firm generalization. Several systems were studied in detail, however, and what was learned is summarized briefly at the end of this section.

6. Raw Measure of Accuracy of Estimates: Raw *F*

The number of cost estimates in each chronology is given in Table 10. For each major article listed there the actual cost was either known from production data or could be determined with a fairly high degree of precision. A rough assessment of the accuracy of the estimates was obtained by computing the ratios of actual to estimated costs:

TABLE 10

LIST OF COST CHRONOLOGIES STUDIED

Flight Vehicle	Number of Estimates in Each Chronology
1. F-84C	2
2. F-84F	1
3. F-86A	1
4. F-86D	2
5. F-89	4
6. F-94C	4
7. F-100	1
8. F-101A	2
9. F-102, 106	6
10. KC-97	3
11. KC-135	3
12. C-130A	1
13. C-133A	1
14. B-47	5
15. B-52	6
16. B-58	4
17. Bomarc	7
18. Falcon	4
19. ICBM (Atlas, Titan)	6
20. Rascal	1
21. SNARK	3
22. Thor	1
	68

Note: Each of the 22 chronologies studied refers to a distinctly different flight vehicle. Although the F-84C and F-84F are similarly numbered, the latter was essentially a different plane and not a simple follow-on from the former. Likewise, the F-86A and F-86D were different planes.

$$\text{Raw } F = \frac{\text{“Actual” cost of the major article}}{\text{Estimated cost of the major article}}.$$

Raw F is the factor that, multiplied by the cost estimate, gives the "actual" cost. The quotation marks are an admission that in many cases the true cost is not known with absolute certainty. These raw cost factors are presented in frequency distribution form in Table 11,

TABLE 11

COST-FACTOR FREQUENCY DISTRIBUTION

(1) Class Intervals,[a] Cost Factors	(2) Frequency of Unadjusted Cost Factors (Raw F)	(3) Frequency of Adjusted Cost Factors[b] (F)
.60–.99	13	14
1.00–1.39	17	23
1.40–1.79	12	10
1.80–2.19	7	5
2.20–2.99	3	6
3.00–3.79	5	4
3.80–4.99	3	2
5.00–9.99	4	4
10.00–19.99	2	–
20.00–39.00	2	–
	68	68
Mean	3.26	1.79
Standard Deviation	5.39	1.34
Root-Mean-Square Error	5.85	1.56

Adjusted Factor closer to unity than Unadjusted Factor:	43 observations
Unadjusted Factor closer to unity than Adjusted Factor:	15 observations
Ties:	10 observations
	68

Notes:

[a] The size of the class intervals varies here.

[b] See Figure 13 for a graphical representation of this distribution.

column (2). If the cost estimates had been substantially correct, the Raw Fs would all have been quite close to unity. The fact that they range from .65 to 30.90 shows how variable the accuracy of the estimates is; the fact that the center of the distribution is substantially above 1 shows that in general the actual cost turned out to be much greater than was expected. The mean of 3.26 and the standard deviation of 5.39 are summary numbers indicating the center and dispersion of the distribution. The root-mean-square error measures the combined effect of the center being away from 1 (the so-called bias of the distribution) and the dispersion.

7. Adjusted Measure of Accuracy of Estimates: *F*

The central task of the empirical analysis of the chronologies is to "explain" the bias and variability of the cost estimates. The analysis is carried out in two stages. In the first stage, the Raw *F*s are adjusted to take into account the two most elementary sources of cost change. First, procurement sometimes occurred as long as 12 years after an estimate had been made. Clearly, allowance for changes in price levels had to be made. And because the early cost estimates were often based upon quite different procurement quantities from those subsequently realized, learning-curve effects had to be taken into account.[10] An estimate of the cost per article of 3,000 flight vehicles would almost certainly be too low as an estimate of the cost per article of 300 flight vehicles, but it should not be considered a bad estimate on that account alone.

Strictly speaking, in appraising the usefulness of early cost estimates one should compare the entire estimated cost-quantity schedule with the entire true cost-quantity schedule. (And for a system analysis, it is the cost-quantity schedule that the analyst needs, for the procurement quantity is a result of the analysis and is not given in advance.) For the purposes of this study, however, it was assumed that the proportionate difference between the two schedules was approximately the same for all quantities. Essentially, this assumption asserts that the inaccuracy observed in the cost estimate would have been about the same regardless of the quantity on which the estimate was based. Thus by using the cost estimator's learning curve when available (and inferring it when it was not) it was possible to modify each cost estimate so that it referred to the quantity for which an actual cost was available.

In the first stage of analysis then, each Raw *F* is converted to an adjusted cost factor, denoted by *F*. The *F* associated with an estimate is a measure of the inaccuracy of the estimate after price-level changes and procurement-quantity differences are taken account of. Column (3) of Table 11 gives the frequency distribution for *F*. The fact that the mean and the standard deviation for *F* are, respectively, closer to unity and smaller than for Raw *F* indicates that (as expected) much of the bias and variability of the cost estimates arose out of price-level changes and procurement-quantity differences. Incidentally, the

---

[10] For a discussion of the learning curve, see Harold Asher, *Cost-Quantity Relationships in the Airframe Industry,* R-291, The RAND Corporation, Santa Monica, California, July 1956; also J. W. Noah and R. W. Smith, *Cost-Quantity Calculator,* RM-2786-PR, The RAND Corporation, Santa Monica, California, January 1962.

latter have the greater effect. Table 11 shows, however, that although Raw F tended to overstate the inaccuracy of an estimate, it was still true that in more than one-third of the cases, F was no closer to unity than Raw F.

8. Model of the Development Process (II); First Variable: Timing Within the Development Program

We now ask, Why are the Fs so variable, and why are they usually greater than unity? Is it possible to derive a formula from the cost chronologies that will help in predicting the Fs for future weapon systems? A good prediction formula might be even more useful than the answers to the questions about causality, but it should be remembered that confidence in an empirical formula must stem from a conviction that the formula is based upon (or is consistent with) reasonable answers to such questions.

The current cost estimate at each step of a flight-vehicle development program is arrived at by costing out the configuration[11] then expected to meet the program's performance requirements. If the requirements impose upon the developer the need to advance the state of the art, it is likely that early in the program his judgment about the final configuration will be based only upon design studies and will therefore be quite tentative. As the program proceeds and additional knowledge is acquired, the current configuration approaches more closely to the final configuration. As the current configuration changes, so will the current cost estimates. Because the revisions are likely to be smaller and smaller as time goes on, and because hardware costing becomes easier to perform as prototype construction advances, it is to be expected that the cost estimates will become better and better. At the end of the development period when procurement begins, the cost estimates should be very good indeed. This implies that the Fs associated with estimates made late in development programs should be distributed more compactly around unity than those associated with estimates made early in the programs. Note that this is only an implication about how the *dispersion* of the Fs changes with time.

The role of time in determining the *bias* of the Fs will now be considered. At the beginning of a program the developer can usually conceive of a number of alternative configurations that might possibly meet the performance requirements. Associated with each configuration would be crude notions of how likely it is that it could be de-

[11] "Configuration" in this context means the detailed specification of all of the physical hardware of the flight vehicle, including the propulsion unit and electronic equipment as well as the airframe.

veloped successfully, what cost that would entail, and how much it might then cost to procure it. A rational development strategy under such circumstances would probably lead the developer to try a relatively cheap configuration first.[12] If this attempt were not successful, another configuration, probably more expensive, would be tried. This trial-and-error approach would be continued until a successful configuration was arrived at. Of course, successive configurations might differ only with respect to one or more components. As the current cost estimate for the article is based upon the current configuration, the early cost estimates would probably be lower than the subsequent ones. Two examples will suffice. An inexpensive guidance system might be contemplated initially. A high pay-off in the form of low cost would justify trying to develop it even if the prospects of success were small. If the system did not achieve an acceptable accuracy, a new (more expensive) system would be developed. In the field of airframes, it might be hoped initially that a certain lift-drag ratio could be attained so that a desired bombing range would be possible with a plane of relatively low weight and therefore low cost. If the developer finds he cannot attain the desired lift-drag ratio, he will try for a somewhat lower ratio, and accept the resulting heavier, more expensive, plane. The essential feature of both these examples is that cost estimates based upon early configurations are likely to be below the actual cost finally realized.

The hypotheses set out above are that, other things being equal, (1) cost estimates made late in a program are likely to be less dispersed around the true value than those made early; and (2) cost estimates made early in a program tend to be lower than the true value, but as the program goes forward this tendency weakens. In Table 12, the hypotheses are confronted by the data of the cost chronologies. Each of the cost estimates was dated with respect to the proportion of the total development period that had already elapsed when the estimate was made.[13] All cost estimates made within the first third of the development period were classified "Early"; those made within the middle third were classified "Medium"; and those

[12] The optimum development strategy would actually depend critically upon detailed information about the overlap of development effort for different configurations. For the present purpose, the strategy need not be spelled out more than to assert the simple probabilistic conclusion about the order in which the configurations would be tried.

[13] The dating of the estimates could not be done with great precision. It was not always easy to determine the beginning and end of a development program, and in fact it frequently was difficult to translate the date of publication of the document in which the estimate appeared into a date for the estimate itself. The end of the development period was defined somewhat arbitrarily. The date of acceptance of the first production article was used as the termination date, primarily because that date was unambiguous and was available for each of the 22 major articles. Frequently further

TABLE 12

ADJUSTED COST FACTORS CLASSIFIED BY TIMING WITHIN THE DEVELOPMENT PROGRAM

	Early	Medium	Late
Number of observations	15	22	31
Mean	2.71	2.09	1.12
Standard deviation	1.91	1.28	.30
Root-mean-square error	2.56	1.68	.32

made within the last third were classified "Late." The means, standard deviations, and root-mean-square errors of F were computed for each of these groupings. The hypotheses imply that as one passes from Early to Medium to Late, the standard deviations and root-mean-square errors should go down and the means should get closer to unity. The statistics in Table 12 agree with the hypotheses. This is not to say, however, that the hypotheses are proved, or that other hypotheses are not also consistent with the data. No doubt various causes are in operation. The hypotheses offered here have been described in some detail, not because they are necessarily true, but because they are plausible for many development programs and they are heuristically suggestive.

9. Second Variable: Technological Advance

The previous sketch of a typical weapon-system development program points to another variable which should help to explain the variability in the distribution of the Fs. The shift from configuration to configuration is a consequence of the initial uncertainty about the form the vehicle must finally take to meet the performance requirements. The magnitude of the technological advance sought in the program will in part determine the degree of initial uncertainty and, therefore, the frequency with which configuration revisions are made. From this argument it follows that, other things being equal, in programs where the magnitude of the technological advance sought is small, early cost estimates should be relatively accurate;

development work was done after that date, and perhaps the first date of operational availability might have been a better date to use. However, if the period defined in this latter way was longer than the period as defined in this study by roughly the same proportion for each of the programs, it would make no substantive difference which definition is used.

TABLE 13

ADJUSTED COST FACTORS CLASSIFIED BY MAGNITUDE OF THE TECHNOLOGICAL ADVANCE SOUGHT IN THE DEVELOPMENT PROGRAM

	Small	Medium	Large
Number of observations	11	18	39
Mean	1.15	1.39	2.15
Standard deviation	.43	.56	1.619
Root-mean-square error	.45	.68	1.99

and bias and variability should be relatively large when the technological advance is great.[14]

To test these propositions, a rough ranking was made of the magnitudes of technological advance sought for each of the 22 major articles examined in this study. A survey of a number of experienced RAND engineers was made in which each respondent was asked to rate subjectively the magnitude of the improvement in the state of the art required for each of the development programs. The survey results were then consolidated into a set of Technological Advance Scores, denoted A, which ranged from approximately 5 to 16.[15] Each major article was then placed in one of three broad Technological Advance groupings: Small, Medium, or Large. The changes observed in the means, standard deviations, and root-mean-square errors as one moves from Small to Medium and then to Large, throw light on whether Technological Advance actually plays the role suggested above. The statistics presented in Table 13, above, are indeed what one would expect.

10. Bivariate Analysis of *t* and *A*

It was argued in the last two sections that both the timing of an estimate within the development program and the magnitude of the technological advance sought in the program promise to be useful vari-

[14] Strictly speaking, it would be the magnitude of the technological advance still to be achieved at the time the cost estimate is made that determined the degree of bias and variability associated with the estimate. In the absence of detailed information on the timing of advances in the state of the art in each of the programs, it is necessary to rely on the assumption that the advance is uniform throughout the development program.

[15] Programs such as those for the C-130A, C-133A, and KC-135 were rated between 5.5 and 8; those requiring major advances, such as SNARK, Bomarc, and the B-58 were rated about 16.

ables in accounting for differences in cost-estimate accuracy. Before examining other possible variables, a point should be made about methodology.

Looking at the explanatory variables one at a time can be misleading. Suppose that in fact timing is important, but technological difficulty is not. If there happened to be a larger proportion of early estimates in the difficult programs than in the easy ones, a result like that in Table 13 would be observed, even though technological difficulty really made no difference. To avoid arriving at a specious conclusion because of a possible intercorrelation between the variables, it is necessary to examine the effect of the variables together.

In Table 14, the means, standard deviations, and root-mean-square errors are given for the *F*s classified by both timing and technological difficulty. For ease of examination, the means and standard deviations are extracted separately from the table and placed in Tables 15 and 16. The hypothesis about bias implies a decline in the means down the columns and an increase in the means across the rows

TABLE 14

ADJUSTED COST FACTORS CLASSIFIED BY BOTH TIME ELAPSED AND MAGNITUDE OF THE TECHNOLOGICAL ADVANCE SOUGHT IN THE DEVELOPMENT PROGRAM

	Technological Advance		
Time	Small	Medium	Large
Early			
Number of observations	1	4	10
Mean	.80	2.15	3.13
Standard deviation	—	.57	2.15
Root-mean-square error	.2	1.28	3.03
Medium			
Number of observations	2	6	14
Mean	1.50	1.32	2.52
Standard deviation	.60	.39	1.41
Root-mean-square error	.78	.50	2.07
Late			
Number of observations	8	8	15
Mean	1.11	1.06	1.16
Standard deviation	.33	.18	.34
Root-mean-square error	.35	.19	.38

Note: — Indicates no estimate possible.

TABLE 15

MEANS OF ADJUSTED COST FACTORS

	Technological Advance		
Time	Small	Medium	Large
Early	.80	2.15	3.13
Medium	1.50	1.32	2.52
Late	1.11	1.06	1.16

Source: Table 14.

in Table 15. Out of the twelve possible comparisons of adjacent cells, all but three are consistent with the hypothesis. When account is taken of the magnitudes of the observed differences and the numbers of observations in the various cells, a crude statistical test reveals that only five of the differences are statistically significant; but in each of the five cases, the comparisons concur with the hypothesis. The entries in Table 16 were surveyed in a similar way to see if the dispersion of the Fs varied from classification to classification in the predicted way. As before, it should be expected that the entries would decline down the columns and increase across the rows. The number of comparisons favorable to the variability hypothesis is again nine. Once more, five of the differences (though not the same five as in the case of the means) are statistically significant; and, again, each of these is in accordance with the hypothesis. Thus, the simultaneous examination of timing and technological advance confirms that each of these variables affects the bias and variability of the Fs.

TABLE 16

STANDARD DEVIATIONS
OF ADJUSTED COST FACTORS

	Technological Advance		
Time	Small	Medium	Large
Early	–	.57	2.15
Medium	.60	.39	1.41
Late	.33	.18	.34

Note: – Indicates no estimate possible.
Source: Table 14.

In considering additional variables, a multivariate approach is used. It is not possible to proceed by cross-classifying into more narrowly defined cells, however, for the cell frequencies in Table 14 are already of minimum size. Instead, the statistical technique of multiple regression analysis is employed. By making the relatively harmless assumption of continuity in the relationship between F and the independent variables, it is possible to improve considerably the explanation of the bias and variability.

11. Third Variable: Length of Development Period

We should now bring out into the open an assumption that has so far been implicit. It makes sense to use F as a measure of the accuracy of an estimate only if the major article for which the cost estimate is initially made is, in an appropriate sense, the same article as the one finally procured. In this study, a cost estimate of a flight vehicle has been interpreted to be an estimate of the cost of procuring the hardware that would meet the Air Force's major performance requirements for the article. If during a development program no substantial change was made in the major performance requirements, it would be proper to compare any cost estimate made during the program with the actual cost. If, however, the major requirements were substantially upgraded after an estimate was made, the value of F computed for the estimate would seriously overstate the magnitude of the estimator's error. A few such estimates were present in the chronologies when they were first compiled, but they were eliminated. Each of the remaining estimates relates essentially to the same major performance characteristics as those found in the articles finally developed.

The major performance requirements initially imposed upon a developer are ordinarily fairly gross and do not specify in fine detail all of the desired characteristics of the article. In the course of the development program, relatively minor additional requirements are usually imposed but they nevertheless tend to increase costs. An example would be innovations designed to increase the comfort and safety of the flight crew over and above that envisioned initially. Also, advances in the state of the art in other development projects and in the nonmilitary sphere frequently lead to additional requirements being set. Because the addition of new, minor requirements can be regarded as an inevitable part of flight-vehicle development, it appears to be justified to include the increased cost in the calculation of F (that is, to use the full actual cost in the numerator).

It is commonly believed that the number of new, minor requirements increases with the length of the development program. Certainly the longer the program, the more opportunities there will be for advances in the state of the art outside of the program; and therefore the greater the number of temptations to improve the vehicle.[16] As a consequence, the Length of the Development Program, L, was selected as an explanatory variable.

12. Fourth Variable: Calendar Date

The chronologies include estimates made as early as 1947 and as late as 1957. As skills improved significantly in virtually all technical fields during that ten-year period, it is reasonable to ask whether there was an improvement in cost-estimating techniques as well. Certainly toward the end of this period cost analysts generally received more complete and earlier basic data than they did at the beginning of the period. As the techniques available to the cost analyst advanced beyond the use of the learning curve, their results, it could be argued, should have improved also.

To test this conjecture, Calendar Date, T, was also selected as an explanatory variable. This variable is an anonymous catch-all for the various influences tending to affect the quality of cost estimates over time. Incidentally, it should be borne in mind that an improvement in the knowledge of how to build a device is quite distinct from an improvement in the knowledge of how to estimate the cost of the device. The early missile development programs yielded a great deal of new technical knowledge which was subsequently utilized in later programs, and the cost estimates in the later programs were more accurate. But this in itself does not mean that cost analysts had become more skilled; part or all of the improvement in estimates might be attributable to the fact that, with the increase of knowledge, the technological advance required in the later programs was less. The better cost estimates resulting in this way from improved technical knowledge are taken into account explicitly by including the variable A in the regression relationship. By including T as well as A, we can measure the separate effect of cost-estimating improvements as such.

13. Regression Results: Algebraic

Previous sections described the four basic variables in terms of which we hope to express an empirical relationship between the ad-

---

[16] On the other hand, it might be argued that, other things being constant, the longer development period might have resulted from an extended effort to simplify the vehicle so it could be procured more cheaply. But, as was pointed out above, only rarely is the possibility of this time-money tradeoff considered after a development program has begun.

justed estimate and the actual cost of major hardware articles. We seek, that is, an equation that will relate F (the ratio of actual cost to adjusted estimate) to the following variables:

- t, the timing within the development program, expressed as the fraction of the program that has already elapsed when the estimate is made;
- A, the measure of the technological advance required by the development program, expressed in terms of a numerical scale ranging from about 5 to 16 for the chronologies studied;
- L, the length of the development program, expressed in months; and
- T, the calendar year in which the estimate is made.

For this purpose we considered a variety of functional forms [17] and adopted equation (1) as the most satisfactory.

$$\log_e F = \alpha_0 + \alpha_1 t + \alpha_2 t \cdot A + \alpha_3 \cdot A + \alpha_4 A^2 + \alpha_5 L + \alpha_6 T + u, \qquad (1)$$

which can also be expressed in the equivalent form:

$$F = Ke^{\alpha_1 t} \cdot e^{\alpha_2 tA} \cdot e^{\alpha_3 A + \alpha_4 A^2} \cdot e^{\alpha_5 L} \cdot e^{\alpha_6 T} \cdot v. \qquad (2)$$

The regression coefficients $K, \alpha_1, \alpha_2, \alpha_3, \alpha_4, \alpha_5$, and α_6, and their standard errors were estimated, as well as the standard error of estimate and the multiple correlation coefficient. Equation (1) with the αs replaced by their estimates (and with calendar year measured as a deviation from 1940) appears as (3):

$$\log_e F = 2.479 + \underset{(.205)}{.097t} - \underset{(.019)}{.032t \cdot A} - \underset{(.189)}{.311A} + \underset{(.007)}{.015A^2} + \underset{(.002)}{.008L} - \underset{(.020)}{.075(T-1940)} + u. \qquad (3)$$

Equation (2) with the αs replaced by their estimates (and with calendar year measured as a deviation from 1940) becomes:

$$F = (11.929) \cdot e^{.097t - .032t \cdot A} \cdot e^{-.311A + .015A^2} \cdot e^{.008L} \cdot e^{-.075(T-1940)} \cdot v. \qquad (4)$$

In (3), the number in parentheses below each estimated regression coefficient is the estimate's standard error. The unbiased multiple correlation coefficient is .698. It is perhaps not evident from the parameter estimates and standard errors given in (3) that (1) is indeed a good choice of functional form. Two of the coefficients appear to

[17] F as well as $\log_e F$ was regressed against the independent variables.

be not significantly different from zero. But each variable (as contrasted with each term) can in fact be shown to be significant when the covariances of the coefficient estimates are taken into account. The residual in (3), u, is the difference between the observed $\log_e F$ and the value of $\log_e F$ predicted by the regression equation. The standard deviation of the residuals, σ_u (the so-called standard error of estimate), which purports to measure the amount of scatter of $\log_e F$ around the regression surface of (3), was .429. Upon examination, however, it was found that though .429 was a measure of the average scatter, the scatter was not the same for both major and minor technological advances.[18] The standard deviation of residuals for the former was .463, but for the latter it was .298. These standard deviations have a particular implication for (4). About two-thirds of all Fs are clustered around the true regression line within bands defined as follows: for major technological advance programs, an upper bound 59 per cent above the regression surface and a lower bound 37 per cent below; and for minor technological advance programs, an upper bound of 30 per cent above the regression surface and 26 per cent below. The standard deviation of residuals of (3) was about the same for all values of t. From this it follows that the standard deviation of the Fs around the regression surface of (4) is proportional to the height of the surface when A is held constant.[19]

14. Hypothesis Testing

Equation (4) is an empirical statement of the relationship between F and the independent variables. As such, it may be thought of as a formula which can be used to correct current cost estimates of major articles now in the early stages of development. How satisfactory it is for this purpose depends upon (a) how well (4) fulfills its role as a concise summary of the relevant aspects of cost inaccuracies in the recent past, and (b) how similar the future is to the past in terms of both development-program cost histories and cost-estimating techniques. If (4) is indeed a good summary and in fact cost-estimating

[18] The estimation of the coefficients of (3) was carried out in accordance with the procedures of the Method of Least Squares. The fact that the $\log_e F$s were more dispersed around the regression line for large values of A than for small ones violates the so-called homoscedasticity condition underlying the method. The consequence of this is not serious, however: the regression coefficients could have been estimated somewhat more efficiently if account had been taken of the lack of homoscedasticity in the estimation process, but the lack of homoscedasticity does not bias the estimates of the coefficients.

[19] From (4), for any given values of t, A, L, and T, $F =$ Predicted $F \cdot v$ where Predicted $F = Ke^{\alpha_1 t} \cdot e^{\alpha_2 tA} \cdot e^{\alpha_3 t + \alpha_4 A^2} \cdot e^{\alpha_5 L} \cdot e^{\alpha_6 T}$. Since we are concerned in the next section

procedures do not change markedly in the near future, we may expect it to be helpful in making decisions about major articles being considered for future procurement.

Either of two points of view may be adopted in relating the coefficients of (4) to the *a priori* hypotheses outlined above. The hypotheses may be taken as tentative assertions which are to be evaluated by judging whether the facts, as summarized in (4), confirm them. Or the hypotheses may be taken as truisms which can be used to verify that (4) makes sense, and therefore may be trusted. In either case, the first step is to see if the hypotheses and the numbers in (4) are consistent.

The hypotheses, expressed as *ceteris paribus* assertions about the variables, were as follows:

1) for increasing values of t, the expected value of F goes down;
2) for increasing values of A, the expected value of F goes up;
3) for increasing values of L, the expected value of F goes up;
4) for increasing values of T, the expected value of F goes down;

---

with the effect on σ_F of changes in t and A, we anticipate that discussion by noting the following:

$$(1)\quad \frac{\partial \sigma_F}{\partial t} = \frac{\partial(\text{Predicted } F)}{\partial t} \cdot \sigma_v + \text{Predicted } F \cdot \frac{\partial \sigma_v}{\partial t}$$
$$= \frac{\partial(\text{Predicted } F)}{\partial t} \cdot \sigma_v + \text{Predicted } F \cdot \frac{\partial \sigma_v}{\partial \sigma_u} \cdot \frac{\partial \sigma_u}{\partial t}.$$

Since $\frac{\partial(\text{Predicted } F)}{\partial t} < 0$ (see footnote 20), $\sigma_v > 0$ and $\frac{\partial \sigma_u}{\partial t} = 0$ (i.e., the standard deviation of residuals of (3) was about the same for all values of t), $\frac{\partial \sigma_F}{\partial t} < 0$.

$$(2)\quad \frac{\partial \sigma_F}{\partial A} = \frac{\partial(\text{Predicted } F)}{\partial A} \cdot \sigma_v + \text{Predicted } F \cdot \frac{\partial \sigma_v}{\partial A}$$
$$= \frac{\partial(\text{Predicted } F)}{\partial A} \cdot \sigma_v + \text{Predicted } F \cdot \frac{\partial \sigma_v}{\partial \sigma_u} \cdot \frac{\partial \sigma_u}{\partial A}.$$

$\frac{\partial(\text{Predicted } F)}{\partial A} > 0$ (for most of the critical range of A; see footnote 20), $\sigma_v > 0$, Predicted $F > 0$, and $\frac{\partial \sigma_u}{\partial A} > 0$ (see text above); so only the sign of $\frac{\partial \sigma_v}{\partial \sigma_u}$ must be obtained in order to find the sign of $\frac{\partial \sigma_F}{\partial A}$. No proof will be given here of the rather evident proposition that if y is a monotonic increasing function of x, then under fairly general regularity conditions imposed upon $f(x)$, the frequency function of x—conditions reasonable to assume for the disturbances of (3)—σ_y will be a monotonic increasing function of σ_x. (In particular, for $f(x)$ normal and $y = \ln x$, $\sigma_y = e^{1/2\sigma_x^2}(e^{\sigma_x} - 1)^{1/2}$ and clearly $\frac{\partial \sigma_y}{\partial \sigma_x} > 0$.)

Therefore, $\frac{\partial \sigma_F}{\partial A} > 0$.

5) for increasing values of t, the standard deviation of F (that is, the standard deviation of residuals) goes down; and
6) for increasing values of A, the standard deviation of F goes up.

It is noteworthy that with only one minor exception, the numerical values of (4) are qualitatively just what is implied by the first four propositions.[20] Inaccuracy does go up with the technological advance of the program for programs above a minimum level of difficulty. Below this level, however, the inaccuracy actually seems to fall.[21] The explanation may well lie in the clumsiness of the Technological Advance scaling system.

Since the standard deviation of F is proportional to the level of F and the level of F decreases with t, it follows that the standard deviation of F goes down with t. Furthermore, as indicated in the last section, the standard deviation of F is greater for major technological advances than for minor ones. Thus, the fifth and sixth propositions are verified.[22]

Having displayed the consistency between the empirical results of the regression analysis and the hypotheses, we turn to the implications of the analysis. Some of the hypotheses are by no means necessarily true even though fairly plausible *a priori* arguments have been mustered in support of them. Nothing has been said about the quantity of resources devoted to cost estimating in various kinds of programs. If a serious cost-estimating effort is made only for programs requiring large technological advances, then estimates made for programs with small and medium advances might very well be inferior to those with large ones. The fact that an optimum development strategy may call for trying relatively cheap configurations first does not mean that the strategy necessarily will be followed. The apparent secular improvement in estimating methods might really be illusory. The position taken here is that, by virtue of the hypothesis testing,

[20] In the language of the calculus, the first four propositions assert: (1), $\frac{\partial F}{\partial t} < 0$; (2), $\frac{\partial F}{\partial A} > 0$; (3), $\frac{\partial F}{\partial L} > 0$; and (4), $\frac{\partial F}{\partial T} < 0$. From (4) it follows that (1) $\frac{\partial F}{\partial t} = (.097 - .032A) \cdot F$ which, for $5 \leq A \leq 16$, is less than zero; (2) $\frac{\partial F}{\partial A} = (-.311 - .032t + .029A) \cdot F$, which for $t = 0$, $A > 10.65$ or $t = 1$, $A > 11.75$ is greater than zero; (3) $\frac{\partial F}{\partial L} = (.008) \cdot F > 0$; and (4) $\frac{\partial F}{\partial T} = -.075\ F < 0$.

[21] For $A < 10.65$, $t = 0$ or $A < 11.75$, $t = 1$, $\frac{\partial F}{\partial A} < 0$. There were 7 major articles and 13 cost estimates in the chronologies below the minimum level.

[22] See footnote 19.

we now really do know more about the causes of inaccuracy of cost estimates. At the same time, the fact that the regression analysis turned up nothing that was awkward to explain makes (4) credible.

15. Regression Results: Graphic

A pictorial representation of (4) will provide a quantitative feeling for the relationship it expresses. Figures 14, 15, and 16 portray graphically the (F,t) profile for a number of different combinations of values of A, T, and L. The profiles show how the F predicted for a cost estimate is related to the time already elapsed in the development program, given the characteristics of the program.

It was to be expected that the profiles would start above unity at $t = 0$ and then drop toward unity as t increased. At the beginning of a development program, an estimate would be biased downward (that is, typically it would be too low) but as time went on the bias of new estimates would diminish. At the end of the program, it was conjectured the (F,t) profile would be close to 1, though perhaps still above it, because by then almost all of the uncertainties in the program would have been overcome. There would then be little reason for expecting systematic downward errors to persist. Whether the profile would be concave upward, concave downward, or linear could not be anticipated in advance. Its being concave upward would mean that though initial estimates were not to be trusted, the bias disappeared fairly quickly so that the estimates would be reliable after the development program was well under way. Its being concave downward would reflect a less happy state of affairs: that cost estimates start out biased downward and improve only slowly until the end of the program when the improvement is finally rapid. We find in Figures 14 and 15 that the profile does drop toward 1, but linearly; that is, the bias diminishes at a fairly uniform rate.

Three types of development programs have been selected for inspection in Figures 14 and 15. Type I is a long-term program (8 years) in which the technological advance sought is large (as, for example, in the SNARK, Bomarc, and B-58 programs). Type II is a program of average length (4½ years) and the technological advance sought is medium (as, for example, in the Thor, B-52, and F-100 programs). Type III is a short program in which the technological advance is quite modest (as, for example, in the KC-97, KC-135, and C-130A programs). The profiles of programs of the three types for the year 1948 appear in Figure 14 and the profiles for 1954 appear in Figure 15. It is immediately obvious that there is virtually no difference

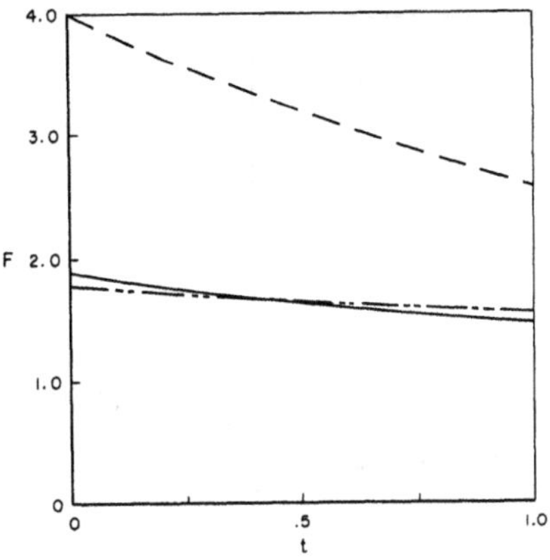

Fig. 14. (F,t) profiles for $T = 1948$

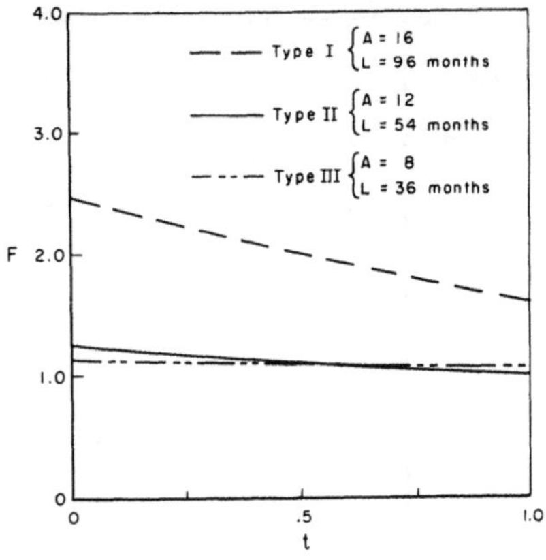

Fig. 15. (F,t) profiles for $T = 1954$

between the Type II and Type III programs, and that by 1954, estimates for these types exhibited no bias. Clearly, it is Type I that is troublesome. We find that, although very early estimates for long and difficult programs were low on the average by a factor of 4 in 1948, by 1954 they were low on the average by a factor of about 2.5. It is reassuring to find that the mean F entry in Table 15 relating to early estimates for difficult programs overstates the amount of bias to be expected at present. Presumably this figure, 3.13, results from many of the extremely low estimates occurring early in the 1947–1957 period.

The year 1954 was selected for Figure 15 because it was in that year that the most recent of the early estimates in the chronologies were made. Extrapolating beyond the period covered in the chronologies is hazardous, to say the least. This is particularly true in view of the fact that the way T is introduced into the functional form of (2) does not enforce the quite natural requirement that the improvement in cost estimating should be incapable of bringing any part of the profile below 1. A sensible, conservative procedure for predictions in the late 1950's might be to take T as equal to 1955 for Type I programs. This will act to compensate for the probable overstatement in (4) of the cost-estimating improvement for the period beyond that covered by the data.

The profile for Type I programs appears again in Figure 16. Here it is accompanied by a .68 confidence band. The breadth of the band for each value of t is a rough index of the accuracy that can be ex-

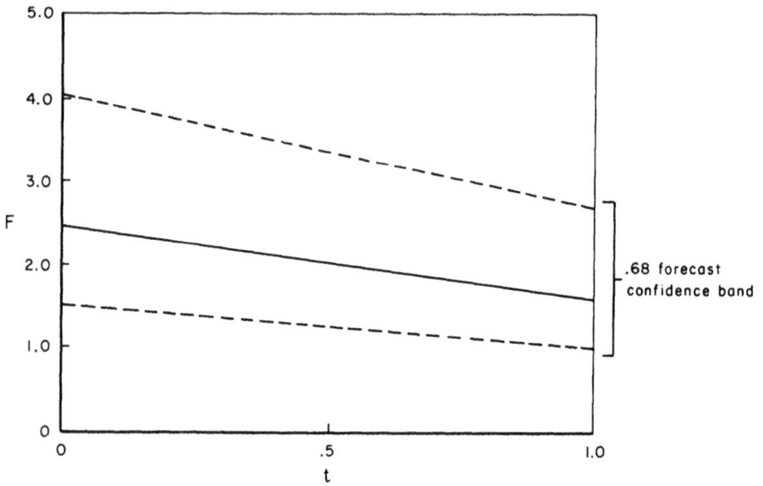

Fig. 16. (F,t) profile for a Type I program $\{A = 16, L = 96\}$ for $T = 1954$ with the .68 forecast confidence band

pected in predicting F in Type I programs at various times during the development period.[23]

16. Fifth Variable: Missiles Versus Aircraft; Sixth Variable: Quantity Adjustment

The effect on F of several additional variables was also examined. It was conjectured that, because missiles are developed somewhat differently from airplanes, the expected F might differ between missile and aircraft programs for which all other program characteristics were similar. When the appropriate regression coefficient was estimated to test this conjecture, it was found that the data did not support it. Similarly, no evidence was found for believing that inaccuracies in making learning-curve adjustments to Raw Fs might be partially responsible for some of the large Fs observed in the chronologies. (This possibility was suggested by the observation that the largest quantity adjustments were associated with particularly poor estimates.)

[23] The precise meaning of the .68 confidence band is somewhat complicated. Essentially it is this: If one makes interval predictions regularly by means of properly constructed confidence bands, about 68 per cent of all such interval predictions will in fact include the true value sought. It is based upon the standard error of forecast.

17. Seventh Variable: Estimator and/or Contractor

We might expect that knowledge of the source of a cost estimate would be helpful in judging its accuracy. But because the cost estimator ordinarily bases his work on contractor-supplied data, it is difficult to distinguish between the inaccuracies attributable to the estimator and those attributable to the contractor. The paucity of data in the chronologies necessarily made any attack on this problem rather inconclusive. By means of regression analysis, RAND-generated estimates were contrasted with those generated elsewhere. No evidence was found for concluding that there was either a meaningful or statistically significant difference between estimates from these two groups. (However, no attempt was made to differentiate between RAND and non-RAND estimates for both the first and second halves of the 1947–1957 period.)

Since all cost estimates ultimately depend upon information supplied by contractors, an attempt was made to see if poor cost estimates were associated with particular contractors among the eleven represented in the set of 22 weapon system programs considered in this study. Unfortunately, with an average of only six observations per contractor, no firm judgment could be made about the comparative reliabilities of the different contractors. It was possible, though, to perform a test relating to contractor reliability which, though it threw only limited light on this subject directly, contributed to the creditability of the regression relationship as a whole.

First, the 68 cost estimates were grouped by contractor. One way of proceeding then would have been to compute the average F for each contractor, and to rank the contractors with respect to cost-estimating accuracy according to the size of their average Fs, with an average F close to unity being best. This method suffers from the serious defect that in such a ranking system contractors assigned to difficult development programs are put at an unfair disadvantage relative to those assigned to easy ones.[24] Cost-estimating accuracy would be confounded with program technological advance. However, one may think of (4) with v ignored (or more properly, with v set equal to unity) as a yardstick that enables one to allow for the uncertainty the

[24] More generally, ranking by average F would be satisfactory only if the cost estimates for individual contractors were random with respect to t, L, and T as well as A. There is no particular reason for thinking there will be lack of randomness as far as t, L, and T are concerned, but there is a presumption that there will be some specialization among contractors with respect to the type of development program.

contractor operated under at the time of each cost estimate. It is easy to see then that the quality of a particular cost estimate is better measured by the cost estimate's estimated regression residual, $\tilde{v}$, the difference between its F and its yardstick value (i.e., the predicted F one gets from (4) if the t, A, L, and T values for the cost estimate are inserted on the right-hand side). In principle, different contractors could be compared on the basis of their average $\tilde{v}$s. If only there were enough observations on each contractor, those with negative average $\tilde{v}$s could be recognized as having done a relatively good cost-estimating job (in the sense of having made reliable estimates themselves, or having supplied good data if the costs in its various programs were actually estimated by others; and those with positive average $\tilde{v}$s could be recognized as having done a relatively poor job – in the same sense).

The sampling fluctuations of the various average $\tilde{v}$s are large because the sample of cost estimates is small, so one would (and should) hesitate to make judgments about individual contractors on the basis of this slim evidence. However, the average $\tilde{v}$s were used in a further statistical test to see if the ranking of contractors by this method was consistent with the prevailing views in the airframe industry about the various contractors. A cost analyst with considerable experience in the airframe industry was asked to supply his estimate of the industry reputation of each contractor for accuracy in cost-estimating. A test of concordance was carried out to see if the "regression-based" ranking conformed to the one implied by this necessarily hearsay "industry reputation" information. The interpretation of the result of this test depends, of course, upon one's willingness to accept the notion that industry reputations are meaningful in this context (and that the cost analyst supplying the information about the reputations was approximately accurate). When dealing with concepts so difficult to quantify as were encountered in this study, one welcomes any independent basis for judging the empirical results; crude as this test is, it helps in judging how much confidence one can have in the regression approach. All in all, it seems reasonable to take the view that the high degree of association found between the two ranking methods helps to validate (4).

18. Eighth Variable: Benchmark Time

The variable t, Time Elapsed in the Development Program, was very important in (4). It was introduced into the equation because of the initial conjecture that the developer learns progressively more and more during the program about the nature of the final configuration. To repeat the fundamental hypothesis, the cost-estimating inaccuracy is primarily a consequence of uncertainty, and as the development program proceeds that uncertainty is dispelled. It may be argued quite reasonably, however, that far from proceeding uniformly, the relevant learning takes place in an intermittent but predictable way. It follows then that a dating scheme based upon development "benchmarks" rather than calendar time might be more satisfactory. One such benchmark would be the first flight of the first test vehicle.[25]

The regression equation analogous to (3) obtained with the benchmark approach is (3′).

$$\log_e F = 3.162 - \underset{(.125)}{.466 t_B^M} - \underset{(.161)}{.551 t_B^L} - \underset{(.140)}{.395A} + \underset{(.006)}{.020A^2} - \underset{(.021)}{.069(T-1940)} + u \qquad (3')$$

where t_B^M and t_B^L are variables that take on the values, respectively, zero and zero if the cost estimate was made before the first flight of the first test vehicle; 1 and zero if the estimate was made after the first flight of the first test vehicle but before acceptance of the first production article; and zero and 1 if the estimate was made after acceptance of the first production article. The unbiased multiple correlation coefficient was .65.[26] Equations (3) and (3′) define practically identical values of $\log_e F$ (and therefore F) at the beginning of the development program; and almost the same values (to the extent a direct comparison is possible) in the middle and at the end of the program. This is true over the entire range of values of A and T. Therefore, (3′) is substantially equivalent to (3) except that it gives a little more insight into the development process. The coefficients (−.466) and (−.551) in (3′) show that most of the decrease in the bias occurs by the time of the first flight of the first test vehicle. The subsequent improvement is very slight.[27]

---

[25] First flight is not a straightforward concept when applied to some missiles. The dates used were selected as corresponding to the first flight of an airplane prototype, that is, when the first major combination of subcomponents were brought together for full test.

[26] The author cannot conceal his disappointment that this "benchmark time" approach did not give a better explanation of $\log_e F$ than the "time-elapsed" one – at least as measured by R^2 – since it seems to get closer to the real underlying relationship.

[27] This is not inconsistent with the finding of linearity in time elapsed. In almost three-fourths of the cases studied, first flight occurred more than one-third of the way through the development program. The reader should bear in mind the rather arbitrary way in which the end of the development period was defined, as explained above in footnote 13.

19. Data Problem: Errors in Measurement

As mentioned earlier, the data used in this study necessarily leave something to be desired. How reliable are conclusions based upon such data? The answer depends in large measure upon just what is wrong with them. Suppose each particular number is subject to error; but the errors, not consistently in one direction, are independent of each other, and are independent of all of the variables. Then the strength of the true relationship between the dependent variable and the independent variables will be *understated* by the strength of the relationship observed between the variables when they are measured with error. It is hard to prove that the errors were really so innocent, but since every effort was made to keep them so, and since there is no specific evidence that they are not, it seems reasonable to assume they are. If this is granted, then the true relationship between F and the independent variables, each measured without error, is even *stronger* than is indicated by the multiple correlation coefficient of .698. That is, if it had been possible to measure the variables more accurately, the multiple correlation coefficient would have been even higher.[28]

The errors probably do make a difference, but a difference which is predictable. There is a slight presumption that each of the regression coefficients of variables subject to error would be farther from zero than the estimated values (negative coefficients being even more negative and positive coefficients being even more positive). For early estimates in Type I development programs (which are of primary interest), this would have the effect of making the expected value of F even larger than indicated by (4). As far as the measurement errors are concerned, therefore, (4) should be an acceptable basis for revising cost estimates, though possibly "conservative" in the sense that the indicated difference between the adjusted estimate and the actual cost would be smaller than the real difference.

20. Data Problem: Randomness

We shall now consider the propriety of analyzing in such detail the 68 estimates that seem to have quite special characteristics. They were selected primarily on the basis of availability. They by no means ex-

[28] The resolution of this paradox is straightforward. A relationship becomes diluted when "noise" is added to the variables it involves. The relationship in the absence of the noise will be stronger than in its presence. For example, a close relationship might exist between the height and weight of men between 20 and 40 years of age. If, however, a large group of men in this age group were weighed with an erratic scale and measured with an awkward and poorly calibrated yardstick, the data would yield an observed relationship between height and weight much less close.

hausted the set of all estimates for the 22 major articles. And the 22 articles were not the only ones developed by the Air Force during the 1947–1957 period. The cell frequencies in Table 13 show an abundance of estimates for articles depending on large technological advances and relatively few depending on medium and small ones; the cell frequencies in Table 12 show that there were fewer early estimates than medium ones, and that late ones were most common of all. These frequencies have important implications for Table 11. Suppose 10 more estimates had been collected. If the data net had caught 10 more early estimates from programs with large technological advances, the means in Table 11 would have been larger. On the other hand, if it had caught 10 more late estimates from programs with small advances, the means would have been smaller. This illustrates the sensitivity of the means of Table 11 to the exact character of the estimates. Since the 68 estimates in the chronologies constitute anything but a random sample of estimates, Table 11 provides an unreliable basis for generalizing about the accuracy of cost estimates. Its usefulness is limited to displaying in compact form the set of Raw *F*s and *F*s of the chronologies and to showing the effects of adjustment for procurement quantity and for price-level changes.

The multiple regression approach, on the other hand, does not require complete randomness of the cost estimates. It is quite all right for the sample of estimates to have particular characteristics either over-represented or under-represented, provided the characteristic is taken into account explicitly in the regression equation. Since t and A do appear explicitly in (4), the cell frequencies of Tables 12 and 13 need cause no concern. Similarly, the inclusion of L in (4) prevents difficulties from arising because the chronologies included a disproportionately large number of long programs. T causes no difficulty in any case because the estimates were spread fairly uniformly over the 1947–1957 period. Randomness is still required, but of a much more restricted sort: it is only essential that the estimates and the programs which they refer to are not atypical with respect to all the other unaccounted for variables. Since there is no evidence that the data of the chronologies fail to fulfill this requirement, it is quite appropriate to use them to arrive at generalizations about the accuracy of cost estimates.

21. Estimation of Independent Variables; Weighting Observations

The discussion of (4) would not be complete without two additional comments. The first is closely related to the data errors considered under Errors in Measurement. The use of (4) in adjusting a cost estimate requires knowledge of the values of t, A, L, and T associated with the estimate. It has already been indicated that for Type I programs caution demands that the value of T should be set at, say, 1955. The values of the independent variables used in deriving (4), though subject to measurement error, were not (we believe) consistently guessed too high or too low. The values of t, A, and L associated with each estimate were available in retrospect and therefore were known more or less accurately. The same cannot be said, however, for the values of t, A, and L that must be estimated for current development programs. Fortunately, the likely mistakes in guessing the values of these variables each lead to the same kind of mistake in predicting F. Typically, at the beginning of a program both the length of the program L and its difficulty A will be underestimated. As a consequence, t will be overestimated. Each of these mistakes leads to an underestimate of F. A safe generalization following from this and from the section on Errors in Measurement is that the overall effect of errors of measurement is to make the estimates of F derived from (4) conservative in the sense that they will be on the low side.

The second comment is concerned with the relative weight given to the various major hardware articles. As Table 10 indicates, the 68 estimates were not spread uniformly over the 22 major articles. The numerical values of (4) were estimated using a computing procedure which gave each estimate equal weight. This, of course, meant that some major articles (for example, Bomarc and the B-52) received much more total weight than others. Weighting the observations so that each article is regarded as equally important [29] would appear to be a reasonable alternative to the procedure followed. There are a number of other equally attractive weighting plans also deserving consideration. For example, weighting each article equally may be less sensible than weighting each article in proportion to the total procurement cost of the major article. But then what quantity would be used, the quantity originally predicted or the final quantity? Perhaps, too, the weighting of each article should be in proportion to the total cost of the system with which it is associated.[30]

---

[29] That is, giving each estimate for a particular major article a weight equal to the reciprocal of the total number of estimates for that article.

[30] The problem of proper weighting arises in another connection also. The cost estimates in the chronologies were generated under a wide variety of conditions for a number of different purposes. The confidence that estimators had in their estimates undoubtedly varied a good deal. If the necessary information had been available, it would have been interesting to see if weighting each observation in proportion to the estimator's belief in its accuracy would have made a difference in the estimates of the regression coefficients.

Reweighting the observations in any of these ways would not necessarily make a difference in the estimates of the regression coefficients. In any case, time did not permit an exploration of the various possibilities.

22. Conclusions About Learning During Development

Almost all the discussion of the empirical analysis so far has centered on the usefulness of (4) as a basis for adjusting current cost estimates in predicting future procurement costs. But what does the empirical analysis tell us about development programs?

It was stated that a cost estimate of a future major article is nearly always obtained by costing out the current configuration (that is, the current picture of what the final configuration will be). Perhaps the difference between the cost estimate and the actual cost can be thought of as a proxy variable representing the amount of learning the contractor must still acquire before completing the development phase of the program. In that case, the slope of the (F,t) profile can be interpreted as an indication of how fast this learning is acquired during the development period. The linearity of the profile means, then, that learning takes place at a uniform rate in time. On the other hand, the benchmark regression analysis indicates that the learning effectively takes place in stages with most of it completed by the time of the first flight of the first test vehicle. The latter view seems more reasonable in view of what is generally known about development programs.

From a different point of view, learning during a major article development program can be thought of as the process of acquiring more precise knowledge about all aspects of the final major article. The information obtained in the empirical analysis of the (F,t) profile and of the scatter of the Fs around the (F,t) profile, tells how fast knowledge accrues about the cost of the final article. The (F,t) profile is useful for adjusting a current cost estimate so that it is no longer biased. It is too much to hope, however, that the debiased estimate will actually be correct. The spread of the $\log_e F$s around the regression surface of (3) shows that in fact the actual cost is ordinarily not the same as the debiased estimate. Debiasing an estimate has the salutary effect of improving it by moving it closer to the true cost *on the average*. But this only means that there is no more reason to think the debiased estimate is too low than to think it is too high. The uncertainty about how much a particular major article will cost depends directly on the amount of scatter around the appropriate (F,t) profile at the value of t corresponding to the timing of the estimate. It was shown under Hypothesis Testing that the scatter of F as measured by the standard deviation of F was proportional to the expected value of F. Since the expected value of F goes down linearly with t, the uncertainty about what the final cost will be is dispelled linearly with t also.

It should be clear that of the two arguments advanced in this section, the former is by far the more speculative. Identifying a cost discrepancy as a measure of ignorance is a heroic assumption, to say the least. The latter argument, however, involves just the right aspect of uncertainty from the standpoint of a person who must make a decision about continuing a development program or terminating it. To the extent that procurement cost is the important consideration in the decision, it is precisely the scatter around the (F,t) profile that is most relevant to the decision.

23. Cost Changes of Major Article Components

It is commonly believed that in programs where total-vehicle cost goes up substantially the cost increases for the airframe are proportionally smaller than those for the propulsion unit and the on-board electronic equipment. A detailed study of several development programs confirmed this belief, by and large; but the differential increase for propulsion and electronic equipment was by no means as uniform or as great as expected, because airframe weights went up significantly, and the airframe cost-per-pound also increased, even after allowing for learning-curve effects. For aircraft, the propulsion-unit cost increases usually resulted from the substitution of a more expensive engine for the one originally planned. The electronic gear increased in price because, typically, a large part of the technological advance envisioned in the program involved guidance and control.

Admittedly, the complete flight vehicle may not be the ideal unit of analysis for an investigation of cost estimates. But the fact that cost-increase patterns of the various components were not the same from major article to major article suggests that the possible improvement obtained by disaggregating to the component level would not be great.

24. The "Changing-configuration" Hypothesis

We have suggested a causal explanation for the fact that cost estimates of major hardware articles tend to be low early in the development program. The argument centers on assumptions about the manner in which cost estimators do their work and the way in which development proceeds. It appears that nearly always a cost estimate for a major article is made on the basis of a physical item – the configuration then being worked on in the development program. A set of performance characteristics as such is hardly ever costed directly.

The fact that cost estimates are usually quite good for programs requiring only small technological advances suggests that the costing of any particular configuration is in itself likely to be fairly accurate. The proximate cause of error in early estimates seems to be the change in configuration between the beginning and the end of the program. A detailed examination of a dozen development programs confirmed that there are indeed many configuration changes in the course of technologically difficult programs. It has been argued that there is a reasonable tendency on the part of contractors to attempt to develop early in a program a configuration that will be cheap at the procurement stage, even if this configuration does not necessarily have the greatest chances of success in fulfilling the performance specification. The consequence of this is that cost estimates generally increase with time as more expensive configurations are developed in the attempt to meet the stated specifications.

25. Conscious Underbidding of Contractors?

We have not discussed so far in this study the possible incentives a contractor might have to present the Air Force with development plans that are intentionally too optimistic with respect to cost. The cost-plus-fixed-fee contractual arrangement for development does not penalize a contractor for underbidding, except to the extent that the fixed fee is based upon the initial cost estimate.[31] Because the contractor's estimate of procurement cost is important in competition for a development contract, there is naturally an incentive to submit low estimates, and it would be surprising if this did not lead sometimes to estimates that are unrealistically low.

This "conscious-underbidding" explanation is obviously different from the "changing-configuration" explanation summarized above. Unfortunately, it is difficult to choose between the two explanations on the basis of the kind of evidence available. The empirical analysis seems to support the changing-configuration hypothesis. But the implications of (4) are also consistent with the conscious-underbidding hypothesis. A contractor's estimate that is too low may be attacked severely by competitors or criticized by the Air Force if it relates to a major article and there is little uncertainty about the probable costs. There is thus a natural policing of the cost estimates for easy development programs. But for programs requiring major technological advances, the underbidding would not be obvious.

---

[31] A common view in the airframe industry is that the profit in a development contract really lies in the production contract that may follow it indicating that even this penalty is probably not taken seriously.

Therefore, technological advance also plays an important role in the conscious-underbidding hypothesis. Conceivably, one might test the underbidding hypothesis by an analysis of contractors' order books to see if the low bids were typically associated with contractors who were particularly in need of Air Force work. However, the practical difficulties of this approach would be insurmountable.

If the various causal hypotheses had exactly the same empirical implications for changes in cost estimates during the development period, then (at least for purposes of prediction) it would not be important to distinguish between the hypotheses. But the empirical implications of the conscious-underbidding and changing-configuration hypotheses are not necessarily identical for the future, even if they have been essentially the same in the past. If the conscious-underbidding hypothesis is correct, future improvements in cost estimating would probably not affect the continued validity of (4), but a change in Air Force-contractor contractual arrangements might very well decrease its validity or invalidate the equation altogether. On the other hand, if the changing-configuration hypothesis is correct, a change in contractual arrangements would make no difference to the validity of the equation, but an improvement in cost-estimating techniques would make the equation obsolete.

The true explanation for observed changes in cost estimates is almost certainly a composite of both hypotheses. But however the reader may assess the relative importance of the two hypotheses, he should find (4) useful so long as there are no important changes in either cost-estimating techniques or in contractual arrangements between the Air Force and its contractors.

C. The Consequences of Cost-estimate Inaccuracies

26. Cost Inaccuracies Versus Other Uncertainties

It has been shown that major-article cost estimates have frequently been quite inaccurate in the past. We now turn to an examination of the consequences of such inaccuracies. First, a comparison will be made between (a) the errors in estimates of weapon-system costs induced by errors in the cost estimates of major articles, and (b) the differences in weapon-system costs resulting from minor differences in operational concept or operational performance.

In planning a weapon system that will become operational five or more years in the future, one must make many rather arbitrary assumptions about what the final system will be like. With different, equally reasonable operational assumptions, the weapon-system cost may differ by large amounts relative to the amount by which the system cost is understated because of an underestimate of the major-article cost. In such cases, the difficulty of specifying the system precisely will create a penumbra of uncertainty about the eventual system cost that will dominate the relatively minor uncertainty arising from the unreliable major-article cost estimate. Where this is true, errors in major-article cost estimates would not be very important. If, however, weapon-system costs were not so sensitive to variations in assumptions, then errors resulting from the use of unreliable major-article cost estimates might turn out to be the dominating consideration. Three examples from the Minuteman weapon system were studied in detail to compare the effects of uncertainties about system specifications and operating assumptions with the effects of uncertainties about the major-article cost. Relatively speaking, the latter were found to be by no means trivial.

27. System Choice and Inaccurate Cost Estimates: Bias

In comparing alternative weapon systems, a system analyst usually tries to compute for each system the cost of carrying out some particular mission. He usually selects as the best system the one that will accomplish the mission at the lowest cost. Because the estimated costs of the major articles in each of the systems are important elements of the total mission costs, errors in the cost estimates could lead to mistakes of selection. In choosing between two systems at the same stage of development where each development program involves the same degree of difficulty, the cost estimates are likely to suffer equally from downward bias. Even so, if the major articles of the two systems do not represent about the same fraction of the total system costs, choosing between the systems without reference to the absolute level of the Fs may lead to incorrect results. But more usually the decision problem involves a choice in which one development program is further from completion or is more difficult technologically than the other. Then a choice between the two systems based upon system costs computed from raw (unadjusted and undebiased) estimates of major-article cost is likely to be wrong. In general, not adjusting cost estimates for bias will lead to a tendency to innovate new systems excessively. In choosing between two systems to perform a given mission, one an entirely new development and the other a follow-on version of a system already in use, failure to debias the major-article costs (by using the appropriate Fs) will cause the new system to appear relatively better than it should.

Another way of comparing two systems is by comparing the effectiveness that can be purchased with a fixed budget through the procurement of each system. The remarks made in the last paragraph are applicable here, but another consideration also arises. This is what, in the language of economics, is called a differential income effect. The effectiveness of a given weapon system may not be proportional to the number of units procured. If the number procured is below a certain limit, the system may lose nearly all its effectiveness; or, to put it another way, its effectiveness may increase quite rapidly when the number of units exceeds a certain limit. A weapon system that depends upon saturation effects is an example of this kind; and if an alternative system is available, the alternative may well be preferable at low budget levels although it may be inferior at high budget levels. Using the F factors to improve the cost estimates is like lowering the budget level. Thus, even if the Fs of two systems are the same, and even if in both systems the major hardware articles represent the same fraction of the total system cost, an "incorrect" budget level (that is, undebiased cost estimates) may lead to a wrong choice. Failing to debias the cost estimates may cause the system analyst to overlook the implications of the differential "income" effects due to changes in the cost of the systems he is comparing.

One more possibility should be mentioned briefly. There are many non-recurring elements in the total weapon systems cost that do not depend upon the scale of operation of the system (such as development costs and headquarters administrative costs). Furthermore, the operating cost of the system does not increase proportionally with the scale of the operation because of economies of scale (particularly in logistic support). Planning a mixed force on the basis of a large budget level will call for procurement of a more varied force than if the budget level is small. The procurement of a system will only be justified if it is operated on a sufficiently large scale to overcome the disadvantages of the high initial costs. Because the effect of ignoring the Fs is to overstate the total budget level actually available, too varied a force may be procured if the estimates are not debiased.

28. System Choice and Inaccurate Cost Estimates: Variance

The last section discussed the possible consequences for weapon system choice of failing to debias estimates. Even if the estimates are debiased, however, they still are not likely to be correct. Therefore, a wrong choice may still be made. Something should be said about the possibility that a system will turn out to be more expensive than a competitor although early in development it appears to be cheaper. We will confine our attention here to a somewhat more restricted question: What is the probability that a *major article* that appears early in development to be cheaper than a competitor will in fact turn out to be more expensive?

Suppose that major articles A and B are being compared and that both require similar degrees of technological advance. If the initial *debiased* cost estimate of B, $\tilde{C}_B$, is greater than that of A, $\tilde{C}_A$, by a factor k ($k > 1$), then the probability that the final cost of B, C_B, will be less than the final cost of A, C_A, is denoted by

$$Pr\{C_B/C_A < 1 | \tilde{C}_B/\tilde{C}_A = k\}.$$

The larger k is, the less likely it is that the apparently cheaper major article will turn out to be the more expensive one. Clearly if k were equal to 1.05 or 1.10, the question of which major article will turn out to be cheaper would still be very much up in the air; if k were equal to 3.00, however, it would be almost certain that A would maintain its superiority. We seek the critical levels of k which separate certainty from uncertainty.

But the similarity of the development programs of the two major articles must be taken into account too. If the two major articles are similar, the cost-increasing difficulties encountered in one program are likely to be encountered in the other also. In that case, A would be likely to remain cheaper even if k was very small. An index of similarity between major articles to be compared, denoted ρ, will be used. The true cost of a major article will be equal to the early cost estimate times the appropriate F from (4), times the residual v. The correlation coefficient ρ measures the joint variation of the residuals for two major articles being compared. (Strictly speaking, it is the correlation between the residuals of (3).) If the development programs were completely different, the residuals would be independent. If the programs were similar, the residuals would be of about the same size with the same sign. But in practice ρ is not likely to be equal to unity, even for closely similar development programs; $\rho = .8$ would characterize a high degree of similarity. Identical development programs would be indicated by $\rho = 1$; completely different development programs would be indicated by $\rho = 0$. Two missile programs that shared, say, guidance and control problems but were quite dissimilar in all other respects might be indicated by ρ of .3 or .4.

We now turn to Figures 17 and 18 below, which, at least in a rough way, express the relationships we are concerned with. Figure 17 gives a set of curves relevant to comparisons of articles requiring minor technological advances; Figure 18 gives the curves to be used with comparisons involving major technological advances. The expression $Pr\{C_B/C_A < 1|\tilde{C}_B/\tilde{C}_A = k;\rho\}$ appears as the vertical scale of Figures 17 and 18 and states the probability that the true cost of B will be less than the true cost of A even though the debiased cost estimate of B is greater than that of A by a factor k; and given that the similarity between the

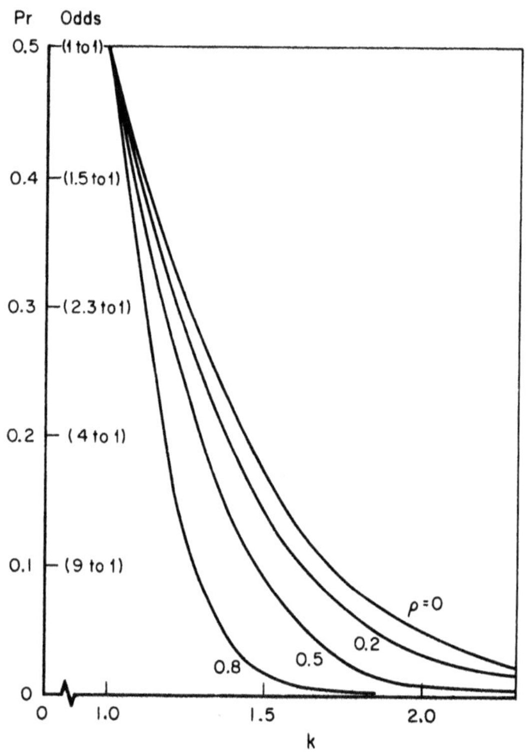

Fig. 17. Comparison of true costs and estimated costs of two articles requiring minor technological advances

Notes:

The vertical scale is the probability

$$Pr\{C_B/C_A < 1|\tilde{C}_B/\tilde{C}_A = k;\rho\}$$

C_A, C_B are true costs of A and B.

$\tilde{C}_A$, $\tilde{C}_B$ are debiased estimates of the costs of A and B.

ρ is the index of similarity between the development programs of A and B.

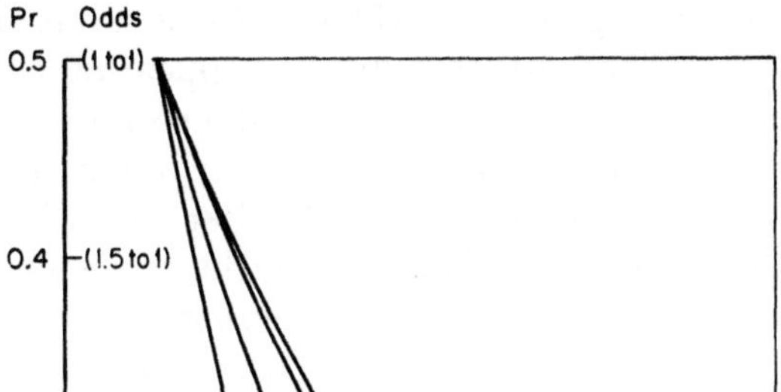

Fig. 18. Comparison of true costs and estimated costs of two articles requiring major technological advances

Note: See Figure 17.

two development programs is stated by the index ρ.[32] The probability values are translated into "odds" values to facilitate understanding of what they mean. The use of the graphs will be illustrated by two examples. If two very different, minor-technological-advance flight vehicles are being compared and the one thought more expensive is estimated, after debiasing, to cost 1.5 times the other, the probability

[32] The probabilities have been computed in the following way. It is assumed that the true cost for any major article—yet to be revealed—is equal to an appropriate F, derived from (4), times the early cost estimate. F is a stochastic variable which is assumed to be log-normal with the parameters ($\log_e F^*$, σ_u), where F^* is the value of F obtained by inserting into the right-hand side of (4) the numbers which describe the cost estimate and the development program. Therefore, at the time of an early cost estimate, the true cost of the major article under consideration is a stochastic variable which is log-normal with parameters ($\log_e F^* \cdot C^{\text{est}}$, σ_u). Let $\theta = C_B/C_A$, where C_A and C_B are the true costs of two major articles to be compared. Then $\log_e \theta = \log_e C_B/C_A = \log_e C_B - \log_e C_A$. Since C_A and C_B are lognormal with parameters ($\log_e F_A^* \cdot C_A^{\text{est}}$, σ_u^A) and ($\log_e F_B^* \cdot C_B^{\text{est}}$, σ_u^B),

that the one appearing cheaper will actually turn out to be the more expensive is .17. (The odds that the one appearing cheaper will remain cheaper are about 5 to 1.) If two rather similar, major-technological-advance flight vehicles are being compared and the one thought more expensive is estimated, after debiasing, to cost 1.3 times the other, then the probability that the one appearing cheaper will actually turn out to be the more expensive is between .28 and .33. (The odds that the one appearing cheaper will remain cheaper are between 2.5 and 2.0 to 1.)

We return now to the question of how large the difference must be between the cost estimates of major articles before we can be confident that the one appearing to be cheaper really will remain so. The answer depends, of course, upon what probability level (or what odds) inspires sufficient confidence. If odds of 4 to 1 are sufficient, then a value of k greater than about 1.7 is required if dissimilar programs of major technological advance are being compared. For the same probability level, if the programs are fairly similar k would have to be at least 1.4 or 1.5.[33]

It may be of interest to mention here that when the United States was still undecided about where to build a canal joining the Atlantic and the Pacific, an important reason for not building it through Nicaragua (a location favored for political reasons) was the fact that the expected cost of building it there was just over one-fourth more than building it across the Isthmus of Panama! Figure 18 provides a very rough estimate of .4 for the probability that in fact the Nicaragua canal would have turned out cheaper.

29. Implications for Cost-effectiveness Studies

In cost-effectiveness studies of alternative systems, it may sometimes be that the best system is better than all others by a whole order of

---

respectively, $\log_e \theta$ is normally distributed with a mean equal to $(\log_e F_B^* \cdot C_B^{\text{est}} - \log_e F_A^* \cdot C_A^{\text{est}})$ and a standard deviation equal to $[(\sigma_u^A)^2 + (\sigma_u^B)^2 - 2\rho\sigma_u^A \cdot \sigma_u^B]^{1/2}$, where ρ is the correlation coefficient describing the relationship between u^A and u^B. If comparisons are made between major articles which both involve the same magnitude of technological advance, the standard deviation reduces to $(2)^{1/2} \cdot \sigma_u \cdot (1-\rho)^{1/2}$, where σ_u is .298 for minor-technological-advance programs and .463 for major-technological-advance programs. (These numbers are the standard deviations of the residuals reported in Section 13.) Let $\tilde{C}_A$ and $\tilde{C}_B$ be the debiased estimates of C_A and C_B respectively; then the mean of $\log_e \theta$ is $\log_e \tilde{C}_B/\tilde{C}_A$. Now let $k = \tilde{C}_B/\tilde{C}_A$. With a table of normal curve areas it is a simple matter to compute the probability that $C_B/C_A < 1$ given k and ρ.

The assumption that F is lognormally distributed is important. If in fact it is far from lognormal, the curves of Figures 17 and 18 are only very rough approximations of the correct ones.

[33] These values of k may be quite sensitive to the exact distribution of F.

magnitude – by so wide a margin that the observed inaccuracies in the major-article cost estimates are unimportant. In such cases neither the debiasing of the major-article estimates nor their comparison (taking variance into account) by the methods of the above section will affect the outcome. On *a priori* grounds, however, one would expect that there would be many cost-effectiveness studies in which none of the alternative systems would display such unquestionable dominance. In these cases the methods presented here should help the analyst to make the right choice.

To test whether the use of debiasing factors would affect the outcome of actual cost-effectiveness studies, three published studies were examined. In this examination, we sought an answer to the question: Would the analysts responsible for the study have come to a different conclusion if they had (a) debiased the major-article estimates and (b) taken account of the remaining cost uncertainties in accordance with the above section? Accepting the other parts of the analysis, we fixed our attention on the estimated cost of the major article. In one of the three studies, the result was to suggest that a different conclusion would have been reached if the analysts had taken into account the bias and variance of the major-article cost estimates. In the other two studies, the other differences between the alternative systems were sufficiently large to dominate the major-article cost uncertainties. The specific results of this examination for each of the three cost-effectiveness studies are as follows:

I: Comparison of Air-breathing Missiles and Aircraft

Reference: G. H. Clement and C. P. Bahrman (editors), *Missile Systems for Strategic Bombardment,* The RAND Corporation, R-248, November 20, 1953.

Rankings for the Early Period

Original Ranking and Cost			Adjusted Ranking and Cost		
Rank	System	Cost [a]	Rank	System	Cost [a]
1.	Guided Missile I [b]	7.5	1.	Current bomber with penetration aid	7.9
2.	Current bomber with penetration aid	7.5	2.	Current bomber alone	9.0
3.	Current bomber alone	9.0	3.	Guided Missile I	14.9

Rankings for the Late Period

1.	Guided Missile II [b]	4.5	1.	Guided Missile II	10.1
2.	Guided Missile I [b]	9.1	2.	Follow-on bomber with penetration aid	17.2
3.	Follow-on bomber with penetration aid	16.5	3.	Guided Missile I	18.0
4.	Follow-on bomber alone	20.0	4.	Follow-on bomber alone	20.0

Result of examination: The rankings of bombardment systems were significantly altered when cost uncertainty considerations were taken into account.

Notes:

[a] Cost is in millions of dollars per unit of effectiveness, that is, for carrying out certain bombing missions.

[b] Guided Missile II was a more advanced missile than Guided Missile I.

II: Comparison of Alternative Bombing Systems

Reference: L. B. Rumph and S. Enke, *Economic Comparison of Intercontinental Airplane Systems for Strategic Bombing,* The RAND Corporation, R-229, March 1, 1952.

In a study of different methods of carrying out bombing missions, the merits of various parasitic and two-stage refueling systems were appraised and a comparison was made of supersonic and subsonic bombers. Although there were differences in the magnitudes of technological advance required by competing alternatives, taking account of cost-estimate uncertainties did not upset the various conclusions reached by the systems analysts.

III: Comparison of Surface-to-surface Rocket and Ramjet Engines for Missiles

Reference: R. W. Krueger, *A Comparison of Long-range Surface-to-surface Rocket and Ramjet Missiles,* The RAND Corporation, R-174, May 1, 1950.

Conclusions	*Results of examination: Is the conclusion upset by cost uncertainty considerations?*
1. ". . . the rocket and ramjet costs are still about the same at short ranges and very heavy payloads. Otherwise at long ranges or light payloads the rocket is clearly superior."	1. No, except that the use of the word "clearly" is only barely warranted.
2. "In conclusion, it may be stated that except for the very restricted case of delivery of heavy, cheap payloads at short ranges, in which instance there exists no preference for either missile type over the other, surface-to-surface rocket missiles are superior to surface-to-surface ramjet missiles for use in long-range bombardment after 1960."	2. No.

These three cost-effectiveness studies were selected only because they were easily available in published form. They were in no sense a random selection from the population of all cost-effectiveness studies, but the fact that they were selected should not suggest that they were particularly good or bad studies in any sense; they simply came readily to hand. Even with these limitations on the nature of the sample, it appears that major-article cost uncertainties can critically affect the outcome of cost-effectiveness studies, although perhaps not so frequently as might have been expected on *a priori* grounds.

30. Implications for Force-structure Projections

In this section we consider the implications for force-structure plans and programs of inaccuracies in the estimated costs of major hardware articles. Projections of force structures extending as far as 10 years into the future are made by a number of Air Force agencies. For such time periods, the projections necessarily involve a number of major weapon systems that are still in the early stages of development when the projections are made. The analysis of cost-estimate bias given above suggests that the budget projections for such time periods may be seriously affected by inaccuracies in the early cost estimates for major hardware articles that require considerable advances in technology. It might be, however, that when aggregated with the costs of a substantial part of the Air Force, these inaccuracies would appear to be only trivial.

To resolve the problem, two long-term projections for the Air Force strategic-force budget were examined. The projections differed in the scales of operation assumed for the various weapon systems from year to year. The first of the two was the more conservative in the sense of involving a smaller total budget. Budget projections for each of these force projections were computed at The RAND Corporation. For each of these for each year of the projection, we computed the percentage of the budget of that year *not* devoted to the procurement of major items of advanced weapon systems.[34] This percentage refers to items of relatively certain cost. The difference between this percentage and 100 per cent refers to the cost of hardware articles for advanced weapon systems that can be regarded as relatively uncertain. Figure 19 shows the annual change in the certain and uncertain shares for both the force structures. It is striking that for both projections a substantial fraction of budget is uncertain almost immediately.

Having thus isolated the uncertain shares of the two projections, we examined the effect of different cost estimates for the uncertain shares. For each year for strategic-force budget projections, we costed the uncertain shares according to three different sets of estimates: (a) Air Force estimates, (b) RAND estimates, and (c) RAND estimates increased by 50 per cent. These were added to the certain shares costed according to RAND estimates. For both strategic forces, the total budget projections vary quite substantially as a result of the different cost assumptions for the ("uncertain") advanced-system articles. Even for the smaller force structure (which, as would be expected, shows the smaller differences between curves), the difference between the RAND and the Air Force estimates amounts to about a half a billion dollars in the earlier years and to nearly a billion dollars in the later years of the period. And if the RAND estimates were too low, the differences between projected budgets and actual budgets would be even greater. This result suggests that an appreciation of the potential

[34] At the cost of some oversimplification, only three weapon systems in these (now somewhat out of date) projections were considered as "advanced": Minuteman, Dyna-Soar, and the B-70.

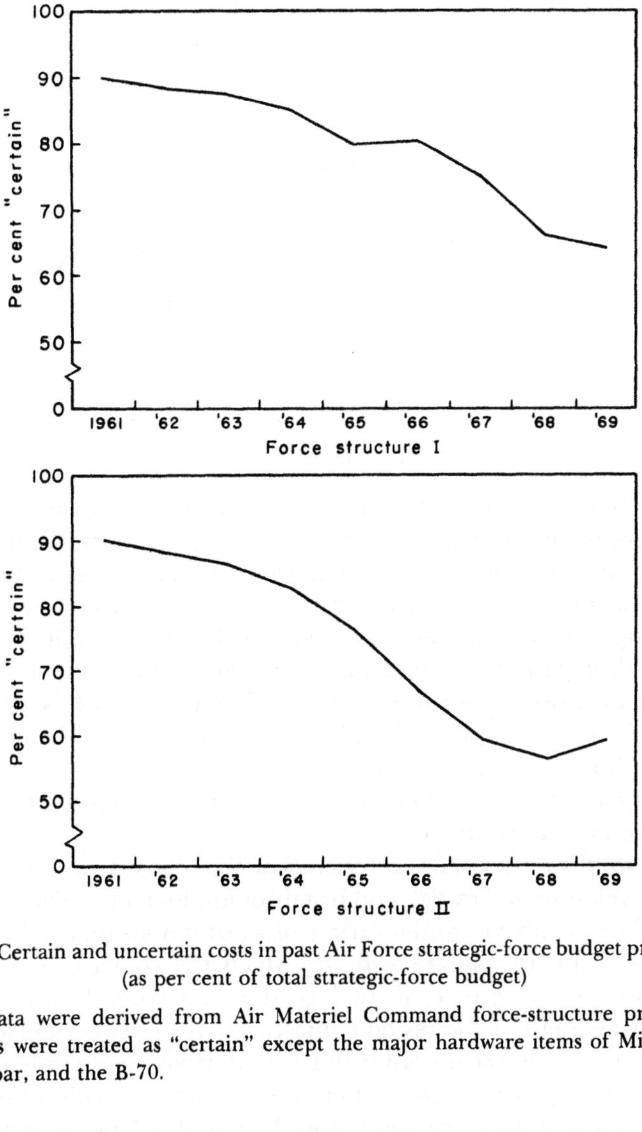

Fig. 19. Certain and uncertain costs in past Air Force strategic-force budget projections (as per cent of total strategic-force budget)

Note: Data were derived from Air Materiel Command force-structure projections. All costs were treated as "certain" except the major hardware items of Minuteman, Dyna-Soar, and the B-70.

biases and their sources as developed in this chapter is important for force-structure budget projections as well as for the cost-effectiveness studies of individual systems.

Chapter 5

TOWARD A NORMATIVE THEORY OF DEVELOPMENT

by Thomas Marschak

A. Introduction

This chapter explores the difficulties of building a normative theory of development – a theory that determines the properties of the "best" conduct of development with some rigor under precise assumptions about the developer's goals and the manner in which he acquires knowledge as development proceeds. Such a theory will, of course, have to deal with models that omit many important elements of development as it occurs in the real world. The models will become progressively more complicated and more realistic, but at the beginning we shall leave out a great deal.

A number of things would be achieved were we to construct a fairly complete normative theory.

1) It would be possible to test reasonable conjectures about what good development strategy and organization look like. That is to say, it would be possible to find a variety of assumptions that yield models simple enough to analyze and for which the conjectures could be demonstrated to be true, if, in fact, they are true. This requires a precise statement of the tested conjectures. If under certain assumptions a tested conjecture is invalid (the development strategy it describes is not good) the developer would have to decide whether or not such assumptions are met before he could accept the tested conjecture in formulating his own development strategy. Among the conjectures we shall test in this manner are that the more one learns in each approach to a development task the more approaches it pays to pursue; and that successive increments in the scale of a development project yield smaller and smaller improvements in the project's payoff, suitably defined.

2) The theory would be a step in finding out what the production

function of the knowledge-producing industry looks like. In particular, the theory would shed light on the critical question of returns to scale in the conduct of research and development, first with respect to individual projects—the most disaggregated research and development efforts—and ultimately by aggregation with respect to the national research and development effort.

3) The theory would identify various areas of ignorance about development in which intensive and critical inquiry would particularly pay off. If certain properties of good development are particularly sensitive to assumptions about how knowledge is acquired, then it is particularly fruitful to make an empirical study of which assumptions are in fact satisfied. Such assumptions might have to do, for example, with the shape of the curve that relates the amount of money spent on development in a particular stage to the decrease in uncertainty (suitably measured) that this spending can bring about.

Since the theory is normative it often might be a poor description of the observed behavior of developers, but that is not its aim. Since developers are presumably interested in improving their performance, they would adopt any improved procedures that a normative theory might generate, and as they did so they would eventually cause the normative theory to become more closely descriptive. From the viewpoint of major economic questions—both macroeconomic questions and questions about the allocation of resources to research and development among firms—the relevant information that the normative study of development might generate is information about the production function of the knowledge industry or of knowledge-producing firms. Like all production functions, these define efficient and attainable input-output combinations; points not on (not satisfying) such a production function are either inefficient or unattainable. A normative theory is, roughly, the theory of how to achieve the points on such production functions.

It would certainly be very useful to construct a descriptive or behavioral theory of current development by observing the actual behavior of developers. But even here a normative theory would be helpful, for it would yield the optimizing behavior that developers would follow if they could. A developer's actual behavior presumably modifies the optimizing behavior to take account of his capacity. Suppose, for example, that the optimizing behavior at some stage of development would require him to compare a certain set of ten thousand alternatives, but, being human, he is able to compare only a thousand. Some information about the larger set may at least usefully characterize the set of alternatives out of which such a human developer will choose. In this way the normative theory might serve as a check on a descriptive theory based purely on observation.

Part B will deal with normative problems in development strategy and Part C will deal rather quickly with some normative problems in development organization. The distinction between the two topics is that problems of strategy could arise in one-man development projects but problems of organization arise only when a project has more than one man.

B. Normative Problems in Development Strategy

1. The Framework

A developer directs the work of bringing to completion an item, and has preferences among the alternative histories that the completed work could exhibit. Except for a brief digression, we shall not be concerned directly with a normative theory governing the behavior of the manager of a development department, in which many different items are simultaneously developed. Even less will be said about the behavior of a firm (or other organization) that devotes resources to activities in addition to development (such as production) to achieve some goal to which all activities contribute. The proposed normative theory would merely be a step in the direction of these much more ambitious theories.

A completed item is described by a number of performance magnitudes.[1] If the developer is asked to state which of two alternative versions of the completed item he prefers, then a knowledge of the performance magnitudes for each version enables him to make the choice.

It is convenient to classify the problems in development strategy that we could consider according to the following four dichotomies.

a) Does the developer divide the space of performance magnitudes into two parts—an unsatisfactory and a satisfactory part—so that his work is finished if, and only if, the item's performance magnitudes lie in the satisfactory part of the space? Or does he divide the space into more than two regions, all of which he is willing to rank? To put it compactly, are the developer's preferences with respect to performance magnitudes two valued or many valued?

b) For the purpose of discussing development strategy do we re-

---

[1] Range, altitude, speed, weight, power, signal-to-noise ratio, and so on. For some purposes the magnitudes may be the characteristics of one or more components of the item.

gard the item being developed as having one component (or as being one giant component) or many components?

c) Must the developer make his decisions about the way he will conduct development before the development starts? Or will there be one or more *review points*, at which the knowledge acquired in the course of development can be brought to bear on new decisions?

d) Does the world outside of the developer's control stay the same during the course of development or does it change? That is to say, does the relevant state of the art change because of work not under the developer's control or do the external data that affect his ranking over the space of performance magnitudes change?

Realism requires, of course, that the second alternative in each dichotomy hold. But we must simplify. Except for the briefest suggestions, we shall, with respect to the first and last dichotomy, look only at problems for which the first alternative holds. With respect to the second and third dichotomies we shall look at both alternatives – single component problems and (briefly) multi-component problems; no review point (or one shot) problems and one and many review point problems.

2. The Developer's Task Under Certainty

In a world of complete certainty the developer knows in what region of the performance space the developed items lie for a given way of pursuing the development. (The term "way" will be discussed below.) But if the developer is to choose between alternative ways he must know more than this. He must know how much time and money will be required until development is complete.

If we now assume two valued preferences we can state the situation more precisely. The developer is to attain a satisfactory version of the item. He can rank the alternative combinations of time and money that suffice to do so. He always prefers less time to more and less money to more but he is willing to trade time and money against each other. For a given item and a given satisfactory region of its performance space, his preferences can be compactly represented by the function $C(M,T)$, which we shall call the time and money cost function; it is defined for all non-negative values of M (money) and T (time). If and only if the combination (M_1,T_1) is preferred to the combination (M_2,T_2), $C(M_1T_1)$ is smaller than $C(M_2T_2)$. The function $C(M,T)$ is ordinal – that is, if C represents the developer's preferences, then so will the transformed function $h(C)$ where h is a non-decreasing transformation of C.[2] The function C is an increasing function of T

[2] That is, for the function h, $x > y$ implies $h(x) \geqq h(y)$.

and of M. We shall henceforth assume $C(M,T) > 0$ for all $M > 0$, $T > 0$.

The developer obtains his ranking of alternative time and money combinations by considering the alternative uses to which money could be put in any time interval and the benefits (net of any borrowing cost) to be derived from each of them. The developer could use M dollars spread over T time units to develop a different item. Or, if the developer works for a customer, then the customer may have such an alternative. Or else the developer may have the alternative of not spending the money on development at all but spending it in some other productive activity or investing it in securities.

At the present level of generality it seems more realistic to let the developer have preferences over all possible time and money combinations than to say he has a fixed budget or is faced with a fixed deadline. More money can always be obtained (at a cost) from somewhere and no deadline is really immutable. (But preferences may exhibit sharp corners; there may be, for example, a value of M such that for fixed T all higher M imply exceedingly high values of C.) It will turn out to be useful in some of the problems we shall look at to consider the budget as fixed and to solve the problem first for this case. In any case, the developer's task under certainty is to conduct the development in such a way that $C(M,T)$ is a minimum.

To make the term "way" more precise we shall introduce the concept of an approach to the task of developing a satisfactory version of the item. An "approach" may be the pursuit of a particular design, or the work of a particular group of people, or the attempt to reach a particular subregion of the satisfactory part of the performance space. In any case, there is an amount of time and an amount of money that would be required if an approach were pursued until it yielded a satisfactory version of the required item. Henceforth we shall let t ($\geqslant 0$) and m ($\geqslant 0$) denote the time and money required to complete an approach. T and M will denote the total time and money expended in the course of development, which might involve the pursuit of several approaches, while $C(M,T)$ always denotes total time and money cost, whether one or more approaches are pursued; $C(M,T) = C(m,t)$ if only one approach, requiring m dollars and t time units, is pursued.

The simplest task we can formulate for the developer under certainty, then, is as follows. The developer is faced with a number of alternative approaches. He knows the time and money each approach would require if it were pursued to completion. He is to pick the approach that has the smallest value of $C(m,t)$, the completion cost when no other approach is used. He then pursues that approach all by itself.

3. The Developer's Task Under Uncertainty

To restate the simplest problem just given for an uncertain world, we suppose that the developer is again confronted initially with a collection of possible approaches. But we must now specify that he does *not* know for a given approach what the time and money cost would turn out to be if that approach were to be pursued by itself and completed. He has, rather, certain beliefs as to the different time and money combinations that might be observed, and these beliefs can be expressed in the form of a probability distribution defined over the possible combinations (m,t).

The probabilities in question are "personal" ones.[3] They may be based on the developer's experience with similar development tasks, his knowledge of the experiences of others, or the opinions of experts in his employ. If necessary the developer can, by conducting an experiment on himself, elicit from himself the personal probability he attaches to an event; for example, that the given approach turns out to require, say, less than t^* time units and m^* dollars to complete. He might ask himself: "Suppose I were given the choice of (1) receiving D dollars if the required time turns out to be less than t^* and the required money less than m^* and nothing otherwise; or (2) receiving D dollars if I draw a red ball and nothing if I draw a black ball from an urn containing a proportion p of red balls and $1-p$ of black balls. What would p have to be in order that I be indifferent between the two options?" The value of p that he chooses determines the required personal probability.

To assert that a developer is simply unable to answer such a question is to accuse him of a degree of ignorance that his observed behavior continually denies. He does, in fact, repeatedly choose between alternative options, each of which can have a number of possible outcomes, and yet he is uncertain which outcome of a given option will in fact be observed. Any developer who is at all consistent and does not make decisions by purest whim is very likely to be repeatedly asking himself, and answering, hypothetical questions of the same form as the one just illustrated (except that both options compared generally have to do with development).

[3] In the sense that has been introduced by L. J. Savage and his followers. See Leonard J. Savage: *The Foundations of Statistics,* New York: John Wiley and Sons, Inc., 1954.

The advocates of personal probability would also suggest that as the developer proceeds with the conduct of development, his initial personal probabilities (attached, for example, to the time and money combinations required by alternative approaches) carry less and less weight in the decisions he makes, while the knowledge he accumulates carries more and more weight. His "prior" personal probabilities, in other words, are replaced by "posterior" ones that reflect both the prior probabilities and the subsequent observations. This is precisely what will occur in our models, but only, of course, when there are one or more review points. In the case of no review points, a useful case to start with in several of the problems that follow, the initial personal probabilities, which characterize the developer's beliefs about alternative approaches before he begins to pursue them, are the sole source of his decisions. He has no opportunity to use the knowledge acquired in the course of pursuing chosen approaches in order to make new decisions.

In the simplest no review point problem under uncertainty, then, the developer is faced with a collection of alternative approaches and for each one he has a (personal) probability distribution over all pairs (m,t) – all the time and money combinations that might turn out to be required in order to complete that approach. Once he chooses an approach from the collection he must complete it. His task is to select one of the alternative approaches. He will clearly never select more than one, for that would yield him more than one satisfactory version of the required item, and one is all he needs. Now it can be shown to follow from very reasonable axioms of behavior that in this situation the developer chooses that approach for which the expected value of $C(m,t)$, computed according to the personal probabilities associated with the possible combinations (m,t) for that approach, is a minimum. This is exactly what we shall assume.

The reasonable axioms that imply this procedure, and the argument that establishes the implication, are given in the book of L. J. Savage.[4] Several simplified accounts of this discussion are also available.[5]

The discussion considers the general question of how a decision-maker ranks the actions open to him when the consequences of these actions depend on which one of a number of alternative states of

[4] *Ibid.*

[5] Jacob Marschak and Roy Radner: *The Economic Theory of Teams,* forthcoming monograph of the Cowles Foundation for Research in Economics, Yale University; H. Raiffa and D. Luce: *Games and Decisions,* New York: John Wiley and Sons, 1958, Ch. 13.

the world prevails. He does not know which state in fact prevails, but he knows the consequences of each action under different sets of circumstances. An action can be thought of as a set of consequences, one consequence corresponding to each state of the world.

The suggested axioms of behavior are constraints on the decisionmaker's choices among the actions. One axiom (the "sure thing principle") essentially says that if two actions yield the same consequence X for some states of the world (but different consequences for other states) and if the decisionmaker prefers the first to the second, then he continues to prefer the first to the second when we replace the consequence X by some other consequence X' so that the two actions still have a common consequence for the same states of the world as before, but this common consequence is now X' rather than X.

This axiom[6] permits one to conclude that the decisionmaker's ranking of actions also implies a ranking of the possible consequences that can be generated by actions and states of the world. This being the case, another axiom (which has been called "independence of tastes and beliefs")[7] then says: Suppose the decisionmaker is faced with two actions. The first yields a bad consequence if one of a certain set Q of states of the world occurs and a good one if a state not in Q occurs. The second action yields the same good consequence if a state of the world in some other set R occurs and the same bad one if a state not in R occurs. Then if the decisionmaker prefers the first to the second he continues to do so if the bad and the good consequence are each replaced by a new consequence, as long as the replacement for the good consequence is still preferred to the replacement for the bad one. To put it another way, the decisionmaker's preferences between the two actions are based solely on his beliefs as to whether the states in Q are more likely to occur than the states in R: he will prefer that action (or take that bet) for which the good consequence is more likely to happen. How good the good consequence is (or how bad the bad one) will not affect his belief, for he is neither a wishful thinker nor a pessimist who regards nature (the chooser of the state of the world) as malevolent toward him.

---

[6] Together with another one, that states the following: Fix a particular state of the world S and generate a ranking of consequences from the decisionmaker's preferences between actions (since an action specifies a consequence for the fixed state S, preference of one action over another implies a ranking of the consequence which the first action yields for S and the consequence which the second action yields). Then the ranking of consequences remains the same if the fixed state S is replaced by the fixed state T.

[7] Marschak and Radner, Ch. I.

These axioms imply first of all that the decisionmaker's beliefs about the possible states of the world can be represented by numbers attached to events (sets of states of the world) and have all the standard properties of probabilities. Some benchmark events are needed, such as the color composition of a set of balls drawn from an urn of known composition, or the resting position of a spinner attached to a circle. By a suitable series of choices between bets—such as the one illustrated above for the case of a developer—the decisionmaker's personal probabilities can then be attached to any other set of collectively exhaustive and mutually exclusive events. The axiom of independence of tastes and beliefs guarantees that it does not matter what we choose as the good and bad consequence in constructing the hypothetical bets that are used to obtain the required personal probabilities from the given benchmark events; in the above illustration concerning the developer, D dollars and zero dollars could be replaced by V dollars and W dollars, respectively, with $W < V$, or by losing your job and not losing your job.

The axioms imply in the second place that there is a way of assigning numbers—utilities—to consequences such that the decisionmaker's preferences between actions can be represented by average or expected utilities, calculated according to the personal probabilities the decisionmaker attaches to events. One action is preferred to another if and only if the expected utility of the first is higher. The assignment of utilities to consequences is, moreover, unique up to a linear transformation—every assignment of utilities that implies the correct ranking of actions is a non-decreasing linear transformation of every other. This means that once an origin (a consequence with a utility of zero) has been picked, the only remaining choice is that of scale (given the chosen origin the utilities under one assignment are constant positive multiples of the utilities under another).

A final implication of the axioms is that if the decisionmaker acquires new knowledge and determines that the possible consequences of actions that he contemplates must lie in some subset of the original set of possible consequences (because some events are now ruled out), then in computing expected utilities for these actions he revises the probabilities attached to events, in accordance with the usual formula for calculating conditional (or *a posteriori*) probabilities from the original unconditional (or prior) ones.

A notable property of the axioms is that the events (or states of the world) to which probabilities are attached need not be repeated events like the tossing of a coin, whose relative frequencies can be taken to be their probabilities. The decisionmaker who obeys the axioms can attach a probability to the event "the moon is made of green cheese" as well as the event "given a development budget of ten million dollars the aircraft described in this brochure will appear one year from now to require (according to best estimates then) another two years to complete but will in fact turn out to take four additional years." Since non-repeated events dominate in the conduct of development, so that beliefs must have a basis other than the observed repetition of identical circumstances, the personal probability approach is peculiarly appropriate to the normative study of development. Indeed there simply is no other approach known at present.

If the developer accepts the axioms we have partly sketched as conditions he would wish his choices among actions to satisfy, then in the no review point problem he will behave as we have indicated. The actions are the approaches, the time and money required for their completion are both the consequences and the unknown states of the world, and the negative of the time and money cost function plays the role of a utility function. The developer chooses that approach out of the collection for which expected time and money cost is a minimum, using personal probabilities to compute the expectations. In the many review point problem, to which we turn in a moment, he will behave in a more complicated manner (he will, in particular, have to revise his probabilities as he acquires new knowledge), but one that follows just as inevitably from the same simple axioms.

Note, incidentally, that we have not by any means ruled out an aversion to risk. The developer might regard any approach in which there is a one-half chance of (m_1,t) and a one-half chance of (m_2,t) as less desirable than an approach in which $[(1/2)(m_1 + m_2),t]$ occurs with certainty. Such preferences are expressed in the shape of the function *C*.[8]

Our assumptions about the developer's task under uncertainty and about the meaning of probability statements in development are now explicit enough so that we may proceed with a detailed survey of problems in development strategy. We begin with the problem of choice among approaches as we have just defined them. We then turn to problems (both no review point or one shot problems and many

[8] A linear *C*-function would imply that the developer has no preference between the two illustrated approaches. A *C*-function that increases with m and increases at an increasing rate – so that a one-half chance of a drop in m below $(1/2)(m_1 + m_2)$ does not compensate for a one-half chance of an equal increase in m above $(1/2)(m_1 + m_2)$ – implies that the developer prefers the second (riskless) approach.

review point problems) in which the definition of approach is broadened in two different directions. Following this we look at the multi-component complication, then, briefly, at the many-valued-preference complication, and even more briefly at the changes-in-the-outside-world complication. We close with a brief digression on the problem that faces the manager of a development department, developing a collection of items.

4. The Pure Parallel Approach Problem with One or More Review Points [9]

4.1. Principal Symbols in this Section

$C(M,T)$ — time and money cost function where M denotes money and T time.

c — the value of $C(m,t)$ for some given approach, where m is the amount of money required to carry it from the Nth review point to completion and t is the time required to carry it through all N review points and thence to completion.

c_n, $n = 1, \ldots, N$ — the estimates of c obtained at the N successive review points.

---

[9] The first discussion of this problem, a discussion of the single review point case, was R. R. Nelson: Uncertainty, Learning, and the Economics of Parallel R&D Efforts, *Review of Economics and Statistics*, Vol. XLIII (November 1961), pp. 351–364. A remark on rigor is in order at this point. We wish to combine accessibility of the argument to readers with generality of the results; in particular we want the results to apply, where possible, to discrete as well as continuous probability distributions. Accordingly a somewhat casual attitude will be taken. The integral $\int f(t)dt$ is defined for all the functions $f(t)$ that arise in the discussion. These functions have a finite number of discontinuities. Thus

$$\int_a^b f(t)dt$$

is to be understood to mean

$$\int_a^{a_1} f_1(t) + \int_{a_1}^{a_2} f_2(t) + \int_{a_2}^{a_3} f_3(t) + \cdots + \int_{a_{n-1}}^{a_n} f_n(t) + \int_{a_n}^{b} f_{n+1}(t),$$

where (1) discontinuities occur at $a_1, a_2, \ldots, a_n$; (2) $f(t) = f_1(t)$ for $a \leqq t < a_1$, $f_2(t)$ for $a_2 \leqq t < a_3$, $f_3(t)$ for $a_3 \leqq t < a_4, \ldots, f_n(t)$ for $a_{n-1} \leqq t < a_n$, $f_{n+1}(t)$ for $a_n \leqq t < b$; and (3) all the summed integrals are Reimann integrals. A function F (always denoted by a capital Latin letter) is called the "probability distribution" of a random variable x if $F(x^*) = Pr(x \leqq x^*)$, or if x is a vector $(x_1,x_2, \ldots ,x_n)$, $F(x^*) = Pr(x_1 \leqq x_1^*, \ldots ,x_n \leqq x_n^*)$, where $x^* = (x_1^*, \ldots ,x_n^*)$. The arguments to follow can all be restated less casually with proper attention to measurability assumptions and with use of Lebesgue integrals throughout.

F	the probability distribution of the random variable $(c_1, \ldots, c_N, c)$; in certain instances other capital Latin letters (but not T, E, or N) also denote such a distribution.
$F_{\gamma n}$	the conditional distribution of c_{n+1} given that $c_n = \gamma$.
q	the number of approaches randomly and independently drawn at the start of development and pursued to review point 1.
w	the looking cost.
Γ, Δ, etc.	a set of approaches available (not previously discarded) at some given review point.
γ, δ, a, b, x, y, etc.	an individual approach available at some given review point, or equivalently (under the Markov assumption) the current estimate for that approach at that review point; these symbols denote the elements of a set Γ, a set Δ, etc.
$T(\Gamma)$, $T(\Delta)$, etc.	an optimal subset of a given set Γ, Δ, etc., at some given review point.
$\tilde{\varphi}_\Gamma^n$, $n = 1, \ldots, N-1$	the lowest attainable expected time and money cost given that (1) review point n has been attained but $n+1$ has not, (2) the set Γ of approaches (that is, of current estimates) is available, (3) a looking cost is to be charged for each of the approaches in Γ that is pursued to $n+1$ and is subsequently charged whenever any approach is pursued one stage further.
φ_Γ^n, $n = 1, \ldots, N-1$	the lowest attainable expected time and money cost given that (1) review point n has been attained but $n+1$ has not, (2) the set Γ is available, (3) a looking cost will not be charged for approaches carried from n to $n+1$ but will be charged for each approach pursued from $n+1$ to $n+2$ and subsequently whenever an approach is pursued one stage further.
$\varphi_\Gamma^N = \tilde{\varphi}_\Gamma^N$	$\min_{\gamma \epsilon \Gamma} \gamma$
$\{a, b, \gamma \ldots\}$	the set of approaches shown within the braces.

$\varphi^n_{\Gamma a}$, $\tilde{\varphi}^n_{\Gamma a}$, $\varphi^n_{\Gamma abx}$, $\tilde{\varphi}^n_{\Gamma abx}$, φ^n_{aby}, $\tilde{\varphi}^n_{aby}$, $\varphi^n_{\{a,b,y\}}$, $\tilde{\varphi}^n_{\{a,b,y\}}$	the same as the definitions of φ^n_Γ, $\tilde{\varphi}^n_\Gamma$, for the set of approaches appearing as a subscript; Γab means the set Γ augmented by the elements a and b. When a term of the form aby appears as a subscript, it means the set $\{a,b,y\}$.
$\nu(\Gamma)$	the number of elements in Γ.
$\theta(q)$	the lowest attainable expected time and money cost if q approaches are drawn at random and pursued at a looking cost to review point 1; thereafter a looking cost is charged whenever an approach is pursued one stage further.
$\bar{\theta}(q)$	$\theta(q) - q$
$\bar{\bar{\theta}}(q)$	$\bar{\theta}(q) - N$

4.2. General Formulation

A developer who is developing a one component item that can be either satisfactory or unsatisfactory must obtain a satisfactory version of the item in a manner that minimizes the expected total time and money cost of development. Total time and money cost is measured by a function $C(m,t)$ of the kind discussed above.

Let the developer be confronted with a number of proposed approaches to the development of the required satisfactory item, where approach is defined in the same manner as before. For each approach there is a unique amount of time and a unique amount of money that would be required if that approach were followed until it yielded a satisfactory item.

Note that an approach, as we shall think of it in this section, does not allow substituting between time and money. Pursuing the same design, for example, but using two different streams of expenditures to do so constitutes, in our present definition, two different approaches. A later section relaxes the definition of approach, and we shall there specifically take into account the fact that the same design may be pursued with alternative degrees of intensity (or that the same group of people may be employed on a schedule further from, or nearer to, an around the clock schedule), and that the outcomes of these alternative efforts bear a special relation to each other.

For each approach the unique true values of the time and money required for completion are unknown to the developer. His initial beliefs concerning the alternative time and money combinations that might be observed for that approach are expressed in a personal probability distribution.

To formulate the general problem of choice among approaches when there are many review points, we go back to a state of knowledge prior to the state we described above in considering the no review point problem. We assume that at the outset the developer is faced with a large, perhaps infinite, collection of possible approaches to his task, and until he engages in some development at some cost in time and money, he finds all these approaches indistinguishable from one another. If we go back early enough in the history of any actual development task there is clearly an initial state of ignorance in which this is approximately true. It will be convenient, and it will not sacrifice generality, to take such an initial state as the starting point of our general problem.

From the many possible initially indistinguishable approaches, then, our developer considers a certain number, and his task will then be gradually to narrow down this number, weeding out the less promising approaches and exploring further the more promising ones. How many approaches he should initially consider will be part of the problem. In the real world consideration of a fixed number of initially indistinguishable approaches corresponds, for example, to the soliciting of design proposals from a number of prospective contractors or project engineers, or the selection of several teams of technical people, each told to formulate an approach to the task. Since development is the acquisition of knowledge, more and more is learned about the time and money needed to complete each approach as it is pursued. The developer is presented with the improved knowledge at each of a sequence of N review points. After the Nth review point further development work is required in order to complete the approach. In many kinds of development there are, in fact, natural stages when the developer takes stock of improved knowledge.

It is important to note that under our assumptions pursuit of an approach is the only way that knowledge can be acquired about it. The developer cannot learn more about the time and money required to complete an approach without in fact coming closer to completing it.

We shall assume, not unrealistically, that all the approaches have the same number of review points. Less realistically, we shall assume that the nth review point, $n = 1, \ldots, N$, occurs at the same point of time in each approach, and that at each review point every approach that is still being pursued must be either discarded forever or else pursued until the next review point. But at least one approach must be pursued to the next review point. The consequence of relaxing the assumption that a discarded approach is discarded forever, of permitting at each review point a sequential selection of the approaches to be pursued further, will be briefly explored somewhat later. Under the present assumption it follows in particular that when the Nth review point (the final one) has been reached, all the approaches that still remain must be discarded except one. That surviving approach will be carried to completion. Carrying two or more approaches beyond the Nth review point would be pointless since there is no further opportunity to stop and compare them and one completed approach is all that is needed.

To fix the ideas, the general problem may now be visualized in a way that gives the developer's personal probability distributions (which in any case have all the standard properties of probability distributions) a somewhat objective or relative frequency interpretation. We shall do so only for convenience and the use of such terms as "random drawing" should not obscure the personal nature of the probabilities and the non-repeated nature of the events to which probabilities are attached.

We can think of the developer, then, as making a random drawing of size q from an urn full of approaches. The number q is the number of initially indistinguishable approaches which he will gradually narrow down. Each approach can be thought of as a ticket on which $N + 1$ pairs of non-negative numbers are written. The pairs are denoted (m_1,t_1), (m_2,t_2), . . . , (m_n,t_n), . . . , (m_N,t_N), (m,t). In the last pair, (m,t), the symbol m will now denote the amount of money required to carry the approach in question from the Nth review point to completion (but not the money required to carry it through the N review points). The symbol t denotes the time required to carry that approach through all N review points and thence to completion. The numbers $m_1, \ldots, m_N$ and $t_1, \ldots, t_N$ comprise sequences of estimates of m and t, respectively. Each ticket (approach) is thus a value of the $(2N + 2)$-dimensional random variable $(m_1,t_1, \ldots ,m_N,t_N,m,t)$. This random variable has a probability distribution which we denote G. Leaving the "urn" interpretation for a moment, G is a personal probability distribution: it expresses the beliefs of the developer about the sequence of costs, for any of the indistinguishable approaches with which he begins.

The pairs of numbers on any ticket he draws are not visible to the developer; they are all covered with tapes. He can remove the tapes on any ticket, one at a time; but the tape covering the nth pair (m_n,t_n) can be removed only if all the preceding tapes have been removed. All tickets for which the developer decides to remove the nth tape must have this tape removed from them at the same time. (In terms of review points, the pairs (m_n,t_n) can be observed only at the

nth review point.) Each time he removes a tape he incurs a money cost of w dollars; we shall refer to this henceforth as the looking cost. Given the initial collection of q tickets, the developer removes the first tape on all of them.[10] Using the knowledge so obtained, he selects a subset of the tickets. For each ticket in this subset the second tape is removed (that is, that approach will be carried to the second review point); all the remaining tickets are discarded forever. Next (at the second review point) the developer looks at the pairs (m_1,t_1), (m_2,t_2) for the surviving tickets and selects a subset of these for which the third tape will be removed (a subset to be carried to the third review point). At the nth stage (review point) the developer looks at the pairs $(m_1,t_1), \ldots, (m_n,t_n)$ for the tickets not yet discarded and decides for which ones to remove the $(n+1)$st tape. Of the tickets still not discarded at the Nth stage (review point), for which the pairs $(m_1,t_1), \ldots, (m_N,t_N)$ are known, just one ticket is chosen as final survivor.

To complete his development task the developer spends an amount of money equal to the sum of two quantities. The first quantity, denoted m^*, is equal to w times the total number of tapes removed from all tickets. The second quantity is equal to the value of m underneath the final tape on the surviving ticket (the true money cost of carrying the surviving approach from the Nth review point and to completion). If C is the time and money cost function introduced earlier, he incurs a total time and money cost of $C(m + m^*,t)$ where t is the second member of the pair under the final tape of the surviving ticket (the true time required to carry the surviving approach through all N review points and thence to completion).

What the developer seeks, for a fixed q, is a policy, a complete set of instructions that tell him at any stage n, for any set of undiscarded tickets (approaches) with any histories $(m_1,t_1), \ldots, (m_n,t_n)$, exactly which ones to discard and which ones to pursue further. Given a policy, the number m^* and the m and t of the surviving approach become random variables whose probability distribution is implied by G, and so, therefore, does the number $C(m + m^*,t)$.

The general pure parallel approach problem is then to find, given a G and a looking cost w, (1) an optimal policy for any fixed initial number of approaches q, that is, a policy for which the expected value of $C(m + m^*,t)$ is not greater than for any other policy; and (2) an

[10] Under our assumption, leaving the first tape unremoved on one of the q tickets is equivalent to drawing a sample of only $q-1$. For since there will be no further opportunity to make use of that ticket (to remove any of its tapes) it might just as well be returned to the urn.

optimal value of the integer q—a number such that when an optimal policy is used no other q yields a lower expected value of $C(m+m^*,t)$. We call this the general N-stage pure parallel approach problem. The word "pure" is used since at least two serious complications can be introduced: the pursuit of different approaches with different intensities, and the sequential selection of approaches, initially and at each review point.

One observation that can immediately be made about the general pure problem is that for fixed q there is always an optimal policy.[11] This is true since for any collection of q tickets (approaches) there is a finite number of ways to proceed at each stage and hence at least one best way.

Other than this there is without doubt little to say about the general problem. The optimal policy can be characterized in several ways that are more compact than our verbal description.[12] But properties of an optimal policy that are interesting from a general economic point of view, or that provide guides to practical computation of an optimal policy, seem very likely to be absent until one further restricts the problem.

The problem can be restricted by (1) placing restrictions on the distributions G, (2) placing restrictions on the time and money cost function C, or (3) replacing the two-dimensional estimates (m_n,t_n) by one-dimensional estimates that are, so to speak, a contraction of the information contained in the two-dimensional estimates. We shall restrict the problem in all these ways, beginning with the third.

A natural contraction of the two-dimensional estimates to one-dimensional estimates consists in replacing each pair (m_n,t_n) by $C(m_n,t_n)$, the time and money cost for the approach in question if the estimates turn out to be correct. $C(m_n,t_n)$ denotes the time and money cost of development if the approach were the only one pursued and were pursued to completion at a money cost of m_n units incurred after the Nth review point (the first N review points being free of money cost), in a total development time (including the N review points) of t_n time units. Instead of obtaining an estimate of t and of m at each review point, the developer now obtains an estimate of $C(m,t)$, namely the number $C(m_n,t_n)$. It is clear that this contraction means a loss of information, by any reasonable definition of "amount of information." It may well be that for a particular collection of approaches

[11] At least if one makes the further assumption that all the conditional expectations implied by the distribution G are finite.

[12] For example, a functional equation, to be satisfied by expected time and money cost under an optimal policy, can, as in all multi-stage problems, be written down. Richard Bellman: *Dynamic Programming*, Princeton: Princeton University Press, 1957.

in the original problem two of them have, at the second review point, the histories (m_1,t_1), (m_2,t_2) and (m_1^*,t_1^*), (m_2^*,t_2^*), respectively, while in the contracted problems they have identical histories, since $C(m_1,t_1) = C(m_1^*,t_1^*)$ and $C(m_2,t_2) = C(m_2^*,t_2^*)$. In the original problem there is then a better basis for choosing between the two approaches than in the new problem and hence it may be that expected time and money cost under an optimal policy is less for the new problem than for the old one.

We shall nevertheless assume henceforth that the contraction has been made and shall let $c_1, \ldots, c_n, \ldots, c_N$ denote the sequence of non-negative one-dimensional estimates for an approach, where $c_n = C(m_n,t_n)$. We let c (equal to $C(m,t)$) denote the true time and money cost for the approach, which takes m money units and t time units to carry from start to finish, when achieving the N review points for the approach costs no money but carrying it beyond the Nth review point does.

An approach is then characterized by the $(N+1)$-dimensional random variable $(c_1, \ldots, c_N, c)$, which has a cumulative distribution function that we call F; F is implied by G. The numbers $c_1, \ldots, c_N$ may be thought of as the products of expert estimators of time and money cost who generate them as the approach is pursued. To obtain the nth estimate the estimators may first make estimates of m and t, and a developer familiar with their procedures and their experience would let the distribution G characterize his beliefs about these underlying estimates. But we assume, in our contracted problem, that the developer does *not* have such familiarity and does not know the underlying distribution G but only the contracted distribution F. Given this somewhat diminished knowledge the developer is to find an optimal policy.

A policy for the contracted problem has the same definition as before, except that the histories to which the developer is to respond when deciding, at the nth review point, which approaches to pursue further, now have the form $c_1, \ldots, c_n$. A true optimal policy for the contracted problem is one for which the expected value of $C(\tilde{m}^* + \hat{m}, \hat{t})$ is a minimum where $\tilde{m}^*$ is the total money spent on looking at all approaches, including the surviving one, at the N review points, $\hat{t}$ is the time required to carry the surviving approach through all N review points and thence to completion, and $\hat{m}$ is the money required to carry the surviving approach from the Nth review point to completion. But we shall now assume that the time and money cost function has the following property: There is a function $\tilde{C}$ defined for all pairs of non-negative real numbers x and y such that for any two values of x, say x' and x'', and any value of y

$$C(x' + x'',y) = \tilde{C}[C(x',y),x''].\tag{1}$$

It then follows [13] that total time and money cost in the contracted problem is given by

$$\tilde{C}(\hat{c},\tilde{m}^*) = C(\hat{\tilde{m}} + \tilde{m}^*,\hat{\tilde{t}}),\tag{2}$$

where $\hat{c} = C(\hat{\tilde{m}},\hat{\tilde{t}})$. Since $\hat{c}$ is the time and money cost of the surviving approach if it were to cost $\hat{\tilde{m}}$ money units after the Nth review point and take altogether $\hat{\tilde{t}}$ time units to complete ($\hat{c}$ is the number under the final tape of the surviving ticket in the contracted problem), calculation of the expected time and money cost for a given policy in the contracted problem, and determination of a true optimal policy for the contracted problem, require only knowledge of the distribution F, not of the underlying distribution G. An optimal policy achieves, for a given q, no higher an expected value of $\tilde{C}(\hat{c},\tilde{m}^*)$ than any other policy.

To make further progress with the contracted problem still more restrictions must be placed on the function C via restrictions on the function $\tilde{C}$. We shall make the strong but extremely conventional assumption that the sum of the looking costs can simply be added (if money is measured in the right units) to the value of $C(m,t)$ of the surviving approach in order to obtain total time and money cost. This means that we assume the function $\tilde{C}$ to be

$$\tilde{C}(x,y) = x + y.\tag{3}$$

According to (1), then, for any two values of M, M' and M'', and any t,

[13] The condition (1) is fulfilled by many reasonable functions C. One sufficient condition for its fulfillment is that indifference contours in the MT-space (lines along which C has a constant value) are vertical displacements of each other when plotted with M on the vertical axis. That is to say, given any two contours the vertical distance between their intersections with the vertical line $T = T^*$ is the same as the vertical distance between their intersections with the vertical line $T = T^{**}$ for any T^*, T^{**}. The situation is as in the diagram. Then we can define $\tilde{C}(x,y)$ (where $x > 0$, $y > 0$) to be the value of

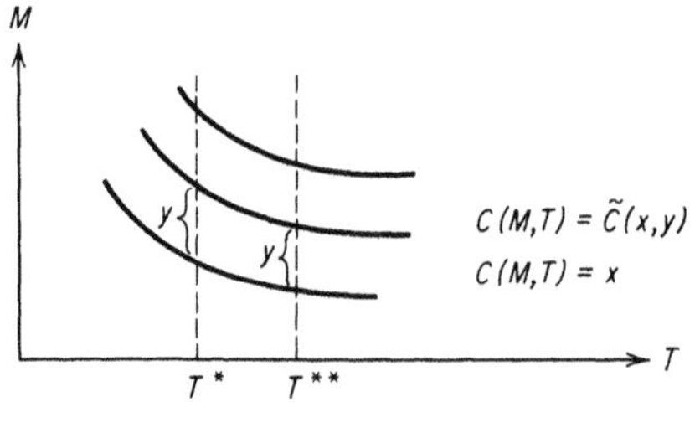

C along (that is, the index of) the contour obtained when we shift up by the distance y the contour $C(M,T) = x$. For this definition of the function $\tilde{C}$ it immediately follows that given any M', M'', T, $\tilde{C}[C(M',T),M''] = C(M' + M'',T)$. This definition of $\tilde{C}$ is illustrated in the diagram.

$$C(M' + M'', T) = C(M', T) + M'',$$

and in particular for the contracted problem

$$C(\hat{\tilde{m}} + \tilde{m}^*, \hat{t}) = C(\hat{\tilde{m}}, \hat{t}) + \tilde{m}^* = \hat{c} + \tilde{m}^*. \tag{4}$$

This is equivalent to assuming that for any fixed completion time T all the time and money cost functions correctly representing the developer's preferences among alternative pairs (M,T), where M is the total money cost of development, are linear in M. All functions C in other words have the form

$$C(M,T) = \delta M + h(T) \tag{5}$$

where δ is some non-negative constant and $h(T)$ is some non-decreasing function. Hence we can choose in particular a function for which δ, the slope with respect to M, is one; to make this choice is to choose the unit in which money is measured. Note that the function h is not required to be linear in T.

The equivalent of this strong additivity assumption has been widely made in analyzing situations wherein a decisionmaker has to decide, at each of a sequence of decision points, to take one of a set of actions or else to acquire more information (at a cost) about the prevailing state of the world, which will determine the consequence of any action. The cost of acquiring information (the looking costs, in our case) and the final consequence are both assumed to be expressible as amounts of some common commodity (for example, money); more of this commodity is preferred to less.

Then the decisionmaker's preferences among alternative actions (gambles) whose possible consequences are amounts of this commodity are given, as usual, by the expected utility of the actions, where the utility of a consequence is now assumed to be a linear function of the commodity amount defining that consequence. If and only if this utility is linear is it correct to say that the decisionmaker always prefers one procedure to another if the first yields a higher expected value of the following random variable: the amount of the commodity defining the final consequence less the cost of acquiring information, or, in other words, the *net* amount with which the decisionmaker is left after the final consequence. If less of the commodity is preferred to more, then the better procedure yields a lower expected value of this random variable.[14]

[14] Among notable recent work making the additivity assumption are Howard Raiffa and Robert Schlaifer: *Applied Statistical Decision Theory,* Boston: Division of Research, Harvard Business School, 1961, and previous work in sequential statistical inference. Without the assumption, the problems considered would be immensely more difficult to study, and it should be no surprise that we have to make the assumption as well.

In our case, when we assume that $C(M,T)$ has the form $M + h(T)$ we are in effect assuming (1) that the inconvenience to the developer of requiring T time units to complete his task is equivalent to the inconvenience to him of spending $h(T)$ money units, and (2) that a linear utility function of money correctly yields his preferences between actions (gambles) whose outcomes are amounts of money. But it is still possible for the non-linear term $h(T)$ to express the fact that as one lengthens the developer's completion time the inconvenience of the delay to him (as measured by the amount of money whose spending is equally inconvenient) increases but at a diminishing rate. This would mean, to be more precise, that he exhibits risk aversion with respect to completion time: he prefers, for example, the certainty of the pair

$$M, \frac{T_1 + T_2}{2}$$

to a one-half chance of (M,T_1) and a one-half chance of (M,T_2). With respect to money, however, the marginal inconvenience is constant and the developer is completely neutral with respect to risk; he pays attention only to expected amounts of money when he chooses between gambles. This is a strong but, as we have observed, a widely made assumption.

We have, then, reached the following restricted form of the original problem: (1) The function C has the form $M + h(T)$. (2) For each approach not yet discarded at the nth review point, an estimate, c_n, of $c = C(m,t)$ for that approach becomes available. (3) The $(N + 1)$-dimensional random variable $(c_1, \ldots, c_N, c)$ has a known distribution function F. (4) For a fixed number, q, of initially chosen and initially indistinguishable approaches one policy is better than another if it achieves a lower expected value of $\hat{c} + m^*$, where m^* equals the looking cost w times the number of times approaches are carried from one review point to the next, and $\hat{c}$ is the value of c for the surviving approach. (5) The problem is to determine an optimal policy given q and an optimal value of q.

It might appear that at each review point the developer obtains from the expert estimators who generate the successive estimates c_n merely a "point estimate" of the true c for each approach. It might appear that such a single number, rather than a whole distribution, describes the developer's beliefs as to where the true c lies for a given approach. This would be unsatisfactory if it were the case, but it is not the case. For the distribution F reflects the developer's beliefs about the way the successive estimates will unfold and the relation they will bear to the true c. In particular, F implies a conditional probability distribution for c following any review point n, that is, a distribution of c given the preceding history $c_1, \ldots, c_n$. Hence, when the developer accepts c_n as an estimate at the nth review point he is permitting the entire conditional distribution to express his beliefs about the true c for the approach in question. But we have so far said little about these conditional distributions and it is now time to discuss them.

4.3. Restricting the Distributions F: Improvement of Estimates in the Pursuit of an Approach

In our formulation of the problem as it now stands nothing is said about the way the successive estimates $c_1, \ldots, c_N$ relate to each other or to the true c for the approach in question. In particular nothing yet implies that the successive estimates become better estimates of c in some appropriate sense, nor that knowing the estimate c_n restricts the probability distribution of the next estimate, c_{n+1}, in some natural way. Both of these properties seem appropriate to require in our model of the learning that occurs as development is pursued. What simple restrictions on F imply them?

We shall argue that two restrictions suffice. We assume first that each is an unbiased estimate of the succeeding estimate in the following sense: [15]

$$E(c_n|c_{n-1}) = c_{n-1},\ n = 2, \ldots, N \quad \text{and} \quad E(c|c_N) = c_N. \tag{6}$$

We call this property the *one stage unbiasedness* property. Second, we assume that the distribution F has the *Markov property*. This means that the conditional distribution of the c_n given $c, \ldots, c_{n-1}$ is uniquely determined by the pair (c_{n-1}, n).[16]

Now note that these two properties together immediately imply the "martingale" property.

$$\begin{aligned} E(c_n|c_1, \ldots, c_{n-1}) &= c_{n-1},\ n = 1, \ldots, N \\ E(c|c_1, \ldots, c_N) &= c_N. \end{aligned} \tag{7}$$

This property means that to find the expected value of the next estimate, c_n, for a given approach we can ignore the entire history of that

[15] In the standard way, E denotes expectation and $E(x|y)$ means the conditional expected value of x given y. Our use of the word "unbiased" differs from the standard usage, but seems appropriate in this context.

[16] Then for two distinct review points, say n', n'', we may have $c_{n'} = c_{n''} = c^*$, while the conditional distribution of $c_{n'+1}$ given that $c_{n'} = c^*$ is quite different from the conditional distribution of $c_{n''+1}$ given that $c_{n''} = c^*$.

approach prior to the most recent estimate; the required expected value is equal to the most recent estimate. It is readily verified that the martingale property in turn implies two other properties: first, another very natural unbiasedness property which we shall call $(N-n)$-stage unbiasedness [17]

$$E(c \mid c_n) = c_n,\ n = 1, \ldots, N, \tag{8}$$

and secondly, the property

$$E(c \mid c_n, c_{n+1}) = c_{n+1},\ n = 1, \ldots, N-1 \tag{9}$$

Property (8) implies that all estimates have the same mean, namely $\bar{c}$, the mean of c, since $Ec = E[E(c|c_n)] = Ec_n$. Property (9) means that of any two successive estimates the earlier one is, in a sense, the less relevant—it can be ignored in forming the conditional expectation of u.

Now the property (9) implies quite by itself that the successive estimates improve in the sense that the squared errors diminish, on the average. That is

---

[17] The proof that the martingale property implies $(N-n)$-stage unbiasedness is as follows. First observe that for $1 \leqq s \leqq n$, $n = 1, \ldots, N+1$,

$$E(c_n|c_s, c_{s+1}, \ldots, c_{n-1}) = \int E(c_n|c_1, \ldots, c_{s-1}, c_s, \ldots, c_{n-1})dF^{1,\ldots,s-1}_{s,\ldots,n-1}$$

$$= \int c_{n-1}dF^{1,\ldots,s-1}_{s,\ldots,n-1} = c_{n-1},$$

where, in general, the symbol $F^{\alpha_1,\alpha_2,\ldots,\alpha_\ell}_{\beta_1,\beta_2,\ldots,\beta_m}$ denotes the conditional probability distribution of the random variable $(c_{\alpha_1}, c_{\alpha_2}, \ldots, c_{\alpha_\ell})$, given $c_{\beta_1}, \ldots, c_{\beta_m}$. We shall prove $(N-n)$-stage unbiasedness, or rather the more general proposition $E(c_{n+r}|c_n) = c_n$, by induction on r. The proposition is true for $r = 1$ (in which case it states our one-stage unbiasedness property) since

$$E(c_{n+1}|c_n) = \int E(c_{n+1}|c_1, \ldots, c_n)dF^{1,\ldots,n-1}_n$$

$$= \int c_n dF^{1,\ldots,n-1}_n = c_n.$$

Suppose the proposition is true for a given r. Then we have, using (10)

$$E(c_{n+r+1}|c_n) = \int E(c_{n+r+1}|c_n, \ldots, c_{n+r})dF^{n+1,\ldots,n+r}_n$$

$$= \int c_{n+r}dF^{n+1,\ldots,n+r}_n$$

$$= E(c_{n+r}|c_n),$$

which, by the induction hypothesis, equals c_n. This completes the proof.

$$E(c_n - c)^2 \geqq E(c_{n+1} - c)^2,\ n = 0, 1, \ldots, N-1. \tag{10}$$

Where c_0 denotes $Ec = \bar{c}$. This is, of course, by no means the only definition of "improvement" that can be proposed. It is nevertheless a reasonable one, and the fact that it is implied by (9) alone means that one could develop a reasonable parallel approach theory without assuming the Markov property; one could assume only (9) and successive estimates would still improve. To see that (9) quite by itself implies (11), write

$$\begin{aligned} E(C_{n+1} - c)^2 &= E[(c_{n+1} - c_n) - (c - c_n)]^2 \\ &= E(c_{n+1} - c_n)^2 - 2E\{E[(c_{n+1} - c_n)(c - c_n)] | c_{n+1}, c_n\} \\ &\quad + E(c - c_n)^2 \\ &= E(c_{n+1} - c_n)^2 - 2E\{(c_{n+1} - c_n)E[(c - c_n) | c_{n+1}, c_n]\} \\ &\quad + E(c - c_n)^2. \end{aligned} \tag{11}$$

Since (9) implies that $E[(c - c_n) | c_{n+1}, c_n] = c_{n+1} - c_n$ we are left with

$$E(c_n - c)^2 - E(c_{n+1} - c)^2 = E(c_{n+1} - c_n)^2 \tag{12}$$

which implies (11) since $E(c_{n+1} - c_n)^2 \geqq 0$. The inequality in (11) is a strict one, moreover, so long as the $(n+1)$st estimate does not equal the nth estimate with probability one.

We summarize the main points in the preceding discussion as

***Theorem 1*. The one stage unbiasedness property (6) and the Markov property imply $(N - n)$-stage unbiasedness (8) and the property $E(u | u_n, u_{n+1}) = u_{n+1}$. The latter property implies, all by itself, improvement of estimates in the sense of (10).**

We shall assume the two basic properties, the Markov and the one stage unbiasedness properties, in the discussion of the N-stage problem below.[18] Some of the results obtained there have their analogues without assuming the Markov property and others do not. Assuming it, at any rate, achieves a major simplification.

Three additional remarks now need to be made. Note first that, according to (12), given c_n the larger the dispersion of c_{n+1} about its mean the greater the gain in knowledge about c as one passes

[18] As it happens, the results of Chapter 4 of this book shed some empirical light on the realism of the $(N - n)$-stage unbiasedness assumption. Those results suggest that estimates may often be biased, but that the bias is sufficiently regular that revised estimates with low bias can be obtained from the original ones. Our assumptions, therefore, may not be unrealistic if we assume that the estimates under discussion are such revised ones.

from c_n to c_{n+1}. Intuitively this might at first seem paradoxical. But the paradox disappears, to put it very roughly, if one realizes that a large dispersion of c_{n+1} about its (conditional) mean means that given c_n it is hard to predict what c_{n+1} will be and what c will be. Therefore knowing what c_{n+1} is constitutes a large gain in information about the approach in question and about its true cost c.

Second, note that nothing in our assumptions prevents the decrease in the expected squared errors $E(c_n - c)^2$ from being different at different n. In particular, it may be that there is early learning—that as n increases the expected squared errors diminish very rapidly for small n but slowly for larger n. This corresponds, in our model, to an empirical conjecture that has been made about real development projects.[19]

Third, it is important to note that acquiring more information about the true c for a given collection of approaches, in the precise sense of replacing poor estimates of c by better ones, with a smaller expected squared error, does not necessarily make the developer better off. It may make him worse off. Consider the following one review point example. The only estimate obtainable for any approach is the initial estimate c_1, and the random variable (c_1,c) has in the first case the distribution F and in the second case the distribution F^*. Under F, (c_1,c) equals

$$(1,2) \text{ with probability } 1/10$$

$$(1,3/4) \text{ with probability } 2/5$$

$$(2,5/2) \text{ with probability } 2/5$$

$$(2,0) \text{ with probability } 1/10$$

Under F^*, (c_1,c) equals

$$(2,2) \text{ with probability } 1/10$$

$$(13/8,3/4) \text{ with probability } 2/5$$

$$(13/8,5/2) \text{ with probability } 2/5$$

$$(0,0) \text{ with probability } 1/10$$

For both distributions one-stage unbiasedness and the Markov property are satisfied. The (marginal) distribution of c is the same for

[19] Burton H. Klein: The Decision Making Problem in Development, in R. R. Nelson, ed., *The Rate and Direction of Inventive Activity: Economic and Social Factors*, Princeton: Princeton University Press, 1962, pp. 477–497.

both distributions. But $E(c_1 - c)^2$ equals 5/8 for F and 49/80 for F^*. (According to (8) this also implies that $E(c_1 - \bar{c})^2 = E(\bar{c} - c)^2 - E(c_1 - c)^2$ is larger for F^* than for F: under F^* more has been learned when c_1 becomes known than under F.) For either distribution the developer picks the surviving approach once he knows the estimates c_1. Since $E(c|c_1) = c$, the optimal surviving approach will clearly be one for which c_1 is not larger than for any other approach. Suppose that the estimate c_1 is available for two approaches (that is, q, the number of initially indistinguishable approaches selected at random, is chosen to be equal to two). Then the developer's expected total time and money cost is equal to $2w$ (the sum of the looking costs for the two estimates) plus the expected value of the minimum of two independent random drawings from the c_1-population.

The expected value of this minimum for the distribution F is $(2)(1/2)^2 + (1)(3/4) = 1.25$ and for F^* it is

$$(2)(1/100) + (13/8)[(8/10)(8/10) + (2)(8/10)(1/10)] + 0 = 1.32.$$

So for $q = 2$, the distribution with the lower expected squared error of the estimate c_1 yet has a worse (higher) value of expected total time and money cost under an optimal policy. Since the results of the next sections imply that there is some looking cost w for which two is in fact the best value of q under either distribution, we obtain, finally, that there exists a w such that the developer is better off with a distribution involving a larger expected squared error for the estimate c_1.

This example implies the following about the general N-stage problem: There exist distributions F and F^* of the random variable $(c_1, \ldots, c_N, c)$ fulfilling one-stage unbiasedness and the Markov Property such that (1) for some n, say n', $E(c - c_n)^2$ is greater for F than for F^*; (2) with respect to all other n the distributions are identical, that is, $\tilde{F}(c_1, \ldots, c_{n'-1}, c_{n'+1}, \ldots, c_N, c) = \tilde{F}^*(c_1, \ldots, c_{n'-1}, c_{n'+1}, \ldots, c_N, c)$, where $\tilde{F}$, $\tilde{F}^*$ denote the marginal distribution of F and F^*, respectively, with respect to the random variable $(c_1, \ldots, c_{n'-1}, c_{n'+1}, \ldots, c_N, c)$; (3) the total expected time and money cost under an optimal policy for an optimal q is less under F than under F^*.

What is displayed here is a common limitation of all convenient and appealing measures of the amount of information that a decisionmaker has. For any such measure it is not the case that more information is always good. Whether an increase in information according to the measure increases the decisionmaker's maximum attainable expected utility depends on the decisionmaker's utility function (which expresses his preferences among outcomes) and on his probability distribution over states of the world. It appears to be the case that for any measure of amount of information[20] one can find some utility function, some probability distribution, and two states of the decision-maker's knowledge (about the true state of the world) such that he is better off in the state containing less information, according to that measure. In the parallel approach problem the utility function (the negative of the time and money cost function) is sufficiently complex and has a sufficiently remote relation to the expected squared error measure of information that it should come as no surprise to find, even in the one stage problem, that "more information" can make the decisionmaker worse off.

One can find examples to show that the same is true for other appealing measures of the change in information as one goes from one distribution of estimates of the true c to another. Such alternative measures include the change in entropy—that is, in the case when c takes only a finite number of values, the difference $\Sigma p(c|c^*) \log p(c|c^*) - \Sigma p(c|c^{**}) \log p(c|c^{**})$, where the c^*s are estimates having one distribution, the c^{**}s are estimates having another, and $p(c|c^{**})$, $p(c|c^*)$ are conditional probabilities. Alternative measures also include the change in the expected range of the true c in problems where an upper as well as a lower bound to c exists—that is, the difference

$$E(c_c^{u*} - c_c^{l*}) - E(c_c^{u**} - c_c^{l**}),$$

where c_c^{u*}, c_c^{l*} denote the highest and lowest possible values of c given that c^* has been observed and c_c^{u*}, c_c^{l**} denote the same given that c^{**} has been observed; the expectations are taken over all c^* and all c^{**}, respectively.

Granting this general limitation of all such simple measures of amount of information, it is still reasonable to require of our formulation of the parallel approach problem that it express improvement of estimates with respect to some simple measure. And this, as we have seen, our formulation rather conveniently achieves.

4.4. *The One Review Point (One Stage) Problem*

We now examine the one review point or one stage version of the problem we have formulated. Although the analysis is close to trivial, the one stage version already suffices to test certain intuitively reasonable conjectures about properties of the good conduct of development, or, more precisely, properties of an optimal policy in the gen-

[20] More accurately, any measure that completely orders states of knowledge about the true state of the world with respect to amount of information, when the number of possible states of knowledge is not trivially small (in a sense that can be made precise for specific decision problems).

eral parallel approach problem. The one stage version also exhibits one striking property whose possible generalization to the N-stage version we shall later study.

To study both the one stage problem and the general N-stage problem we shall need a basic result which we denote, for convenience, the Fundamental Lemma.

Fundamental Lemma. Let there be given n random variables. The ith, $i = 1, \ldots, n$, has a probability distribution $F_i(x)$ such that $F_i(x) = 0$ for $x \leqq 0$, and such that the mean, Ex_i, is finite. Denote by z the minimum of a random sample of n independent observations, where the ith observation in the sample comes from the ith population, $i = 1, \ldots, n$. Then

$$Ez = \int_0^\infty \prod_{i=1}^n [1 - F_i(t)]dt.$$

Proof: For any random variable x and any probability distribution G satisfying the conditions on the F_i, it is well known that [21]

$$Ex = \int_0^\infty [1 - G(x)]dx.$$

Now if z has the probability distribution $F(z)$ then

$$\begin{aligned} F(z^*) &= Pr(z \leqq z^*) = 1 - Pr(z \geqq z^*) \\ &= 1 - [1 - F_1(z^*)][1 - F_2(z^*)] \cdots [1 - F_n(z^*)]. \end{aligned}$$

Hence $$Ez = \int_0^\infty [1 - F_1(z)] \cdots [1 - F_n(z)]dz.$$

Now in the one stage case the developer has drawn q approaches, each characterized by the numbers (c_1,c) where $E(c|c_1) = c_1$. As we noted above, the surviving approach is to be chosen at the first and

[21] If G is continuous, with $G(x) = \int_0^x g(t)dt$, then a proof is as follows:

$$\begin{aligned} \int_0^\infty [1 - G(x)]dx &= \int_0^\infty \left[\int_x^\infty g(y)dy\right] dx \\ &= \int_0^\infty \left[\int_0^y g(y)dx\right] dy \\ &= \int_0^\infty \left[\int_0^y dx\right] g(y)dy \\ &= \int_0^\infty yg(y)dy = Ey. \end{aligned}$$

For G not continuous a reformulated version of this argument holds.

only review point. At this point the estimates c_1 are available for all q approaches and the optimal survivor is one for which c_1 is not larger than for any of the other q approaches. The developer's expected total time and money cost is then qw plus the conditional expected value of c given that c_1 equals the minimum of a random drawing of q from the c_1 population. But by one stage unbiasedness this equals qw plus the expected value of this minimum itself. Hence by the Fundamental Lemma, optimal expected time and money cost [22] for a given q is

$$qw + \int_0^\infty [1 - F_1(t)]^q \, dt,$$

where F_1 denotes the distribution of c_1.

Observe next that the expected value of the minimum of q independent drawings from the same population declines as q declines but at a decreasing rate. That is, for any integer $q > 0$ and any distribution G whatever, with finite mean and $G(t) = 0$ for $t < 0$,

$$\int_0^\infty [1 - G(t)]^q \, dt - \int_0^\infty [1 - G(t)]^{q+1}$$
$$- \left\{ \int_0^\infty [1 - G(t)]^{q+1} \, dt - \int_0^\infty [1 - G(t)]^{q+2} \, dt \right\}$$
$$= \int_0^\infty [1 - G(t)]^q [G(t)]^2 \, dt > 0.$$

This immediately implies that for any looking cost w there is in the one stage problem a unique optimal value of q. If q is less than this value then increasing q by one decreases $\int_0^\infty [1 - F_1(t)]^q \, dt$ by more than w. But increasing q beyond its optimal value decreases $\int_0^\infty [1 - F_1(t)]^q \, dt$ by less than w. Once the unique optimal number of initially indistinguishable approaches is reached it is not worthwhile to add more; until it is reached it is worthwhile. It follows also that for each q there is some looking cost w^* such that for all $w \leqq w^*$, q is the optimal number of approaches to pursue to the first review point.

Determination of the optimal q, which we denote $\hat{q}$, completely solves the one stage problem. It only remains to see if there are interesting simple relationships between $\hat{q}$ or the optimal expected time and money cost and certain parameters of the distribution F.

---

[22] We shall use the term "optimal expected time and money cost" to denote expected total time and money cost under an optimal policy.

One important question is this: how does the optimal number of approaches pursued change as the average amount learned in any one approach increases—as, very roughly, the productivity of the available approaches increase?

Ordinary economic intuition suggests that $\hat{q}$ would increase, at least as long as Ec did not much change. For in a profit maximizing firm producing, say, a single output with a single factor of production (whose price is given to the firm), a technological change that increases the output of a single unit of the factor would also increase the output of n units of the factor. Hence the previously optimal level of output (and the previous amount of the factor used) would no longer be optimal, and more of the factor of production would now be used than before. In our case $-qw - \int_0^\infty [1 - F_1(t)]^q \, dt$ corresponds roughly to profit, $-\int_0^\infty [1 - F_1(t)]^q \, dt$ to output, and approaches are the factor of production, their price remaining always w. Intuition might suggest that increasing the amount learned in a single approach corresponds to a technological improvement that raises the output of one or of n units of this factor of production. If we regard $E(c_1 - \bar{c})^2 = E(\bar{c} - c)^2 - E(c_1 - c)^2$ to be a reasonable measure of average amount learned in attaining the first review point, we might not hesitate to recommend to the developer the following:

Rule of Thumb. If, when you turn from one development task to another, $\bar{c}$ (the initial information about the true costs of the available approaches, as well as the mean of these costs) remains roughly the same, while $E(c_1 - \bar{c})^2$ (the average amount learned from an approach) increases, then do not decrease the number of approaches you pursue. If the looking cost w is sufficiently small, you should increase the number of approaches you pursue.

Would he be right in recommending this rule? The answer is: without further knowledge of the distributions, *no.* The same illustration we used above to show that decreasing the expected squared error of estimates may be bad also shows the general invalidity of this rule of thumb. For both F and F^*, $Ec = 3/2$. As we saw, more is learned, in the sense of the rule of thumb, in attaining the first review point under F^* than under F. Expected total time and money cost when $q = 1$ is $w + 3/2$ for both distributions. When $q = 2$ it is $2w + 1.25$ for F and $2w + 1.32$ for F^*, a drop of $.25 - w$ for F and $.18 - w$ for F^*. Thus if w equals .2, for example, at least two approaches should be pursued to the first review point under F, but under F^*, where more is learned, not more than one should be pursued. Moreover, any looking cost w sufficiently small to justify two or more approaches under F^* justifies at least as many under F.

As suggested earlier, we could let amount learned be measured in alternative ways: average change in conditional entropy (a measure of the change in uncertainty about c as one passes from no knowledge of an approach to knowledge of c_1); or change in the expected range of c. We can then again construct illustrations violating the rule of thumb, as revised to incorporate one of these new measures of amount learned.

We have here our first illustration of an important task of normative theory: to check on intuitively plausible rules by making precise the terms used in the rules (terms such as "amount learned"), and determining general conditions under which the precisely stated rules are good ones.

To complete the task in the present case we ought briefly to investigate conditions under which one (or both) of the proposed rules of thumb is correct. One condition [23] under which the rule is correct is this: c_1 is always some linear transform $rz + s$ of a random variable z whose mean is zero and whose variance is 1. More precisely there exists a distribution (a cumulative density function) $G(z)$ with mean 0 and variance 1 such that for the distribution $F_1(x)$, according to which c_1 is distributed, there exist numbers $r \geqq 0$, $s \geqq 0$ such that for any x, $F(x) = G[(z - s)/r]$. Our requirement that $F_1(x) = 0$ for $x \leqq 0$ imposes the further condition that $G(z) = 0$ for $z \leqq -s/r$.

Under these conditions, $Ec_1 = s$ and $E(c_1 - Ec_1)^2 = E(r^2z^2 + 2rsz + s^2 - s^2) = r^2$. But it can also be easily shown that $Ex_n = rEz_n + s$ where x_n, z_n denote, respectively, the minimum of a sample of size n from the x-population and the z-population. Hence the expected value of the total time and money cost to completion when q approaches are pursued is $qw + rEz_q + s$. Since $Ez = 0$, clearly $Ez_q < 0$. For a fixed q and fixed $Ec_1 = s$, therefore, $qw + rEz_q + s$ decreases, and for small enough w the optimal q increases if and only if $E(c_1 - Ec_1)^2 = r^2$ increases. The rule of thumb holds.

The suggested condition on the probability distribution of c_1 is sufficiently lenient to allow a large variety of shapes for the distribution, since the class of distributions having mean 0 and variance 1 displays great variety. For example, the density function of c_1, although meeting the above condition, can have one mode, two modes,

[23] First noted by R. Nelson in Uncertainty, Learning, and the Economics of Parallel R&D Efforts, *Review of Economics and Statistics,* Vol. XLIII (November 1961), pp. 351–364.

symmetry, asymmetry, positive slope, negative slope, and so on. Nevertheless the condition is a special one, which the developer probably has no *a priori* inclination to agree to.

Yet, if he accepts the other assumptions of the one review point problem (and we conjecture that in many cases he would) he must accept the condition (or some equally special one) and the definition of "amount learned" (or some equally convenient and reasonable one) if his rule of thumb is to be generally valid. It is the contribution of models and analyses like the above to show the developer the hidden conditions under which certain cherished, reasonable, and useful rules of thumb are valid and those under which they are not; and so to encourage the developer to probe his own beliefs about alternative sets of conditions, abandoning the rule of thumb if that is, for him, the most honest answer.

4.5. The N-Stage Problem [24]

We shall examine several further rules of thumb that have meaning only for problems of more than one stage. But first we shall establish useful properties of the optimal policy for the N-stage problem as we have thus far restricted it and under several further restrictions. Our restrictions so far were given in the summary at the end of Section 4.4 and in the two assumed properties, the one stage unbiasedness property (6) and the Markov property.

4.5.1. A Very General Result. We note first one easily obtained result that holds even without our assuming these two properties. We state it as

***Theorem 2*. Given at stage n, $n = 1, \ldots, N$, any collection of approaches, with any history of preceding estimates, the lowest attainable expected total time and money cost is a continuous and strictly increasing function of the looking cost w.**

Proof: That optimal expected time and money cost is strictly increasing in w is obvious: for all possible succeeding histories of the approaches that remain at stage n, exactly the same responses are available to the developer after an increase in w as before, but each response costs strictly more with respect to looking and yields the same expected time and money cost for the surviving approach.

---

[24] The proofs of Theorems 2 and 5 of this section, and the counter example under "Diminishing Returns and Stronger Properties" below, are largely due to J. A. Yahav. A compact discussion of the results of this section, in a somewhat more general setting, appears in a joint paper by Thomas Marschak and J. A. Yahav: The Sequential Selection of Approaches to a Task, *Management Science*, May 1966.

To show continuity, compare two values of the looking cost, say w and $w + \epsilon$ ($\epsilon > 0$). Now consider (1) $\varphi(w)$, which denotes the optimal expected time and money cost when w is the looking cost: a best subset of the approaches available at n is chosen—call this subset ψ—and best subsets are also chosen at all subsequent review points. Now if $w + \epsilon$ is the looking cost, then it is possible (though not generally optimal) to pursue the same subset ψ from review point n to $n + 1$ and to narrow down the approaches pursued thereafter in exactly the same way as an optimal policy does when w is the looking cost. The expected time and money cost achieved in this way is not greater than $\varphi(w) + \epsilon(N - n)\nu(\psi)$, where $\nu(\psi)$ denotes the number of approaches in ψ.

We have, therefore,

$$\varphi(w) \leqq \varphi(w + \epsilon) \leqq \varphi(w) + \epsilon(N - n)\nu(\psi).$$

By taking ϵ suitably small, $\varphi(w + \epsilon) - \varphi(w)$ can be made arbitrarily close to zero. This establishes continuity from the right, and a symmetric argument [25] establishes continuity from the left.

The property of continuity with respect to looking cost is of interest in itself and is important for several extensions of the parallel approach problem as we have defined it. Suppose, in particular, one wants to allow for the possibility that pursuing more expensive approaches (spending more in looking, which also means spending more on development itself, prior to the last review point) yields a better final item. A completed approach, for example, not only yields, at a certain time and money cost, an item that is satisfactory with respect to the performance magnitudes defining the original task but yields a satisfactory item of a certain grade in terms of some other magnitude. This grade is to be balanced against the total time and money cost in assessing the completed program. If the balancing just consists in subtracting the time and money cost from the grade (when measured in suitable units) then the developer wants an optimal policy (in our previous sense) for each w and an optimal choice of w—a value of w such that the grade corresponding to that w minus the optimal expected time and money cost for that w is a maximum with respect to w. For the making of this calculation, and also

[25] The symmetric argument proves continuity from the left by establishing the inequality

$$\varphi(w - \epsilon) < \varphi(w) < \varphi(w - \epsilon) + \epsilon(N - n)\nu(\psi^*)$$

where ψ^* is a subset of the approaches available at n which is an optimal subset for the looking cost $w - \epsilon$. A stronger property than continuity is in fact proved: $\varphi(w)$ satisfies a Lipschitz condition at all w. But φ is not differentiable with respect to w.

for the economically interesting uniqueness of an optimal w, a first condition is that expected time and money cost as a function of w does not jump at any value of w.

Another context in which varying the looking cost is important is closely related to the complication to be discussed below. We may permit increasing the looking cost to buy a more nearly completed item at stage N. Following stage N, that is to say, the more intensive (costly) has been each look prior to stage N, the less the time and money required to complete the development task. For appropriate assumptions about the manner in which increasing w shifts the probability distribution of the true time and money cost c, the continuity property is again crucial.

From this point on, changes in the looking cost w will play no further role in the analysis. There will be no loss in generality if we simply take the unit in terms of which money is measured to be the cost of looking. Except when an explicit statement to the contrary is made, the looking cost is henceforth assumed to be one.

4.5.2. Notation. We now introduce some notation appropriate to our assumption that the one stage unbiasedness property and the Markov property hold. We shall let capital Greek letters, Γ, Δ, and so on, denote *sets* of approaches; lower-case Greek or Latin letters will be used to denote single approaches (elements). Also, a symbol such as Γa, Δxy, will denote the set composed of a set (Γ or Δ) augmented by the indicated elements (a or x and y). A symbol such as $\{a\}$, $\{x,y\}$, $\{\gamma_1,\gamma_2, \ldots ,\gamma_n\}$ denotes the set composed of the elements within the braces. The symbol $\nu(\Gamma)$ denotes the number of elements in the set Γ.

Under the Markov assumption all the relevant information about an approach at review point n is given by the current estimate c_n. Hence at stage n a set Γ of approaches is completely identified, for the purposes of subsequent decisions, by the current estimates for the approaches in Γ. We can therefore speak interchangeably of the approaches contained in Γ and the current estimates contained in Γ. Moreover, having the set Γ at review point n, with $N-n$ review points remaining, can just as well be thought of as having attained the first review point in an $(N-n)$ stage problem, with Γ comprising the set of first estimates.

The symbol $\tilde{\varphi}^n_\Gamma$, $n = 1, \ldots, N-1$, will mean the expected total time and money cost given that (1) review point n has been attained but review point $n+1$ has not, (2) the set Γ of the nth estimates is known, (3) a charge for looking will be made henceforth (none having yet been made), and (4) an optimal policy is to be applied henceforth (its first application will be the selection of an optimal subset of the approaches in Γ to be pursued to review point $n+1$). The symbol $T(\Gamma)$ will denote an optimal subset of the approaches (current estimates) in Γ given that some review point n has been attained; the number n will be clear from the context in which the symbol is used.

The symbol φ_Γ^n, $n = 1, \ldots, N-1$ will denote the expected total time and money cost given that (1) review point n has been attained but review point $n+1$ has not, (2) the entire set Γ of approaches with known n^{th} estimates is to be pursued to review point $n+1$, (3) a looking cost is to be charged beginning at review point $n+1$ (that is, there is no charge for carrying Γ from n to $n+1$) and (4) an optimal policy is to be applied starting at review point $n+1$ (its first application will be selection of an optimal subset of the set of $\nu(\Gamma)$ approaches whose $(n+1)$st elements are available, this subset to be carried to review point $n+2$).

Thus we have

$$\tilde{\varphi}_\Gamma^n = \varphi_{T(\Gamma)}^n + \nu[T(\Gamma)],\ n = 1, \ldots, N-1 \tag{13}$$

where $T(\Gamma)$ is an optimal subset of Γ, that is, $\varphi_{T(\Gamma)}^n + \nu[T(\Gamma)] \leqq \varphi_\Delta^n + \nu(\Delta)$ for all sets $\Delta \subseteq \Gamma$. We also have

$$\varphi_\Gamma^n = E\tilde{\varphi}_{\Gamma^*}^{n+1},\ n = 1, \ldots, N-1 \tag{14}$$

where Γ^* is a random variable, namely the set of $(n+1)$st estimates for the approaches whose n^{th} estimates comprise Γ.

Symbols such as $\varphi_{\Gamma a}^n$, $\tilde{\varphi}_{\Gamma a}^n$, $\varphi_{\Gamma ab}^n$, $\varphi_{\Delta xy}^n$, φ_{abx}^n, $\varphi_{\{a,b,x\}}^n$, have the meanings just given for the sets given as subscripts. We shall also let $F_{\gamma n}$, $n = 1, \ldots, N$ denote the conditional distribution of the estimate c_{n+1} given that the estimate γ is observed at review point n ($F_{\gamma N}$ if the distribution of c given that $c_N = \gamma$).

If an optimal policy is used, if $\Gamma_1, \ldots, \Gamma_N$ is the sequence of estimate sets obtained in applying it, and if Γ_1 is a random drawing of q from the population of initial estimates c_1, then optimal expected total time and money cost is given by

$$\theta(q) = \left[E \sum_{n=1}^{N} \nu(\Gamma_n) + \min_{\gamma \epsilon \Gamma_N} E(c \mid c_N = \gamma)\right],$$

which, because of one stage unbiasedness, equals

$$E\left[\sum_{n=1}^{N} \nu(\Gamma_n) + \min_{\gamma \epsilon \Gamma_n} \gamma\right].$$

We then also have for any N-stage problem, including the case $n = 1$,

$$\theta(q) = E[q + \tilde{\varphi}^1_{\Gamma_1}]$$

where we may define, for the sake of completeness, $\tilde{\varphi}^N_\Gamma = \varphi^N_\Gamma = \min_{\gamma \in \Gamma}$. We are first interested in optimal policies given the size q of the initial set. An initial looking cost of q is incurred before the optimal policy is applied (the first application is the choice of an optimal subset $T(\Gamma_1)$ to be pursued to the second review point at a looking cost of $\nu[T(\Gamma_1)]$).

4.5.3. The Ordering Property. We are now in a position to ask the first obvious question about an optimal policy: is it always true that low estimates are good, that is, if it is optimal to pursue a collection of r approaches, out of a large set, from one review point to the next, must they always be the lowest ranking approaches (estimates)? The answer, possibly surprisingly, is *not in general.* There is no general validity to another appealing rule of thumb: "If one stage unbiasedness and the Markov assumption are satisfied a set of approaches can always be improved or at least never damaged by substituting an approach with a lower current estimate for an approach with a higher one." Consider the following simple counter example.

There is one review point remaining and the available approaches are of two kinds: some have the current estimate $c_{N-1} = 48$ and some the current estimate $c_{N-1} = 50$. The conditional probability distribution of c_N given that $c_{N-1} = 48$ is

$$c_N = \begin{cases} 47 \text{ with probability } 1/3 \\ 48 \text{ with probability } 1/3 \\ 49 \text{ with probability } 1/3 \end{cases} \tag{15}$$

The conditional probability distribution of c_N given that $c_{N-1} = 50$ is

$$c_N = \begin{cases} 100 \text{ with probability } 1/3 \\ 50 \text{ with probability } 1/3 \\ 0 \text{ with probability } 1/3 \end{cases} \tag{16}$$

Now compare two pairs of approaches to be pursued to the Nth review point, when the survivor is to be chosen: the pair {48,48} and the pair {50,50}. The survivor is the approach whose estimate c_N is the smaller. If the pair {48,48} is chosen then the expected value of the survivor's c_N and true cost c is $47\frac{5}{9}$. But if the pair {50,50} is chosen the expected value of the survivor's c_N and true cost c is $27\frac{7}{9}$. Thus the pair of approaches with worse current estimates is the better pair.

If lowness of current estimates does not provide a reliable guide for choice among approaches, there would seem to be little hope for a simple optimal policy having simple properties. We now consider a restriction on the distribution F which is a sufficient condition for the exclusion of examples such as those just shown. It is a sufficient condition, that is to say, for what we shall call the ordering property.

The ordering property is that for any stage Γ, any stage n, and any two approaches with current estimates δ, δ^* such that $\delta^* < \delta$ (δ^* is "better" than δ), $\tilde{\varphi}^n_{\Gamma\delta^*} \leqq \tilde{\varphi}^n_{\Gamma\delta}$ and $\varphi^n_{\Gamma\delta^*} \leqq \varphi^n_{\Gamma\delta}$ (the set $\Gamma\delta^*$ is not worse than the set $\Gamma\delta$). The restriction that implies the ordering property will also play a crucial role in our subsequent results. We first need a definition.

Definition. A set M of probability distributions $F(t)$ is a *monotonic set* if

1) Each has a finite mean.
2) If $F(t)$ is in M, $F(t) = 0$ for $t < 0$.
3) If $F(t)$ and $G(t)$ are in m and if $F(t)$ has a mean not higher than $G(t)$, then $F(t) \geqq G(t)$ for all t.

Note that any subset of a monotonic set is a monotonic set and that no two distinct distributions in a monotonic set have the same mean. An example of a monotonic set is provided by any distribution $G(t)$ (with $G(t) = 0$ for $t < 0$) in which the mean is simply a location parameter. Allowing the mean to shift to the right preserves the shape of the distribution and decreases the mass (probability) to the left of any fixed t. Shifting to the right then generates a monotonic set, namely a family of distributions $G_\mu(t)$ (the subscript denotes the mean) such that if $\mu^{**} > \mu^*$, $G_{\mu^*}(t) = G_{\mu^{**}}[t - (\mu^{**} - \mu^*)]$.

The family of triangular distributions, of which three (with means μ^*, μ^{**}, μ^{***}) are shown in the figure, are a monotonic set of this

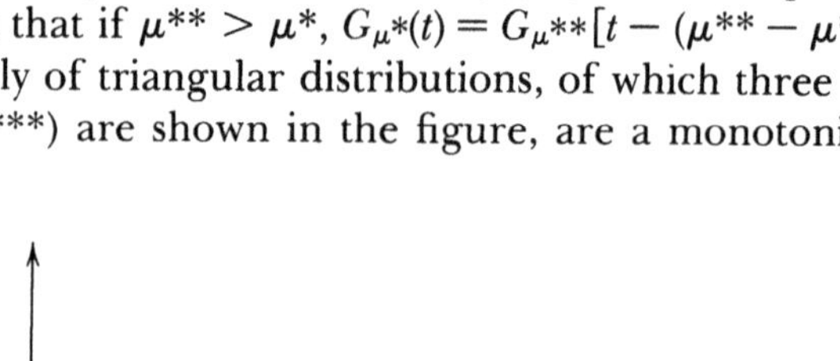

kind; so are the set of all exponential distributions, the set of all rectangular distributions with a common lower bound, and a great many others. Monotonic sets of discrete distributions are also easily constructed. If we assume that the conditional distributions $F_{n\gamma}$—the distributions of the estimate c_n given that $c_{n-1} = \gamma$—form a monotonic set we are still permitting them, and the distribution F, a great deal of variety.

We can now prove the following theorem.

Theorem 3. **Let the distribution F define an N-stage parallel approach problem. Let F have the Markov property and the one stage unbiasedness property (6). In addition let F be such that for any n, $n = 1, \ldots, N-1$, the set of all conditional distributions $F_{\gamma n}(t)$ is monotonic. At some stage n let Γ be a set of approaches for which n^{th} estimates are available and consider the two sets $\Gamma\delta$ and $\Gamma\delta^*$, where $\delta^* < \delta$. Then**

$$\tilde{\varphi}^n_{\Gamma\delta^*} \leqq \tilde{\varphi}^n_{\Gamma\delta} \tag{17}$$

and

$$\varphi^n_{\Gamma\delta^*} \leqq \varphi^n_{\Gamma\delta}. \tag{18}$$

Proof: The proposition "$\delta^* < \delta$ implies (18) for any set Γ" is certainly true for $n = N-1$. For it follows from the Fundamental Lemma and from the monotonicity assumption that

$$\begin{aligned}\varphi^{N-1}_{\Gamma\delta^*} &= \int_0^\infty \left\{\prod_{\gamma\epsilon\Gamma}[1 - F_{\gamma N}(t)]\right\}[1 - F_{\delta^* N}(t)]dt \\ &\leqq \int_0^\infty \left\{\prod_{\gamma\epsilon\Gamma}[1 - F_{\gamma N}(t)]\right\}[1 - F_{\delta N}(t)]dt = \varphi^{N-1}_{\Gamma\delta}.\end{aligned}$$

Now suppose the proposition "$\delta^* < \delta$ implies (18) for any set Γ" is true for some n. We shall first show (Step I) that the proposition "$\delta^* < \delta$ implies (17) for any set Γ" is then also true for n. This will next be shown (Step II) to imply that "$\delta^* < \delta$ implies (18) for any set Γ" is true for $n-1$. We will then have established by induction that $\delta^* < \delta$ implies both (17) and (18) for all n and for any set Γ.

Step I. The following two cases are possible:

(i) There exists an optimal subset of $\Gamma\delta$ containing δ, say the subset $\hat{\Gamma}\delta$. Then, applying (18), the subset $\hat{\Gamma}\delta^*$ of $\Gamma\delta^*$ is at least as good as $\hat{\Gamma}\delta$ (yields at least as low an expected total time and money cost) even when we now add the cost of looking incurred in stage n. We have

$$\tilde{\varphi}^n_{\Gamma\delta} = \varphi^n_{\hat{\Gamma}\delta} + \nu(\Gamma) + 1 \geqq \varphi^n_{\hat{\Gamma}\delta^*} + \nu(\Gamma) + 1 \geqq \tilde{\varphi}^n_{\hat{\Gamma}\delta^*}$$

and "$\delta^* < \delta$ implies (17)" is true for n.

(ii) There exists an optimal subset of $\Gamma\delta$ not containing δ, say the subset $\Gamma^{\#}$. But $\Gamma^{\#}$ is also a subset of $\Gamma\delta^*$, so that

$$\tilde{\varphi}^n_{\Gamma\delta} = \varphi^n_{\Gamma^{\#}} + \nu(\Gamma^{\#}) \geqq \tilde{\varphi}^n_{\Gamma\delta^*}.$$

Again, "$\delta^* < \delta$ implies (17)" is true for n.

Step II. We need the following lemma:

Let $G(t)$, $H(t)$ form a monotonic set and let $E_G t < E_H t$, where E_G, E_H denote expectation under the distributions G and H, respectively. Let $m(t)$ be a function of T such that $E_G m(t)$, $E_H m(t)$ are finite and $t^* > t^{**}$ implies $m(t^*) \geqq m(t^{**})$. Then

$$E_G m(t) \leqq E_H m(t).$$

To prove this, let $G^*(m^*)$ denote $P_G[m(s) \leqq m^*] = P_G(s \epsilon S)$, where S is the set $\{s | m(s) \leqq m^*\}$ and P_G, P_H denote probability under the indicated distribution. By the assumption on the function m

$$G^*(m^*) = P_G[s \leqq m^{-1}(m^*)] = G[m^{-1}(m^*)]$$

for some number $m^{-1}(m^*)$. Similarly,

$$H^*(m^*) = H[m^{-1}(m^*)],$$

where $H^*(m^*)$ denotes $P_G(s \epsilon S)$. But

$$G[m^{-1}(m^*)] \geqq H[m^{-1}(m^*)].$$

Hence $G^*(x) \geqq H^*(x)$ for all x, and therefore

$$E_G m(t) = \int_0^\infty [1 - G^*(x)]dx$$

$$\leqq \int_0^\infty [1 - H^*(x)]dx = E_H m(t),$$

which proves the lemma.

Now consider the function

$$m(\beta) = \tilde{\varphi}^n_{\Gamma\beta}.$$

We have shown that under the induction hypothesis "$\delta^* < \delta$ implies (18) for n and any Γ," $0 \leqq \beta^* \leqq \beta^{**}$ implies $m(\beta^*) \leqq m(\beta^{**})$. Now let Γ' be a collection of approaches available at stage $n - 1$, that is, a collection of $(n - 1)$st estimates, and let $\delta^{*\prime}$, δ' be two more such estimates, where $\delta^{*\prime} < \delta'$. Let Γ be a fixed collection of nth estimates for the approaches in Γ'. Let δ^*, δ denote, respectively, random variables, namely the nth estimate for an approach whose $(n - 1)$st estimate is $\delta^{*\prime}$ and the nth estimate for an approach whose $(n-1)$st estimate is δ'; δ^* has the distribution $F_{\delta^{*\prime},n-1}$ (with mean $\delta^{*\prime}$) and δ the distribution $F_{\delta',n-1}$ (with mean δ'). Moreover, $F_{\delta^{*\prime},n-1}$, $F_{\delta',n-1}$ form a monotonic set, with the former distribution having the lower mean. It follows from the lemma just proved that

$$E_{F_{\delta',n-1}} m(\delta) \geqq E_{F_{\delta^{*\prime},n-1}} m(\delta^*).$$

Each side of this inequality is a function of the fixed collection Γ. Now letting Γ be a random variable and taking expectations on either side of the inequality, we obtain, finally, that under the induction hypothesis for any Γ', δ', $\delta^{*\prime}$, with $\delta^* < \delta'$,

$$E\tilde{\varphi}^n_{\Gamma\delta^*} \leqq E\tilde{\varphi}^n_{\Gamma\delta}, \qquad \text{or}$$

$$\varphi^{n-1}_{\Gamma'\delta^{*\prime}} \leqq \varphi^{n-1}_{\Gamma'\delta'}, \qquad \text{which is (18)}$$

for $n-1$. The induction is complete and the theorem proved.

Note the pattern of the proof, for it will recur. A pair of propositions, $\mathscr{P}^n$ and $\tilde{\mathscr{P}}^n$ are to be proved. The proposition $\mathscr{P}^n$ concerns expected total time and money cost, net of all looking cost prior to stage $n+1$, when certain sets of approaches are pursued from stage n to stage $n+1$ and an optimal policy is applied from stage $n+1$ on. The proposition $\tilde{\mathscr{P}}^n$ is the same proposition when looking costs are incurred from stage n on, and an optimal policy is applied to the sets in question, starting at stage n. One first proves that $\mathscr{P}^n$ holds for $n = N-1$. Then follow two steps: (1) the proof that $\mathscr{P}^n$ implies $\tilde{\mathscr{P}}^n$ and (2) the proof that $\tilde{\mathscr{P}}^n$ implies $\mathscr{P}^{n-1}$. Both $\mathscr{P}^n$ and $\tilde{\mathscr{P}}^n$ are then established by induction for all n.

For brevity we shall use the word "monotonicity" to mean that for $n = 1, \ldots, N-1$, the conditional distributions $F_{\gamma n}$ form a monotonic set. Theorem 3 establishes that the ordering property follows from monotonicity. Monotonicity implies, in other words, that if an optimal subset of the available approaches at some stage n contain r approaches they must have the r lowest-ranking current estimates for the available approaches.

4.5.4. Diminishing Returns and Stronger Properties. We next investigate whether or not the major property of the one-stage problem holds also in the N-stage problem: is it again true that as one increases q, the number of initially indistinguishable approaches in the initial set Γ_1, the successive drops in $E\varphi^1_{\Gamma_1}$, the expected value of the optimal expected total time and money cost given the initial set, never increase but always decrease or stay the same?

The answer is *not in general,* and yet another appealing rule of thumb that asserts this *diminishing returns* property with respect to q is invalid unless further restrictions are accepted.

The following is a counter example. There are two review points ($N = 2$) and $c_1 = 42 + 1/3$ with probability 4/5, $42 + 4/9$ with probability 1/5. Given that $c_1 = 42 + 1/3$, c_2 equals 44, 42, or 41, each with probability 1/3. Given that $c_1 = 42 + 4/9$, c_2 equals $77 + 1/9$, $50 + 1/9$, or 1/9, each with probability 1/3. To present the counter example we need not specify the conditional distribution of c. We shall let the looking cost be 14. (This makes the calculations a little more convenient; a counter example with a looking cost of 1 can clearly be obtained from the present one by dividing all values of c_1 and c_2 by 14.)

Using the same notation as before, we have the following expected time and money costs.

$$\varphi^1_{\{42+1/3\}} = 42 + 1/3$$

$$\varphi^1_{\{42+4/9\}} = 42 + 4/9$$

$$\varphi^1_{\{42+1/3,\ 42+1/3\}} = 41 + 1/3$$

$$\varphi^1_{\{42+4/9,\ 42+4/9\}} = 25 + 1/3$$

$$\varphi^1_{\{42+1/3,\ 42+4/9\}} = 28 + 7/27$$

$$\varphi^1_{\{42+1/3,\ 42+1/3,\ 42+1/3\}} = 41 + 10/27$$

$$\varphi^1_{\{42+4/9,\ 42+4/9,\ 42+4/9\}} = 15 + 25/27$$

$$\varphi^1_{\{42+1/3,\ 42+1/3,\ 42+4/9\}} = 27 + 22/27$$

$$\varphi^1_{\{42+1/3,\ 42+4/9,\ 42+4/9\}} = 18 + 71/81.$$

In each of the above equalities the number on the right is simply the expected value of the minimum when one random drawing is made from each of the c_2 populations in the set of populations comprising the subscript on the left of the equality.[26]

For a looking cost of 14, we can then easily verify that the following are optimal subsets of sets of approaches whose first estimate is known:

$$T(\{42 + 1/3\}) = \{42 + 1/3\}$$

$$T(\{42 + 4/9\}) = \{42 + 4/9\}$$

[26] Thus in the third equality, $41 + 1/3$ is the expected value of the minimum of 2 drawings, each from the conditional probability distribution of c_2 given that $c_1 = 42 + 1/3$.

$$T(\{42+1/3, 42+1/3\}) = \{42+1/3\}$$

$$T(\{42+4/9, 42+4/9\}) = \{42+4/9, 42+4/9\}$$

$$T(\{42+1/3, 42+4/9\}) = \{42+1/3, 42+4/9\}$$

$$T(\{42+1/3, 42+1/3, 42+1/3\}) = \{42+1/3\}$$

$$T(\{42+4/9, 42+4/9, 42+4/9\}) = \{42+4/9, 42+4/9\}$$

$$T(\{42+1/3, 42+4/9, 42+4/9\}) = \{42+4/9, 42+4/9\}$$

$$T(\{42+1/3, 42+1/3, 42+4/9\}) = \{42+1/3, 42+4/9\}.$$

We can now compute the expected value of $\tilde{\varphi}^1_{\Gamma_1}$ when the size q of Γ_1 (the initial randomly drawn collection of approaches, whose first estimates all become known) varies from $q=1$ to $q=2$ to $q=3$. We use the relation

$$\tilde{\varphi}^1_{\Gamma_1} = \varphi^1_{T(\Gamma_1)} + 14\nu[T(\Gamma_1)].$$

For $q=1$ we take the average of $\tilde{\varphi}^1_{\Gamma_1}$ for both of the possible one element initial sets Γ_1 and we obtain

$$4/5(42+1/3+14) + 1/5(42+4/9+14) = 56+16/45.$$

For $q=2$ we average $\tilde{\varphi}^1_{\Gamma_1}$ over the three possible two elements sets Γ_1 and obtain

$$16/25(42+1/3+14) + 1/25(25+1/3+28) + 8/25(28+7/27+28) = 56+74/225.$$

For $q=3$ we do the same for the four possible three-element sets Γ_1 and obtain

$$1/125(25+1/3+28) + 64/125(42+1/3+14) + 48/125(28+7/27+28) + 12/125(25+1/3+28) = 55+1117/1125.$$

The drop in optimal expected time and money cost is $6/225 = 30/1125$ as we pass from $q=1$ to $q=2$, but it is greater, namely $378/1125$, as we pass from $q=2$ to $q=3$. The crucial diminishing returns property is violated.

The question is now again: under what additional natural conditions on the joint probability distribution of the estimates does the property hold?

The answer to this question is not completely known. What we shall show is quite surprising: when one passes from $q=1$ to $q=2$ to

$q = 3$ then the monotonicity condition implies diminishing returns and several stronger properties as well, but for q greater than three then even with monotonicity the diminishing returns property and the stronger properties can be violated.

The first of the stronger properties implying diminishing returns is a property we call *non-complementarity*. It is defined as follows:

Definition: The distribution $F(c_1, \ldots, c_N, c)$ exhibits non-complementarity at stage n of the N-stage problem if for any set of approaches Γ and any pair of approaches α, β for which n^{th} estimates are known

$$\tilde{\varphi}_{\Gamma}^{n} - \tilde{\varphi}_{\Gamma\alpha}^{n} \geqq \tilde{\varphi}_{\Gamma\beta}^{n} - \tilde{\varphi}_{\Gamma\alpha\beta}^{n}. \tag{19}$$

The inequality asserts that the improvement in total expected time and money cost due to adding the approach α to the set Γ of available approaches is not less than the improvement when α is added to the larger set $\Gamma\beta$. Note also that (19) can be written

$$\tilde{\varphi}_{\Gamma}^{n} - \tilde{\varphi}_{\Gamma\alpha\beta}^{n} \leqq \tilde{\varphi}_{\Gamma}^{n} - \tilde{\varphi}_{\Gamma\alpha}^{n} + \tilde{\varphi}_{\Gamma}^{n} - \tilde{\varphi}_{\Gamma\beta}^{n}.$$

In other words it cannot be the case that the improvement due to adding both α and β together to Γ is greater than the sum of the improvement when α alone is added and the improvement when β alone is added. It cannot be that α and β possess (in the presence of Γ) some sort of complementarity which (for some looking cost) would make it worthwhile to add them jointly to Γ but not worthwhile to add either one separately to Γ.

It is easy to see that what we have called "diminishing returns" is implied for any N and any distribution F such that (19) is satisfied at $n = 1$. Consider a drawing of size q from the population of first estimates and regard this q-element set Γ_1 as fixed. Now consider the expected effect of adding to Γ_1 first another drawing, α, from the population of first estimates and then a second drawing β. Both α and β are random variables. Now let $\Delta_1(\alpha)$ denote $\tilde{\varphi}_{\Gamma_1}^{1} - \tilde{\varphi}_{\Gamma_1\alpha}^{1}$; let $\Delta_2(\alpha,\beta)$ denote $\tilde{\varphi}_{\Gamma_1\alpha}^{1} - \tilde{\varphi}_{\Gamma_1\alpha\beta}^{1}$; let $\Delta(\alpha,\beta)$ denote $\Delta_1(\alpha) - \Delta_2(\alpha,\beta)$. Suppose a value of (α,β) occurs, namely $(\bar{\alpha},\bar{\beta})$, for which $\Delta(\alpha,\beta) \leqq 0$. Then with the same probability or probability density there occurs the pair $(\bar{\beta},\bar{\alpha})$. Non-complementarity at $n = 1$ implies

$$\Delta_2(\bar{\alpha},\bar{\beta}) \leqq \Delta_1(\bar{\beta}).$$

But

$$\Delta_1(\bar{\beta}) + \Delta_2(\bar{\beta},\bar{\alpha}) = \Delta_1(\bar{\alpha}) + \Delta_2(\bar{\alpha},\bar{\beta}).$$

Hence

$$\Delta_2(\bar{\beta},\bar{\alpha}) \leqq \Delta_1(\bar{\alpha})$$

and therefore

$$\Delta_2(\bar{\alpha},\bar{\beta}) - \Delta_1(\alpha) \leqq \Delta_1(\bar{\beta}) - \Delta_2(\bar{\beta},\bar{\alpha})$$

or

$$\Delta(\bar{\beta},\bar{\alpha}) \geqq -\Delta(\bar{\alpha},\bar{\beta}).$$

It follows that $E\Delta(\alpha,\beta) \geqq 0$. If we now let Γ_1 be a random variable rather than fixed we obtain

$$E(\tilde{\varphi}^1_{\Gamma_1} - \tilde{\varphi}^1_{\Gamma_1\alpha}) \geqq E(\tilde{\varphi}^1_{\Gamma_1\alpha} - \tilde{\varphi}^1_{\Gamma_1\alpha\beta})$$

where the expectations are taken over all q-element sets Γ_1 and all pairs (α,β). This is precisely the diminishing returns property with respect to the initial number, q, of approaches whose first estimates are known.

In the previous two-stage counter example to the diminishing returns property, non-complementarity is, of course, violated at $n = 1$. To be precise,

$$\tilde{\varphi}^1_{42+1/3} - \tilde{\varphi}^1_{\{42+1/3,42+4/9\}} = 42 + 1/3 + 14 - (28 + 7/27 + 28) = 2/27,$$

but

$$\tilde{\varphi}^1_{\{42+1/3,42+4/9\}} - \tilde{\varphi}^1_{\{42+1/3,42+4/9,42+4/9\}} = 28 + 7/27 + 28 - (25 + 1/3 + 28)$$
$$= 2 + 25/27.$$

The pair of approaches $(42 + 4/9,\ 42 + 4/9)$ possesses a complementarity which makes the drop in optimal expected time and money cost when both are added to the approach $(42 + 1/3)$ more than twice the drop when one only is added.

Observe now that if non-complementarity is satisfied at a particular stage n, then we know one very important aspect of the optimal procedure at that stage. For if non-complementarity holds then so does a weaker property, which for distributions possessing the ordering property we shall call *ordered non-complementarity.*

Definition. The distribution $F(c_1, \ldots, c_N, c)$ possessing the ordering property exhibits ordered non-complementarity at stage n of the N-stage problem if (19) holds for $\alpha \leqq \beta$ and for α not less than the largest member of Γ.

If ordered non-complementarity holds at stage n then the following is an optimal procedure: List all the approaches for which n^{th} estimates are known, in increasing order of the estimates (that is, from best to worst). Proceed down this list, calculating each time the drop in expected total time and money cost caused by adding the next approach. As soon as an approach is reached for which the drop is less than one (the cost of looking) all the preceding approaches in the list constitute an optimal subset, to be pursued one stage further. If such an approach is not reached before the list of available approaches is exhausted, then all of them are an optimal subset.

The marginal improvement caused by adding an approach not better than the preceding ones declines (or stays the same), in other words, as more approaches are added. This means that either an approach is reached whose marginal improvement is not enough to justify the looking cost or else all the available approaches are worth carrying to the next stage.

We now proceed to show that monotonicity implies non-complementarity at all stages (and hence ordered non-complementarity and diminishing returns with respect to q) when q equals 3, so that there are never more than three approaches at any stage and the set Γ in the preceding definitions always has just one element. To do so we shall need several additional concepts. First we shall need the concept of non-complementarity at stage n when all the approaches in question are pursued, free of looking cost, to the next stage, at which looking costs start to be assessed and an optimal policy is applied. When this is the case at stage n we have

$$\varphi_{\Gamma}^{n} - \varphi_{\Gamma\alpha}^{n} \geqq \varphi_{\Gamma\beta}^{n} - \varphi_{\Gamma\alpha\beta}^{n} \tag{19)*$$

(which is (19) without the tilde (~) over the φs). In the second place we shall need to speak of a different kind of non-complementarity than the one so far defined. We shall call this *non-complementarity with respect to quality*. It is defined for any F having the ordering property.

Definition. A distribution $F(c_1, \ldots, c_N, c)$ possessing the ordering property exhibits non-complementarity with respect to quality at stage n of the N-stage problem of $x < y$ implies for any δ

$$\tilde{\varphi}_{\delta y}^{n} - \tilde{\varphi}_{\delta x}^{n} \leqq \tilde{\varphi}_{y}^{n} - \tilde{\varphi}_{x}^{n} \tag{20}$$

and for any δ, Δ

$$\tilde{\varphi}_{\Delta\delta y}^{n} - \tilde{\varphi}_{\Delta\delta x}^{n} \leqq \tilde{\varphi}_{\Delta y}^{n} - \tilde{\varphi}_{\Delta x}^{n}. \tag{21}$$

To state the property in words: if the quality of an approach is improved, by substituting x for y, then the improvement in expected time and money cost is not greater when the substitution is performed in the presence of a given set (Δ or the empty set) than when it is performed in the presence of a larger set ($\Delta\delta$ or $\{\delta\}$). There is no possibility of a complementarity between the improved approach y and the extra approach δ such that the substitution is worth more when δ is added than when it is not.[27] The inequality (20) expresses non-complementarity with respect to quality when Δ is the empty set. Again, there will be occasion to use the properties (20), (21) with all approaches carried to the next stage and with no looking cost or choice of optimal subsets until the next stage—that is, with the tilde (~) removed. The inequalities are then

$$\varphi^n_{\delta y} - \varphi^n_{\delta x} \leqq \varphi^n_y - \varphi^n_x, \qquad x < y, \tag{20)*$$

$$\varphi^n_{\Delta\delta y} - \varphi^n_{\Delta\delta x} \leqq \varphi^n_{\Delta y} - \varphi^n_{\Delta x}, \qquad x < y. \tag{21)*$$

We can now proceed to prove that non-complementarity ((19) and (19)*) holds when Γ has a single element γ, and that non-complementarity with respect to quality holds when Δ is the empty set ((20) and (20)*).

***Theorem 4.* Let the distribution $F(c_1, \ldots, c_n, c)$ satisfy the Markov and one stage unbiasedness properties and let it possess monotonicity (for each n, $n = 1, \ldots, N - 1$, the conditional distributions $F_{\gamma n}$ form a monotonic set). Then at any stage n there is non-complementarity when Γ is a one element set γ and non-complementarity with respect to quality when Δ is the empty set. That is to say, we have for any γ, α, β:**

$$\tilde{\varphi}^n_\gamma - \tilde{\varphi}^n_{\gamma\alpha} \geqq \tilde{\varphi}^n_{\gamma\alpha} - \tilde{\varphi}^n_{\gamma\alpha\beta}, \tag{22}$$

$$\varphi^n_\gamma - \varphi^n_{\gamma\alpha} \geqq \varphi^n_{\gamma\alpha} - \varphi^n_{\gamma\alpha\beta}, \tag{22)*$$

and for any δ, x, y, $x < y$, (20) and (20)*.

Proof: The pattern of proof is similar to that of Theorem 3. We prove (Step I) that (22)*, (20)* hold for $n = N - 1$; then (Step II) that for fixed n, (22)*, (20)* imply (22), (20); and finally (Step III) that if (22), (20) hold for a fixed n then (22)*, (20)* hold for $n - 1$. This completes the inductive proof. The complete proof is somewhat lengthy and contains some observations of independent interest. It is given as an Appendix, pp. 315–321.

A very straightforward proof, which uses Theorem 4 and has three steps, analogous to the three of Theorem 4, also establishes that when Δ has one element, non-complementarity with respect to quality holds in both its forms, (21) and (21)*, at every stage. There is not sufficient

[27] As we shall observe below, non-complementarity with respect to quality is "stronger" than non-complementarity in the sense that "(21) holds for all F, n, N (or all n, N and monotonic F)" implies "(19) holds for all F, n, N (or all n, N and monotonic F)."

interest in that proof to justify its presentation here. It is worth noting, however, that the proposition it yields is the strongest of all the ones we establish, since non-complementarity with respect to quality for all monotonic distributions and all j-element sets Δ (j an integer $\geqq 1$) implies non-complementarity for all monotonic distributions and all j-element sets Γ.

To see this note that given any F and any Γ, α, β, and n (with $\alpha > \beta$, say) one can always invent a sufficiently bad approach $e > \alpha$ so that for the monotonic distribution F^*, a modified and always constructable form of F that allows for the possibility of e, we have

$$\tilde{\varphi}^n_{\Gamma e}(F^*) = \tilde{\varphi}^n_{\Gamma}(F)$$

$$\tilde{\varphi}^n_{\Gamma\alpha}(F^*) = \tilde{\varphi}^n_{\Gamma\alpha}(F)$$

$$\tilde{\varphi}^n_{e\beta}(F^*) = \tilde{\varphi}^n_{\Gamma\beta}(F)$$

$$\tilde{\varphi}^n_{\Gamma\beta}(F^*) = \tilde{\varphi}^n_{\Gamma\beta}(F),$$

where the symbol in parentheses denotes the distribution with respect to which the indicated expected time and money cost is calculated. The approach e is so bad that it is never used. Then, making the above substitutions, non-complementarity for F, Γ, α, β becomes non-complementarity with respect to quality for F^*, Γ, α, β, e ((20) takes the form (21) with the role of Δ played by Γ, that of δ by β, that of y by e, and that of x by α). Thus if we knew non-complementarity with respect to quality for all monotonic distributions, where Δ has a fixed number of elements, then we would also know non-complementarity for all monotonic distributions when Γ has the same number of elements.

In fact, however, monotonicity implies both properties only for one element[28] sets Γ and for zero element sets Δ. We could show this by providing a counter example to the weakest of the properties we have so far mentioned, the property of diminishing returns with respect to q, when q exceeds three.

Then the stronger properties – non-complementarity and non-complementarity with respect to quality – could not hold either. But that would still leave open the possibility that a useful property even weaker than diminishing returns might be implied by monotonicity for $q > 3$.

---

[28] For the very special class of monotonic distributions in which there are at any stage just two kinds of approaches (a good and a bad kind) non-complementarity can be shown to hold for Γ a two element set and non-complementarity with respect to quality for Δ a two element set. The proof follows the three step pattern of Theorem 4. For its Step II the proof requires examination of a very large number of subcases.

Before stating such a weaker property it will be convenient to introduce slightly changed notation. Recall that we defined above

$$\theta(q) = q + \tilde{\varphi}^1_{\Gamma_1},$$

where Γ_1 is the initial q-element set of estimates c_1. Now define $\overline{\theta}(q) = \theta(q) - q$, that is, $\overline{\theta}(q)$ is the best attainable expected time and money cost when looking cost is one, q approaches are drawn at random, and no charge is made for obtaining their initial estimates.

Then a weaker property than diminishing returns is the following: for any q and any positive integer m, $\theta(q) - \theta(q+1) < 1$ implies $\theta(q) - \theta(q+m) < m$. We shall call this property *limited diminishing returns.* If it holds, and if we have found a size q of the initial drawing such that adding another approach drops optimal expected time and money cost by less than 1 (the looking cost), then adding m approaches drops time and money cost by less than m. Hence if such a q is determined it is the optimal q. Clearly diminishing returns implies limited diminishing returns.

We now give a fairly complicated counter example in which the distribution is monotonic, but in which even limited diminishing returns fails to hold. All of our stronger properties then also fail to hold. In this counter example, $N = 2$. The initial estimate can take on three values 0, α, and γ, with probabilities $(1/10)^k$, $1/100[1-(1/10)^k]$ and $99/100[1-(1/10)^k]$ respectively. If $c_1 = 0$ then $c_2 = 0$ with probability one. If $c_1 = \alpha$ then c_2 equals b with probability 4/5 and $b + 40$ with probability 1/5. If $c_1 = \gamma$ then c_2 equals b with probability 1/2 and $b + 40$ with probability 1/2. The conditional distributions of c given c_2 play no role in the example. It is easily seen that the distribution of (c_1,c_2,c) is monotonic with $0 < \alpha < \gamma$. We let the cost of looking equal one. We then have at stage $N-1$

$\tilde{\varphi}_{\alpha\alpha\gamma\gamma\gamma\ldots\gamma} = \varphi_{\alpha\alpha} + 2 = 3.6 + b$, where the number of γs in the subscript is three or more;

$\tilde{\varphi}_{\alpha\gamma\gamma\gamma\ldots\gamma} = \varphi_{\alpha\gamma\gamma\gamma} + 4 = 5 + b$, where the number of γs is three or more;

$\tilde{\varphi}_{\gamma\gamma\gamma\gamma\gamma\ldots\gamma} = \varphi_{\gamma\gamma\gamma\gamma\gamma} + 5 = 6.25 + b$, where the number of γs is five or more;

$\tilde{\varphi}_{\alpha\alpha\alpha\ldots\alpha} = \varphi_{\alpha\alpha\alpha} + 3 = 3.32 + b$, where the number of αs is three or more;

$\tilde{\varphi}_{0\Gamma} = \varphi_0 + 1 = 1$ for any set Γ.

To obtain these equalities we use the fact that at stage $N-1$ it must be the case for any monotonic distribution that adding to a collection of approaches, without charge, a new approach no better than any in the collection decreases the expected time and money cost by not more than does adding the worst approach in the existing collection to all the others in the collection. We use the fact, that is to say, that at $N-1$ we have ordered non-complementarity. This fact is an immediate consequence of the Fundamental Lemma.

We then have, as best attainable expected time and money cost for random initial drawings of five, six, and seven approaches

$$\begin{aligned}\bar{\theta}_5 = 1 - [1-(1/10)^k]^5 \\ &+ [1-(1/10)^k]^5\{(99/100)^5(6.25) \\ &+ \tbinom{5}{1}(99/100)^4(1/100)(5) \\ &+ \tbinom{5}{2}(99/100)^3(1/100)^2(3.6) \\ &+ (3.32)\sum_{i=3}^{5}\tbinom{5}{i}(99/100)^{5-i}(1/100)^i \\ &+ b\}\end{aligned}$$

$$\begin{aligned}\bar{\theta}_6 = 1 - [1-(1/10)^k]^6 + [1-(1/10)^k]^6\{(99/100)^6(6.25) \\ &+ \tbinom{6}{1}(99/100)^5(1/100)(5) \\ &+ \tbinom{6}{2}(99/100)^4(1/100)^2(3.6) \\ &+ (3.32)\sum_{i=3}^{6}\tbinom{6}{i}(99/100)^{6-i}(1/100)^i \\ &+ b\}\end{aligned}$$

$$\begin{aligned}\bar{\theta}_7 = 1 - [1-(1/10)^k]^7 \\ &+ [1-(1/10)^k]^7\{(99/100)^7(6.25) \\ &+ \tbinom{7}{1}(99/100)^6(1/100)(5) \\ &+ \tbinom{7}{2}(99/100)^5(1/100)^2(3.6) \\ &+ (3.32)\sum_{i=3}^{7}\tbinom{7}{i}(99/100)^{7-i}(1/100)^i \\ &+ b\}.\end{aligned}$$

We can use large binomial tables to obtain each of the products in the above expressions. We then obtain, to nine decimal places,

$$\bar{\theta}_5 - 2\bar{\theta}_6 + \bar{\theta}_7 = [1 - (1/10)^k]^5[-.000008861 + 2(1/10)^k(.012571372) - (1/10)^{2k} + (1/10)^{2k}(6.162228705) + (1/10)^{2k}b].$$

Now suppose we can find a value of b and a value of k such that $\bar{\theta}_5 - \bar{\theta}_6$ equals $1 - \epsilon$, where ϵ is positive but extremely small, while $(\bar{\theta}_5 - \bar{\theta}_6) - (\bar{\theta}_6 - \bar{\theta}_7) = \bar{\theta}_5 - 2\bar{\theta}_6 + \bar{\theta}_7$ is less than -2ϵ. Then we have found our counter example. But in fact inspection of the above expressions reveals that we can easily do so. For example, set $k = 10$ and solve the equation $\bar{\theta}_5 - \bar{\theta}_6 = 1$ for b, where b is rounded off to nine decimal places. This value of b is 987437489 and since, being rounded off, it is slightly less than the true solution to $\bar{\theta}_5 - \bar{\theta}_6 = 1$, that must mean that for this value of b, $\bar{\theta}_5 - \bar{\theta}_6$ is slightly less than one, but by an amount less than 10^{-8}. If we now insert this value of b and the value $k = 10$ into the expression for $\bar{\theta}_5 - 2\bar{\theta}_6 + \bar{\theta}_7$ we see that the term $-.000008861$ will dominate in that expression. In fact, the value of $\bar{\theta}_5 - 2\bar{\theta}_6 + \bar{\theta}_7$ turns out to be, to ten decimal places, $-.0000088609$ which is far larger in absolute value than $2 \cdot 10^{-8}$.

Thus for $b = 987437489$ and $k = 10$, it is not worth the looking cost to add a sixth randomly drawn initial approach but it is worth twice the looking cost to add both a sixth and a seventh. It is clear that if we want to replace the approach that has $c_1 = c_2 = 0$ by one in which $c_1 = c_2 = \delta > 0$ we can always choose a δ sufficiently small that the counter example is preserved.

The considerable delicacy of the counter example stems from the fact that we essentially confine it to two point distributions, which are easy to manipulate. If we admitted three or four point distributions we could certainly find examples where one does not need computation to many decimal places, but they would be much more laborious to construct. What is the essential reason that the above distribution does yield a counter example? The main point is that for five drawings one will get, at stage $N - 1$, with rather high probability, a combination of a and γ which, when followed by the sixth and seventh drawings, exhibits a strong complementarity. With one stage left to go it is, perhaps surprisingly, possible to construct examples of complementarity—that is, examples in which $\tilde{\varphi}_\Gamma - \tilde{\varphi}_{\Gamma a} - \tilde{\varphi}_{\Gamma b} + \tilde{\varphi}_{\Gamma ab} < 0$, *provided* Γ *has five or more elements.* It was such an example upon which the counter example just given was erected. When Γ has four or fewer elements it can be shown, by rather tedious study of subcases (and study in each subcase of the integrand in the integral that forms part of the expression for $\tilde{\varphi}_{\Gamma} - \tilde{\varphi}_{\Gamma a} - \tilde{\varphi}_{\Gamma b} + \tilde{\varphi}_{\Gamma ab}$) that non-complementarity holds at stage $N - 1$.

In the example just given the strong complementarity that occurs with sufficiently high probability to cause the failure of limited diminishing returns has the following form. Although the addition of the first approach (approach a) to the set Γ leaves a and most or all of Γ in an optimal subset, the further addition of the second approach (approach b) knocks out most of Γ from the optimal subset. The optimal subset of the set Γab is composed of a and b plus few or no elements of Γ. The saving in looking cost due to knocking out the elements of Γ outweighs the possible inferiority of the small optimal subset of Γab compared with the large optimal subset of Γa. The saving in looking cost, that is to say, is substantially larger than the quantity $\varphi_{T(\Gamma a)} - \varphi_{T(\Gamma ab)}$, which may be negative. ($T(\Gamma a)$,$T(\Gamma ab)$ denote optimal subsets.) The result is that the net improvement due to adding a to Γ is less than the net improvement due to adding b to Γa.[29] This sort of knocking out is, we may conjecture, the only way complementarity can occur in monotonic distributions. It is easy to verify that it cannot occur for monotonic distributions when Γ has only one element.

There has also been constructed a counter example to limited diminishing returns and non-complementarity with $N = 3$, Γ containing two elements, and q equal successively to two, three, and four. It is a counter example in which c_1, c_2, c_3, and c are the four successive states of a Markov chain containing ten possible state values and satisfying our monotonicity and one stage unbiasedness conditions. Needless to say, a computer is needed to compute the relevant expressions, and the particular complementarities that cause the counter example cannot be easily detected, as they could in the more instructive counter example just given.

4.5.5. A Summary. We can informally summarize our results as follows: For distributions possessing the ordering property we distinguish five properties denoted P_1, P_2, P_3, P_4, P_5. All of them have to do with the successive addition of new approaches to existing ap-

---

[29] A simple example in which this occurs is the following. (The counter example presented above was, in fact, constructed from it, after some modification.) We are at stage $N - 1$. There are three possible approaches. For each of them c_N will be either zero or 100. For approach γ, c_N equals 100 with probability 1/10; for approach δ, c_N equals 100 with probability 1/5; and for approach λ, c_N equals 100 with probability 1/2. The set Γ is $\{\gamma\lambda\lambda\lambda\lambda\}$ and the approach δ plays the role of both the approaches a and b in our definition of non-complementarity. The cost of looking is 1/4. Then $\tilde{\varphi}_{\Gamma} = \varphi_{\Gamma} + 6/4 + 5/16 + 6/4$, $\tilde{\varphi}_{\Gamma\delta} = \varphi_{\gamma\delta\lambda\lambda} + 4/4 = 1/2 + 1$, and $\tilde{\varphi}_{\Gamma\delta\delta} = \varphi_{\lambda\delta\delta} + 3/4 = 4/10 + 3/4$. Therefore $\tilde{\varphi}_{\Gamma} - 2\tilde{\varphi}_{\Gamma\delta} + \tilde{\varphi}_{\Gamma\delta\delta} = -3/80$.

proaches. The properties are limited diminishing returns (P_1), diminishing returns (P_2), ordered non-complementarity (P_3), non-complementarity (P_4), and non-complementarity with respect to quality (P_5). (The properties P_3, P_4, P_5 occur in two forms—with or without a tilde in our notation.)

We have the following chain of implication: "P_5 holds for all F" $\Rightarrow$ "P_4 holds for all F" $\Rightarrow$ "P_3 holds for all F" $\Rightarrow$ "P_2 holds for all F" $\Rightarrow$ "P_1 holds for all F." The chain still holds if the words "for all monotonic F" replace the words "for all F" and also if the words "when not more than q approaches are initially drawn" are added to each statement in the chain, where q is an integer $\geqq 3$. The monotonicity condition implies the ordering property. For $q = 3$ (that is, for the successive addition of two approaches to one existing approach), monotonicity also implies the strongest proposition, P_5 (with a one-element set Δ), and hence all the other (weaker) ones. But for the case of more than one existing approach, monotonicity does not imply even the weakest of the five properties. There is an enormously sharp distinction between the case of one existing approach (with a second and a third added to it) and the case of more existing approaches. The sharpness of the distinction is a most unexpected result. If a developer never deals with more than three approaches his optimal policy displays very strong and appealing properties so long as the monotonicity condition is fulfilled. If he deals with more than three then monotonicity implies none of them at all.[30] One could hardly ask for a more striking example of the ability of analysis to refute intuition.

4.5.6. Upper and Lower Bounds for the Optimal Number of Approaches. The counter example just presented raises the alarming possibility that there is no way of determining the optimal number of initially drawn approaches short of comparing all possible values of q. In fact at least one upper bound to the optimal value of q can be given.

First observe that we change nothing essential in the pure parallel approach problem if we assume that one approach may be carried free through all N stages. Since at least one approach must be pursued through all N stages, all choices (of q and of approach subsets) that are optimal under this assumption are optimal without it. We shall be concerned with the curve that, under this assumption, gives the best attainable expected time and money cost for each q. We denote this curve $\bar{\bar{\theta}}(q)$, where $\bar{\bar{\theta}}(q) = \bar{\theta}(q) - N$. ($\bar{\theta}(q)$ denoted best attain-

[30] Except the ordering property.

able expected time and money cost, when no charge is made for the initial drawing of approaches, before we made the assumption of one free approach.)

Consider now two other functions of q that, unlike $\bar{\bar{\theta}}(q)$, are easily calculable. Let $\theta'(q)$ denote the optimal expected payoff when the surviving approach is to be chosen at review point 1 and $\theta''(q)$ the payoff when all q approaches are pursued free of looking cost to review point N, at which the survivor is chosen. It is clear that under the Markov and one stage unbiasedness assumptions $\theta'(q)$ and $\theta''(q)$ both approach the horizontal line Z units above the horizontal axis as q becomes large; $Z \geqq 0$ is the smallest value of t such that $Pr(u \leqq t) = 0$. It is also clear that with respect to the positive integers q, both $\theta'(q)$ and $\theta''(q)$ have positive second difference, since each equals the expected value of the minimum of q independent drawings from a fixed population. Finally, for all integers $q \geqq 1$, $\theta'(q) \leqq \bar{\bar{\theta}}(q) \leqq \theta''(q)$ and (under our assumption that one approach is free) $\theta'(1) = \bar{\bar{\theta}}(1) = \theta''(1)$. The situation must be as in the diagram below where three

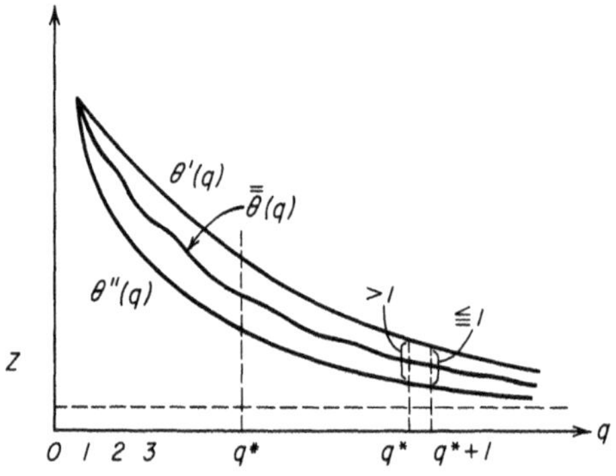

curves are smoothly drawn through the integer points for which the three functions are defined.

The difference $\theta'(q) - \theta''(q)$ increases at first, but starts to decrease at the integer $q\#$. The integer $q^* + 1$ is the first integer beyond $q\#$ for which $\theta'(q) - \theta''(q) \leqq 1$. The integer q^* *is the required upper bound* since $\bar{\bar{\theta}}(q)$ cannot be decreased by more than one (the cost of another randomly drawn approach) for q greater than q^*.

An integer q^* certainly exists and is, in fact, not difficult to compute (using two integrals of the form given in the Fundamental Lemma, one dealing with the population of estimates c_N and the other with the population of estimates c_1). Note that this upper bound does not depend on monotonicity, though it does depend heavily on the

Markov, one stage unbiasedness, and $(N-n)$ stage unbiasedness properties. Its existence is reassuring. It is clear, moreover, that exactly the same notion can be used to construct an upper bound to the rank of the worst approach that will be contained in the optimal subset of any s-element set of approaches (ranked from best to worst) at any stage. This upper bound may well be s.

Now what about a lower bound? At any stage, given any collection of approaches and given the ordering property, is there some relatively simple way of finding some approach in the ordered list of approaches (ordered from best to worst) such that we can be sure that all approaches better than that one must be included in at least one optimal subset?

We note first that such a simple lower bound always exists when the collection of approaches consists of just two approaches. The developer can pretend at any stage n that there is only one stage left—that the surviving approach is to be chosen at the next stage. He can then ask, under this "myopic" assumption: is it worthwhile to add the worse of the two approaches to the better one? If the answer is "yes" then it is also the case that the true optimal subset at stage n consists of both approaches. The true improvement must be at least as great, since in particular the survivor can always be chosen at the next stage even when it doesn't have to be, since $E(c|c_n) = c_n$ and since we may assume one approach to be free. Hence when there are just two approaches the myopically optimal subset is always contained in the true optimal subset. The same argument applies, of course, to the initial random drawing of approaches. If $q = 2$ yields a lower value of $\bar{\theta}(q)$ than $q = 1$ when we assume the first stage to be the last then it will *a fortiori* yield a lower value when we do not make this assumption.

When we pass to more than two approaches the same simple lower bound does not work. Counter examples satisfying monotonicity can then be found in which the true optimal subset may be contained in the myopically optimal subset instead of the other way around.

A weaker lower bound, just as simple to calculate, does however exist. Let us denote by $F_{n\gamma}^N$ the conditional distribution of c_N given that $c_n = \gamma$. Further define

$$\hat{\varphi}_\Gamma^n = \int \prod_{i \in \Gamma} [1 - F_{ni}^N(t)]dt.$$

Thus $\hat{\varphi}_\Gamma^n$ denotes the expected value of the smallest c_N when *all* the approaches in Γ are carried to stage N. Then if one pretends, at stage n, that all the approaches in Γ have to be carried (free of charge) to stage N at which point the survivor is picked, and if under this assumption adding the approach a to Γ decreases the expected value of the survivor's time and money cost by *more than* $N-n$, then a is worth adding to Γ *without* the assumption. We state this as

Theorem 5. **For any monotonic distribution $F(c_1, \ldots, c_N, c)$, any stage n and any collection of approaches Γ, $\hat{\varphi}^n_\Gamma - \hat{\varphi}^n_{\Gamma a} > N - n$ implies $\tilde{\varphi}^n_\Gamma - \tilde{\varphi}^n_{\Gamma a} > 0$ for any approach a.**

Proof: Let $T_n(\Gamma)$ denote a surviving subset of approaches at stage N, given that Γ is available at stage N and an optimal policy is applied from stage N on. If there are several (equally good) surviving subsets let $T_n(\Gamma)$ denote the lowest ranking one when these several subsets are "lexicographically" ordered. Let $L_n(\Gamma)$ denote the total looking cost incurred in reaching stage N, starting with Γ at stage n, applying an optimal policy from stage n on, and whenever there is more than one optimal subset, selecting the one with fewest elements. Let a^n denote the value of the estimate c_N of an approach whose n^{th} estimate is a. The set $T_n(\Gamma)$, $L_n(\Gamma)$, and a^n are random variables. Finally, define

$$\overset{*}{\varphi}{}^n_{\Gamma a} = EL_n(\Gamma) + N - n + E \min_{\gamma \in \{T_n(\Gamma), a^n\}} \gamma.$$

Then, since $\overset{*}{\varphi}{}^n_{\Gamma a} \geqq \tilde{\varphi}^n_{\Gamma a}$; it suffices to prove that

$$\hat{\varphi}^n_\Gamma - \hat{\varphi}^n_{\Gamma a} > N - n \text{ implies } \hat{\varphi}^n_\Gamma - \overset{*}{\varphi}{}^n_{\Gamma a} > 0.$$

To prove this observe that it follows from the Fundamental Lemma that for any fixed subset of Γ, say Λ,

$$\hat{\varphi}^n_\Lambda - \hat{\varphi}^n_{\Lambda a} \geqq \hat{\varphi}^n_\Gamma - \hat{\varphi}^n_{\Gamma a}. \tag{23}$$

Now $T_n(\Gamma)$ is a subset of the approaches in Γ (and of their N^{th} estimates). It is a subset that is selected stochastically from Γ, but since for every subset the inequality (23) holds, we must also have

$$E \min_{\gamma \in T_n(\Gamma)} \gamma - E \min_{\gamma \in \{T_n(\Gamma), a^n\}} \gamma \geqq \hat{\varphi}^n_{\Gamma a} - \tilde{\varphi}^n_{\Gamma a} > N - n. \tag{24}$$

But

$$\begin{aligned} \tilde{\varphi}^n_\Gamma - \overset{*}{\varphi}{}^n_{\Gamma a} &= E\left[\min_{\gamma \in T_n(\Gamma)} \gamma + L_n(\Gamma)\right] \\ &\quad - E\left[\min_{\gamma \in \{T_n(\Gamma), a^n\}} \gamma + L_n(\Gamma) + N - n\right] \\ &= E \min_{\gamma \in T_n(\Gamma)} \gamma - E \min_{\gamma \in \{T_n(\Gamma), a^n\}} \gamma - (N - n). \end{aligned}$$

Hence, by (24), $\tilde{\varphi}^n_\Gamma - \overset{*}{\varphi}{}^n_{\Gamma a} > 0$.

Thus we have, when the ordering property holds, a set that must be contained in the true optimal subset of a given collection of approaches. When the ordering property holds, then for a not smaller than the largest element of Γ, $\tilde{\varphi}^n_\Gamma - \tilde{\varphi}^n_{\Gamma a}$ implies $\varphi^n_\Gamma - \varphi^n_{\Gamma a} > 1$. We go down the list of approaches in the given collection, ordered from best to worst, asking for each approach in the list whether the drop in expected time and money cost due to adding the approach is greater than $N - n$ if we pretend that all the better approaches and the added approaches are to be pursued free of charge to $N - n$. As soon as we reach an approach for which the answer is "no" we can be sure that the answer is "no" for all worse approaches, and we stop. We have then found a subset that must be contained in the optimal subset, since by Theorem 5 all the approaches in the subset were worth the looking cost when added to the preceding ones. If we are lucky we have also exhausted the entire collection and then we know that it is optimal to pursue the entire collection one stage further. The procedure can also be used, of course, to obtain a lower bound to the optimal number of approaches to draw at random initially.

4.6. Computation of an Optimal Policy

For a known monotonic distribution $F(c_1, \ldots, c_N, c)$ the actual carrying out of an optimal narrowing down of an initial set of approaches, and the actual computation of the optimal q, are in general very complex. For more restricted Fs simplifications of the computations are no doubt possible. Our knowledge so far tells us that we begin the narrowing down at any stage n by listing the approaches for which current estimates are known from best to worst.

The situation is then straightforward when there are only two or three approaches. We can apply the sharp myopic lower bound when there are only two approaches, and for the case of both two and three we can apply the upper bound described above and Theorem 4 as well. Theorem 4 implies that we have an optimal subset as soon as we reach a number of approaches (going down the list of three from best to worst) such that adding one more (the next best one) decreases expected time and money cost by less than one.

When there are more than three approaches we can apply the upper bound described and the lower bound (less sharp than the myopic one) of Theorem 5. Beyond this the situation is difficult. In principle, however, the computation of φ^n_Γ is always possible for any n and any Γ. This is true since φ^n_Γ is the expected value of the minimum of s random variables, namely the variables $\tilde{\varphi}^{n+1}_{\Delta^*}$, where Δ is one of the s possible subsets of Γ, and Δ^* is the set of $(n+1)$st estimates corresponding to that subset. Each variable $\tilde{\varphi}_{\Delta*}^{n+1}$ can in turn be defined in a similar way with respect to stage $n + 2$, and so on. In principle, a vastly complex but finite computation of φ_Γ^n and hence $\tilde{\varphi}_\Gamma^n$ is possible for any n. In principle, therefore, given any initial drawing of q approaches, an optimal policy can always be constructed. It requires the computation at each stage of the expectation of each of a finite number of very complicated random variables.

4.7. An Additional Remark and Some Unsettled Questions

There is at least one further rule of thumb that one might intuitively expect an optimal policy to display but that can readily be shown not to hold.

Consider the following rule of thumb, having to do with "wasteful duplication."

> The more widely *dispersed* (dissimilar) are the estimates observed at a given review point, the more approaches should be pursued to the next review point. Dispersion may be measured, for example, by the average of the squared deviations of the estimates from their mean.

The rule may appear, at first sight, reasonable enough. If, for example, all the approaches pursued up to the given review point yielded the same estimate at that review point then it might seem likely that the approaches have very similar time and money costs to completion and that to pursue more than one or two of them any further is wasteful duplication.

A simple example shows the rule to be invalid. Suppose that among the collection of possible approaches there is one that dominates all the others and reveals itself unambiguously at the nth review point. In other words, this approach has, at the nth review point, the estimate c_n^*, and no other approach has the same estimate. Its true time and money cost to completion, moreover, also equals c_n^* and this is less than the true time and money cost for all other approaches. Then if an approach is observed to have the estimate c_n^* at the nth review point, all other approaches are immediately dropped, no matter how much variety there may be among their estimates. If, on the other hand, a collection of identical, or nearly identical, estimates not including c_n^* are observed, then, in general, more than one of them is (under an optimal policy) pursued further.

The point is that the rule of thumb expresses too crudely the intuitive notion that wasteful duplication should be avoided. Avoiding wasteful duplication not only means avoiding the pursuit of approaches whose true costs are nearly identical, it also means avoiding the pursuit of additional approaches when it is quite certain the best possible approach has already been found.

The revised intuition suggests a revised rule of thumb:

If among the observed estimates c_n at the nth review point there is not one that unambiguously identifies the approach for which c is known not to exceed the c of any possible approach, then the more widely dispersed are the observed c_ns, the more approaches should be pursued to the next review point.

But the revised rule is obviously invalid too. For it is, of course, easy to construct monotonic (and other) distributions F such that if at some review point a pair of approaches with current estimates (a,a) are available it is optimal to pursue both of them, but if the more diverse pair (a,b) are available $(b > a)$ then it is optimal to pursue only one of them. For neither of the two estimates need it be the case, moreover, that they unambiguously identify a dominating approach.

It appears difficult to translate the rather strong intuitive notion that there is something that can be called "wasteful duplication" and that ought to be avoided into a precise and true property of an optimal policy.

We now consider very briefly several of the numerous open questions in the pure parallel approach problem.

1) Suppose the Markov assumption is dropped. Then the monotonicity of F can still be defined as before: F is monotonic if for any collection of approaches at any stage n the conditional distributions of $(n + 1)$st estimates—when each conditional distribution is now a distribution of c_{n+1} given a preceding history $c_1, \ldots, c_n$—form a monotonic set. How many of our preceding results are now implied by monotonicity?

2) What assumptions other than monotonicity imply the properties P_1 to P_5?

3) If one returns to the non-contracted form of the problem, in which there are two-dimensional estimates (m_n,t_n) for each approach, are there any simple properties of an optimal policy for simple nonlinear (for example, quadratic) time and money cost functions?

4) Can one prove propositions about the effect of varying the relative weight given to time in the time and money cost function on interesting properties of the optimal policy? Can one make precise and test conjectures, that is to say, about the peculiarities of crash programs in which completion time has a very high weight?

5) Consider the following appealing variant of the pure parallel approach problem. Not only is the vector of an approach's succes-

sive estimates a random variable, but also N, the dimension of this vector, is a random variable. A problem is defined by a family of distributions $F^1(c_1)$, $F^2(c_1,c_2)$, . . . , $F^N(c_1,c_2, \ldots ,c_N)$, . . . , and a distribution $G(N)$. An approach will exhibit, upon completion, the history $(c_1,c_2, \ldots ,c_N,N)$, where $c_1, \ldots , c_{N-1}$ are estimates of c_N and c_N is the true time and money cost of the approach. The random variable N is the number of time periods required to complete the approach and therefore to know the true cost c_N. The variable N becomes known for an approach only after it has been pursued through N review points; at review point N the current estimate is accompanied by an unmistakable signal whose meaning is that c_N is the true time and money cost and development is over.

At each stage the developer has to decide, as before, which approaches to pursue further (at a fixed looking cost) and which to drop. He stops as soon as one of the approaches has yielded its c_N. His goal, as before, is to minimize the expected time and money cost of completion. The question now is: what assumptions lead to propositions about the optimal policy analogous to those we have proved? A good starting point for this more complex non-truncated problem is the following special case: for each N with probability one, $c_N = KN$ and c_n, $n < N$, equals Kn (the time and money cost of an approach is simply a constant times the number of periods required to complete it; the nth estimate is simply the same constant times the number of elapsed, uncompleted periods).

5. The Parallel Approach Problem with Sequential Selection of Approaches at Each Review Point

We consider now one of the major ways in which the previous model departs from reality and shall discuss quite briefly how the model might accordingly be generalized. We have assumed that at each review point the developer looks at the cost estimates available for all the approaches that have been carried up to the review point, decides which of them to pursue further, and then begins to do so. But the developer is, in fact, under no compulsion, at the given review point, to decide once and for all, solely on the basis of the cost estimates, which of the approaches he will pursue further.

Suppose the developer has carried a number of approaches to the nth review point. He can then, for example, pursue the best approach (the one with the lowest cost estimate) to its $(n + 1)$st review point, when a more accurate cost estimate becomes available, while keeping the other approaches – the second best one, the third best one, and so on – at a temporary standstill. If the more accurate cost estimate for the best approach turns out to be sufficiently high, he may then return to the temporarily halted approaches and pursue the second best one to *its* $(n+1)$st review point. He may thereupon return to the third best approach and pursue it to its $(n+1)$st review point, and so forth. To make things still more complex the approaches could be staggered: the developer, having returned to the second best approach and resumed it, might at the same time pursue the best approach still further (to its $(n+2)$nd review point) in order to get a still more accurate cost estimate for it. He would do this, to put it crudely, so as not to waste time.

Finally, in the preceding sentences the word "best" could be replaced by the words "r_1 best"; the words "second best" by the words "next r_2 best"; the words "third best" by "next r_3 best"; and so forth. The developer could, that is to say, explore a sequence of batches of approaches, carrying one batch at a time to the $(n+1)$st review point and then deciding whether or not to carry the next batch to the $(n+1)$st review point. There would be an economy in the pursuit of a batch of r approaches to the $(n+1)$st review point compared with the pursuit of the r approaches one by one—namely that it takes $1/r$ times as long to carry the batch one review point further as it does to carry the approaches one by one to the $(n+1)$st review point.

We have sketched, clearly, an extraordinarily complicated and almost totally unexplored sequential decision problem—even when the staggering and batch complications are ruled out. Yet it is a problem that could probably be attacked with existing tools. We conclude our discussion of it by considering the very simplest case—the one review point case.

5.1. Sequential Selection of Approaches in the One-review-point Case

The developer has available prior to the first review point a population of initially indistinguishable approaches. Each approach is characterized by two numbers: c, its true time and money cost to completion, and c_1, an estimate of c (where $E(c/c_1) = c_1$). The developer's problem is not to choose a number of approaches to be pursued to the first review point. Rather he carries a sequence of approaches, one at a time, to the first review point (he randomly draws a sequence of approaches from the population of approaches). When he decides to pursue no more approaches to the first review point, then he selects that approach among those he has pursued for which c_1 is a minimum. He carries that approach to completion. Every time he pursues an approach to the first review point he expends one time unit and a fixed money cost, which we take to be one.

Under our earlier assumption about the form of the time and money cost function we can regard this time and money expenditure as having a money equivalent. Let the money equivalent be s money units.

What the developer wants, then, is a stopping rule: a rule that tells him for a given collection of c_1s, one for each approach pursued to the first review point so far, whether or not to pursue an additional approach to the first review point. For a particular sequence of c_1s—say, $c_1^1, \ldots, c_1^r$—the expected total time and money cost of development is

$$\bar{\varphi}_r \equiv \min(c_1^1, \ldots, c_1^r) + sr.$$

The optimal stopping rule is one which minimizes $E\bar{\varphi}_r$, where the expectation is taken with respect to r (which is itself a random variable for a given rule) as well as with respect to the r values of c_1.

We assume, as before, that the developer knows F_1 the probability distribution of the c_1. For a known F_1 with a finite mean μ the problem of finding an optimal stopping rule has been given a general solution.[31] The optimal rule, in our case, is this:

If $s < \mu$, stop as soon as you have a c_1 for which $c_1 < \alpha$ where α is the root of the equation

$$\int_0^\alpha (\alpha - x)dF_1(x) = s. \tag{25}$$

If $s \geqq \mu$, pursue one approach only. Under this rule the expected value of $\bar{\varphi}_r$ can be shown to be exactly α when $s < \mu$ (and μ otherwise).

It is clear that if it took no time, but only money, to pursue an approach to the first review point then the expected total money cost of development under the optimal stopping rule is less than when the developer operates under the constraints assumed in Section 4 and chooses, once and for all, the optimal number of approaches, say $\hat{q}$, to pursue to the first review point. For the expected money cost obtained for $\hat{q}$ can always be duplicated under the sequential arrangement by pursuing a sequence of $\hat{q}$ approaches. But when we allow the pursuit of an approach to the first review point to take time, then the sequential arrangement (using the optimal stopping rule) may or may not be better than the non-sequential one. The batch economy mentioned above now comes into play. If the developer is forced to pursue approaches one by one he may be worse off than if he is

[31] F. Chow and Herbert Robbins: A Martingale System Theorem and Applications, *Proceedings of the Fourth Berkeley Symposium on Probability and Statistics*, Berkeley: University of California Press, 1961.

never allowed to do so. The best arrangement is to permit him to do either and, in fact, to permit him to pursue a sequence of batches of approaches as well (he may decide to pursue just one batch, in which case he is satisfying the constraints of the previous section).

By way of illustration, let the money equivalent of one time unit now be β, so that $s = \beta + 1$, and let the random variable c_1 have a rectangular distribution from zero to L ($L > 0$). Then the solution of (25) becomes

$$\alpha = \begin{cases} \sqrt{2L(\beta+1)} & \text{if } \beta + 1 < L/2 \\ L & \text{if } \beta + 1 \geqq L/2 \end{cases}$$

and the upper term is also the expected total time and money cost of development under the optimal stopping rule when $\beta + 1 < L/2$.

Now suppose the developer is faced with the constraints of the previous section. He must choose a number of approaches, call it n, to be pursued to the second review point. It is easily established, using the Fundamental Lemma, that the expected value of the minimum of a sample of size q from a population that is rectangularly distributed between 0 and L is $L/(q+1)$. Hence the $\hat{q}$ which the developer seeks is that value of q for which $L/(q+1) + \beta + q$ is a minimum. Treating q as continuous, and differentiating and solving the conditions for a minimum, we obtain

$$\hat{q} = \sqrt{L} - 1.$$

For simplicity, assume $\sqrt{L}$ is an integer greater than $\beta + 1$. (If $\sqrt{L} \leqq \beta + L$ then the optimal thing to do is simply to pick one of the initially indistinguishable approaches and pursue it to completion—since the time and money cost of carrying an additional approach to the second review point is greater than or equal to the maximum drop in time and money cost, from the first review point to completion, that could be gained by doing so.)

If $\sqrt{L} - 1$ is the number of approaches carried to the first review point, then the expected total time and money cost of development when sequential exploration of approaches is forbidden is

$$\beta + 2\sqrt{L} - 1.$$

Hence for $\beta + 1 < L/2$ the constraint that the developer has to carry approaches to the first review point in the sequence is preferred to the constraint that he must once and for all choose a number of approaches to carry to the second review point if and only if

$$\sqrt{2L(\beta+1)} < \beta + 2\sqrt{L} - 1 \qquad (26)$$

which is satisfied for all β smaller than a number that depends on L. If development time is sufficiently cheap to the developer, he prefers the former constraint to the latter. (For $\beta + 1 \geqq L/2$ only one approach is ever pursued in the sequential case, and the latter constraint is therefore preferred or at least indifferent to the former one.)

It is clear that whether or not (26) is satisfied, the developer is best off of all if he is permitted to carry a sequence of batches of approaches to the second review point, and his optimal decision will then in general be to pursue such a sequence, composed of more than one batch.

5.2. *Rules of Thumb*

What can now be said about the rules of thumb we investigated in Section 4? Suppose the developer has to choose a sequence of approaches to be carried to the first review point one at a time. Is it now true that the more the developer learns by pursuing an approach to the second review point the more approaches he pursues, on the average, when he uses an optimal stopping rule?

Consider the simple case in which the variable c_1 has a two point probability distribution. It takes the value a with probability p and b with probability $1 - p$, where $0 < a < b$. There are, clearly, only two possible stopping rules having the form of the optimal rule as given by (25). *Rule 1* says "Pursue just one approach to the second review point (that is, stop when you have an approach for which $c_1 \leqq \alpha$, where α is a number greater than or equal to b)." *Rule 2* says "Keep pursuing approaches to the second review point until you have one for which $c_1 = a$ (that is, stop when you have an approach for which $c_1 \leqq \alpha$, where α is a number less than b and greater than or equal to a)."

Under Rule 1 the expected time and money cost to completion is $ap + b(1 - p) + s \equiv \mu + s$ (μ is the mean value of the c_1s). Under Rule 2, the expected time and money cost to completion is a plus s times the expected number of approaches that have to be pursued to the review point until one is obtained for which c_1 equals a. This expected number is $p + 2(1 - p)p + 3(1 - p)^2p + 4(1 - p)^3p + \cdots$. As is easily established, the sum of this convergent series is simply $p/[1 - (1 - p)]^2 = 1/p$. The expected time and money cost to completion under Rule 2 is, therefore, $a + s/p$.

Rule 2, then, is the optimal stopping rule if $a + s/p < \mu + s$ or

$$a + s\left(\frac{1 - p}{p}\right) < \mu. \tag{27}$$

Rule 1 is optimal if the inequality is reversed (if the inequality becomes an equality the two rules are equally good). Now it is easy to verify that given a μ we can find two triples (a,b,p) such that (i) for both of them $0 < a < b$, (ii) $ap + b(1-p) = \mu$ for both of them, (iii) the first has a higher variance, (iv) the inequality (27) is satisfied for both of them, and (v) p is larger for the first than for the second.[32] The two triples would then define two-point distributions of the variable c_1 having the same mean; the first has a higher variance and yet $1/p$, the expected number of approaches pursued under the optimal stopping rule, is less than for the second distribution. Although more is learned in pursuing an approach to the second review point—using reduction in expected squared error as a measure of learning—the expected number pursued is smaller. The rule of thumb of Section 4.3, appropriately restated to fit the present context, again lacks general validity.

It is safe to state, moreover, that the invalidity remains if we permit free choice of sequences of batches of any size, since we can find triples for which the optimal size batch throughout the sequence is 1—the case just considered.

Finally, by expanding the example just considered one can show that if the rule of thumb is restated for the case of a many review point problem, with a sequential selection of the approaches to be carried from the first to the second review point, from the second to the third, and so on, then that rule will also be generally invalid.

6. The Pursuit of Approaches with Different Intensities

There is a second severe departure from reality in the pure parallel approach model of Section 4. The possibility is ignored that a particular design, or the work of a particular group, may be pursued, in any period of time, at different intensities—that is, using different amounts of money. Formally the pursuit of the same design or the work of the same group at different intensities had to be considered in Section 4 as the pursuit of different approaches, and the model said nothing about the peculiar way such different approaches are related to each other.

We shall now consider this possibility. As a start we shall (1) consider one shot development problems, wherein the only decision the developer makes is made once and for all at the beginning of development (at the first review point) and (2) redefine "approach" for the one shot case so that an approach can now be pursued with different intensities.

[32] For example, the two triples (1.5, 1/2) and (1, 7, 2/3), both with mean $\mu = 3$, satisfy conditions (i) to (v) for $q = 1$.

6.1. One Shot Development Problems Wherein an Approach May Be Pursued with Different Intensities

We consider a developer whose task, as in all the discussions so far, is to achieve a satisfactory version of an item. He has available a number of approaches. An approach is now defined as "a collection of probability distributions of time to completion, one distribution for each alternative budget devoted to the approach."

We shall concentrate on the case of two available approaches. The first is defined by a family of probability distributions: the family $F(b_1,t_1)$, where b_1 is a parameter and t_1 is a random variable; $F(b_1,t_1)$ gives the probability attached (by the developer) to the event "completion of the first approach (achievement of a satisfactory version of the required item, using that approach) in not more than t_1 time units when a total budget of not more than b_1 is made available to the group pursuing that approach." The second approach is characterized by the family of distributions $G(b_2,t_2)$, to be interpreted analogously. The times t_1 and t_2 are the respective random variables in these two distributions; the numbers b_1 and b_2 are parameters of the distribution functions.

Now for every total development budget—denoted by B—that the developer contemplates using for the development task, he wants the division of the budget as between the two development approaches to be optimal. To be able to define "optimal" more easily, we shall assume that once the budget B of a particular approach has been determined, that amount of money is permanently committed. As soon as one approach is completed, development ceases and no part of the budget committed to the uncompleted approach can be recovered; it is lost forever even though the approach is to be dropped.

We recall now our general assumption that the developer is not faced with a rigid total budget limitation nor with a time deadline he dares not transgress. He is faced rather with alternative uses (for example, other development tasks) for the money that he could devote to speeding up the development task we are considering. The alternative uses imply a preference ordering over the alternative time and money combinations that can turn out to be required in completing the task in question. We have let the function $C(M,T)$ define the preferences (and any non-decreasing function of C defines them equally well); we have called C the total time and money cost of development.

In the present case, then, the developer wants to find budgets

b_1 and b_2, for the two available approaches, such that $EC\{b_1 + b_2, \min [t_1(b_1), t_2(b_2)]\}$ is smaller than for any other b_1, b_2, where $t_1(b_1)$, $t_2(b_2)$ denote the actual times to completion for the two approaches when the given budgets are available. One important general question is this: under what conditions on the function C and the probability distributions F and G does there exist a unique optimal total budget $b_1 + b_2$, and under what conditions can it easily be found? This is the question we shall chiefly consider.

We first assume that C is linear in T and M and increasing in both. The expenditure of time T has, in other words, a money equivalent that is a linear function of T. Under this assumption, the expected value of C for given budgets b_1, b_2 can be written

$$b_1 + b_2 + aE \min [t_1(b_1), t_2(b_2)].$$

It follows that for any total budget B the optimal allocation of the budget between the two approaches is to devote an amount $\hat{b}(B)$ to the first approach and an amount $B - \hat{b}(B)$ to the second approach such that

$$\varphi[B,\hat{b}(B)] \equiv E \min \{t_1[\hat{b}(B)], t_2[B - \hat{b}(B)]\}$$

is less than $\varphi[B,b]$ for any other b, $0 \leqq b \leqq B$. (It is not possible to reallocate the budget B, that is to say, in such a way as to decrease the expected value of the time to completion of the approach that is completed first.)

Now suppose we knew that the function $\varphi[B,\hat{b}(B)] \equiv \hat{\varphi}(B)$ had the following diminishing returns shape:

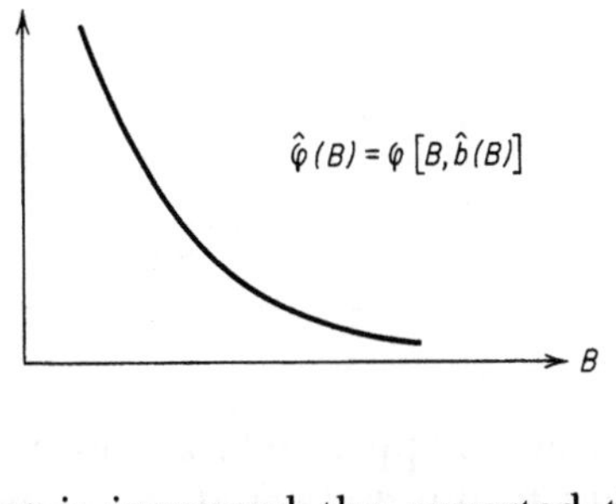

As the total budget is increased the expected time to completion (when the total budget is optimally allocated) declines, but at a diminishing rate; each increment in the budget drops the expected time to completion by less than the preceding increment. We know from our assumption about C that the developer's preferences among the combinations of $\hat{\varphi}$ and B can be represented by straight indifference lines; the higher the indifference line on which a given combination lies the worse the combination is. The optimal budget B^* is, then, that one for which the corresponding point on the $\hat{\varphi}$-curve lies on the lowest indifference line; this occurs at the tangency point shown in the following diagram.

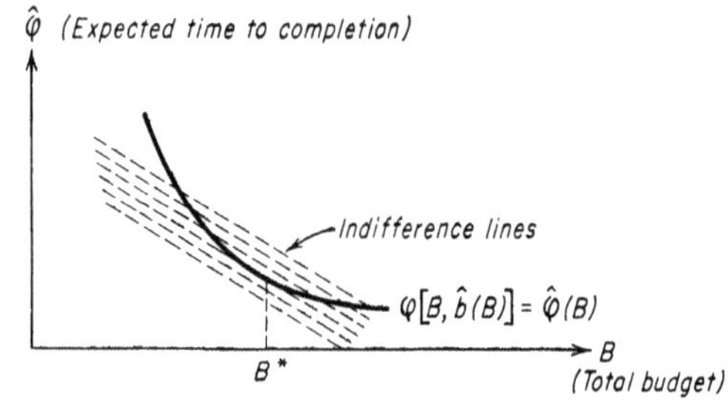

The existence and uniqueness of an optimal budget is then established.[33]

If, on the other hand, the $\hat{\varphi}$-curve is concave to the origin (exhibits increasing returns) then there may be more than one optimal budget. The curve cannot be everywhere concave or it would have to intersect both axes which would mean that a zero budget still permits a finite completion time and that a zero completion time is obtainable with a finite budget. But the curve might be concave to the right of some small value of B, say δ, and to the left of some large value, say Δ, as in the diagram below.

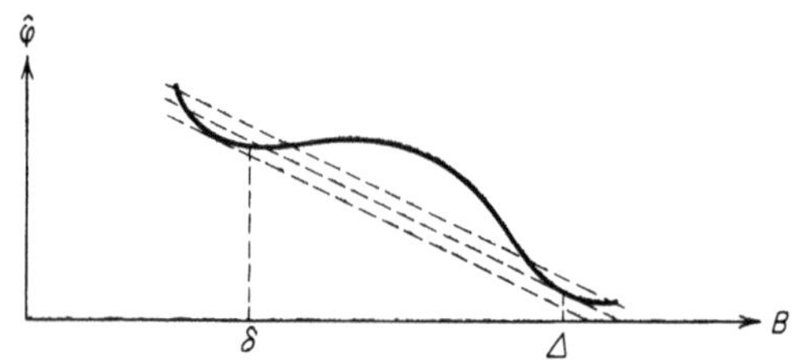

If the indifference lines happen to be as shown, then δ and Δ would both be optimal budgets. But this would be a coincidence and a curve such as that just shown would be nearly as reassuring from the stand-

[33] Provided that the $\hat{\varphi}$-curve is in fact asymptotic to both axes, as shown. If the curve is not defined below some (very low) B or above some (very high) B, then the pathological case is possible in which no tangency point occurs.

point of uniqueness of optimal budget as the convex curve of the previous figure. Typically the optimal budget would be either δ or Δ depending on the slope of the indifference lines.

If there are many concave regions and many convex ones in the $\hat{\varphi}$-function, as indicated in the figure below, then the possibility of

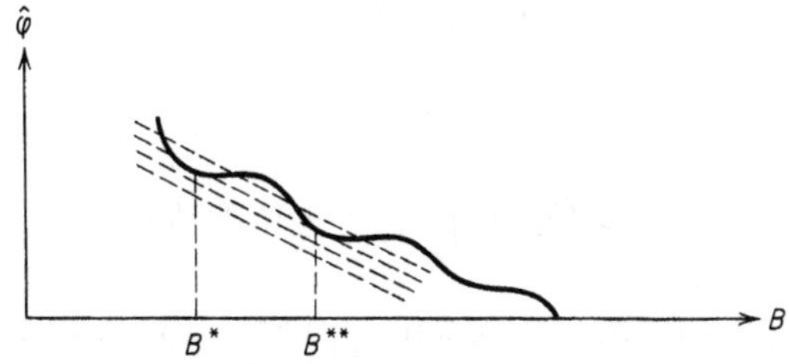

more than one optimal budget is more serious. It is still, however, not the general case; there is generally a finite number of tangency points and the one on the lowest indifference line defines a unique optimal budget. What would make this case alarming, however, is the difficulty of finding the optimal budget. If the developer knows that he is in the case of the concave $\hat{\varphi}$-curve with one tangency point he can approximate the optimal budget by computing the expected time $\hat{\varphi}$ for a low B, then considering a number of successive increments in B and determining for each of them whether the drop in $\hat{\varphi}$ is worth the increase in B. He can make the approximation as close as he wishes. If he knows that he is in the case of the second figure he needs only to make the computation for two values of B $-\delta$ and $\Delta-$ whose location he either knows or can approximate. But if he knows that he is in the case of the third figure and does not know the number of humps nor their location, he must then compute the entire φ-function in order to find the optimal budget.

It is, therefore, of considerable interest to find, for each of these three cases, general conditions under which the developer can be sure he is in the given case. In searching for these conditions, one is also led to propositions about the function $\hat{b}(B)$ which gives the optimal allocation of the budget B between the two approaches. In particular it becomes possible to investigate an important, intuitive, plausible rule of thumb—that the optimal division of the budget is not to devote all of it to one approach.

We are interested, then, in finding for a number of classes of distributions $F(t_1,b_1)$, $G(t_2,b_2)$, (1) the function $\hat{b}(B)$ (where B equals $b_1 + b_2$), and (2) whether the function $\hat{\varphi}$ is of the type shown in the first, second, or third of the three figures above. But we shall confine the present discussion to some initial steps.

6.1.1. The Case of Two Indistinguishable Approaches. First, let $\mu_1(b_1)$ denote the expected time to completion of the first approach if the budget b_1 is made available to it, that is,

$$\mu_1(b_1) = \int_0^\infty [1 - F(t_1,b_1)]dt.$$

Similarly, let

$$\mu_2(b_2) = \int_0^\infty [1 - G(t_2,b_2)]dt.$$

Suppose now (a) that for each approach the distribution of times to completion is uniquely determined by its mean – once we know the expected time to completion we know also the probability density attached to all possible completion times. (For example, the distribution of completion times might be a rectangular one with zero probability for non-negative times; each member of this class of distributions is uniquely determined by its mean.) Suppose, moreover, (b) that the same family of probability distributions of time to completion characterizes both approaches. Suppose, finally, (c) that the function relating the expected times to completion to the money spent is the same non-increasing function $\mu(b)$ for each approach, that is, that for any $b \geqq 0$, $\mu_1(b) = \mu_2(b) = \mu(b)$. Assumptions (a) to (c) imply that the developer's *a priori* knowledge of the two approaches gives him no grounds for preferring one to the other (were he forced to choose either one or the other). They are, in fact, indistinguishable.

If b_1 and b_2 are given, then, the time to completion for the first approach has a probability distribution $F(t,b_1) = H[t,\mu(b_1)]$ and the time to completion for the second approach has the distribution $G(t,b_2) - H[t,\mu(b_1)]$, where t is the random variable and $\mu(b_1)$, $\mu(b_2)$ are parameters uniquely identifying the distribution of t. We shall make another assumption: (d) that the function $H(t,\mu)$ is twice differentiable with respect to μ for $\mu > 0$ and that $\mu(b)$ is twice differentiable for $b > 0$. The first and second derivatives are denoted $\mu'(b),\mu''(b)$, respectively.

Then for a fixed total budget B, of which $b \leqq B$ is assigned to the first approach, the expected time to completion of development is, by the Fundamental Lemma,

$$\varphi(B,b) = \int_0^\infty \{1 - H[\mu(b),t]\}\{1 - H[\mu(B - b),t]\}dt.$$

We have to clarify the meaning of $\mu(0)$ and of $H[t,\mu(0)]$. When a zero budget is assigned to an approach it takes an infinite amount of time to complete that approach. The most convenient assumptions expressing this fact are the following two. First, we assume

$$\lim_{b\to 0} \mu(b) = \infty$$

(that is, $\mu(b)$ can be made as large as desired by taking b small enough). Secondly, for the family of distributions $H[\mu(b),t]$ characterizing an approach, we define $H[\mu(0),t]$ for any $t > 0$, to be the limit of $H[\mu(b),t]$ as b goes to zero, and we assume this limit to equal zero. That is, by taking b small enough, the probability that the completion time exceeds any given non-negative number t can be made as close as desired to one. We then have for the expected completion time when the first approach gets all of a total budget B, and the second gets none,

$$\varphi(B,0) = \int_0^\infty \{1 - H[\mu(B),t]\}\,dt.$$

As remarked in the proof of the Fundamental Lemma, the integral is another way of writing the expected value of the random variable whose distribution is given by $H[\mu(B),t]$, and hence $\varphi(B,0) = \mu(B)$.

We now want to find $\hat{b}(B)$—the optimal portion of the budget B to assign to the first approach, $0 \leqq \hat{b}(B) \leqq B$. A first step is to see for what value of b the partial derivative of $\varphi(B,b)$ with respect to b is zero. For under additional conditions this value of b will be that value b between zero and B for which $\varphi(B,b)$ is a minimum. We write

$$0 = \frac{\partial\varphi}{\partial b} = \int_0^\infty (\{1 - H[\mu(b),t]\}H_\mu[\mu(B-b),t]\mu'(B-b)$$
$$- \{1 - H[\mu(B-b),t]\}H_\mu[\mu(b),t]\mu'(b))\,dt, \quad (28)$$

where the symbol $H_\mu(y,t)$ denotes

$$\frac{\partial H(\mu,t)}{\partial\mu}$$

evaluated at $\mu = y$.

We first note that for $b = B/2$, the two large terms in the integral become identical, so that (28) is satisfied for $b = B/2$. The derivative of the expected development time with respect to the portion of the total budget spent on the first project is always zero when this portion is exactly half. But now observe that the function $\varphi(B,b)$ is completely symmetrical about $b = B/2$. For $\varphi(B,b) = \varphi(B,B-b)$. Since the two approaches are indistinguishable, to devote b dollars to the first and $B - b$ to the second is the same as devoting $B - b$ to the first and b to the second. It is clear that if the φ-curve has a second derivative of constant sign then it must have one of the three shapes in the following diagram:

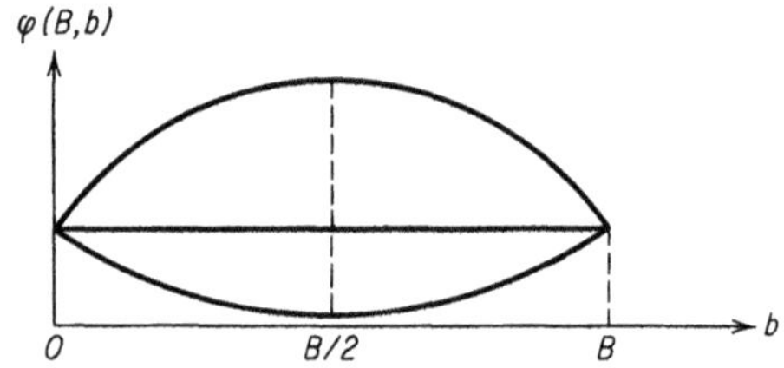

We have, then, the following result:

> If for any B the derivative of $\varphi(b,B)$ with respect to b (the marginal drop in expected completion time as the budget of the first approach is increased) is everywhere negative between $b = 0$ and $b = B/2$, then the optimal budget for the approach is $\hat{b}(B) = B/2$. If the derivative is positive in this interval, the optimal budget is $\hat{b}(B) = 0$ (or equivalently $\hat{b}(B) = B$). If the derivative is zero in this interval all budgets are equally good. (29)

It then becomes important to find interesting conditions on the functions μ and H under which the derivative is everywhere positive, negative, or zero between $b = 0$ and $b = B/2$. A glance at (28) reveals that the only broad and easily established conditions of this kind must specify the sign of the first and second derivatives of $H(\mu,t)$ with respect to μ (for all t) and the sign of the second derivative of the function μ.

We consider one such condition on $H(\mu,t)$. Suppose that

$$H_\mu(\mu,t) < 0 \text{ for all } t > 0,\ \mu > 0$$

and

$$\frac{\partial^2 H(t,\mu)}{\partial \mu^2} \equiv H_{\mu\mu}(\mu,t) > 0 \text{ for all } t > 0,\ \mu > 0. \qquad (30)$$

These conditions are satisfied by certain monotonic sets of distributions (to use our earlier concept). They are satisfied, for example, when $H(\mu,t)$ is the exponential distribution, that is $H(\mu,t) = 1 - e^{-\mu t}$ for $t > 0$.

As far as conditions on the function μ are concerned, three interesting ones to investigate are the following.

1) $\mu(b)$ exhibits diminishing returns $\mu''(b) > 0$ (31a)

2) $\mu(b)$ exhibits increasing returns. This has to be defined in a slightly more complicated way than just satisfaction of $\mu''(b) < 0$ for all $b \geqq 0$ (the definition symmetrical to (31a)). For we want $\mu(0)$ to be infinite and this cannot be the case if $\mu''(0) < 0$. A natural definition of "increasing returns" is:

$$\mu''(b) < 0 \text{ for } \epsilon < b < B^*, \tag{31b}$$

where ϵ is small and B^* is very large, larger than any budget that arises in the analysis. The μ-curve, that is to say, has the shape shown in the figure. The curve has an inflection point at ϵ. We shall assume

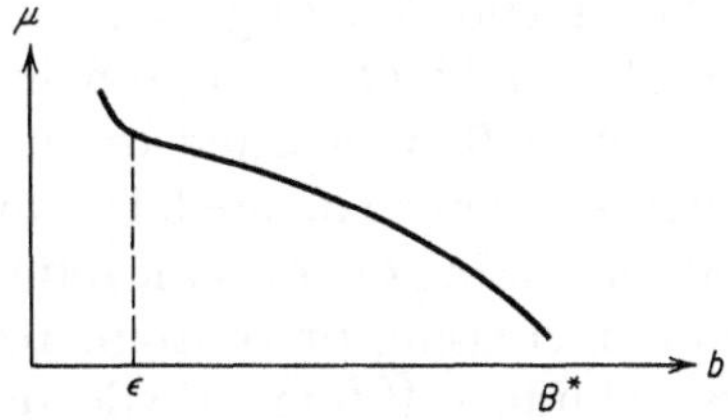

that at least ϵ has to be devoted to each approach in the increasing returns case.

3) $\mu(b)$ exhibits constant returns. We define this case analogously:

$$\mu''(b) = 0 \text{ for } \epsilon < b < B^*. \tag{31c}$$

Now for the case of increasing returns, if (30) is satisfied, then we have for $\epsilon < b \leqq B/2$,

$$1 - H[\mu(b),t] > 1 - H[\mu(B-b),t] > 0,$$
$$H_\mu[\mu(B-b),t] \leqq H_\mu[\mu(b),t] < 0$$

and

$$0 < \mu'(b) \leqq \mu'(B-b).$$

Hence from (28) we see that $d\varphi(B,b)/db > 0$ for $\epsilon < b < B/2$, so that the optimal allocation of the total budget is to devote all (but ϵ) of it to one approach.

If there are constant returns in the μ-function, then under the conditions (30) the optimal allocation consists in devoting all (but ϵ) of B

to one approach. This is perhaps somewhat surprising. When each successive increment in an approach's budget changes expected completion time by the same amount, one might have thought that all divisions of the total budget between the two approaches would be equally good.[34]

If the μ-function exhibits decreasing returns then the conditions (30) do not by themselves imply anything about the optimal allocation of the budget. As the discussion of Section 6.1.2 below will imply, one can find families of distributions satisfying (30) and decreasing returns functions μ, such that the optimal allocation consists in devoting all the budget to one approach; and one can find others such that the optimal allocation consists in devoting some of the budget to each approach.

Let us now check to see whether, when conditions (30) hold, the knowledge of this fact, and the knowledge of $\hat{b}(B)$, yield information about the shape of the function relating total budget to expected development time when the total budget is optimally allocated. If all but ϵ of the given total budget B is allocated to one approach, the expected time to completion is approximated, for small ϵ, by $\mu(B)$. Then under conditions (30) increasing or constant returns to the budget of an approach do imply increasing or constant returns, respectively, with respect to the total budget. If there are decreasing returns to the budget of an approach, then the conditions (30) do not by themselves imply either decreasing or increasing or constant returns.

It is unfortunate that there are no general propositions for the diminishing returns case ($\mu'' > 0$) for families of distributions in which H_μ, $H_{\mu\mu}$ satisfy (3). The diminishing returns case seems likely

[34] The conditions (30) can be restated so that strict differentiability and twice differentiability of the function $H(\mu,t)$ with respect to μ are no longer required. If, in particular, we require only that $H(\mu,t)$ possess for all $\mu > 0$ a left-hand derivative $H_\mu(\mu,t)$ and the function $H_\mu(\mu,t)$ possess for all $\mu > 0$ a left-hand derivative $H_{\mu\mu}(\mu,t)$ then the results just given for the original conditions (30), still hold when $H_\mu(\mu,t)$, $H_{\mu\mu}(\mu,t)$ are interpreted as left-hand derivatives in the statement of these conditions. Thus, for example, the reinterpreted conditions (30) are satisfied when $H(\mu,t)$ is rectangular:

$$H(\mu,t) = \begin{cases} \dfrac{t}{2\mu}, & 0 \leqq t \leqq 2\mu \quad \text{or} \quad 0 \leqq t/2 \leqq \mu \\ 1, & t > 2\mu \quad \text{or} \quad t/2 > \mu \end{cases}$$

The function $H(\mu,t)$ has no derivative with respect to μ at $\mu = t/2$ but it does have a left-hand derivative there. The function $H_\mu(\mu,t)$ has a discontinuity at $t/2$, but also has a left-hand derivative there. Since the reinterpreted conditions (30) are satisfied, we have that for $\mu(b)$ exhibiting increasing or constant returns and for rectangular $H(\mu,t)$ the optimal allocation of B consists in spending all but ϵ of it on one approach.

to be empirically the most important one. If, moreover, we were to incorporate the pure parallel approach problem of Section 4 into the present problem we might be able to demonstrate the condition $\mu'' > 0$. For we could interpret the allocation of a larger and larger budget to an approach as the assignment of more and more initially indistinguishable groups of people, each group costing the same, to the pursuit of the same approach; at some review point all but one of the groups is dismissed. At each review point new estimates of each group's completion time become available. It may be that if the distribution of these estimates meets a stronger condition than the monotonicity condition of Section 4, then under an optimal policy the expected completion time for the approach drops, but at a diminishing rate, as the number of groups is increased.

There are certainly families of distributions $H(\mu,t)$, twice differentiable with respect to μ, for which $H_\mu < 0, H_{\mu\mu} \geqq 0$ fails to hold. If the developer feels that he is dealing with such a family, but he does not know which one, then the curve $\varphi(b,B)$ may, for all the developer knows, rise and fall many times. All he knows about it is that it is symmetrical about $B/2$ and has a zero derivative at $B/2$. He may be unable to find the optimal budget $\hat{b}(B)$ for the first approach or the shape of the curve $\varphi[B,\hat{b}(B)]$.

Thus all rules of thumb, however intuitively appealing, that purport to give either the optimal allocation of a budget, or the shape of the curve relating expected time to optimally allocated total budget, and that require knowledge of nothing but the shape of the μ-function, have no general validity. The rule "don't put all eggs in one basket, but allocate something to each approach, at least when there are diminishing returns in the μ-function" is not generally valid. And neither is the rule "the curve relating expected completion time to optimally allocated total budget has increasing, constant, or diminishing returns according as the μ-function itself has increasing, constant, or diminishing returns." Progress toward usable and valid rules lies only in the exploration of particular families of probability distributions, and the rules found will require of the developer that he explicitly decide whether or not the probability distribution confronting him belongs to these families. The case of the family of rectangular distributions discussed in footnote 34 is solved below.

6.1.2. The Case of Two Initially Different Approaches. Suppose now that the two approaches available to the developer are not initially indistinguishable. The expected time to completion for an approach budget of b is given by the function $\mu_1(b)$ for the first approach and $\mu_2(b)$ for the second. It is fairly clear that no interesting results can be obtained unless we further specify the relation between these two functions.

We shall explore the following assumption: For all b, $\mu_1(b)$ bears a constant ratio to $\mu_2(b)$. Specifically $\mu_1(b) = k\mu_2(b)$, where $k < 1$. The first approach is then the better approach in the sense that it yields a lower expected completion time for any approach budget. But it by no means follows that all of any total budget should be allocated to it. We assume again that for either approach completion time has a distribution $H(\mu,t)$, uniquely determined by μ.

For any total budget B the expected completion time is, if b is allocated to the first approach ($0 \leqslant b \leqslant B$),

$$\bar{\varphi}(k,b,B) = \int_0^\infty \{1 - H[k\mu_2(b),t]\}\{1 - H[\mu_2(B - b),t]\}\,dt.$$

We want to determine the optimal portion $\hat{b}(B)$ of a given total budget B to be allocated to the first approach, $0 \leqslant \hat{b}(B) \leqslant B$. Without knowing anything further about the functions H and μ_2, nothing can be concluded about $\hat{b}(B)$ except, of course, that it cannot equal zero (since allocating B to the first approach is better than allocating nothing to it and everything to the second). In general we cannot even assert that $\hat{b}(B) < B/2$.

First case: $H(\mu,t)$ rectangular, $\mu(b)$ a rectangular hyperbola. Accordingly we investigate a still interesting but highly specific pair of assumptions.

1) $H(\mu,t)$ is a rectangular distribution with mean μ, that is,

$$H(\mu,t) = \begin{cases} \dfrac{t}{2\mu}, & 0 \leqq t \leqq 2\mu \\ 1, & t > 2\mu. \end{cases}$$

2) The function $\mu(b)$ characterizing an approach is a rectangular hyperbola; it has the form $\mu = k/b$. For the two approaches in question we can write [35]

$$\mu_1^{(b)} = \frac{k_1}{b}$$

$$\mu_2^{(b)} = \frac{k_2}{b}.$$

[35] In all that follows the μ-function could be generalized somewhat by introducing an exponent. We could have $\mu(b) = k/b^w$ (where $w > 0$) and all the following results would be preserved.

Now it quickly follows from the Fundamental Lemma that if one drawing is taken from a non-negative rectangular population with mean μ_1 and another from a non-negative rectangular population with mean μ_2, where $\mu_1 \leqslant \mu_2$, the expected value of the minimum of the two drawings is $\mu_1 - \mu_1^2/3\mu_2$. Accordingly, the expected time to completion when b out of a budget B is allocated to the first approach and $B - b$ to the second is

$$\bar{\varphi}(k_1,k_2,b,B) = \begin{cases} \varphi_1(k_1,k_2,b,B) = \dfrac{k_1}{b} - \dfrac{k_1^2(B-b)}{3b^2k_2} \text{ if} \\ \dfrac{k_1}{b} \leqq \dfrac{k_2}{B-b} \left(\text{or equivalently if} \right. \\ \left. b \geqq \dfrac{Bk_1}{k_1+k_2}\right) \\ \varphi_2(k_1,k_2,b,B) = \dfrac{k_2}{B-b} - \dfrac{bk_2^2}{3k_1(B-b)^2} \text{ if} \\ \dfrac{k_1}{b} \geqq \dfrac{k_2}{B-b} \left(\text{or equivalently if} \right. \\ \left. b \leqq \dfrac{Bk_1}{k_1+k_2}\right), \end{cases}$$

where $0 \leqq b \leqq B$.

Note the following symmetry: $\bar{\varphi}(k_1,k_2,b,B) = \bar{\varphi}(k_2,k_1,B-b,b)$. In words: to devote b to the first approach and $B - b$ to the second when the first approach is characterized by k_1 and the second by k_2 is the same as devoting $B - b$ to the first and b to the second when the first is characterized by k_2 and the second by k_1.

Let us now investigate the shape of the $\bar{\varphi}$-curve (which is differentiable for $0 \leqslant b < B$) by looking at the derivatives of its two parts. We obtain

$$\frac{\partial\varphi_1}{\partial\varphi} = \frac{k_1^2(2B-b) - 3k_1k_2b}{3k_2b^3}, \quad \frac{k_1B}{k_1+k_2} \leqq b \leqq B,$$

$$\frac{\partial\varphi_2}{\partial b} = \frac{k_2}{(B-b)^2}\left[1 - \frac{k_2(b+B)}{3k_1(B-b)}\right], \quad 0 \leqq b \leqq \frac{k_1B}{k_1+k_2}.$$

Hence

$$\frac{\partial\varphi_1}{\partial b} \begin{Bmatrix} > \\ = \\ < \end{Bmatrix} 0 \text{ according as } \frac{k_1}{k_2} \begin{Bmatrix} > \\ = \\ < \end{Bmatrix} \frac{3b}{2B-b}, \quad \frac{k_1B}{k_1+k_2} \leqq b \leqq B,$$

and

$$\frac{\partial \varphi_2}{\partial b} \begin{Bmatrix} > \\ \equiv \\ < \end{Bmatrix} 0 \text{ according as } \frac{k_1}{k_2} \begin{Bmatrix} > \\ \equiv \\ < \end{Bmatrix} \frac{B+b}{3(B-b)}, \quad 0 \leqq b \leqq \frac{k_1 B}{k_1 + k_2}.$$

Suppose now that $k_2/k_1 < 1$, that is, in the k_1k_2-space the point (k_1,k_2) lies in the positive quadrant and, if the k_1-axis is vertical, on or above the line $k_1 = k_2$. For brevity write $\lambda = k_2/k_1$. Then if

$$0 < b < \frac{k_1 B}{k_1 + k_2} = \frac{B}{1+\lambda}, \text{ or } \frac{b}{B} < \frac{1}{1+\lambda},$$

it is also true that

$$\frac{b}{B} < \frac{3-\lambda}{\lambda+3}.$$

For if $0 < \lambda < 1$ then

$$0 < \lambda - \lambda^2$$

and

$$\lambda + 3 < 3 + 2\lambda - \lambda^2$$

or

$$\lambda + 3 < (1+\lambda)(3-\lambda),$$

whence

$$\frac{1}{1+\lambda} < \frac{3-\lambda}{\lambda+3}.$$

But $b/B < (3-\lambda)/(\lambda+3)$ implies $1/\lambda > (b+B)/3(B-b)$. Hence, if $0 \leqslant b < k_1B/(k_1+k_2)$ and $0 < \lambda < 1$, we have

$$\frac{\partial \varphi_2}{\partial b} > 0.$$

Continuing with the case $0 < \lambda < 1$, we find that $\partial\varphi_1/\partial b$ can be either negative or positive for

$$\frac{k_1 B}{k_1 + k_2} < b \leqslant B.$$

But note that if $\partial\varphi_1/\partial b$ is negative at some b between $k_1B/(k_1+k_2)$ and B, then it must be negative at all higher b up to $b = B$. This is so since $3b/2B - b$ is an increasing function of b (up to $b = B$).

We conclude that for the case $k_2/k_1 < 1$ the $\bar{\varphi}$-curve has one of the following two shapes:

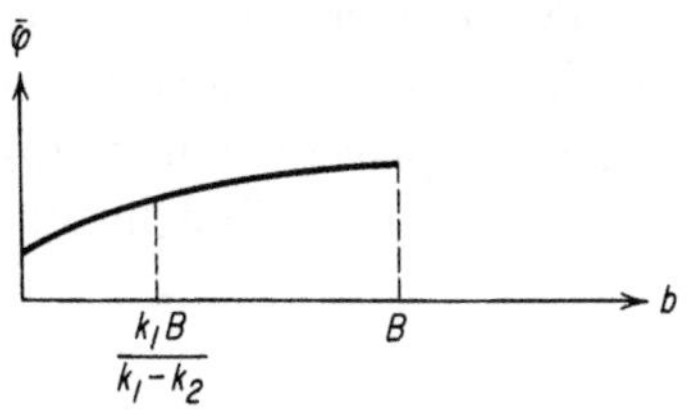

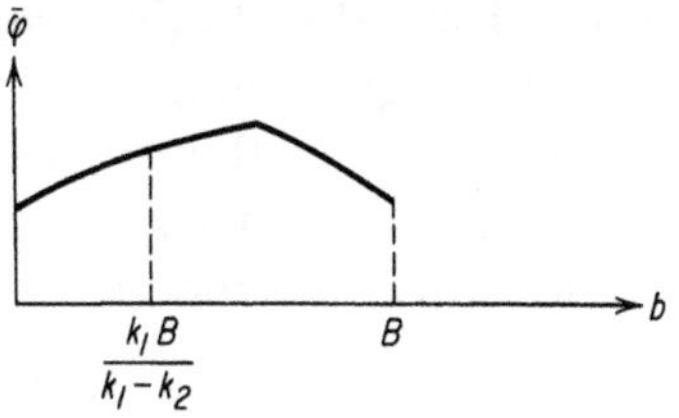

If the first figure applies, the optimal amount to allocate to the first approach (the one whose expected completion time is higher for every approach budget b) is $\hat{b}(B) = 0$. All of B goes to the second approach. For this optimal allocation the expected completion time is $\bar{\varphi}(k_1,k_2,0,B) = k_2/B$. If the second figure applies, then, the intersection of the $\bar{\varphi}$-curve with the line $b = B$ must occur at a value of $\bar{\varphi}$ higher than $\bar{\varphi}(k_1,k_2,0,B) = k_2/B$. For otherwise we would have $\bar{\varphi}(k_1,k_2,B,B) = k_1/B < k_2/B$, which is false. So when the second figure applies it is also true that $\hat{b}(B) = 0$.

However, by the symmetry of the φ-function we immediately have a similarly complete result for the case $k_1/k_2 < 1$. In this case $\hat{b}(B) = B$.

Finally, in the case $k_1 = k_2$ the φ-function looks like

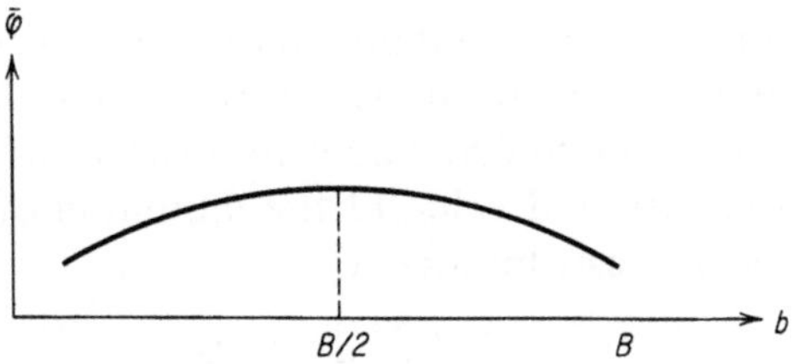

The two halves of the $\bar{\varphi}$-function are perfectly symmetrical about $b = B/2$ and at $b = B/2, \dfrac{\partial \varphi_1}{\partial b} = \dfrac{\partial \varphi_2}{\partial b} = 0$. The optimal allocation consists in devoting the entire budget to either of the two (indistinguishable) approaches.

To summarize: The optimal allocation of any total budget B consists in devoting all of it to approach one if $k_1 \leqq k_2$, approach two if $k_2 \geqq k_1$.

Second case: $H(\mu,t)$ triangular, $\mu(b)$ a rectangular hyperbola. We now investigate the same situation for a case in which the distributions of completion time are not a family of flat rectangular distributions but instead are distributions with a unique mode or peak. Such distributions might well be regarded as more realistic; we shall investigate whether or not the greater realism changes the possibly surprising "all eggs in one basket" result of the rectangular case. Specifically, we let $H(\mu,t)$ be triangular:

$$H(\mu,t) = \begin{cases} \dfrac{t^2}{2\mu^2}, & t \leqq \mu \\ 1 - \dfrac{(2\mu - t)^2}{2\mu^2}, & \mu < t \leqq 2\mu \\ 1, & t > 2\mu. \end{cases}$$

The corresponding probability density function $h(\mu,t)$ is as in the figure:

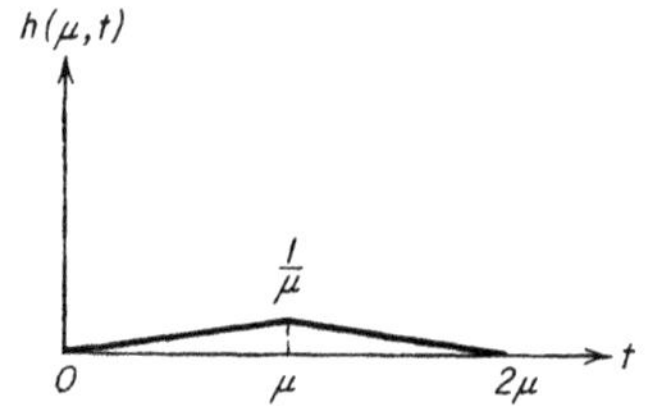

We first obtain from the Fundamental Lemma, after considerable computation, the following result. Given two triangular distributions of the kind shown in the figure, one with mean r and the other with mean s, $r \leqq s$, the expected value of the minimum of two drawings, one from each of the distributions, is

$$r - \tfrac{1}{4}(r^3/s^2), \quad \text{if} \quad 2r \leqq s,$$

and a more complicated expression (which we can ignore for the present purpose) if $2r > s$. It follows that in studying the curve $\bar{\varphi}(k_1,k_2,b,B)$, which gives the expected completion time when b dollars goes to the first approach and $B - b$ to the second, we can divide the interval $0 \leqq b \leqq B$ into four sub-intervals. In the interval

$$0 \leqq b < \frac{k_1 B}{2k_2 + k_1}$$

we have

$$\frac{2k_2}{B - b} < \frac{k_1}{B}$$

so that the second approach has the smaller (or not larger) mean completion time and twice this mean is less than the mean completion time for the first approach. Hence $\bar{\varphi}$ takes the form $r - \frac{1}{4}(r^3/s^2)$ with $r = \frac{k_2}{B-b}$, $s = \frac{k_1}{b}$. In the interval $\frac{k_1 B}{2k_2 + k_1} \leqq b < \frac{k_1 B}{k_2 + k_1}$, we have $\frac{k_1}{b} \geqq \frac{k_2}{B-b}$ and $\frac{2k_2}{B-b} > \frac{k_1}{b}$ so that the second approach has the smaller (or not larger) mean completion time and twice this mean is greater than the mean of the first approach. Hence $\bar{\varphi}$ takes the more complicated form which we have not given. The function $\bar{\varphi}$ also takes this form for the interval

$$\frac{k_1 B}{k_2 + k_1} \leqq b < \frac{2k_1 B}{k_2 + 2k_1}.$$

For here

$$\frac{k_1}{b} \leqq \frac{k_2}{B-b} \quad \text{and} \quad \frac{2k_1}{b} > \frac{k_2}{B-b}$$

so that the first approach has smaller mean completion time and twice this mean is greater than the mean of the second approach. Finally, in the interval

$$\frac{2k_1 B}{k_2 + 2k_1} \leqq b \leqq B$$

$\bar{\varphi}$ again has the form $r - \frac{1}{4}(r^3/s^2)$ with $r = k_1/b$ and $s = \frac{k_2}{B-b}$. For here $\frac{2k_1}{b} \leqq \frac{k_2}{B-b}$; the first approach has smaller mean completion time and twice this mean is less than the mean completion time for the second approach.

The intervals really are adjoining but non-overlapping intervals, since for any $k_1 > 0$, $k_2 > 0$, $B > 0$,

$$0 < \frac{k_1 B}{2k_2 + k_1} < \frac{k_1 B}{k_2 + k_1} < \frac{2k_1 B}{k_2 + 2k_1} < B.$$

Now we can find b, B, k_1, k_2 such that $\min\,[\bar{\varphi}(k_1,k_2,0,B), \bar{\varphi}(k_1,k_2,B,0)] > \bar{\varphi}(k_1,k_2,b,B)$, while $\bar{\varphi}(k_1,k_2,0,B) = k_2/B$ and $\bar{\varphi}(k_1,k_2,B,0) = k_1/B$. If for example $k_1 = 2$, $k_2 = 3$, and

$$b = \tfrac{3}{5}B < \tfrac{4}{5}B = \frac{2k_1 B}{2k_1 + k_2},$$

then

$$\bar{\varphi}(k_1,k_2,b,B) = \frac{k_2}{B-b} - \frac{1}{4}\frac{b^2}{k_1^2}\frac{k_2^2}{(B-b)^3} = \frac{15B}{2} - \frac{9315}{128B}$$

which is less than min $(k_1/B,k_2/B) = 2/B$ if $B^2 < 4/15 + 621/64$. Hence it can happen that allocation of some positive part of the total budget B to each approach is optimal.

It is possible but more complicated to show that if one of the ks is sufficiently greater than the other then it is optimal to allocate all of B to one of the approaches. We omit the demonstration here. The fact is, in any case, that the surprising optimality of the all eggs in one basket allocation may hold even when we replace the rectangular distributions by the more natural triangular ones. When we do so, however, the allocation may also be non-optimal.

6.1.3. A Case of *n* Initially Indistinguishable Approaches. We explore now an n-approach generalization of the above two-approach problem for indistinguishable rectangular distributions. Suppose the developer has n approaches available but his *a priori* knowledge affords no relevant basis for distinguishing between them. Let the μ-function characterizing each approach again be $\mu(b) = k/b$ and let the distribution $H(\mu,t)$ again be rectangular.

For a given total budget B the developer is to choose n approach budgets $b_1, \ldots, b_n$ $(0 \leqq b_i \leqq B, i = 1, \ldots, n)$ such that $\Sigma b_i = B$ and such that expected completion time is a minimum. From the Fundamental Lemma we see that expected completion time is given by

$$\bar{\varphi}(b_1, \ldots, b_n, B) = \int_0^{\min(b_1,\ldots,b_n)} \left(1 - \frac{tb_1}{2k}\right)\left(1 - \frac{tb_2}{2k}\right) \cdots \left(1 - \frac{tb_n}{2k}\right) dt.$$

It is easily verified, from the Lemma, that the expected value of the minimum of a sample of n from a non-negative rectangular population with mean μ is $2\mu/(n+1)$, so that in the present case

$$\bar{\varphi}\left(\frac{B}{n}, \ldots, \frac{B}{n}\right) = \frac{2kn}{B(n+1)}.$$

On the other hand, if any of the b_i are equal to B, then $\bar{\varphi}$ takes the value k/B. Since $n > 1$, $2n/(n+1) > 1$ and hence $2kn/B(n+1) > k/B$. To assign all of the total budget to one approach yields a lower expected completion time than dividing it equally among the n approaches.

This suggests that the optimal allocation assigns the total budget to one approach, just as was the case for $n = 2$. This can in fact be proved. The central idea of the proof is that if, in the n-dimensional space of the bs, one moves in any direction away from $(B/n, \ldots, B/n)$ while remaining on the hyperplane $\Sigma b_i = B$ and in the positive orthant, then the value of $\bar{\varphi}$ continually declines until one of the axes is reached; at this point all of B is devoted to some one approach and $\bar{\varphi}$ is as low as it is possible to make it.

6.1.4. A Case of *n* Approaches Not Initially Indistinguishable. Combining the preceding two problems we have n approaches i, each characterized by a different number $k_i > 0$; for the ith approach, expected completion time when b dollars is spent on it is b/k_i. Using a proof that combines elements of the proof just sketched for the $k_i = k$ case with a generalization of the proof we gave for the case $n = 2$, $k_i \neq k_2$, we can show the following: The optimal allocation of any budget B consists in devoting all of it to the best approach – an approach i^* for which $k_i \geqslant k_{i^*}$, $i \neq i^*$.

6.1.5. Implications. What are the implications of the results we have obtained in the one shot problems we have studied in which the expected completion time of an approach depends on its budget in a manner defined by a rectangular hyperbola, while the completion time for a given budget has a rectangular probability distribution? In the first place, we have a case in which heavy initial commitments are good (the central issues in the histories of Chapter 3). In the second place, the optimality of allocating the entire total budget to one approach remains unaffected by the size of the total budget; no matter how large it is it never pays to assign any of it to a second approach. Finally, these statements are true even though each approach's μ-function exhibits diminishing returns, and, moreover, as "sharply" diminishing returns as we wish. (The sharpness can be arbitrarily increased by choosing large enough ks.) Intuition might have granted the preceding statements for the case of μ-functions exhibiting increasing or constant returns, but that they are true for the case of diminishing returns seems surprising.

To what extent are these results due to certain peculiar properties of the rectangular distribution? The most disturbing (unrealistic) property of the rectangular distribution is its flatness. The case of triangular distributions allows us to assert that we can construct distributions in which there is a peak (in the density function) and in which the two statements still hold. This is perhaps not surprising; for introducing an arbitrarily slight peak into the rectangular distribution would not be expected to reverse the results we have obtained.

Let the probability distribution remain rectangular, on the other hand, and consider the μ-functions. We know that if the μ-functions were not hyperbolas but horizontal straight lines beginning at some very small value of b, say ϵ, then it would certainly not be optimal to devote all of any total budget to one approach. If we very slightly smooth out such a μ-function as in the following figure, we get a

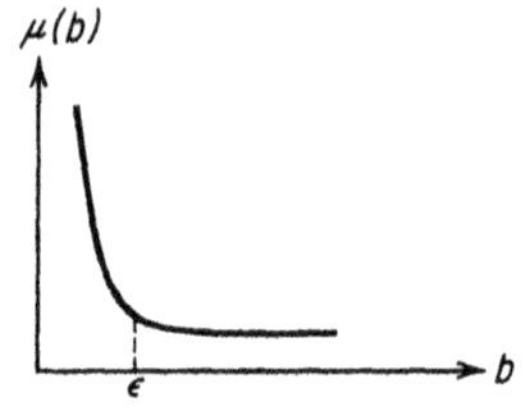

function exhibiting diminishing returns and such that $\mu(0)$ is infinite.[36]

For a collection of approaches characterized by functions such as this, the preceding statements would not hold for every total budget even though the probability distributions of completion times remain rectangular.

We can summarize the general import of the cases studied by simply remarking that the extent to which one can rigorously defend the prescription "avoid heavy initial commitments" is still very little understood even for the relatively simple context of one shot problems.

6.1.6. Other Directions in Which the One Shot Problem May Be Generalized. Two directions of generalization that we have not explored should be recalled. First, we can drop the assumption that once we know the amount spent on an approach we know not only its expected time to completion but also the entire probability distribution of completion times. We can permit the spending of b dollars on an approach to purchase one of several alternative probability distributions of completion times and we can let these alternative distributions differ with respect to parameters other than the mean. Second, we can permit an approach that is not completed (because another approach is completed first) to have a salvage value. Some of the budget initially assigned to the approach is refunded to the developer; how much of it depends on the time the approach has been under way. We shall not explore these complications here but only remark that their introduction would reinforce the statement in the previous paragraph.

6.2. Many Review Point Problems in Which an Approach May Be Pursued with Different Intensities

There are a number of ways of transforming the one shot problem we have considered into a many review point problem, wherein a sequence of development decisions are made. We consider first the

[36] That is, $\lim_{b \to 0} \mu(b) = \infty$.

simplest many review point problem that still follows closely the spirit of the pure parallel approach problem of Section 4 (which was a many review point problem without the possibility of varying the intensity of an approach).

6.2.1. A One Review Point Problem. Suppose that the approaches available to the developer meet the assumptions of Section 6.1.3 and that they differ only with respect to the constant k. Once the developer knows k for an approach he knows the probability distribution of completion times for any proposed budget b to be assigned to that approach; the mean of this distribution is k/b. But initially, let us suppose, the developer does not know the value of k for any approach. Initially he is faced with a collection of indistinguishable approaches. For any approach he can, after the expenditure of a certain amount of time and money, learn the value of k. He learns it at the first review point. His problem is (a) to decide the number n of initially indistinguishable approaches that he will pursue to the first review point, at which k becomes known for each of them; and (b) to decide at that point, on the basis of the ks, how much of any total budget B (the total amount remaining to him at that point) to assign to each of the approaches that are available at the first review point. Answers to (a) and (b) are needed to determine an optimal total budget to be spent on pursuing approaches up to the first review point and pursuing selected approaches beyond the first review point.

As before, progress in solving the problem cannot be made without further assumptions. Suppose we make the same assumptions as in 6.1.3: The μ-function is a rectangular hyperbola and the probability distributions of completion time for an approach whose budget is fixed are rectangular.

The developer, then, starts, in effect, by taking n drawings from the population of the ks; the ith drawing is k_i, which defines $\mu(b) = k_i/b$, the expected completion time for the ith approach when b dollars are spent on it from the first (and only) review point on. We know from 6.1.3 that the optimal allocation of the budget B that the developer has left at the review point consists in devoting all of it to an approach with the lowest k. But now let the developer be given a total budget B^* to be spent on carrying approaches to the review point and carrying the surviving approach from the review point to completion. Assume that it costs one unit of money to pursue an approach to the review point and that it takes one time unit to reach the review point; assume that no approach can be completed before the review point is reached. Then, for a given total budget $B^* > 1$, any (integer) value of n such that $0 < n < B^*$ can be chosen. For a given value of m the expected completion time (beyond the compulsory time unit that gets the developer to the review point) is given by

$$\theta(n,B^*) = \frac{E \min (k_1, \ldots, k_n)}{(B^* - n)}.$$

For a given B^* the developer, knowing the probability distribution of the ks, wants to find an integer n, $0 < n < B^*$ (call it $\hat{n}(B^*)$) that minimizes $\theta(n,B^*)$. But we know that no matter what the probability distribution of the ks, $E \min (k_1, \ldots, k_n)$ decreases as n increases, but at a diminishing rate. We can write $g(n) = E \min (k_1, \ldots, k_n)$ and can momentarily treat n as continuously variable (rather than discrete) and gn as differentiable in order to see what can be said about the shape of $\theta(n,b^*)$ and about $\hat{n}(B^*)$. We have, then, $g'(n) < 0$, $g''(n) > 0$. Also

$$\frac{\partial\theta(n,B^*)}{\partial n} = \frac{g(n)}{(B^* - n)^2} + \frac{g'(n)}{(B^* - n)}.$$

For $0 < n < B^*$ this is $\begin{Bmatrix} > \\ = \\ < \end{Bmatrix}$ 0 according as

$$B^* \begin{Bmatrix} \geq \\ = \\ < \end{Bmatrix} n - \frac{g(n)}{g'(n)}.$$

However, the term $n - g(n)/g'(n)$ increases as n increases (its derivative with respect to n is $[g(n)g''(n)]/[g'(n)]^2 + 2$, which is positive). It follows that once an n is found for which $B^* < n - g(n)/g'(n)$ (and hence $\partial\theta/\partial n < 0$), the same inequality holds for all higher n up to $n + B^*$. Hence the function $\theta(n,B^*)$ must look, as far as its first derivative is concerned, either like this:

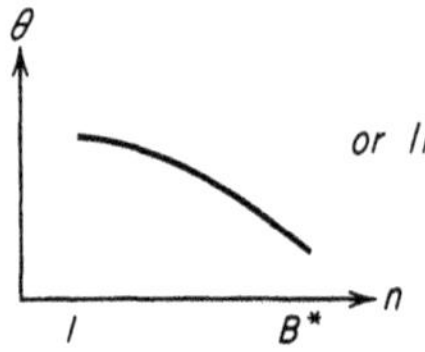

or like this:

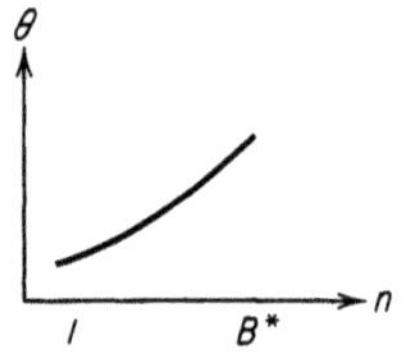

or like this:

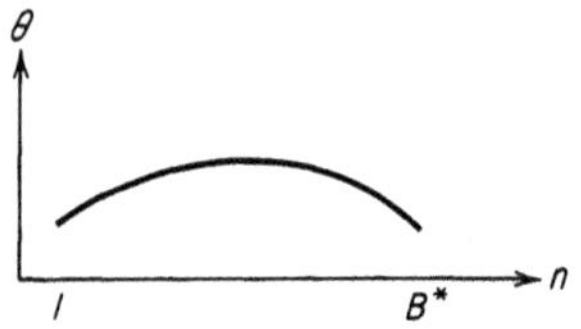

It cannot look like this:

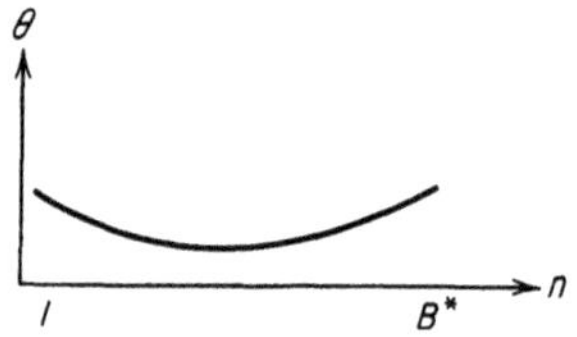

Thus $\hat{n}(B^*)$, the optimal number of approaches to pursue to the review point, is either 1 or else it is B_I^*, the largest integer less than B^* (the largest number of approaches that can be pursued to the review point while there is still some money left over with which to pursue some of them beyond the review point).

Now $\hat{n}(B^*) = 1$ if

$$\frac{g(1)}{B^* - 1} < \frac{g(B_I^*)}{B^* - B_I}$$

and $\hat{n}(B^*) = B_I^*$ if the inequality is reversed. Writing $B_I^* = B^* - \epsilon$ where $0 < \epsilon \leqq 1$, this inequality can be written

$$\epsilon g(1) < g(B^* - \epsilon)(B^* - 1). \tag{32}$$

Now for integers n, $g(n)$ – the expected value of the minimum of a sample of size n from a non-negative population – goes to the population's lower bound (the number below which values occur with probability 0) as n goes to infinity. Depending on how fast $g(n)$ goes to this lower bound the term $ng(n)$ goes, as n goes to infinity, either (a) to some finite non-negative number N (N may be zero if the lower bound is zero), or (b) to infinity.

Consider what happens as we make the total budget B^* larger and larger, while restricting it, for simplicity, to integer values, so that $\epsilon = 1$ in (32). If the distribution of the ks is such that (a) holds, then there is some total budget such that for all higher budgets (all higher values of B^*) the optimal number of approaches to carry to the review point is one if $g(1) < N$ and $B^* - 1$ if $g(1) > N$. If (b) holds there is some total budget such that for all higher budgets the optimal number of approaches to pursue to the review point is one.

We note that if the population of the ks is itself rectangular with mean[37] $g(1)$, then (32) becomes

$$\epsilon g(1) < \frac{2g(1)}{B^* - \epsilon + 1}(B^* - 1)$$

or

$$\epsilon < \frac{2B^* - 1}{B^* - \epsilon + 1}$$

or

$$B^* > \frac{\epsilon^2 - \epsilon - 2}{\epsilon - 2}. \tag{33}$$

[37] The expected value of a minimum of a sample of one is, of course, the same as the mean.

Since the right-hand term is less than one, (33) is satisfied no matter what B^* is, so long as it is greater than one (it need not be an integer). Thus no matter how large B^* is and no matter what the mean (or variance) of the rectangular distribution of the ks, the optimal number of approaches to carry to the review point is one.

Returning to the case of an unspecified k population, observe that when $n(B^*) = 1$, we have

$$\theta[\hat{n}(B^*), B^*] = \frac{g(1)}{B^* - 1},$$

which decreases at a decreasing rate as B^* increases. When $\hat{n}(B) = B_I^*$, we have $\theta[\hat{n}(B), B] = [g(B_I^*)]/(B^* - B_I)$. If we consider only integer values of B^*, then $B^* - B_I$ is always one and again the function decreases at a decreasing rate. (For non-integer values the function θ fluctuates above and below the curve that connects the values of θ for integer values of B^*.)

We can conclude, in any case, that for large enough B^* (and in the case of a rectangular distribution of the ks for any B^*) further increasing the total budget decreases expected development time, but (when the budget is optimally allocated both initially and at the review point) each increase decreases the expected development time by less than the preceding one. This, as we have seen, is a most helpful property in the finding of an optimal budget.

The cases in which the optimal number of approaches to carry to the review point is one (as when the k population is rectangular) are quite remarkable. In these cases the opportunity to acquire information before finally committing one's budget to the best approach (at the second review point) is totally discarded. The intuitively appealing stricture against heavy initial commitments is doubly violated; the final approach is selected at the very start and the entire budget is devoted to it.

Note finally that the intuitively appealing rules of thumb which we examined in the pure parallel approach problem are generally invalid here, just as they were there.

First consider two k populations having the same mean, but different variances. It is reasonable to speak of the high-variance case as the one in which the developer learns more about an approach from carrying it to the first review point. But as we saw earlier, it is not necessarily true that the expected value of the minimum of a sample of size n is smaller for the high variance population than for the low variance population. It is not generally true, therefore, that if, for a given total budget, it pays to pursue a given number of approaches in the low variance case up to the first review point, it pays even more to do so in the high variance case. In interpreting "pays to pursue a given number" we must now allow for the fact that the money saved on the approaches not pursued to the first review point is used instead to carry more intensively beyond the first review point those approaches that are carried to the first review point. The generally invalid rule of thumb is, then: "The more you learn in pursuing an approach to the first review point, the more of any total budget you should spend on pursuing approaches to the first review point."

Second, the rule of thumb discussed at the end of Section 4 would say, in the present context, "the more widely dispersed are the ks characterizing the approaches available at the first review point, the more nearly equal should be the division of the money remaining at the first review point among the approaches available." This is certainly false in the present case since the optimal decision is to devote all the remaining money to the approach with the lowest k.

6.2.2. A Many Review Point Problem. To formulate (but not to solve) the many review point extension of the preceding problem is a simple matter. An approach is characterized now by N numbers $k_1, \ldots, k_N, k$. The numbers k_n become known at the nth review point. To carry an approach from one review point to the next costs a constant amount of time and money—say one money unit and one time unit. No variation in the intensity with which an approach is pursued is possible until review point N. At that point different budgets can be assigned to an approach to be used to carry it to completion; the higher the budget the lower the expected time required beyond review point N until the approach is completed. The number k_N completely determines, for the approach which it characterizes, (1) the relation between expected completion time and money spent beyond the Nth review point (the μ-function); and (2) the probability distribution of time to completion for each alternative amount of money spent beyond the Nth review point (the probability distribution is uniquely determined by its mean).

6.2.3. Other One and Many Review Point Problems. More realistically, we could let the developer vary the intensity with which an approach is pursued before review point N. Then the more money spent on an approach following a review point n and prior to $n+1$ the more is learned in that interval; the more accurate is the developer's knowledge at $n+1$ of the completion times consequent upon alternative expenditures following $n+1$. But also the more money spent between n and $n+1$ the less there is left to do until a satisfactory version of the required item is obtained, and the lower, therefore, is the expected completion time for any given expenditure following $n+1$.

To make precise this much more complex problem, let us consider the case $N = 1$. Initially the developer may now choose an amount of money (call it a_1) to be spent on a given approach. But initially all approaches are indistinguishable. At review point 1, which occurs after one time unit, he observes, for the given approach, an estimate $k_1(a_1)$ whose distribution depends on a_1. He then chooses the remaining amount of money (call it a_2) to be spent on that approach.

Let us be very specific. Let the true probability distribution of times to completion for a given approach when a_1 and a_2 are spent on it be the rectangular distribution whose mean is $k/(a_1 + a_2)$. "Nature" chooses k and the developer will never know exactly what k is. He does know initially a family of joint probability distributions (taken over all approaches) of $k_1(a_1)$ and k, one distribution for each value of a_1. His knowledge of these families of joint probability distributions tells him (1) that $E[k/k_1(a_1)] = k_1(a_1)$, and (2) that $E[k_1(a_1) - k]^2$ is a certain decreasing function of a_1. The greater a_1, the amount spent on carrying an approach to the first review point, the more accurate on the average is the statement that the true k equals the estimate $k_1(a)$.

Given a total budget B^* the developer has to decide at the start of development how many of the initially indistinguishable approaches to pursue to the first review point and how much to spend on each of them. At the first review point, using the signals observed for the approaches that have been pursued to the first review point, he must decide how much of the remaining money to assign to each of these approaches. The time it takes to complete the approach that is completed first is the total time required for development. The developer wants to make both decisions so as to minimize the expected development time.[38]

We shall not reformulate this one review point problem for less specific assumptions, nor solve it for the specific assumptions just given. And we shall not take the space to formulate the general many review point version of the problem. We remark only that one could propose so many promising investigations of specific problems in the simpler classes considered in 6.1, 6.2, and 6.3, that study of the problems in the complex class just described should probably receive a low priority.

7. Multi-component Problems

We have so far assumed the developer's task to be the completion of a satisfactory version of an item, where "satisfactory" means that

[38] Note that if a_1 is sufficiently large compared with the unknown k (if $k/a_1 < 1$), then development may be completed before the first review point occurs.

the item's performance magnitudes lie in a satisfactory part of the performance space. But we have not allowed for one of the important complexities of development, namely, that an item is made up of a number of components, each of which can have one of many alternative sets of characteristics and each of which can be developed in a number of ways.

Let us in fact assume that a finished component can be completely described by a group of numbers; and let each number be a value of a distinct variable called a characteristic of the component. Component i has the θ_i characteristics $v_1^i, \ldots, v_{\theta_i}^i$, denoted, for brevity, by the vector V_i. If the item has s components, then a particular collection of the s vectors $(V_1, \ldots, V_s)$ completely describes the final item and completely determines its performance. The space of the vectors $V = (V_1, \ldots, V_s)$ may in fact be regarded as being itself the performance space, although for some purposes (for example, the next section) it seems more natural to define the performance space as a different space. Whether or not it is different, the satisfactory region in the performance space defines a satisfactory region S in the V-space. The region S may be thought of, to use terms that actually arise in development, as a region of properly mated (or matched) components. The vectors V outside this region define components that do not fit together sufficiently well to give a satisfactory performance for the complete item.

We shall assume that the location of the region S in the V-space is completely known to the developer before development starts. In some important real cases, of course, the knowledge of where S lies is improved as development proceeds. But it is a helpful and, in many cases, a realistic simplification to assume that it is not.

What the developer does not know at the start of development is how costly (in time and money) it will be to attain any particular point in S. For component i's characteristics he may choose a value of V_i that appears very easy to attain, but if, as a result, the requirement that the vector V of all component characteristics lie in S forces another component j to take a value of V_j that is very costly to obtain, then the choice of the easy V_i is a poor one. On the other hand, it is equally risky to choose for each component i a value of V_i that, according to some independent criterion, appears good—for example, to choose large values of $v_1^i, \ldots, v_{\theta_i}^i$ because large values of these characteristics seem generally desirable. To do so may guarantee that the resulting V lies in S, but it may guarantee this at an excessive cost. Whatever his initial choice of V is, the developer can also choose, in general, the effort (money) he will devote to obtaining each of the components V_i. He also has, in general, the option of learning more (at some cost) about the effort required to obtain each alternative V in S before finally deciding on the V to aim for and the effort to be devoted to the V_i making up that V.

In order to clarify these issues we shall briefly explore some very special and simple two component problems.

7.1. *A One Shot, Two Component Problem*

Let the item under development have two components, 1 and 2. Let component 1 be completely described by a single characteristic x and component 2 by a single characteristic y. In the xy space let the satisfactory region S be as shown in the diagram below. It is desirable,

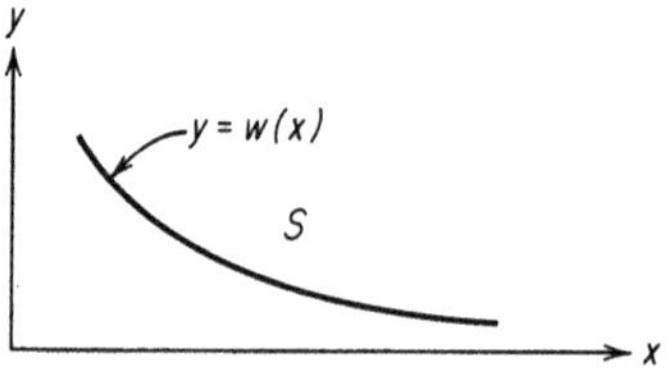

that is to say, to have high values of both characteristics. The lower boundary of S is an indifference curve. Along the curve, x and y can be traded against each other in the manner usually assumed for two commodities (consumed, say, by a household). Points in S above the boundary are actually better than points on the boundary, but our developer troubles himself only with two-valued preferences and is content to be anywhere within the region S. The equation of the concave boundary curve is $y = w(x)$, where w is differentiable for $x > 0$.

Suppose there is available at the start just one approach to each component. An approach to a component will now be defined by a collection of probability distributions of times to completion; to a given value of the characteristic and a given value of the budget to be devoted to the component, there corresponds one probability distribution in the collection. (Attainment of the given value of the characteristic is called "completion" of the development of the component.)

Specifically, we assume that the developer knows for component 1 a function $\mu_1(x,b)$, decreasing in b and giving the expected completion time when x is the value of the component's characteristic and b is its budget. We assume, as in the previous section, that there is a family of one-parameter probability distributions $H_1(\mu_1,t_1)$ giving the distribution of the component completion time. The parameter μ_1 is the mean completion time. For component 2 there are two analogous functions $\mu_2(y,b)$ and $H_2(\mu_2,t_2)$.

Then, if the developer is given a total development budget B, and if he chooses characteristics x and y, and devotes b of the budget to component 1 and the remainder, $B - b$, to component 2, the time to completion of the item's development will be the time required to complete both components, and the expected time to completion of the item will be

$$\bar{\bar{\varphi}}(x,y,b,B) = E \max (t_1,t_2).$$

Given a B the developer wants $\bar{\bar{\varphi}}$ to be a minimum. He wants to choose values of x, y, b—call them $\hat{x}(B)$, $\hat{y}(B)$, $\hat{b}(B)$—such that $[\hat{x}(B),\hat{y}(B)]$ is in S, $0 < b \leqslant B$, and, for any (x,y) in S and any b, $0 < b \leqslant B$,

$$\bar{\bar{\varphi}}(x,y,b,B) \geqslant \bar{\bar{\varphi}}[\hat{x}(B),\hat{y}(B),\hat{b}(B),B].$$

If we assume that for all (x,y), t_1 and t_2 have a common upper bound T (above which values of t_1 and t_2 occur with probability zero), then it follows that [39]

$$\bar{\bar{\varphi}}(x,y,b,B) = T - \int_0^T H_1[\mu_1(b,x),t]H_2[\mu_2(b - b,y),t]dt. \tag{34}$$

Assume the existence of such a T, and suppose further that for a fixed budget assigned to component 1 (and hence a fixed mean completion time μ_1) the probability of achieving the value x in a time less than or equal to a positive number t^* becomes smaller when x is increased, for any t^*.[40] The higher the intended characteristic x, in other words, the "harder" it is to achieve. Assuming H_1, H_2 to be differentiable with respect to μ_1, μ_2, respectively, and the functions μ_1, μ_2 with respect to x and y, respectively, we have

$$\frac{\partial H_1[\mu_1(b,x),t]}{\partial x} < 0, \qquad \frac{\partial H_2[\mu_2(b,x),t]}{\partial y} < 0$$

and also

$$\frac{\partial \mu_1(b,x)}{\partial x} > 0, \qquad \frac{\partial \mu_2(b,y)}{\partial y} > 0.$$

It now follows from (34) that the developer loses nothing by constraining his component characteristics to be *on* the boundary curve

[39] From a lemma that one can obtain from the Fundamental Lemma, giving an expression for the expected value of the maximum of several independent drawings, each from a different population.

[40] Except for t^* equal to the upper limit T. For this t^* the probability just defined is always equal to 1.

$v = w(x)$. (If they are above the curve, $\bar{\bar{\varphi}}$ can be diminished by pulling them down to it.) So minimization of $\bar{\bar{\varphi}}(x,y,b,B)$ can be replaced by minimization of

$$\hat{\bar{\bar{\varphi}}}(x,b,B) \equiv T - \int_0^T H_1[\mu_1(b,x),t]H_2\{\mu_2[B-b,w(x)],t\}\,dt.$$

This is to be minimized with respect to x and b, subject to the constraints $x \geqslant 0$, $0 < b \leqslant B$. Let us briefly consider particular functions H_1, H_2, μ_1, μ_2, w meeting all the above assumptions.

Let the functions μ_1, μ_2, w be rectangular hyperbolas and let the probability distributions H_1, H_2 be rectangular. That is, let

$$\mu_1(b,x) = \frac{x}{b}, \quad \mu_2(b,y) = \frac{ky}{b}, \quad y = w(x) = \frac{\mu}{x},$$

where k and μ are positive constants and

$$H(\mu_1,t_1) = \begin{cases} \dfrac{t_1}{2\mu_1}, & 0 \leqq t_1 \leqq 2\mu_1 \\ 1, & t_1 > 2\mu_1 \end{cases}$$

$$H(\mu_2,t_2) = \begin{cases} \dfrac{t_2}{2\mu_2}, & 0 \leqq t_2 \leqq 2\mu_2 \\ 1, & t_2 > 2\mu_1. \end{cases}$$

We obtain from the Fundamental Lemma that the expected value of the maximum of two drawings, one from each of these two populations is, if $\mu_1 \leqslant \mu_2$,

$$\frac{\mu_1^2 + 3\mu_2^2}{3\mu_2}.$$

Now the means of the two rectangular distributions are x/b and $k\mu/x(B-b)$ for a fixed total budget B, of which b is devoted to the first component. Hence we have for the expected completion time for both components

$$\hat{\bar{\bar{\varphi}}}(x,b,B) = \begin{cases} \varphi_1(x,b,B) \equiv \dfrac{xk\mu}{3b^2(B-b)} + \dfrac{k\mu}{x(B-b)} \text{ if } x^2 \leqq \dfrac{bk\mu}{B-b} \\ \left(\text{or equivalently, if } b \leqq \dfrac{x^2B}{k\mu + x^2}\right); \\ \varphi_2(x,b,B) \equiv \dfrac{xk\mu}{3(B-b)^2 b} + \dfrac{k\mu}{xb} \text{ if } x^2 > \dfrac{bk\mu}{B-b} \\ \left(\text{or equivalently, if } b > \dfrac{x^2B}{k\mu + x^2}\right). \end{cases}$$

Now fix x (and B) and consider the best amount to be allocated to the first component. Since both φ_1 and φ_2 become infinite at $b=0$ and at $b=B$, some of the budget must be devoted to each component. We have

$$\frac{\partial\varphi_1(x,b,B)}{\partial b}=\frac{xk\mu}{3(B-b)^2}\left[\frac{2}{b^2(B-b)}-\frac{2}{b^3}-\frac{k\mu}{x}\right],$$

so that

$$\frac{\partial\varphi_1}{\partial b}\left\{\begin{matrix}\geq\\=\\<\end{matrix}\right\}0 \text{ according as } \frac{1}{b^2(B-b)}-\frac{1}{b^3}\left\{\begin{matrix}\geq\\=\\<\end{matrix}\right\}\frac{k\mu}{2x}.$$

Also

$$\frac{\partial\varphi_2}{\partial b}\left\{\begin{matrix}\geq\\=\\<\end{matrix}\right\}0 \text{ according as } \frac{1}{b(B-1)^2}-\frac{1}{(B-b)^2}\left\{\begin{matrix}\geq\\=\\<\end{matrix}\right\}\frac{k\mu}{2x}.$$

Each of these derivatives is zero at values of b that solve a quartic equation. There may be as many as four such (real) values and so we cannot exclude the possibility that for some k, μ, x, and B, the derivative of φ_1 with respect to b vanishes four times for b between 0 and $x^2B/(k\mu+x^2)$, and the derivative of φ_2 with respect to b vanishes four times for b between $x^2B/(k\mu+x^2)$ and B. The analytical difficulties of writing the optimal b as a function of x, μ, k, and B are not trivial.

Note that no matter what k, μ, x, and B are it is never optimal to divide the budget exactly equally between the two components. For both derivatives are always negative at $b=B/2$, so that $\hat{\hat{\varphi}}$ cannot be at a minimum there. This is a somewhat surprising result.

7.2. *Many Review Point, Two Component Problems*

Let us now make all the assumptions of the preceding highly specific problem except the assumption that the number k is initially known to the developer. Except for this he knows initially all that he was previously assumed to know. The number k measures, roughly speaking, the difficulty of getting to a particular value of the second component's characteristic (y) compared with the difficulty of getting to the same value of the first component's characteristic. The developer initially knows only the probability distribution of k (and hence its expected value).

At some time and money cost (say C^*) he can find out what k in fact is. Or, alternatively, he can choose to save C^* and to make his final budget commitments to each component, and his final choice of component characteristics, using only his initial knowledge of the distribution of k. To do the latter optimally may or may not mean to make the choice of budgets which would be optimal if k were exactly equal to its expected value; whether it means this or not depends on the distribution of k.

We can here test, then, a rather primitive but precise form of the viewpoint that has been cogently argued with respect to early specification of the components. The view is as follows: Early specification of components permits early component matching and this achieves certain economies. These economies are generally outweighed, however, by the risk that the component specifications, chosen when the developer knows little about their relative difficulty compared with alternative specifications, will turn out to be very costly.[41] In the present context the economies of early matching are simply the saving of C^*.

It is rather clear in the present problem that knowledge of k will be worth some part of a total budget B to the developer for any distribution of k (in which more than one value of k has positive probability). For the optimal values of x and b depend on k. Moreover, since some money goes to each component in an optimal allocation, we cannot get, if we assume the distribution of k to be rectangular, an analog of the result of 6.2.2, in which it never paid to improve the initial knowledge. For that result depended heavily on the fact that in the optimal allocation no money at all goes to each of its alternative uses except one (the alternative uses were approaches in the problem of 6.2.2).

To this extent the above problem supports the view just described. It would be considerably more complicated to support a more refined version of this view: that the proportion of a total budget which the optimizing developer devotes to improving his knowledge of k increases if his uncertainty about what k is, measured by its variance, say, increases while the expected value of k remains unchanged.

We could, of course, allow the developer's knowledge of k to increase not just once but at a succession of review points. At each review point he would have to decide whether to acquire more knowledge (acquire a still more accurate estimate of k) or to make a final choice of component budgets and characteristics. And we could allow (analogously to 6.2.3) for the fact that the work of acquiring such improved knowledge would probably be generalized development work on each component, so that there would be the less left to do the later the review point at which the final choice of component characteristics and budgets is made. These extensions (to the case of

---

[41] Costly with respect to time if a total budget is given.

two review points, say) would be quite complicated even for our simple case, but they would certainly be feasible.

We could, finally, incorporate in principle all the elements of the problems of Sections 4, 5, and 6 into a multi-component problem. A specific component characteristic (or set of characteristics when the component's vector V_i has more than one dimension) could be attained using a number of alternative approaches. These could be pursued with different intensities following each review point, and the choice of intensities at each review point could be performed sequentially.

7.3. *Problems of Choosing Performance Specifications*

Closely related to multi-component problems are problems of choosing a point in the space of the total item's performance magnitudes, or rather in the satisfactory part of that space. The total item is again regarded as having one component. At some point in its development, the item's precise performance magnitudes have to be decided on.

The distinguishing mark of these problems is that the developer cannot, in general, separately choose the efforts to be devoted to improving each performance magnitude. (He can do so if each performance magnitude is simply the characteristic describing a separate component, but our one component assumption rules out this possibility.) Rather, it is the effort devoted to reaching a point in the satisfactory part of the performance space—that is, reaching all coordinates of this point—that can be varied.

To be general (and realistic), however, we must let the developer choose, at a given stage of development (a given review point), not a point in the satisfactory part of the space but a subregion of the satisfactory part. To a given choice of subregion and a given budget to be spent on further development there corresponds, at the given review point, a probability distribution of times to completion. "Completion" means attainment of some point in the subregion. Presumably, the narrower is a subregion, at a given review point and for a given budget, the more widely dispersed (more risky) is the probability distribution of completion times.

Given an initial total budget, at each review point the developer has to choose a subregion and the amount of the remaining budget to be devoted to it prior to the next review point. The work for which this amount is spent both narrows the dispersion of the probability distributions associated with the subregion and brings attainment of the point in the subregion closer in time. We conjecture that under reasonable assumptions the size of the optimally chosen subregions will shrink—that, in fact, the nth one will be properly contained in the $(n-1)$st. Needless to say some highly specific assumptions would have to be made in order to explore the conjecture.

Note, finally, that the possibility of choosing subregions rather than points could be incorporated into R-component problems. The developer would successively choose R subregions, the ith one lying within the ith component's characteristic space.

8. Further Refinements for the Case of Two Valued Preferences

8.1. Interdependence Between Approaches

In reality, when several approaches are pursued (simultaneously or in sequence) each of them is not pursued in total isolation; nor would such isolation be generally optimal for the developer. The pursuit of an approach from one review point to the next, say, yields various kinds of knowledge which would assist the pursuit of another approach. The exchange of knowledge between two approaches prior to a given review point might improve the accuracy of the estimates made for each of them at the review point; and it might, for each of them, leave less to do until completion.

How could we take interdependence formally into account, under the assumption that the intensity with which an approach is pursued cannot be varied, for the one review point problem? We could still let an approach be characterized by the numbers (c_1,c) and could still regard the q initially chosen approaches as q independent drawings from a population of vectors (c_1,c). The numbers c_1 and c for an approach are now, respectively, the estimated cost at the first review point and the true cost if that approach alone were pursued from the first review point on. It would still be true that at the first review point a single surviving approach is to be chosen.

But now if q approaches, characterized by the vectors $(c_1^1,c^1), \ldots,$ (c_1^q,c^q), are pursued to the first review point, then the estimated cost to completion for the ith one must be, at the second review point, some function of the numbers characterizing all q approaches. In particular it may be a function $f_q^i(c_1^1, \ldots, c_1^i, \ldots, c_1^q)$ of the signals the q approaches would yield at the first review point if each of them were pursued in isolation. At the first review point the approach selected to be the survivor is then that approach i for which f_q^i is a minimum. Presumably the function f_q^i still gives great weight to the argument c_1^i—an intrinsically good (bad) approach will have a low (high) estimated cost no matter what it may learn from the other approaches. The actual values of the arguments of the functions f_q^i (the c_1^i) will never be known to the developer, who observes only the values of the functions f_q^i. But from the forms of the functions f_q^i and from the probability distribution of the vectors (c_1^i,c) it should be possible for the developer to deduce the optimal number of approaches to pursue to the second review point.

8.2. The Scheduling of Events in the Pursuit of an Approach

Consider the pursuit of a single approach—the attempt to follow a design, or the development plan of a particular group of people. When the approach is brought to completion and its history is to be written, it will be seen to have been composed of a sequence of events. The list of events is, of course, arbitrary, but if the item developed is one of a large class of items, then, presumably, there exists a list of more or less standard events. An event may be satisfactory completion of a component, or the passing of a well-defined milestone in the development of a component or of the whole item (for example, completion of certain standard tests). In estimating at some review point the amount of time that an approach requires to completion (for a given budget) the developer might very well start by trying to list the events still to come. If he is reasonably confident of what those coming events are, he may then observe that some events cannot occur until certain others have taken place; that the date at which an event is achieved may, to some extent, be made earlier (perhaps at a cost); and that there are certain critical events whose early achievement is likely to be particularly helpful since their late achievement would hold up to the completion of many other events and hence the completion of the approach.

It is these observations that have led to the techniques for the management of development for which the most general term is "network methods." The events to be achieved can be portrayed in a network, as in the following diagram:

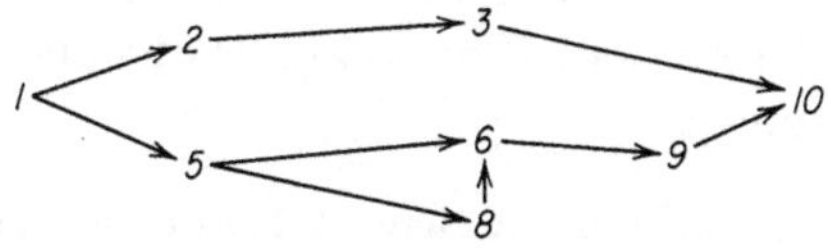

The initial event in the approach pursued has to be event 1. For any other given events it is true that the preceding event (located at the tail of the arrow which points to the given event) has to precede the given event. (Thus event 3 cannot occur before event 10, 5 cannot occur before 6 and 8, but 6 and 8 can occur in either order.) An arrow in the diagram, leading from one event to another, also portrays an activity, namely, the activity of proceeding from achievement of the first event to achievement of the second.

Associated with a given network is a well-defined optimization problem. The earlier literature on network methods was often notable for its lack of precision and clarity, and this is partly because the optimization problem was so seldom referred to. In much of the more recent discussion, the deficiency has been remedied.[42]

An approach is given and a set of events whose achievement constitutes completion of the approach is given. The set of events is partially ordered and the ordering can be portrayed in a network. An event can be called by a number and the numbering system made to be consistent with the given partial ordering—that is, if event i must precede event j then it must also be true that $i < j$.[43] (This is the case in the diagram above.)

The duration y_{ij} of the activity leading from event i to event j, $i < j$, can be chosen, subject to some constraints, by the developer. Let the constraints on a given y_{ij} be simply that there is a lower limit d_{ij} and an upper limit D_{ij}:

$$d_{ij} \leqq y_{ij} \leqq D_{ij}. \tag{35}$$

To speed up the activity leading from k to j, however, costs money; let $a_{ij}(y_{ij})$ be the money cost of achieving the duration y_{ij}, where $a'_{ij} < 0$. In addition to the activities, the developer can choose occurrence times t_i; t_i is the number of time units from the start of the approach at which event i occurs. The choice of durations and occurrence times must meet the constraint

$$y_{ij} \leqq t_j - t_i, j > i. \tag{36}$$

Then, for any given choice of the t_i the completion time of the approach is t_i^*, where $i < i^*$ for all events i (i^* is the terminal event—the completion of the approach). The total cost of a given set of durations and occurrence times is

[42] See especially D. R. Fulkerson: A Network Flow Computation for Project Cost Curves, *Management Science,* Vol. 7 (January 1961), pp. 167–178, and J. E. Kelley, Jr.: Critical-path Planning and Scheduling: Mathematical Basis, *Operations Research,* Vol. 9 (May–June 1961), pp. 296–320. The first paper on network methods that explicitly formulated an optimization problem was apparently that of J. E. Kelley, who considered the problem discussed here.

[43] But the converse is not true; if $i < j$ it does not follow that i must precede event j.

$$C = \sum_{\substack{i<i* \\ i<j*}} a_{ij}(y_{ij}).$$

For a given completion time $t_{i*} = T$ the developer's optimization problem is to choose occurrence times and duration such that C is a minimum subject to the constraints (35) and (36); let $C(T)$ denote this minimum.[44] If the functions a_{ij} are linear, then the developer has, for each given completion time, a linear programming problem. It is a straightforward consequence of the ordinary theory of linear programming that in any such problem there is some completion time T^* such that for all completion times $T \geqslant T^*$ the problem has a solution. For all $T \geqslant T^*$, moreover, the minimum cost $C(T)$, attained when the best durations and occurrence times are used, has a most useful shape: $C(T)$ decreases with t and is convex and piecewise linear:

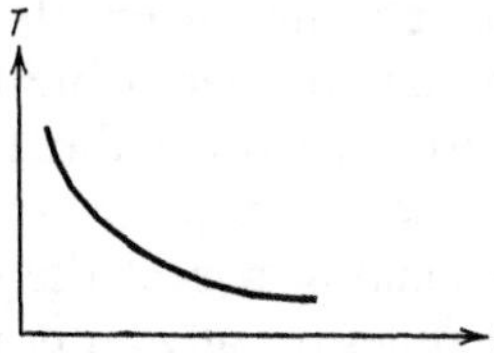

As we saw in the introduction to Section 6, this means that if the developer were faced with just a single approach and had to decide how much money to spend on it (how much to speed up its completion) then for rather natural sorts of time and money cost functions (with concave indifference contours) there is a unique optimal amount of money to be spent on the approach.

The above well-defined optimization problem can in principle be enlarged to take some account of uncertainty. The cost $a_{ij}(y_{ij})$ of getting from event i to event j in y_{ij} time units can be made random; in particular we might assume $a_{ij}(y_{ij}) = \bar{a}_{ij} + \mathscr{E}_{ij}$, where $\bar{a}_{ij}$ is a constant and $\mathscr{E}_{ij}$ is a random variable. We then have a stochastic linear programming problem of a class whose investigation is under way.

If the (non-stochastic) optimization problem we have described is too difficult to solve there is still a technique that may be useful to the

[44] Note that the numbers a_{ij}, d_{ij}, D_{ij} may be used to express some special properties of the network in question. Thus, in the network of the figure the activity (3,5) is one whose duration we do not want directly to choose (for 5 may in fact occur before 3). We express this by letting the cost a_{35} be 0 for all values of y_{35} (so that y_{35} does not enter the function being minimized). A similar statement is true of the activity (5,9), which is composed of two activities, (5,6) and (6,0), whose durations are to be directly chosen (so that direct choice of the duration of (5,9) would be superfluous).

developer. He may guess at a set of occurrence times for which the time and money cost of completing the approach seem reasonable. He may then find a critical path through the network for this set of occurrence times. This is a path proceeding through the network from left to right; if the duration times separating the events along the path are added up they exactly equal the completion time of the approach. It follows that if any of the chosen occurrence times along the path are not achieved (if the duration of an activity on the path is allowed to slip beyond the time chosen) then the completion time for the whole approach will suffer – it will be greater than the intended time. For events off the path there may be slack – some slippage can occur without holding up the approach's completion time; the amount of available slack can be computed for each activity of the path. The critical path can thus be made into a useful control device for the developer who has chosen a completion time for the approach. He pays particular attention to insuring that the events on the critical path do not slip, allocating more money to their achievement if necessary; he does not need to supervise as closely the events (perhaps many thousand of them) off the critical path.

It is control techniques making use of the critical path, given an initial choice of occurrence times for all events, that have occupied the bulk of the earlier literature on network methods. In particular, an element of uncertainty about the achievement of the chosen occurrence times was introduced into some of the literature and some of the network techniques used in practice.[45] The developer asks the engineers and scientists who are to work on the approach to give three estimates – optimistic, most likely, and pessimistic – for the time that will be required to achieve a serially connected activity. (A serially connected activity is the activity of proceeding from one event in the network to an event immediately to its right, connected to the first event by an arrow.) Presumably – although the point was often glossed over – the estimates are to be made under the assumption that a given amount of money is made available for the activity. Then highly specific assumptions are made about the probability distribution of the time that will turn out to be required for a given activity, for example, that the distribution is a Beta distribution uniquely determined by the three estimates. It is thus possible to obtain the expected

[45] Notably the first network technique, PERT (Program Evaluation Review Technique), originally described in D. G. Malcolm, J. Y. Roseboom, C. E. Clark, and W. Fazar: Application of a Technique for Research and Development Program Evaluation, *Operations Research,* Vol. 7 (September–October 1959), pp. 646–669.

time to completion of the approach and the variance of the completion time.

It is unfortunately the case, however, that if this procedure is followed, if activities are then subdivided into subactivities that comprise them so as to obtain a more detailed network, and if the procedure is again applied to the new network, then different (equally reasonable) ways of subdividing will lead to different estimates of expected completion time. This is a disturbing property.

The fundamental difficulty in using the network formulation in development tasks is, of course, that very often the list of events that have to occur before an approach is completed simply cannot be written down in advance. Often only the crudest guesses can initially be made, for example, as to the list of components that will have to be developed, and as to which components will have to precede which.

Network methods clearly have a limited usefulness for much less ambitious aims than the scheduling of an entire approach, culminating in a fully developed item. They would be useful at or near the last of a sequence of review points, when little development remains to be done, uncertainty is small, and the remaining events can be fairly precisely listed. They could be used at such review points to estimate the completion time for alternative approaches and alternative approach budgets. We conjecture that, before much longer, experience will cause developers to restrict the use of network methods to such a less ambitious role.

9. Many Valued Preferences

We shall say very little about development problems in which the developer ranks more than two regions of the performance space. Formally, in such problems, we can think of the developer's total preferences as summarized by a function $V(M,T,\pi)$ where M and T are again the money and time required to develop the item in question and π is the vector of performance magnitudes characterizing the developed item. The better is a triple (M,T,π), the higher is V.

Consider first the simplest one shot (no review point) problem. The developer is confronted with alternative approaches and he cannot vary the intensity with which any of them is pursued. An approach is characterized by a probability distribution over the triples (M,T,π) that will turn out to be observed when the approach is pursued to completion; M will be the amount of money required to complete the approach, T the amount of time, and π the vector of performance magnitudes for the item the approach yields. The developer is to pick an approach out of those available for which $EV(M,T,\pi)$ is a maximum. If the available approaches are initially indistinguishable (have the same value of $EV(M,T,\pi)$) he picks one at random.

Next consider the problem that is the analog of the one review point problem of Section 4. Let there be a review point at which more information becomes available for any approach pursued to the review point, more information about the true value of $V(M,T,\pi)$ if that approach were the only one ever pursued. Let the lower case symbol $v(m,t,\pi)$ now denote the value of V that would be obtained if only one approach were ever pursued, if m dollars and t time units were expended on it and if it yielded a performance vector π. Let $\bar{v}$ denote the signal observed for an approach at the review point and assume that $E(v/\bar{v}) = \bar{v}$. Let one money unit and one time unit be required to pursue any approach to the review point.

Observe now that it is no longer reasonable, as it was in the pure parallel approach problem (and in all the two valued preference problems), to assume that once one approach is completed all others are dropped. For an uncompleted approach might yield a better item than the completed one and so might be worth completing. If, on the other hand, we want to stay in the one review point case, then we cannot allow the developer to base his decision as to whether or not to continue uncompleted approaches once one approach has been completed on the value of m, t, and π observed, at what amounts to a second review point, for the completed approach. We must therefore assume either (1) that all uncompleted approaches do have to be dropped once one approach is completed, so that at the first and only review point only one surviving approach is picked; or else (2) that all approaches not dropped at the review point have to be completed. Though neither assumption is very satisfactory we briefly explore both.

If we make assumption (1) we have, formally, the problem of Section 4 again. The developer picks, at the second review point, that approach for which $\bar{v}$ is largest. The optimal number of approaches to pursue to the second review point is determined in precisely the manner described in Section 4.[46]

If, however, we make assumption (2) then the situation is very different. Let q approaches be pursued to the first review point and let $p \leqslant q$ of these be chosen, at the review point, to be pursued to completion. Let the total completion times that turn out to be required for these p approaches be $t_1, \ldots, t_p$; let the total amounts of money that

[46] Except for a change in sign, since it is now a large V that is desired.

turn out to be required to pursue them from the first review point to completion be $m_1, \ldots, m_p$ and let the final performance vectors be $\pi_1, \ldots, \pi_p$. Then the developer's total payoff is

$$\max_{i=1,\ldots,w} V[\max(t_1, \ldots, t_p), \sum_{i=1}^{w} m_i + q, \pi_i].$$

The developer has to choose (a) the number q and (b) a rule which tells him, given the information he has at the first review point, the number p and the p approaches to be completed. The choice of (a) and (b) is to maximize the expected value of the above expression.

Two things are clear. First $p = 1$ will not in general be the optimal choice of p. Second, if the best p is greater than 1 then it is not necessarily true that the p approaches chosen should be the ones with the p highest values of $\bar{v}$. And this is so even if we make the V-function linear (analogously to our linearization of the C-function in Section 4).

Thus let π be one dimensional and let V have the form $V = \alpha M + \beta T + \gamma\pi (\alpha < 0, \beta < 0, \gamma > 0)$. An approach is then characterized by a value of (m,t,π) and a value of $\bar{v}$, which is the estimate observed at the review point of the quantity $\alpha m + \beta t + \gamma\pi$. The true amounts of time and money, t and m, required to complete the approach, and the true performance π that it yields will never be known unless the approach is completed. Over all approaches there is a probability distribution of the four dimensional variable $(m,t,\pi,\bar{v})$. Suppose q is taken to be 3 and $p = 2$. We can find probability distributions of $(m,t,\pi,\bar{v})$ and values of α, β, γ, such that the best choice of two approaches at the second review point is not the two approaches (out of those available) for which $\bar{v}$ is largest.

For example, let the joint probability distribution be such that $\bar{v}$ is a perfect estimate ($\bar{v}$ always equals $\alpha m + \beta t + \gamma\pi$), and let $\beta = -1$, $\alpha = -1$, and $\gamma = 1$. Let the probability distribution assign probability ½ to the vector $Q_1 = (m_1, y_1, \pi, \bar{v}_1)$ and ½ to the vector $Q_2 = (m_2, t_2, \pi_2, \bar{v}_2)$ where $m_1 > m_2$, $t_1 > t_2$, $\pi_1 > \pi_2$, and $\bar{v}_1 > \bar{v}_2$.

The three approaches pursued to the review point can be either (a) three Q_1s, or (b) three Q_2s, or (c) one Q_2 and two Q_1s, or (d) one Q_1 and two Q_2s. Each of these four cases occurs with probability ¼. We compare Rule I: "Choose the two approaches for which $\bar{v}$ is highest" with Rule II: "Choose the two approaches for which $\bar{v}$ is lowest." In cases (a) and (b) both rules yield the same payoffs. In case (d) under Rule I and in case (c) under Rule II, the payoff is the same (namely, $\pi_1 - m_1 - m_2 - t_1$). So expected payoff under Rule I is higher or lower than expected payoff under Rule II according as the payoff in case (c) under Rule I is higher or lower than the payoff in case (d) under

Rule II, that is, as $\pi_1 - 2m_1 - t_1$ is greater or less than $\pi_2 - 2m_2 - t_2$.

However, we can find values of the πs, ms, and ts such that $\pi_1 - 2m_1 - t_1 \leqslant \pi_2 - 2m_2 - t_2$ and at the same time all the inequalities assumed above are satisfied. (For example: $\pi_1 = 201$, $\pi_2 = 100$, $m_1 = 100$, $m_2 = 1$, $t_1 = 2$, $t_2 = 2$, for which $\bar{v}_1 = 99$, $\bar{v}_2 = 98$.) For such values Rule II is better than Rule I when three approaches are available at the second review point and two of them are to be selected for completion. We can certainly construct probability distributions of $(m,t,\pi,\bar{v})$ for which this remains true and for which $\bar{v}$ is not a perfect estimate of v. These probability distributions, moreover, may be such that the conditional distributions of v given $\bar{v}$ form a monotonic set. Such monotonicity does not imply an ordering property with respect to the estimate ($\bar{v}$) as it did in the problem of Section 4.

A better procedure, of course, would be not to insist, given that three approaches have been carried to the review point, that exactly two approaches be pursued from the review point to completion. Better still would be a rule based not on the knowledge of $\bar{v}$ but directly on the knowledge that presumably is used to obtain $\bar{v}$—that is, on some estimate, for each approach that is available at the review point, of its true t, its true m, and its true π.

The role of the estimate $\bar{v}$ is, in any case, certainly drastically different from the role of c_1 in Section 4. Not only is $\bar{v}$ not very interesting information, but if it is available the approaches chosen to be pursued beyond the second review point should not necessarily have a better $\bar{v}$ than the approaches dropped, even under a monotonicity assumption.

If we turn to problems in which intensities can be varied, we have similarly drastic differences as compared with two-valued preference problems. We could redefine an approach, for example (analogously to Section 6), as a family of probability distributions. Each member of the family is defined for a given value of m, the amount of money made available for pursuit of the approach; the (multi-dimensional) random variable corresponding to the given m is the vector (π,t)—the performance that turns out to be obtained and the time that turns out to be required when m dollars are made available.

It would be more satisfactory not to insist that t and π be uniquely determined once m is fixed. Presumably the time over which the amount m is spread affects the performance attained. Or, to put it in another way, a number of performance vectors can be attained with m dollars; they will differ in the time interval required for their attainment. Then an approach is either (a) a family of probability distributions of time to completion, each member of the family defined by a pair (m,π); or (b) a family of probability distributions of performance vectors, each member of the family defined by a pair (m,t). But if we are to formulate a one shot problem in which several initially indistinguishable approaches are available and a total budget is given (as in 6.1), then we must take definition (b). For since the best of the performance vectors finally attained for the completed approaches will be chosen, where "best" means "maximizing V given the *total* time and money spent on all approaches," we cannot choose the item's performance in advance if there is ever to be any advantage at all in preserving more than one approach.

The analog of the problem of 6.1 then becomes, under definition (b), as follows: The developer is faced with two initially indistinguishable approaches and a fixed total budget B. He must choose an amount of money b to be devoted to the first approach, with $B - b$ going to the second. He must also choose durations t_1 and t_2 for the two approaches. The choice of b, π_1, π_2 is to be such that expected payoff is a maximum. For a given choice expected payoff is

$$E \max \{V[\max (t_1,t_2),B,\pi_1], V[\max (t_1,t_2),B,\pi_2]\}$$

where the probability distribution of π_1 is determined by t_1 and b and that of π_2 by t_2 and $B - b$.

This is a far different problem from that of 6.1. And the extension of the two cases of fixed and variable approach intensities to many review points yields problems equally different from the many review point problems we have looked at above.

10. Changes in the World Outside the Developer's Control

With respect to this final and perhaps most difficult complication we make only one remark. Suppose that for any of the problems discussed above an optimal policy has been found. Under this policy the number of approaches pursued by the developer from a given review point n to the next review point is a random variable. Consider the expected value of this number and call it E_n. If we let the outside world change during the course of development, this must mean that the parameters defining the developer's personal probability distributions considered so far—distributions over the time, performance, or money outcomes of the available approaches—must themselves be thought of as random variables with personal probability distributions reflecting the developer's beliefs about the outside world. The changes in the outside world, that is to say, have added a new uncertainty to the existing uncertainty, which was the intrinsic technical uncertainty of the development task.

We might now expect the following to be a reasonable conjecture: If the given problem is solved again, taking into account the new uncertainty, then under the revised optimal policy the expected number of approaches E'_n pursued from review point n to review point $n + 1$ is greater or at least not smaller than E_n. The case for the exploration of more than one alternative is strengthened by the introduction of outside uncertainty. Reasonable as the conjecture seems, the results of Sections 4, 5, and 6 should make us wary of accepting it as true in general.

To get true and interesting propositions about optimal development decisions while we allow for outside uncertainty doubtless requires that we specify this uncertainty quite narrowly. The probability distribution of the outside disturbances has to be added to the existing technical uncertainty. For the student of development to choose such a distribution and to assert that the choice is reasonable requires boldness, to say the least.

11. Project Selection Problems

We conclude our list of problems with a glance at a problem that does not arise in the completion of a single development task or project. But it is a problem appearing widely in the literature on R&D management, and the difference between it and single project decision problems is worth mentioning.

A developer is given, let us say, a total development budget. He is confronted with a number of different development projects or tasks. He has to choose how much of the budget to allocate to each (zero may be allocated to some). Presumably there is some measure of the value of a collection of projects, the total profit which they eventually earn, for example. The precise value of this measure is not known until all the chosen projects have been completed.

But the crucial novelty of the project selection problem, as compared with our single project problems, is that this measure of value is additive; each completed project contributes something to the total value and the value function can be written so that the value is the sum of the project contributions. If the value of a collection of projects were instead equal to the value of the best project in a collection, the problem would formally belong precisely in the same class as those we have formulated. Problems in which value, or payoff, is an additive function of the activities that contribute to value, and among which choice is to be made, are somewhat more familiar than the problems that we have looked at, in which payoff depends on the best of the activities.[47]

12. Previously Explored Sequential Decision Problems Related to the Parallel Approach Problem

We conclude our discussion of the pure and generalized parallel approach problems by surveying very briefly several problems that have been discussed in the literature of statistical decision theory and that appear closely related to the parallel approach problems.

12.1. The Sequential Design of Experiments

To describe this class of problems we consider an example given by Chernoff.[48]

It is desired to compare the efficacy of two drugs. Two experiments are available, E_1 with the first and E_2 with the second drug (on a group of subjects, say). The outcome of each experiment is success or failure. Success has an unknown probability (frequency) P_1 in the first experiment and P_2 in the second. The choice is to be made between two alternative hypotheses: the hypothesis that $P_1 > P_2$ and the hypothesis that $P_1 \leqslant P_2$. (In a simpler version of the problem one hypothesis is $P_1 = p^*$, $P_2 = p^{**}$ and the other is $P_1 = p^{**}$, $P_2 = p^*$; no other pairs of probabilities are possible.) The experimenter is faced with a sequence of decision points. At each point in the sequence he can decide, on the basis of the outcomes of the experiments so far performed, (a) to accept the first hypothesis, (b) to accept the second, (c) to postpone a choice and instead conduct experiment E_1 again, (d) to conduct E_2 again. There is a fixed cost for each repetition of an experiment. There is a penalty function that assigns one penalty to the acceptance of the first hypothesis when the second is true and another penalty to acceptance of the second hypothesis when the first is true. Finally the experimenter attaches an *a priori* (personal) probability to the first hypothesis being true and another probability to the second being true (the two probabilities sum to one).

The experimenter seeks a rule that tells him at each decision point, for each possible set of accumulated experimental outcomes, which

[47] One problem with an additive payoff with respect to the choices made and that depends also on some uncertain (non-chosen) parameters is the stochastic linear programming problem. It might turn out that project selection problems could usefully be put into stochastic linear programming form.

[48] Herman Chernoff: The Sequential Design of Experiments, *Annals of Mathematical Statistics,* Vol. 30 (September 1959), pp. 755–770.

decision to take.[49] The results are not applicable or generalizable to our picture of a development task for one main reason: the available experiments, in this class of problems, remain the same at every decision point. Each of the available experiments changes the (posterior) probabilities the decisionmaker attaches to the alternative hypotheses in the same way at every decision point.[50] But it is the essence of development that at different decision points the available experiments are different. The developer's knowledge changes in a different way as a result of his efforts early in development than it does as a result of his efforts late in development, and he cannot perform experiments of the latter kind without first having performed experiments of the former kind.[51]

12.2. Sequential Selection of That Event Having the Highest Probability Among a Finite Number of Events

The most relevant form of the problem is this:

There are k random variables each with a different *unknown* distribution. One observation is taken from each and the maximum of the k observations is noted. The decisionmaker wants to choose that population out of the k populations for which the probability that it yields the maximum of the k observations is higher than for any other population. Formally the problem is identical to the following. One out of k possible events can occur and the event having the highest probability of occurrence is to be found. For example, a roulette wheel can yield one of 36 numbers; which has the highest probability associated with it? The ith event in the original problem, $i = 1, \ldots, k$, is the event that the observation from the ith population is the largest of the k observations.

Let $p_1, \ldots, p_k$ be the true probabilities of the k events, $\Sigma p_i = 1$. A sequential procedure has been found[52] such that for any set of true

[49] Optimal rules here have been characterized by Herman Chernoff: The Sequential Design of Experiments, *Annals of Mathematical Statistics,* Vol. 30 (September 1959), pp. 755–770 and by Dorian Feldman, Contributions to the "Two Armed Bandit" Problem, *Annals of Mathematical Statistics,* Vol. 33 (September 1962), pp. 847–856.

[50] To be more precise: let $Z_1, Z_2, \ldots, Z_n, \ldots$ denote a fixed sequence of experimental outcomes actually obtained in one repetition of the problem. Now consider the rth stage of another repetition of the problem. Let the sequence of r experimental outcomes observed up to that stage be the members of some subset of the set $\{Z_1, Z_2, \ldots, Z_n, \ldots\}$. Then no matter how this subset is chosen, the rule for determining the posterior probability at stage r is the same.

[51] Performing an experiment might correspond in our context to pursuing an approach from one review point to the next.

[52] Robert E. Bechhofer, Salah Elmaghraby, and Norman Morse: A Single Sample Multiple Decision Procedure for Selecting the Multinomial Event Which Has the Highest Probability, *Annals of Mathematical Statistics,* Vol. 30 (March 1959), pp. 102–119.

ps for which the ratio of the largest p to the next largest is some number θ, the probability of correctly selecting the most probable event when the procedure is followed is greater than p^*; and such that the expected number of sets of k observations required to achieve this is not larger than for any other sequential procedure. For any pair θ, p^*, that is to say, an optimal sequential decision procedure is known. At each decision point, the decisionmaker takes a set of k observations and then either selects the event with highest probability or decides to take another set of observations.

In the development context, the procedure could be applied only in the following sort of case. The developer has available a number of alternative approaches, say the proposals of each of k groups (k companies), to complete the task which faces him. He wants to choose the group that is most likely to achieve the task at least cost. He will not, of course, ask the k groups repeatedly to complete the task. But he may ask them repeatedly to perform some preliminary part of the task—for example, to prepare some design (a different one at each repetition) from which he then makes the best possible cost estimate. The procedure would then allow him to choose, with a preassigned probability of being right, the group that best performs the preliminary task (proposes designs that will be cheaper than the designs proposed by others according to the developer's own estimate). And the developer may feel that the winning group is likely to be also the group that would best (most cheaply) perform the complete development task.

This is certainly a somewhat far-fetched application. But the procedure has the great appeal of requiring no knowledge of the probability that group i is the best group in a given repetition, other than a knowledge of the ratio of the highest probability to the next highest. Only very modest demands are made on the developer's capacity to elicit personal probabilities from himself. The procedure, and related versions of the general problem, certainly deserves further attention in the development context.

12.3. Stochastic Approximation

In the original form of this problem there is an experiment defined by a parameter controlled by the experimenter, and an outcome.[53] The outcome is a random variable having a different probability distribution for each value of the parameter. The probability distribution associated with each parameter is unknown to the experimenter. He

[53] D. Monro and H. Robbins: A Stochastic Approximation Model, *Annals of Mathematical Statistics,* Vol. 22 (June 1951), pp. 400–407.

nevertheless wants to find that value of the parameter for which the expected value of the outcome is either (a) equal to some value[54] or (b) a maximum over all possible values of the parameters.[55] A sequence of experiments is formulated which is shown to yield convergence to the required value of the parameter. At the nth step in the sequence the experiment is performed for a value of the parameter that is a certain function of the number n and of the outcome of the $(n - 1)$st experiment. If a large enough number of experiments in the sequence is performed the probability that the outcome of the last experiment lies within some preassigned distance of the required value of the parameter can, under fairly general conditions, be made as close to one as is desired.

Considerable further generalization of this result has been obtained[56] but not, it appears, in a direction that makes the result more relevant to the context of development. The best use of the result we have described for the development context is not in the pure parallel approach problem but rather in a problem that combines (in a very elementary way) both of the main complications of the problem we considered.

Suppose the developer has available a single approach that can be pursued with different intensities (different budgets). Suppose, however, he is to start with one project, namely the pursuit of the approach at one budget level. Then he can initiate a second project (the same approach started afresh but for a different budget) when he knows something more about the first project; he can initiate a third project when he knows something more about the second; and so forth.[57] (This is a variant of the sequential complication discussed in Section 5.)

Each project is then an experiment in the given sense. The parameter is the project's total budget and the outcome might be the first good estimate of the total required development time when the given total budget is available. The sequential process described would then (in the limit) identify that project whose expected estimated completion time is (a) equal to some given amount, or (b) lowest.

---

[54] J. Kiefer and J. Wolfowitz: Stochastic Estimation of the Maximum of a Regression Function, *Annals of Mathematical Statistics*, Vol. 23 (June 1952), pp. 462–466.

[55] Aryeh Dvoretzky: On Stochastic Approximation, *Proceedings of the Third Berkeley Symposium on Probability and Statistics*, Berkeley: University of California Press, 1956, Vol. I, pp. 39–56.

[56] Notably by K. L. Chung, On a Stochastic Approximation Method, *Annals of Mathematical Statistics*, Vol. 25 (June 1954), pp. 463–483.

[57] The approach may be identified with a particular company. Each repetition of the approach may involve a different group within the company.

In another interpretation it might be that many approaches are available (in the sense of our previous discussion) but that each one is identified with some physical design parameter; the approach consists in developing a version of the required item that displays that value of the design parameter (and is satisfactory with respect to performance). The experiment consists in choosing a value of the parameter and then, for example, pursuing the approach for a specified time period using a specified amount of money (the same time period and amount of money for each experiment). The outcome is an estimate of the true time and money cost to completion. The sequential procedure identifies, in the limit, that value of the design parameter for which the expected estimated cost either is a minimum or else equals a specified amount.

In both of these interpretations, however, there is a major difficulty. The sequential procedure that has been examined in the literature so far does not yield any knowledge, at each stage, of the number of additional experiments that will be needed before the required value of the parameter can be estimated with a specified accuracy. Yet such knowledge would be essential for the experimenter (developer) to whom each experiment has a cost (in the case of the developer, a time and money cost). He needs such knowledge in order to decide when his estimate of the required parameter is sufficiently accurate so that further experiments are not worth their cost. Presumably the cost-of-experimentation complication will eventually be introduced into the study of stochastic approximation, which will be treated as a sequential decision problem; but so far this has not been done.

12.4. The Theory of Search

Here too a decision problem is missing in most (but not all) of the literature. In the original papers of B. O. Koopman [58] an object is hidden in some physical (Euclidean) space (for example, at some point on the real line). The probability that it lies in any fixed region of this space is given by a probability distribution over the coordinates of this space. A search activity can be undertaken. In this activity, the search effort devoted to a particular region determines, according to a specific rule, the probability of finding the object in the region if in fact it is there. Given the rule and given the original probability distribution, the problem is to allocate a given search budget (a fixed amount of

[58] B. O. Koopman: The Theory of Search, *Operations Research,* Parts I and II, Vol. 4 (May–June and September–October 1956), pp. 324–346 and 503–531, and Part III, Vol. 5 (September–October 1957), pp. 613–626.

search effort) over the region so as to maximize the probability of finding the object.

One might think of a very straightforward and simpleminded translation of this problem into a development context: the space in which search occurs is the space of design characteristics of the item being developed and there exists one unknown point somewhere in the space that would characterize a satisfactory item. This interpretation has little appeal, not only because more than many points, not just one, characterize a satisfactory item (a complication which a generalization of the original search problem would allow for), but above all because there are no responses to changing knowledge as search proceeds.

One could turn the search problem into a sequential decision problem in a variety of ways, and some of these might fit the development context reasonably well. For example, there might be a number of hidden objects (a number of satisfactory design points) distributed over the space according to a known probability law. A search budget is given and is spent, a little at a time, in searching the space. At each of a sequence of decision points, a policy tells the searcher where to look next. An optimal policy maximizes the probability of finding one of the objects, given the budget. Better still let the budget not be fixed and let there be a time and money cost function indicating the searcher's preferences over the alternative combinations of time and money (effort) that can turn out to be required to find one of the objects. At each decision point the searcher decides how much money (effort) to spend and in what regions to spend it. If he follows an optimal policy he minimizes expected time and money cost.

Appealing as these versions of the problem may sound no work bearing on them has yet appeared. It is not clear that in studying development they have any advantage over our generalized parallel approach problem and they may well turn out to be more difficult.

12.5. The General Theory of Dynamic Programming

David Blackwell[59] has developed a general theory of dynamic programming, in contrast to the previous rather piecemeal accumulation of solutions, or solution algorithms, for numerous special dynamic programming problems.[60] In the general problem a decisionmaker responds at successive decision points, to successive states of a system.

[59] David Blackwell: Discrete Dynamic Programming, *Annals of Mathematical Statistics*, Vol. 33 (June 1962), pp. 719–726, and Discounted Dynamic Programming, Vol. 36 (February 1965), pp. 226–235.

[60] See also Richard Bellman: *Dynamic Programming*, Princeton: Princeton University Press, 1957, and Ronald A. Howard: *Dynamic Programming and Markov Processes*, Cambridge, Massachusetts: The M.I.T. Press, 1960, p. 136.

At the nth decision point the decisionmaker is to choose an act from a set A of acts.[61] This choice has two consequences: First, the decisionmaker receives a current payoff, which is a function of n, of the current state, and of his chosen act. Second, the system passes to a new state, which confronts the decisionmaker at decision point $n + 1$; the probability distribution of the new state depends on both the state and the act chosen at decision point n.[62] The problem is to find an optimal policy that maximizes the expected value of the sum of all current payoffs, or if the number of decision points is infinite, the discounted sum (without discounting, the sum might be infinite under some policies).

Some general results are obtained. Among the most interesting are certain general conditions under which there is a stationary optimal policy which assigns the same act to a given state no matter what the number, n, of the current stage. Thus in our pure parallel approach problem a myopic policy (which always pretends that there is just one stage left to go) is stationary. From the point of view of development, the difficulty with these results is that they require the number of nontrivial decision points to be infinite.[63] In a number of development problems, as we have seen, it is reasonable to suppose that the problem be over at a terminal stage N. If, on the other hand, one allows sequential selection of approaches, initially and at each of the N stages, then one has in effect, converted the N-stage problem into one whose number of stages is itself a random variable. For a stage is then a point at which the developer decides to add another approach to the set of those for which estimates of a certain kind are available. It is possible that some of the present and future results of the general theory of dynamic programming may have application in this case.[64]

13. Limitations of Problems Based on the Approach Concept

The central notion throughout our survey of the elements of a normative theory of development strategy was that there are a num-

---

[61] Not permitting a different set, A_n of possible acts at each decision point n does not really involve a loss of generality. If we take A to be a set containing all A_n then by suitable choice of payoff function we can make choice of an act outside A_n at stage n so undesirable that it does not occur under an optimal policy.

[62] And may, therefore, depend on all preceding states and acts, since the state at n may be defined to include the entire preceding history.

[63] There is a trivial formal way to turn a finite stage problem into an infinite stage problem. We could suppose that after the terminal stage N, only a null act yields a payoff that is not extremely bad. For this null act payoff is zero for all states. Then the decisionmaker, and the system, stand still after stage N. But this extension violates other conditions needed for the main results to hold.

[64] Or in the case of the non-truncated variant of the pure parallel approach problem suggested in 4.7 above.

ber of approaches to a development task and the main function of development strategy is to respond to changing knowledge by changing the relative effort devoted to alternative approaches. "Approach" is a very broad term. If completed, an approach would exhibit a certain history; the worth of the history would depend on the total time and money that completion required.

Our survey suggests that most if not all problems of development strategy can be formulated as problems in which the essential decisions are choices between approaches. But development work is learning. If these formulations are to be useful as ultimate guides to policy the probability distributions defining the problems must reflect the true nature of the learning that occurs in the main areas of technology. Which distributions do so and which do not is a massive empirical question whose exploration has barely begun.[65]

Our survey has touched very lightly on the major complications that realistic models would have to incorporate. We have been content, in several instances, with looking at fixed budget problems, when choice of the budget is itself part of a more realistic problem. The sequential selection, the variable intensity, the component matching, and the many valued preference complications have been dealt with only by very special illustrations. But we have already been able to look at simplified but precise formulations of intuitively reasonable rules of thumb, and found that only very special assumptions justify them—a finding that will certainly remain even when the rules are reformulated in much more complicated (and realistic) contexts. And we have treated rather completely the pure parallel approach problem, which, simplified as it is, seems a very natural place to begin. If the survey stimulates others to begin exploring some of the many roads it suggests, it will have served its purpose.

C. Normative Problems in Development Organization

1. General Normative Models of Organizations

The analysis of precise normative models is a relatively novel way of studying organizations. If one attempts to study the development project in this way one encounters further novelties, for the development project is a peculiar organization differing in several fundamental ways from the main organization models studied so far by normative organization theorists.

---

[65] The study reported in Chapter 4 of this book may be regarded as a first contribution to this task.

Let us summarize these models briefly, so as to be able to identify the peculiarities of the development project. In the main models studied[66] the members of the organization repeatedly take actions in the face of a changing and not perfectly predictable environment, whose current state may not be completely known to all members although each member has some partial knowledge of its current state. At any moment of time the environment that prevails and the members' actions that are in force (the organization's action vector) imply an outcome (for example, a level of profits) experienced by the organization at that moment. The organization's members share common preferences among the alternative outcomes. It is particularly convenient if these preferences can be represented by a payoff function that assigns a number to each environment-action vector pair: if, and only if, an environment and an action vector imply an outcome preferred to the outcome implied by another environment and action vector, the first pair yields a higher value of the payoff function than the second pair.

One then seeks ways in which the members can respond to their changing knowledge of the environment so as to yield a sequence of new actions. One is interested in good ways of responding that on the average yield actions achieving a high value of the payoff function. But a good way of responding in this sense may be a costly one to pursue; it may require much computation and communication. Thus one is ultimately interested in ways of responding to the environment that are good in a net sense, ways that yield a high average net payoff, where net payoff is obtained from payoff as originally defined in such a way as to take account of the computation and communication costs incurred by the organization.

To specify the problem completely not only must one specify the payoff function and the probability law governing the changing environment, but one must also make precise the ways of responding to the changing environment that are open to the organization. Among the possibilities are the following:

1) One may restrict the organization to making a one-shot response to each new environment. Each member of the organization observes

---

[66] The relevant efforts are the "theory of teams" (Jacob Marschak and Roy Radner: *The Economic Theory of Teams,* forthcoming monograph of the Cowles Foundation for Research in Economics, Yale University) and the study of "adjustment processes" in economies and other organizations (Kenneth J. Arrow and Leonid Hurwicz: Decentralization and Computation in Resource Allocation, in W. Phoutts, ed., *Essays in Economics and Econometrics,* Chapel Hill: University of North Carolina Press, 1960, pp. 34–104, and Thomas Marschak, "Centralization and Decentralization in Economic Organizations," *Econometrica,* Vol. 27 (July 1959), pp. 399–430.)

some part of the new environment and the members are permitted a single opportunity to send some part of their specialized knowledge to other members. Following this sole interchange, each member looks at his total knowledge of the new environment (derived from his observation and from the interchange) and decides on a new action, which he takes. The new actions remain in force until the environment changes again. One seeks rules telling each member, following any new environment, what part of his knowledge to send to each other member and what action to take given his knowledge after the interchange. Rules that require a fairly complete interchange (highly centralized rules) followed by very elaborate computations may achieve good actions but their operating costs (for communication and computation) will be high. Rules whose average net payoff is high are sought.

2) One can permit the organization's response to a new environment to be a sequence of interchanges and of revised actions. Following each interchange each member revises (improves) his actions on the basis of his accumulated knowledge. At the interchange the information he sends to other members may include his last revised action. Again, we seek rules that prescribe the entire sequence following any new environment and are good in a net sense.

In both setups, measurement of the net performance of a proposed set of rules must take into account, in general, not just the cost of the equipment (human or mechanical) needed to carry out the computation and communication the rules require, but also the speed with which the equipment does so. A slow one shot response in the first setup is bad since actions appropriate to the new environment will be delayed a long time (until the interchange has occurred and a new action vector has been computed). In the meantime, some inappropriate action vector (the old one for example) is in force. The longer the delay, the longer this inappropriate action vector is in force. Similarly, in the second setup, the longer the time elapsing between the successive improved actions in a sequence, the lower the average gross payoff the sequence achieves.

In both setups, then, the costs that must be taken into account in order to obtain the average net payoff yielded by a proposed set of rules must include the penalty due to delay and the cost of equipment, when the equipment chosen is just costly (elaborate) enough to reduce the delay penalty to an optimal level. Still more costly equipment would reduce the delay penalty still further but there would be no net gain in doing so. In both setups the delay penalty for any given rules, and hence also the optimal delay, depend on the probability law that governs the changing environment. This is true since, following any environment, the penalty due to having in force an inferior action vector instead of the action vector that would be best for that environment (a situation that persists until action vectors closer to the best one have been generated) depends on what the environment is.

2. Normative Models of the Development Project

Let us now turn to the development project. Here one can raise very difficult and important normative questions even though the organization is assumed to function once only and to disappear once its development task is completed. It was essential in the general model just described that the organization repeatedly draw new environments and be designed in such a way that its responses to them be, on the average, good ones from now into the indefinite future. The sequence of environments is unknown (though the probability law governing it is not), for if the sequence were known in advance the organization could compute its entire sequence of future responses once and for all at the start of its life, and could then, having been programmed, dissolve itself. How fast this once and for all computation is performed would not in general matter much since the computation time would be insignificant compared with the infinite (but perfectly predictable) future that stretches before the programmed organization.

In the case of the simplest model of a development project, the environment is also unknown at the start of the organization's life. The environment consists of all the unknown determinants of the difficulty of various approaches to the development task. Only *one* environment is ever drawn by the organization, but even so it does matter a great deal how one designs the organization, which will disappear once it has completed its response to the environment. A well designed organization completes its development task at a low average cost, where the averaging is now performed not over future environments facing the organization but over all the development-task environments that the organization could draw at the start of its life. The cost will include (as we have seen) both a time and a money component, but, unlike the general model considered above, the time component – the penalty due to delay in completing the task – does not depend on the environment that has been drawn. Completing the task slowly is undesirable, if the money spent is kept constant, because certain benefits yielded by the completed item (for example, profits) are forgone until it is completed. But the magnitude of these benefits need have nothing to do with the project's environment, which is the technical difficulty of the development task.

Of course we could study models of development organizations –

development laboratories, for example—in which the organization is perpetual, and its purpose is to deal with an imperfectly predictable stream of development tasks with changing benefits due to their prompt completion. Such a model would fall into the general class discussed above. The point is, however, that we need not deal with this more general and difficult class in order to raise pertinent and quite sufficiently difficult questions of development organization.

We now give an extremely simple illustration of a model of a development project facing an unknown environment at the start of its life and disappearing forever once its development task is completed. Even in this simple case some interesting normative questions of project organization can be studied. The project will, at the start, draw three approaches to its development task from a population of approaches. Each approach is characterized by a true time and money cost c, a first estimate c_1, and a second estimate c_2. We make the same assumptions about the distribution of the random variable (c_1,c_2,c) as we made above in Section 4.5 of Part B (monotonicity, one-stage unbiasedness, and the Markov assumption). The environment is the collection of three vectors (c_1,c_2,c) that have been drawn.

For each approach, c_1 equals a with probability p and b with probability $1-p$. Given that c_1 equals a, c_2 zero with probability q and u with probability $1-q$. Given that c_1 equals b, c_2 equals zero with probability r and c with probability $1-r$. Since we assume that $E(c/c_2)=c_2$ the possible values of c play no role in the analysis. We assume $a<b$ and $q>r$.

The project is composed of two developers (or two development groups). Developer 1 is in charge of the first two of the three approaches and Developer 2 is in charge of the third. We assume that each developer must pursue at least one approach until the second review point, when the second estimate (c_2) is available. But Developer 1 may or may not choose to pursue both of his approaches to the first or to the second review points.

We shall compare two modes of project organization. The first is centralized. Each developer fully informs the other of his current estimates at all review points. The second is decentralized. Neither developer knows the other's estimates until the second review point; at this point all current estimates are pooled and the surviving approach is chosen. The centralized organization is, of course, the better of the two if it does not incur greater communication costs. Presumably, however, it does incur greater communication costs since it requires more interchanges of information. The extra communication cost involves both time and money. For a given expenditure of money on the interchanges (on the human and mechanical communication equipment that performs them), they can be made to require not more than a certain length of time. For a larger expenditure they would require less time. If the time and money cost function has the additive form described in 4.5 of Part B, then the best money expenditure on communication equipment and the resulting communication time must both be added to the time and money cost (c) of the surviving approach to obtain the organization's total time and money cost when its task is complete. We shall assume to begin with that only the extra approach of Developer 1 incurs a looking cost (w) when it is pursued from one review point to the next; the other two approaches are free.

We shall explore the following central question: does the gross advantage of centralization (or full information)—the advantage before communication costs are taken into account—go up or down as the organization passes from the use of just two of its three approaches to the use of all three? By the use of an approach we mean its pursuit until at least review point 2. If all three are used, that means that Developer 1 exercises his option to pursue a second approach. We also ask the converse question: is the improvement due to the third approach greater for the centralized organization? Put another, broader way, the questions become one: is more fully shared information a substitute for or a complement of additional approaches?

Table 17 shows Developer 1's estimate of the drop in lowest attainable gross expected time and money cost (gross because communication costs are ignored) when, at review point 1, an additional approach is added to the single approach pursued by him and is then used by him (is pursued to review point 2), just as is his original approach. Developer 2 always carries an approach to review point 2 in any case. The table considers the decentralized and the centralized organizations and for the latter it considers all possible combinations of values of c_1 for the two original approaches (one pursued by each developer) to which the extra approach is to be added. In the centralized organization Developer 1's estimate of the drop due to using the added approach is exact, since he knows the exact value of c_2 for Developer 2's approach. In the decentralized organization he does not know Developer 2's c_1 and his estimate is an average of the drop when Developer 2's c_1 equals a and the drop when it equals b. The terms "a approach" and "b approach" used in the table mean approaches for which $c_1 = a$ and $c_1 = b$, respectively.

To illustrate the calculations that yield the table, consider Case 1

TABLE 17

THE VALUE OF AN ADDITIONAL APPROACH IN A CENTRALIZED AND IN A DECENTRALIZED PROJECT ORGANIZATION

Case Number $i =$	Probability of This Case When Existing Approaches and Added Approach Are Drawn at Random $\pi_i =$	Approach Added at Review Point 1, to Developer 1's Existing Approach and Used by Him	Developer 1's Existing Approach	Developer 2's Existing Approach in Centralized Organization	Drop in Gross Expected Time and Money Cost as Perceived by Developer 1: Centralized Organization $\lambda_i =$	Drop in Gross Expected Time and Money Cost as Perceived by Developer 1: Decentralized Organization $\eta_i =$	Is $\lambda_i < \eta_i$ or $>\eta_i$?
1	p^3	a	a	a	$c(1-q)^2q-w$	$c(1-q)q(1-r+pr-pq)-w$	$<$
2	$p^2(1-p)$	b	a	a	$c(1-q)^2r-w$	$c(1-q)r(1-r+pr-pq)-w$	$<$
3	$p^2(1-p)$	a	b	a	$c(1-r)(1-q)q-w$	$c(1-r)q(1-r+pr-pq)-w$	$<$
4	$p(1-p)^2$	b	b	a	$c(1-r)(1-q)r-w$	$c(1-r)r(1-r+pr-pq)-w$	$<$
5	$(1-p)^3$	b	b	b	$c(1-r)^2r-w$	$c(1-r)r(1-r+pr-pq)-w$	$>$
6	$p(1-p)^2$	b	a	b	$c(1-r)(1-q)r-w$	$c(1-q)r(1-r+pr-pq)-w$	$>$
7	$p(1-p)^2$	a	b	b	$c(1-r)^2q-w$	$c(1-r)q(1-r+pr-pq)-w$	$>$
8	$p^2(1-p)$	a	a	b	$c(1-r)(1-q)q-w$	$c(1-q)q(1-r+pr-pq)-w$	$>$

(line 1 of the table). In the centralized organization the drop in gross expected time and money cost because of the addition of an *a* approach to two *a* approaches is the drop in the expected value of the minimum of the c_2s. This is equal to $c(1-q)^2$, the expected value when two *a* approaches are used, minus $c(1-q)^3 + w$, the expected value when in addition an extra *a* approach is used (at a looking cost of w) by Developer 1. The drop is therefore $c(1-q)^2 q - w$. In the decentralized organization, Developer 2's estimate of the drop equals his estimate of expected gross time and money cost when he uses one *a* approach, knowing that Developer 2 either has an *a* approach (with probability p) or a *b* approach (with probability $(1-p)$), minus his estimate of expected gross time and money cost when he uses two *a* approaches. This is $p(1-q)^2c + (1-p)(1-q)(1-r)c$ minus $p(1-q)^3c + (1-p)(1-q)^2(1-r)c + w$, which simplified to $c(1-q)q(1-r+pr-pq) - w$. For the remaining cases the calculations are completely analogous. It is then easily verified that our assumption that $q > r$ implies the inequalities shown in the last column with respect to the drops in the centralized and decentralized organizations. The first column, finally, gives the probability with which each case occurs given that all three approaches (the two existing ones, and the extra one) are independently drawn from the population of initially indistinguishable approaches.

To answer the question of whether giving Developer 1 a randomly drawn extra approach decreases gross expected time and money cost by more in the decentralized organization than it does in the centralized organization we must consider a number of possible cases, each one imposing a different restriction on the values of q, r, c, and w. The cases differ with respect to the optimal subset chosen by the centralized organization, at review point 1, out of three approaches with known values of c_1. In each case all ordered triples of approaches —ordered with respect to the value of c_1—are considered. For convenience a bar over a letter (over a possible value of c_1) indicates that the approach with that value of c_1 is included in the centralized organization's optimal subset; if there is no bar the approach is not included. Our assumption that two approaches are free and our previous results on the pure parallel approach problem, when monotonicity is satisfied and there are never more than three approaches, tell us that the possible cases are the following:

Case I:	$\bar{a}\bar{a}a$	*Case II:*	$\bar{a}\bar{a}\bar{a}$	*Case III:*	$\bar{a}\bar{a}a$
	$\bar{a}\bar{a}b$		$\bar{a}\bar{a}\bar{b}$		$\bar{a}\bar{a}b$
	$\bar{a}\bar{b}b$		$\bar{a}\bar{b}\bar{b}$		$\bar{a}\bar{b}\bar{b}$
	$\bar{b}\bar{b}b$		$\bar{b}\bar{b}\bar{b}$		$\bar{b}\bar{b}\bar{b}$

Case IV:	$\bar{a}\bar{a}a$	*Case VI:*	$\bar{a}\bar{a}\bar{a}$
	$\bar{a}\bar{a}b$		$\bar{a}\bar{a}b$
	$\bar{a}\bar{b}b$		$\bar{a}\bar{b}b$
	$\bar{b}\bar{b}\bar{b}$		$\bar{b}\bar{b}\bar{b}$
Case V:	$\bar{a}\bar{a}\bar{a}$	*Case VII:*	$\bar{a}\bar{a}\bar{a}$
	$\bar{a}\bar{a}b$		$\bar{a}\bar{a}b$
	$\bar{a}\bar{b}b$		$\bar{a}\bar{b}\bar{b}$
	$\bar{b}\bar{b}b$		$\bar{b}\bar{b}\bar{b}$

Consider Case I first. The extra approach is never used by the centralized organization so that the drop in expected time and money cost due to adding it is zero. The value of $\lambda_1, \ldots, \lambda_8$ in the table is zero or negative. The decentralized organization, however, may use the extra approach when Developer 1's two approaches have the c_1 values given in cases (5)–(8) of the table. In those cases we may have $\eta_i > 0$ even though $\lambda_i < 0$. Then the drop due to the third approach would be greater for the decentralized organization than for the centralized organization.

Next consider Case II. This is the opposite extreme: the centralized organization always uses the extra approach, and the drop in expected time and money cost after adding it is

$$\sum_{i=1}^{8} \pi_i \lambda_i.$$

The decentralized organization, on the other hand, has to use the extra approach in cases (1)-(4), for then $\lambda_i > 0$, $\eta_i > 0$, but in some or all of cases (5)–(8) it may not use it. So for the decentralized organization the drop in expected time and money cost because the third approach was added may be as little as

$$\sum_{i=1}^{4} \pi_i \eta_i.$$

Values of q, r, c, and w can very well be chosen so that we remain in Case II while the drop for the decentralized organization is

$$\sum_{i \epsilon I} \pi_i \eta_i,$$

where I is some subset of $[1,2, \ldots ,8]$, and this is less than

$$\sum_{i=1}^{8} \pi_i \lambda_i.$$

(For example, if $p = 1/2$, $q = 1/2$, $r = 1/4$, and $w < 25c/256$, then $\lambda_i > 0$,

$i = 1, \ldots, 8$; $\eta_i > 0$, $i = 5,6$; $\eta_i < 0$, $i \neq 5,6$; and

$$\sum_{i=1}^{8} \pi_i \lambda_i = \frac{75}{512} c - w > \frac{125}{1024} c - 3/4w = \sum_{i=5,6} \pi_i \eta_i.)$$

So in Case II the third approach may be worth less to the decentralized than to the centralized organization. The remaining cases display a similarly mixed picture and we shall not go into them here.

It remains to investigate whether the gross advantage of centralization over decentralization (without taking account of communication costs) increases or decreases when one passes from the case of two randomly drawn approaches available at review point 1 to the case of three randomly drawn approaches. For this purpose we must alter the previous assumptions in one respect. We now assume that in the decentralized organization Developer 1 must pursue one approach to the second review point (as does Developer 2), but Developer 1 incurs a looking cost for every approach he uses including the compulsory one. Developer 2's single approach is free. In the centralized organization, Developer 1 also incurs a looking cost for every approach he uses, but he has no compulsory approach: he may pursue no approaches if he wishes. Under this modified assumption, our previous conclusion (that the gain due to a third approach may be either larger for the decentralized organization or smaller) is certainly preserved. At the same time the modified assumption does yield a gross advantage for centralization in the two approach case; under our earlier assumption the two modes of organization would be indistinguishable in this case.

The gross advantage of centralization in the two approach case arises because it is sometimes optimal for Developer 1 in the decentralized organization to pursue no approach further than review point 1, even though Developer 1 in the centralized organization is forced to pursue one to review point 2. The gross advantage in the three approach cases may take two different forms; for each triple of c_2 values one or the other of these forms will be displayed. In the first form, the advantage arises because it is not optimal for the fully informed Developer 1 of the centralized organization to pursue his extra approach while the incompletely informed Developer 1 of the decentralized organization does pursue it. The advantage takes the second form when the centralized Developer 1 pursues the extra approach but the decentralized Developer 1 does not. When the triple of approaches is such that the advantage is of the first kind it is easily seen to be greater than the advantage of centralization when only the first two of that triple of approaches are available at review point 1. But when the triple is such that the advantage takes the second form, then it may be smaller than the advantage when only the first two of the triple are available. One can choose p, q, r, w, and c so that the cases in which the two approach advantage is greater than the three approach advantage outweigh those in which it is less, and one can choose p, q, r, w, c so that the reverse is true.

Thus even in the simple situation we have studied we cannot say that more fully shared information and more approaches must be substitutes or that they must be complements. Moreover, it is possible for the value of more fully shared information to go up (down) as approaches are added, while the value of more approaches goes down (up) as the sharing of information increases.

If information sharing and approaches were substitutes or complements in interesting classes of problems, that would be a suggestive result for those who design project organizations. It might be worthwhile, therefore, to search for interesting conditions on the basic probability distribution—even in the three approach, two-review point case—implying that the two commodities are substitutes or complements. Many other questions bearing on the design of project organizations can be studied in the same spirit. One of them, for example, would be: does the advantage of centralization increase in crash projects, that is, in projects whose time and money cost function gives a high weight to time? In the pure parallel approach context, the question is whether the errors decentralized developers make (because of incomplete information) in estimating the gain from further pursuing approaches increase as the weight given to time increases. (Recall that the estimates c_n, on which the developer bases his decisions, are estimates of c, which is a weighted combination of the money required beyond the last review point and the time required.)

We have provided only the sketchiest introduction to the normative study of models of project organization. As in the case of normative problems in strategy, a large but not too forbidding area of suggestive, unexplored, and partly solvable problems awaits the student of development.

Appendix

PROOF OF THEOREM 4, CHAPTER 5, SECTION 4.5

The statement of the theorem and a brief description of the three steps in the proof are given in the text.

We now proceed to the three steps.

Step (I). By the Fundamental Lemma,

$$\begin{aligned}\varphi_{\gamma}^{N-1} - \varphi_{\gamma\alpha}^{N-1} &= \int [1 - F_{\gamma,N-1}(t)]dt - \int [1 - F_{\gamma,N-1}(t)][1 - F_{\alpha,N-1}(t)]dt \\ &= \int [1 - F_{\gamma,N-1}(t)]F_{\alpha,N-1}(t)dt \\ &\geqq \int [1 - F_{\gamma,N-1}(t)][1 - F_{\beta,N-1}(t)]F_{\alpha,N-1}(t)dt \\ &= \varphi_{\gamma\beta}^{N-1} - \varphi_{\gamma\alpha\beta}^{N-1}.\end{aligned}$$

Also if $x < y$ then by monotonicity $F_{y,N-1}(t) \geqq F_{x,N-1}(t)$ and hence

$$\begin{aligned}\varphi_{y}^{N-1} - \varphi_{x}^{N-1} &= \int \{[1 - F_{x,N-1}(t)] - [1 - F_{y,N-1}(t)]\}dt \\ &= \int [F_{y,N-1}(t) - F_{x,N-1}(t)]dt \\ &\geqq \int [1 - F_{\gamma}(t)][F_{y,N-1}(t) - F_{x,N-1}(t)]dt \\ &= \varphi_{\gamma y}^{N-1} - \varphi_{\gamma x}^{N-1}.\end{aligned}$$

Step (II). Step II falls into two parts: Part A is the proof that at any n (22)*, (20)* imply (22). Part B is the proof that (22)*, (20)* imply (20).

Part A. A number of cases have to be considered to achieve this part. The number is considerably cut down by the following general observation, which applies to a set Γ of any size (not just a one element set) and is of some independent interest.

Suppose that for some stage n the following condition is met: if for any set Γ and any approach α, $T(\Gamma\alpha)$ is an optimal subset of $\Gamma\alpha$ then

$$T(\Gamma\alpha) \cap \Gamma \subseteq T(\Gamma) \tag{A1}$$

for some optimal subset $T(\Gamma)$ of Γ.[1]

In other words, an approach that remains part of an optimal subset when the extra approach α is added to those available (an approach good enough to withstand the addition of α) is also part of an optimal subset in the absence of α. If (A1) were known for stage n then non-complementarity at that stage could immediately be established for a number of cases.

First, consider the case in which for all optimal subsets $T(\Gamma\alpha)$, $\alpha \notin T(\Gamma\alpha)$. Then also, by (A1) for any optimal subset $T(\Gamma\alpha\beta)$, $\alpha \notin T(\Gamma\alpha\beta)$. Hence $\tilde{\varphi}^n_\Gamma - \tilde{\varphi}^n_{\Gamma\alpha} = \tilde{\varphi}^n_{\Gamma\beta} - \tilde{\varphi}^n_{\Gamma\beta\alpha} = 0$ and non-complementarity is established.

Second, suppose that for all optimal subsets $T(\Gamma\alpha\beta)$, $\alpha \notin T(\Gamma\alpha\beta)$. Then $\tilde{\varphi}^n_{\Gamma\beta} - \tilde{\varphi}^n_{\Gamma\beta\alpha} = 0$ and we have non-complementarity.

Third, suppose that for all optimal subsets $T(\Gamma\beta)$, $\beta \notin T(\Gamma\beta)$. Then also $\beta \notin T(\Gamma\alpha\beta)$ for all optimal subsets $T(\Gamma\alpha\beta)$. Hence $\tilde{\varphi}^n_\Gamma - \tilde{\varphi}^n_{\Gamma\alpha} = \tilde{\varphi}^n_{\Gamma\beta} - \tilde{\varphi}^n_{\Gamma\alpha\beta}$.

Fourth, suppose that for all optimal subsets $T(\Gamma\alpha\beta)$, $\beta \notin T(\Gamma\alpha\beta)$. Then $\tilde{\varphi}^n_{\Gamma\alpha\beta} = \tilde{\varphi}^n_{\Gamma\alpha}$ and since $\tilde{\varphi}^n_{\Gamma\beta} \leqq \tilde{\varphi}^n_\Gamma$, we have $\tilde{\varphi}^n_\Gamma - \tilde{\varphi}^n_{\Gamma\alpha} \geqq \tilde{\varphi}^n_{\Gamma\beta} - \tilde{\varphi}^n_{\Gamma\beta\alpha}$.

If (A1) holds for a stage n and we wish to establish non-complementarity for that stage we can then confine our attention to cases in which

α is in an optimal subset of $\Gamma\alpha$, β is in an optimal subset of $\Gamma\beta$, and α and β are in an optimal subset of $\Gamma\alpha\beta$.[2] (A2)

Observe now, however, that if at stage n (19)* is true ((19)* becomes (22)* when Γ is a one element set $\{\gamma\}$) then (A1) holds at stage n. To see this note that (19)* implies (just as did (19)) the optimality of the procedure described in the text for construction of an optimal subset (proceeding down the ordered list of approaches until adding the next approach is not worth the looking cost). Next suppose for some optimal subset $T(\Gamma\alpha)$; $\alpha \in T(\Gamma\alpha)$ (if not, (A1) holds trivially). Let Γ be the set $\{\gamma_1, \ldots, \gamma_r\}$, where $\gamma_1 \leqq \gamma_2 \leqq \ldots \gamma_r$. Let $T(\Gamma)$ be a subsequence of $\gamma_1, \ldots, \gamma_r$, namely $\gamma_1, \ldots, \gamma_{r^*}$, $r^* \leqq r$.

[1] The symbol $\cap$ denotes the intersection of two sets.

[2] In addition we can dispense with the case in which every optimal subset $T(\Gamma)$ is a proper subset of Γ (a case which only arises when Γ has more than one element). For then there exist optimal subsets $T(\Gamma\alpha)$, $T(\Gamma\beta)$, $T(\Gamma\beta\alpha)$ such that $T(\Gamma\alpha) \cap \Gamma \subset T(\Gamma)$, $T(\Gamma\beta) \cap \Gamma \subset T(\Gamma)$, $T(\Gamma\alpha\beta) \cap \Gamma \subset T(\Gamma)$. Hence nothing is changed if we everywhere replace Γ by the set $T(\Gamma)$, which is an optimal subset of itself. When Γ has more than one element therefore one can confine one's attention to cases in which Γ is an optimal subset of itself.

Let $\Gamma\alpha$ be, when similarly ordered, the sequence $\gamma_1, \ldots, \gamma_{r^{**}}, \alpha, \gamma_{r^{**}+1}, \ldots, \gamma_r$. Then an optimal subset $T(\Gamma\alpha)$ must be the ordered sequence $\gamma_1, \ldots, \gamma_{r^{**}}, \alpha, \ldots, \gamma_{\hat{r}}$, where $\hat{r} \leqq r^*$ and $\gamma_{\hat{r}} \leqq \gamma_{r^*}$. To see this note that $\{\gamma_1, \ldots, \gamma_{r^*}\}$ is carried to the next stage and then $\{\gamma_1, \ldots, \gamma_{r^*}, \gamma_{r^*+1}\}$ is carried to the next stage the drop in expected optimal time and money cost is less than one (the looking cost) since $\{\gamma_1, \ldots, \gamma_{r^*}\}$ is optimal. If $\{\gamma_1, \ldots, \gamma_{r^{**}}, \alpha, \ldots, \gamma_{r^*}\}$ is carried to the next stage and then $\{\gamma_1, \ldots, \gamma_{r^{**}}, \alpha, \ldots, \gamma_{r^*}, \gamma_{r^*+1}\}$ is carried to the next stage then the drop in expected time and money cost is *a fortiori* less than one, because of (19)*. So whatever members of Γ are contained in the optimal subset $T(\Gamma\alpha)$ are also contained in $T(\Gamma)$, an optimal subset of Γ. Thus (19)* implies that (A1) holds at stage n.

To return now to the case of a one element Γ, since we assume (22)* and (20)* at stage n as the induction hypothesis, we know that (A1) holds at stage n and we can now, in establishing (22), confine the discussion to just the cases satisfying conditions (A2). This we now proceed to do.

Since we want to prove the non-negativity of $\tilde{\varphi}^n_\gamma - \tilde{\varphi}^n_{\gamma\alpha} - \tilde{\varphi}^n_{\gamma\beta} - \tilde{\varphi}^n_{\gamma\alpha\beta}$, which is symmetric in α and β, we may as well assume henceforth that $\alpha \leqq \beta$ (for if we have established the non-negativity for $\alpha \leqq \beta$ then by interchanging α and β we can establish it also whenever $\alpha \geqq \beta$). Moreover if $\gamma \leqq \alpha \leqq \beta$, (22) follows at once. For if (A2) is to be satisfied then for $\gamma \leqq \alpha \leqq \beta$, $T(\{\gamma,\alpha\}) = \{\gamma,\alpha\}$ is an optimal subset (since if α is in an optimal subset of $\{\gamma,\alpha\}$ then so must be the better approach γ). Similarly $T(\{\gamma,\beta\}) = \{\gamma,\beta\}$ and, by the optimality of the procedure described in the text for construction of optimal subsets, $T(\{\gamma,\alpha,\beta\}) = \{\gamma,\alpha,\beta\}$ is an optimal subset. But this means that (22) becomes identical to (22)* (the looking costs cancel out).

If $\alpha \leqq \gamma \leqq \beta$ then by the same argument $T(\{\gamma,\beta\}) = \{\gamma,\beta\}$ is an optimal subset. Again, by the optimality of the construction procedure, $T(\{\gamma,\alpha,\beta\}) = \{\gamma,\alpha,\beta\}$ must be an optimal subset. But this further implies that $T(\{\alpha,\gamma\}) = \{\alpha,\gamma\}$ is an optimal subset, since if proceeding down the list of approaches from α to γ and then to β is worth twice the looking cost, then proceeding from α to γ alone must (by (22)*) be worth at least the looking cost. So again (22) coincides with (22)*.

For the remaining cases, then, we assume[3] $\alpha \leqq \beta \leqq \gamma$. The cases are distinguished by different assumptions about the optimal subsets

[3] The same arguments establish that if we want to show that (19)* (together with (21)*) implies (19) for the general case in which Γ is a set with many elements, then we may as well assume, in addition to the conditions (A2) that $\alpha \leqq \beta$ and that α is not less than the largest element in Γ.

of the sets $\{\alpha,\gamma\}$, $\{\beta,\gamma\}$, $\{\alpha,\beta,\gamma\}$, consistent with (A2). The assumed optimal subsets are identified by equalities of the form $\bar{\varphi}_\Gamma^n = \varphi_{T(\Gamma)}^n + \nu[T(\Gamma)]$.

Case (a)

$$\bar{\varphi}_{\alpha\gamma}^n = \varphi_\alpha^n + 1 \tag{i}$$

$$\bar{\varphi}_{\beta\gamma}^n = \varphi_\beta^n + 1 \tag{ii}$$

$$\bar{\varphi}_{\alpha\beta\gamma}^n = \varphi_{\alpha\beta}^n + 2. \tag{iii}$$

We also have, of course, $\bar{\varphi}_\gamma^n = \varphi_\gamma^n + 1$. Complementarity (the denial of (22)) would imply

$$\varphi_\gamma^n - \varphi_\alpha^n < \varphi_\beta^n - \varphi_{\alpha\beta}^n - 1.$$

But (20)* implies

$$\varphi_{\gamma\beta}^n - \varphi_{\alpha\beta}^n \leqq \varphi_\gamma^n - \varphi_\alpha^n.$$

Combining, we get

$$\varphi_{\gamma\beta}^n < \varphi_\beta^n - 1$$

or

$$1 < \varphi_\beta^n - \varphi_{\gamma\beta}^n. \tag{iv}$$

But (iv) contradicts (ii), for if (iv) were true $\{\beta\}$ would not be an optimal subset of $\{\gamma,\beta\}$. Hence (22) holds for this case.

Case (b)

$$\bar{\varphi}_{\alpha\gamma}^n = \varphi_{\alpha\gamma}^n + 2 \tag{i}$$

$$\bar{\varphi}_{\beta\gamma}^n = \varphi_{\beta\gamma}^n + 2 \tag{ii}$$

$$\bar{\varphi}_{\alpha\beta\gamma}^n = \varphi_{\alpha\beta}^n + 2. \tag{iii}$$

Complementarity would imply

$$\varphi_\gamma^n - \varphi_{\alpha\gamma}^n - 1 < \varphi_{\beta\gamma}^n - \varphi_{\alpha\beta}^n.$$

But (i) implies

$$\bar{\varphi}_\alpha^n - \bar{\varphi}_{\alpha\gamma}^n \geqq 1.$$

Combining, we obtain

$$\varphi_\gamma^n - \varphi_\alpha^n < \varphi_{\beta\gamma}^n - \varphi_{\beta\alpha}^n,$$

which contradicts (20)*.

Case (c)

$$\tilde{\varphi}^n_{\alpha\gamma} = \varphi^n_{\alpha} + 1 \quad \text{(i)}$$

$$\tilde{\varphi}^n_{\beta\gamma} = \varphi^n_{\beta\gamma} + 2 \quad \text{(ii)}$$

$$\tilde{\varphi}^n_{\alpha\beta\gamma} = \varphi^n_{\alpha\beta} + 2. \quad \text{(iii)}$$

(20)* immediately implies non-complementarity.

Case (d)

$$\tilde{\varphi}^n_{\alpha\gamma} = \varphi^n_{\alpha} + 1 \quad \text{(i)}$$

$$\tilde{\varphi}^n_{\beta\lambda} = \varphi^n_{\beta} + 1 \quad \text{(ii)}$$

$$\tilde{\varphi}^n_{\beta\lambda} = \varphi^n_{\alpha} + 1. \quad \text{(iii)}$$

Non-complementarity immediately follows.

We have then shown that for all possible cases (20)*, (22)* implies (22). This completes Part A of Step II.

Part B. An optimal subset of $\{\delta, x\}$ can be $\{\delta\}$ or $\{x\}$ or $\{\delta, x\}$. An optimal subset of $\{\delta, y\}$ can be $\{\delta\}$ or $\{y\}$ or $\{\delta, y\}$. There are thus nine possible combinations but, using the fact that $x < y$, three of them can immediately be disposed of: If $\{\delta, x\}$ is an optimal subset of itself then $\{y\}$ cannot be an optimal subset of $\{\delta, y\}$ unless $\{\delta, y\}$ is an optimal subset also (which is a case we shall consider). If y were an optimal subset of $\{\delta, y\}$, that would mean $x < y \leqq \delta$, so that if δ is worth adding to x then (by (20)*) it is *a fortiori* worth adding to y. If $\{\delta\}$ is an optimal subset of $\{\delta, x\}$ but $\{\delta, x\}$ and $\{x\}$ are not, then $\delta < x < y$ and neither $\{\delta, y\}$ nor $\{y\}$ can be optimal subsets of $\{\delta, y\}$.

We are left with the following six cases.

Case (1)

$$\tilde{\varphi}^n_{x\delta} = \varphi^n_{x\delta} + 2, \qquad \tilde{\varphi}^n_{y\delta} = \varphi^n_{y\delta} + 2.$$

Then (20) simply coincides (after cancellation of the looking costs) with (20)*.

Case (2).

$$\tilde{\varphi}^n_{x\delta} = \varphi^n_{x\delta} + 2, \qquad \tilde{\varphi}^n_{y\delta} = \varphi^n_{\delta} + 1.$$

Then the denial of (20) would be

$$\varphi^n_y - \varphi^n_x < \varphi^n_{\delta} - \varphi^n_{x\delta} - 1.$$

But the assumptions of the case also imply

$$\varphi_\delta^n - \varphi_{y\delta}^n \leqq 1.$$

Combining, we obtain

$$\varphi_y^n - \varphi_x^n < \varphi_{y\delta}^n - \varphi_{x\delta}^n,$$

which contradicts (20)*.

Case (3)

$$\bar{\varphi}_{x\delta}^n = \varphi_x^n + 1, \qquad \bar{\varphi}_{y\delta}^n = \varphi_{y\delta}^n + 2.$$

The denial of (20) becomes

$$\varphi_y^n - \varphi_x^n < \varphi_{y\delta}^n - \varphi_x^n + 1.$$

But we also have

$$\varphi_x^n - \varphi_{x\delta}^n \leqq 1$$

which, after combining, again yields the contradiction of (20)*.

Case (4)

$$\bar{\varphi}_{x\delta}^n = \varphi_x^n + 1, \qquad \bar{\varphi}_{y\delta}^n = \varphi_\delta^n + 1.$$

The denial of (20) becomes

$$\varphi_y^n - \varphi_x^n < \varphi_\delta^n - \varphi_x^n,$$

or $\varphi_y^n < \varphi_\delta^n$, which contradicts the assumption $\bar{\varphi}_{y\delta}^n = \varphi_\delta^n + 1$.

Case (5)

$$\bar{\varphi}_{x\delta}^n = \varphi_x^n + 1, \qquad \bar{\varphi}_{y\delta}^n = \varphi_y^n + 1.$$

Denial of (20) becomes

$$\varphi_y^n - \varphi_x^n < \varphi_y^n - \varphi_x^n,$$

which is false.

Case (6)

$$\bar{\varphi}_{x\delta}^n = \varphi_\delta^n + 1, \qquad \bar{\varphi}_{y\delta}^n = \bar{\varphi}_\delta^n + 1$$

and the right hand side of (20) is zero, which makes (20) true.

We have then shown, for all possible cases, that (20)*, (22)* imply (20). Part B of Step II is completed.

Step III. Suppose (22) holds at stage n, that is, for any α, β, γ,

$$\bar{\varphi}_\gamma^n - \bar{\varphi}_{\alpha\gamma}^n - \bar{\varphi}_{\beta\gamma}^n + \bar{\varphi}_{\alpha\beta\gamma}^n \geqq 0.$$

Now consider, at stage $n-1$, any triple of approaches with current estimates α', β', γ'. Then the nth estimates for these three approaches are random variables α, β, γ. Since, by definition,

$$\varphi_{\Delta'}^{n-1} = E\tilde{\varphi}_{\Delta}^{n}$$

where Δ' is any set of $(n-1)$st estimates and Δ the corresponding set of nth estimates, we have

$$\varphi_{\gamma'}^{n-1} - \varphi_{\alpha'\gamma'}^{n} - \varphi_{\beta'\gamma'}^{n} + \varphi_{\alpha'\beta'\gamma'}^{n} = E(\tilde{\varphi}_{\gamma}^{n-1} - \tilde{\varphi}_{\alpha\gamma}^{n} - \tilde{\varphi}_{\beta\gamma}^{n} + \tilde{\varphi}_{\alpha\beta\gamma}^{n})$$

which is $\geqq 0$ since the expression in parentheses is $\geqq 0$ for every possible value of (α,β,γ). Thus (22) at stage n implies (22)* at stage $n-1$.

To show that (20) at n implies (20)* at $n-1$ one goes through an argument completely analogous to the argument used to establish an analogous result in the proof of Theorem 3.

We write (20) in the form

$$\tilde{\varphi}_{y}^{n} - \tilde{\varphi}_{\delta y}^{n} \geqq \tilde{\varphi}_{x}^{n} - \tilde{\varphi}_{\delta x}^{n}.$$

Each side of this inequality can be written as a value of the function

$$h(\lambda) = \tilde{\varphi}_{\lambda}^{n} - \tilde{\varphi}_{\delta\lambda}^{n}$$

with the left side of the inequality being the value h takes for a value $\lambda = y$ and the right side of the inequality the value h takes for the lower value $\lambda = x$. To show that for any $\delta', x', y', x' < y'$,

$$\varphi_{y'}^{n-1} - \varphi_{\delta'y'}^{n-1} \geqq \varphi_{x'}^{n-1} - \varphi_{\delta'x'}^{n-1}$$

it suffices to show, by the argument of Theorem 3, that if δ, y, x are the nth estimates for the approaches with $(n-1)$st estimates δ', x', y', and if we fix δ, then $h(\lambda)$ is a non-decreasing function of λ. But this is precisely what the induction hypothesis (20) says.

The required induction is therefore complete.[4]

[4] Note that the monotonicity assumption (which allows us to use the argument of Theorem 3) enters at this final point, as well as in Step I. It is not directly used in Step II.

INDEX

SELECTED RAND BOOKS

Arrow, Kenneth J. and Marvin Hoffenberg, *A Time Series Analysis of Interindustry Demands,* Amsterdam: North-Holland Publishing Company, 1959.

Bellman, Richard (ed.), *Mathematical Optimization Techniques,* Berkeley and Los Angeles: University of California Press, 1963.

Bergson, Abram, *The Real National Income of Soviet Russia Since 1928,* Cambridge, Mass.: Harvard University Press, 1961.

Buchheim, Robert W. and the Staff of The RAND Coporation, *The New Space Handbook: Astronautics and Its Applications,* New York: Vintage Books, A Division of Random House, Inc., 1963.

Chapman, Janet G., *Real Wages in Soviet Russia Since 1928,* Cambridge, Mass.: Harvard University Press, 1963.

Dantzig, G. B., *Linear Programming and Extensions,* Princeton, N.J.: Princeton University Press, 1963.

Dorfman, Robert, Paul A. Samuelson, and Robert M. Solow, *Linear Programming and Economic Analysis,* New York: McGraw-Hill Book Company, Inc., 1958.

Dresher, Melvin, *Games of Strategy: Theory and Applications,* Englewood Cliffs, N.J.: Prentice-Hall, Inc., 1961.

Ford, L. R., Jr. and D. R. Fulkerson, *Flows in Networks,* Princeton, N.J.: Princeton University Press, 1962.

Harris, Theodore E., *The Theory of Branching Processes,* Berlin, Germany: Springer-Verlag, 1963.

Hirshleifer, Jack, James C. DeHaven, and Jerome W. Milliman, *Water Supply: Economics, Technology, and Policy,* Chicago: University of Chicago Press, 1960.

Hitch, Charles J. and Roland N. McKean, *The Economics of Defense in the Nuclear Age,* Cambridge, Mass.: Harvard University Press, 1960.

Johnson, William A., *The Steel Industry of India,* Cambridge, Mass.: Harvard University Press, 1966.

Liu, Ta-Chung and Kung-Chia Yeh, *The Economy of the Chinese Mainland: National Income and Economic Development, 1933–1959,* Princeton, N.J.: Princeton University Press, 1965.

Lubell, Harold, *Middle East Oil Crises and Western Europe's Energy Supplies,* Baltimore: The Johns Hopkins Press, 1963.

McKean, Roland N., *Efficiency in Government Through Systems Analysis: With Emphasis on Water Resource Development,* New York: John Wiley & Sons, Inc., 1958.

McKinsey, J. C. C., *Introduction to the Theory of Games,* New York: McGraw-Hill Book Company, Inc., 1952.

Moorsteen, Richard, *Prices and Production of Machinery in the Soviet Union, 1928–1958,* Cambridge, Mass.: Harvard University Press, 1962.

Nelson, Richard R., Merton J. Peck, and Edward D. Kalachek, *Technology,*

Economic Growth, and Public Policy, Washington, D.C.: The Brookings Institution, 1967.

Novick, David (ed.), *Program Budgeting: Program Analysis and the Federal Budget,* Cambridge, Mass.: Harvard University Press, 1965.

Quade, Edward S. (ed.), *Analysis for Military Decisions,* Chicago: Rand McNally & Company; Amsterdam, North-Holland Publishing Company, 1964.

Rosen, George, *Democracy and Economic Change in India,* Berkeley and Los Angeles: University of California Press, 1966.

Williams, J. D., *The Compleat Strategyst: Being a Primer on the Theory of Games of Strategy,* New York: McGraw-Hill Book Company, Inc., 1954.

Wolf, Charles, Jr., *Foreign Aid: Theory and Practice in Southern Asia,* Princeton, N.J.: Princeton University Press, 1960.

GPSR Compliance

The European Union's (EU) General Product Safety Regulation (GPSR) is a set of rules that requires consumer products to be safe and our obligations to ensure this.

If you have any concerns about our products, you can contact us on ProductSafety@springernature.com

In case Publisher is established outside the EU, the EU authorized representative is:

Springer Nature Customer Service Center GmbH
Europaplatz 3
69115 Heidelberg, Germany

Batch number: 10682411

Printed by Printforce, the Netherlands